SPIES FOR NIMITZ

SPIES FOR NIMITZ

JOINT MILITARY INTELLIGENCE IN THE PACIFIC WAR

Jeffrey M. Moore

Naval Institute Press

ANNAPOLIS, MARYLAND

Naval Institute Press
291 Wood Road
Annapolis, MD 21402

Library of Congress Cataloging-in-Publication Data
Moore, Jeffrey M., 1968–
    Spies for Nimitz : joint military intelligence in the Pacific War /
Jeffrey M. Moore.
    p. cm.
    Includes bibliographical references and index.
    ISBN 1-59114-488-4 (alk. paper)
    1. World War, 1939–1945—Military intelligence—United States. 2.
World War, 1939–1945—Campaigns—Pacific Area. 3. United States.
Navy. Joint Intelligence Center, Pacific Ocean Areas—History. I. Title.
    D810.S7M577 2003
    940.54'8673'099—dc22

                            2003015494

    Printed in the United States of America on acid-free paper ∞
        11 10 09 08 07 06 05 04   9 8 7 6 5 4 3 2
                        First printing

To the founders of the United States' intelligence community and
the heroes of the Pacific War who fought so hard for so long
and sacrificed so much, and to my colleagues at the
Pentagon who were there on 11 September 2001:
the best and the finest this country has to offer.

We will never forget.

CONTENTS

FOREWORD

Intelligence is a complex and often misunderstood military science. All too frequently, military operations are labeled as intelligence successes or failures without a full understanding of the role intelligence really played. More often than not, however, it is the "failure" that takes center stage. Nevertheless, to begin to understand intelligence and the role it plays, it is important to recognize up front what it is expected to accomplish, and just as important, what it is not.

In its most basic form, the purpose of intelligence is to reduce uncertainty for policy makers, planners, and commanders, so they can make and execute plans or policies with greater confidence and less risk. The complete elimination of uncertainty, on the other hand, however noble the concept may seem, is futile, as history has shown many times over. Therefore, the first rule of intelligence is that it is intended to reduce uncertainty, not eliminate it. There are simply too many intangible factors, such as weather, mechanical failure, and human failure, to assume that good intelligence will guarantee operational success all by itself.

Second, intelligence alone should be thought of as nothing more than a tool. Irrespective of how well balanced, how sharp, or how well suited for the task the tool may be, it will not necessarily produce the desired results when in the hands of an inexperienced or careless user. The same can be said for intelligence. Unless the intended user is willing to devote resources to obtain the necessary intelligence, knows how to integrate it into the planning process, or is willing to act upon it in the absence of complete certainty, then intelligence—no matter how good it may be—is worthless.

What, then, constitutes an intelligence success? There are three main ingredients. Intelligence successes are a combination of (A) good intelligence, (B) the integration of good intelligence into the decision-making process, and (C) good luck. Good intelligence comes from efficient use of collection assets, a comprehensive analysis of available material, a concise assessment, and proper dissemination. It alone, however, is not enough to guarantee an intelligence success. And this is key. Even the best intelligence can be worthless if it is not acted upon or is used improperly. And finally, there is the factor of good luck. Luck or chance often plays a part in discovering vital data on the enemy and may result from coming across a crucial enemy document in a seized bunker, receiving the defection of important enemy personnel, or capitalizing on the blunder of one's opponent.

The battle of Midway in 1942 is a classic example of how all three factors combined to produce a true intelligence and operational success. The actual intelligence work, breaking the Japanese naval code and determining Midway as the target of the attack, was excellent. But it was only part of the success. Admiral Nimitz took an enormous risk by acting on this intelligence, sending his three carriers to Midway and leaving Hawaii virtually defenseless. Failure to act on the intelligence would have resulted in a profoundly different outcome to the battle of Midway. And finally, there was the blind luck that the American aviators found the Japanese fleet at just the right time and place.

Another good example is the raid on the Entebbe airfield in Uganda in July 1976 by Israeli commandos. Their goal was to rescue 103 hostages from a French jet airliner that had been hijacked by the Palestinian Liberation Organization en route from Israel to France. The raid included approximately 150 Israeli commandos that flew 2,500 miles in four C-130 cargo planes escorted by Phantom jet fighters to the objective. They rescued the hostages within an hour after landing, with a loss of just one Israeli soldier and three hostages. This spectacular victory combined excellent intelligence on the objective, the willingness to accept great risk, and more than a little good luck.

What, on the other hand, constitutes an intelligence failure? The phrase "intelligence failure" reflects incompetence or indicates that the intelligence process has suffered a breakdown. Additionally, if intelligence is inadequate, is it automatically a failure? Not necessarily.

There are essentially four kinds of intelligence failures. First, there are those that result from errors in the intelligence process—direction, collection, processing (which includes analysis), and dissemination. In World War II, for example, Allied imagery analysts combed every square foot of the Normandy beachhead prior to the D-Day invasion in June 1941. Yet their preoccupation with finding German units, equipment, and supplies precluded them from predicting the very obstacle that would bring the Allied advance to a near halt—the hedgerows. Their error was one based on poor direction, which, in turn, had a negative impact on collection and processing. Similarly, a message indicating that an attack on Pearl Harbor was imminent was actually sent up the chain of command but was not acted upon because of a failure in the dissemination process.

The second type results from the commander's failure to heed intelligence. Custer's Indian Scouts were so certain that they were walking into an ambush of overwhelming proportions that they actually conducted a "Death Dance" the night before the fateful attack. Custer, out of ignorance or arrogance, simply refused to accept their counsel. Likewise, Gen. Douglas MacArthur, in this case almost certainly out of sheer arrogance, refused to accept or believe that thirty Chinese divisions had crossed the Yalu River into North Korea in 1950. (Approximately thirty divisions in ten field armies crossed the Yalu between 15 October and 15 November.) Despite overwhelming intelligence to the contrary, he split his force, the Eighth Army and X Corps, and ordered them to continue the advance to the Yalu. Both units had to retreat in the face of the "phantom" Chinese divisions.

The third type of intelligence failure can be attributed to a decision made by a commander, which in hindsight and peaceful reflection could be considered imprudent in terms of the effect on intelligence. For example, the decision by Admiral Turner to install cameras on bombers rather than on separate photo reconnaissance aircraft when such aircraft were available contributed to very narrow coverage of Iwo Jima through 1944 and 1945. As a result of this and other problems, photo reconnaissance missions completely missed the large concentrations of weapons and fortifications on the north end of the island.

Fourth, some intelligence failures result not from bad intelligence operations, but from effective deception on behalf of the enemy. In 1945, the Japanese on Okinawa carried out a complete change of their defensive plan within twenty-four days of battle, no small achievement for over a hundred thousand troops. This massive movement of men and matériel was conducted with excellent operational security, much of it under darkness, and went completely undetected by U.S. intelligence. In a more recent example, in May 1998, India conducted a series of underground nuclear tests that the United States learned about only when the Indian government publicly announced them. An Indian nuclear researcher said later, "It's not a failure of the CIA. It's a matter of their intelligence being good, our deception being better."

In addition, there are phenomena pertaining to war that have a negative impact on the intelligence process because of adverse circumstances of war or chance. For example, bad weather such as clouds can obscure a target from photo reconnaissance platforms. (The term *platforms* refers to aircraft, ships, and vehicles.) Similarly, some types of terrain and foliage can mask an enemy's weapons positions from intelligence collection technologies. Furthermore, administrative organs that impact intelligence but that are separate from it can misplace valuable intelligence personnel and therefore hamper the intelligence process. Such phenomena can result in inadequate intelligence, but they do not always constitute failures.

There are several references to intelligence failures and inadequate intelligence in this book. It is important to understand the cause of these failures and inadequacies and under which category they fall. This is not an attempt to lay blame outside the intelligence camp or to exonerate the Joint Intelligence Center, Pacific Ocean Areas (JICPOA), but to isolate the cause of the intelligence problem in order to prevent such an occurrence from happening again. Too often, intelligence failures and inadequacies lead to not only knee-jerk changes of intelligence policies, but also changes in leadership, management philosophies, and organizational structures. This is often unnecessary. Too little attention is directed at the root cause of the problem—whether it was a commander's disregard for intelligence, a successful deception effort on behalf of the enemy, or the successful execution of a disinformation campaign. However, when these things happen, we should not be traumatized. We should take objective steps to solve whatever problems we face, especially now that intelligence is becoming increasingly sophisticated—chiefly taking the form of foreign denial and deception operations. As of 2001, we are more susceptible to information operations and manipulation than in years past. So, we need to research why mistakes happen and what we can do to prevent a recurrence. More important, we will never learn the right lessons and take the appropriate corrective measures if our default reaction is simply to cry "intelligence failure."

This book gives clear and concise examples of intelligence successes, failures, and inadequacies. And although the subject matter is now nearly sixty years old, the lessons are as valid as if they occurred just yesterday. Unfortunately, I can't say that we as a nation have learned from these lessons. It is time that we started paying attention.

BRIG. GEN. MICHAEL ENNIS
Head, United States Marine Corps Intelligence Activity
Headquarters, USMC, Arlington, Virginia

PREFACE

This book is a concise and detailed study of the history, operational procedures, and exploits of the United States' top secret Pacific War intelligence agency: the Joint Intelligence Center, Pacific Ocean Areas, or JICPOA. Located in the Makalapa Crater adjacent to Pearl Harbor, JICPOA was the United States' first effective, all-source intelligence unit. All-source intelligence is intelligence derived from numerous sources, such as communications, photographs, enemy documents, and prisoner of war interrogations. JICPOA's major contribution to history was its role in helping U.S. forces achieve victory in a bloody war with the Japanese. It operated from 7 September 1943 until the war ended in the summer of 1945. The unit primarily served Adm. Chester Nimitz, Pacific Fleet Commander in Chief, and his area of operations—the Central Pacific and western and southern parts of the Pacific as well. JICPOA also provided intelligence support for the strategic bombing campaigns in China, Formosa (Taiwan), and Japan, and it supported Gen. Douglas MacArthur's attack on the Philippines.

However, MacArthur, who mainly operated throughout the large landmasses of the Southwest Pacific Areas (SWPA), relied on a separate intelligence infrastructure for his information needs. Maj. Gen. Charles Willoughby, MacArthur's G-2, ran this intelligence infrastructure. It consisted of four organizations: the Allied Translator and Interpreter Section (ATIS), the Central Bureau, the Allied Intelligence Bureau (AIB), and the Order of Battle Section—all based in Australia. ATIS translated documents, interrogated prisoners of war, and provided linguists to SWPA combat units. The Central Bureau supplied MacArthur with radio intelligence, and the AIB afforded him human intelligence from spies. It also ran a series of special operations in theater. MacArthur did not believe that photo interpretation was as useful as captured documents and prisoner interrogations, so it took a backseat to other forms of intelligence.[1] Perhaps because of this,

Willoughby supervised most photo interpretation himself. Finally, the Order of Battle Section, formed in 1942, analyzed information regarding Japanese units, leadership, tactics, and weapons.[2]

JICPOA, in contrast, employed over a thousand intelligence specialists in a single organization who were assigned to various sections. Their jobs ranged from analyzing Japanese radio traffic and studying photographs of enemy-held islands, to accompanying infantry forces on beach assaults to process vital combat intelligence. JICPOA worked closely with Pacific Fleet intelligence echelons as well. (The term "fleet intelligence" refers here to all U.S. Navy and Marine intelligence activity in the Pacific, distinct from JICPOA.) JICPOA focused all of its efforts on keeping U.S. military commanders and combat echelons abreast of Japanese military activity, and its intelligence reached all branches of the Pacific Fleet, including the Marines (administratively referred to as "Fleet Marine Forces.")

Certain historians have mentioned JICPOA in their books. The official Marine Corps records of the Pacific War make reference to JICPOA in several volumes. Rear Adm. Edwin T. Layton briefly mentioned JICPOA in his book *And I Was There,* a riveting account that focused most of its pages to code-breaking and behind-the-scenes intelligence activities from Pearl Harbor to the Battle of Midway. W. J. Holmes, JICPOA's second in command, discussed JICPOA and other Pacific intelligence organizations in *Double Edged Secrets.* However, Holmes's book is more of a personal memoir of his war years than a technical study of the organization he served. Numerous other books such as *Ultra in the Pacific* and *The American Magic* are excellent works on radio intelligence units in the Pacific War and tell a vital part of our nation's military history. Yet, no historian has thoroughly examined the history of JICPOA. This book fills that gap.

JICPOA's operational procedures are relevant to today's intelligence community. Its methods of direction, collection, processing, and dissemination—the intelligence cycle—are the same basic methods used by intelligence organizations all over the world. Furthermore, the problems it faced in executing its missions are similar to those that U.S. intelligence agencies presently face.

This book also examines how JICPOA's all-source intelligence influenced the Central Pacific island-hopping campaigns under Admiral Nimitz. For each island targeted for assault, JICPOA produced an information bulletin that supplied intelligence on the island's geography, shore and beach conditions, roads, port facilities, wharves, airstrips, and enemy order of battle. Operations planners used information bulletins when devising attack plans to seize these islands—specifically, when determining where to land the attack force, how many troops to use to seize an island, and how much air and naval fire support to apply to reduce the enemy's main defenses.

It is not the goal of this book, however, to single out JICPOA as the one decisive impetus behind the Central Pacific island campaigns. Such undertakings were the result of a combination of competently led and well-trained troops, a clearly defined mission, and efficient logistical networks. Accurate intelligence was but one of the many necessary ingredients. The reader must constantly keep this in mind throughout this book. Intelligence had a tremendous impact on the Pacific island campaigns, but it did not necessarily make or break them. The marines, army troops, and sailors who fought on these islands took them away from the Japanese by effective use of violent force. This was the primary reason for the success of the campaigns.

Nor is it the goal of this book to criticize the Pacific intelligence community as a failure for those campaigns where intelligence did not accurately portray the actual enemy situation. An intelligence failure is when ineptitude infects the intelligence cycle and results in dismal consequences. This is different from an inability to complete the intelligence cycle thoroughly, even if the results may be equally dismal. The inability to complete the cycle is circumstantial; it may be due to time constraints, scant reconnaissance assets, low reconnaissance technology, a lack of collected data for analysts to work with, and any of myriad odd events associated with war. Compounding these difficulties is the enemy's effort to hide their intentions from the opponent's intelligence services. It is also pertinent to note that the failure of one portion of the intelligence cycle does not mean that the whole process has broken down. For example, signals intelligence for a particular operation might falter, but photographic and document intelligence for the same operation might generate fantastic results.

Such issues bring up numerous questions. Is it an intelligence failure when the enemy expertly camouflages defensive positions to such an extent that photo interpreters cannot see the positions? Does this mean that the photo interpreters are incompetent or not trained well enough? Or does it mean that their reconnaissance technology is not advanced enough to produce clear imagery of what is happening on the objective? What if radio interceptors are tuned into frequency "A" while the enemy reveals his secret defense plans on frequency "D?" What if document analysts have hundreds of documents to analyze, few language specialists on hand, and little or no time to complete their work? Is it possible, perhaps, that events beyond the control of intelligence specialists sometimes plague their work to the point of infection? Even so, intelligence personnel are trained and paid to get effective intelligence to the people who need it on time. Are we making excuses for the intelligence community if it does not perform to exemplary standards? In order to answer these questions, it is important to understand the tasks that intelligence specialists must complete, the environment in which they work, and the science of their trade.

Unfortunately, at the end of World War II, JICPOA closed down before it had the opportunity to analyze how its intelligence impacted the Pacific island assaults. During the war, it did produce a few after-action studies of seized islands, but these primarily mapped out enemy defenses and served as background information on general Japanese defensive tactics. Similarly, the bulk of the Pacific Fleet's after-action intelligence reports on Pacific campaigns do contain assessments of how intelligence performed during particular battles, but they were not comprehensive studies and often lacked depth. Furthermore, authors of these reports followed different formats that presented information in a variety of ways. Some assessments of the same campaign contradict one another. For example, one for Peleliu remarked that photographic intelligence for that battle was quite good, and another said it was bad. For these reasons, among others, most of the conclusions drawn here concerning the effectiveness of JICPOA's intelligence are mine.

To draw my conclusions, I have used comparison and contrast methodologies, primarily between the official Marine Corps records of Pacific campaigns and JICPOA's information bulletins. The Marine Corps records provided detailed information on each campaign, such as what happened during the landing phase, how combat progressed ashore, and decisive moments during each battle. In essence, they revealed battlefield successes, failures, and difficulties. JICPOA's information bulletins on each targeted island disclosed what was known about the objectives before U.S. forces attacked them. By comparing these two types of documents, it was possible to discover how intelligence impacted the various phases of each battle.

For example, if a naval preliminary bombardment destroyed most of the beach defenses of a particular target and JICPOA had located most of those beach defenses before the battle, presumably JICPOA's intelligence was helpful to the bombardment. Such a situation occurred on Guam. Similarly, if, upon landing, marines received heavy artillery fire from the interior of an island and JICPOA had not located main-force enemy artillery sectors on that island, the presumption would be that JICPOA's information was not effective for the preliminary bombardment—as did occur on Saipan.

Finally, this is not only a technical study of U.S. military intelligence. It is also a study of U.S. military evolution, a chronicle of struggle, determination, and courage. Before World War II, few operations planners valued intelligence units or the personnel assigned to them. During World War II, however, intelligence went from being a little-understood military science to one of the most vital commodities in the United States' vast arsenal, and the intelligence specialist went from being the misfit line officer to the invaluable sage. Ultimately, as a result of World War II, the United States would change from being one of the only major world powers that neglected intelligence to a nation that would come to hold it as a vital service.

Overall, this book focuses on the true nature of military intelligence—what it is, where it comes from, and how it can be used. Analyzing how military intelligence impacted the Pacific War, specifically the Central Pacific drive, helps to reveal the true nature and purpose of intelligence, a concept that is unclear to most outside of the intelligence community. Over the years, many in the press, the government, and even the military have come to expect the impossible from intelligence—that it provide a god's-eye view of the activities that surround us, especially those of the enemy. However, enemy activity is dictated by human behavior, and human behavior is impossible to correctly predict on a continual basis. The purpose of military intelligence is not to provide an all-seeing view of the enemy, but to decrease the inherent uncertainty of military operations by providing information about the enemy that helps the commander achieve his or her goals.

Intelligence and the Amphibious Assault:
Basic Concepts

Intelligence

Intelligence is one of the most vital ingredients in war and operations planning. Around 400 B.C., the Chinese general Sun Tzu wrote in *The Art of War:* "Know the enemy and know yourself; in a hundred battles you will never be in peril. When you are ignorant of the enemy but know yourself, your chances of winning or losing are equal. If ignorant of both the enemy and yourself, you are certain in every battle to be in peril."[3]

Carl von Clausewitz, in his posthumously published book *On War,* described intelligence as "all the knowledge we have on the enemy and his country; therefore, in fact, the foundation of all our ideas and actions."[4]

According to *U.S. Naval Intelligence Naval Doctrine Publication (NDP) 2,* a joint U.S. Navy–Marine Corps intelligence manual, there are three primary types of intelligence: strategic, operational, and tactical. Strategic intelligence helps senior-level policy makers prioritize national objectives and provides information on foreign countries' national objectives, capabilities, and intentions. In the late 1930s, for example, the White House and War Department were missing specific strategic intelligence on Japanese military plans to seize Southeast Asia for its oil and other natural resources. Had they known, they might have been able to direct the U.S. military to blunt Japanese attacks throughout the region and avert the seizure of the Philippines and the attack on Pearl Harbor.

Operational intelligence provides information to senior operations planners who design theater or regional military operations. This includes identifying major objectives to be seized, exploited, or destroyed. In the Pacific War, for example, operational intelligence helped Adm. Chester Nimitz decide what island groups to attack and what specific islands to occupy.

Tactical intelligence supports the conduct of the attack or defense in the battlespace by furnishing information on the enemy's order of battle. This includes troop strength, weapons, the type and location of defensive fortifications, or the scope of the enemy's attack formations. For example, during the island-hopping campaigns in the Central Pacific, photo interpreters analyzed aerial photographs of enemy air bases for tactical intelligence on Japanese defensive fortifications to support naval and aerial bombardment missions. Whatever the type of intelligence support, they all have something in common—each type provides information on the enemy's capabilities and intentions.[5]

Although during World War II JICPOA's intelligence influenced decision making at the strategic level, its main contribution was to the operational and tactical levels where operations planning and execution took place. Fundamentally, JICPOA helped operations planners decide how much force to apply to seize an objective, which entailed inflicting the maximum amount of destruction on the enemy at the least expense to U.S. commanders and in a minimum amount of time.

There are several variations of the intelligence cycle, but they are all similar. *U.S. Army Field Manual 34-3, Intelligence Analysis,* states that "intelligence operations follow a four-phase process known as the intelligence cycle" and that the process is continuous.[6] According to FM 34-3, the cycle consists of direction, collection, processing, and dissemination. In the direction phase, the commander dictates the intelligence mission, prioritizes information requirements, and establishes a due date for the intelligence product. This phase is vital, because it establishes what operations planners need to know, how the information will be collected, and when it will be delivered for use. In the collection phase, units or individuals collect data on the enemy or terrain through various means—human reconnaissance, intercepting radio signals, interrogating prisoners of war, analyzing captured documents, etc. During the processing phase, analysts assess, integrate, and deduce data for its value to the operation at hand. This is where information becomes intelligence, a pivotal stage. Analysis requires thoughtful application by intelligent personnel who also possess common sense and at least a familiarity with the enemy and their processes. The U.S. Army asserts that phase three is also when the information is produced, or packaged, for the end user. Afterward, in phase four, the intelligence is forwarded to specific end users who then apply it to operations planning and execution.[7]

The Intelligence Cycle. Naval Intelligence, Naval Doctrine Publication 2

The U.S. Navy's *NDP 2* states that intelligence is a five-step process that consists of planning and direction, collection, processing, production, and dissemination. The Marine Corps also uses this sequence. It essentially is the same as the U.S. Army's version, except that the USN divided the cycle differently.[8] JICPOA used a similar process—direction, collection, prioritization, processing, production, and dissemination. JICPOA's process differed slightly from the armed services' doctrines stated above because it supported a rapid operational tempo, and information overload was sometimes a problem. Accordingly, it applied prioritization to certain types of data after the collection phase. (The USA, USN, and USMC doctrines also use prioritization, but within other phases.) For example, if operation "A" produced thousands of captured documents, JICPOA's linguists would scan through them and pick out the documents pertinent to operation "B," the next island assault. This type of occurrence—adapting to the circumstances of the war—happened frequently because, unlike the current U.S. armed forces, JICPOA did not have an intelligence doctrine when the war began. It had to develop one as the war progressed.

Indeed, on the eve of World War II, the United States did not have substantial intelligence assets. Each branch of the military had its own intelligence unit, but none was capable of supporting large offensive operations. This was a direct result of historical neglect. The United States had never put real effort into establishing an effective intelligence echelon. That is not to say that the United States did not have intelligence capabilities during past wars, because it did. For example, Gen. George Washington ran his own human intelligence operations during the American Revolution, Gen. Ulysses S. Grant relied on an unextraordinary wartime intelligence agency run by Allan Pinkerton during the Civil War, and the U.S. Navy established the Office of Naval Intelligence in 1882. However, these were small intelligence services with limited assets, and while they sometimes did provide crucial intelligence, overall, they lacked effectiveness.

Most U.S. commanders through history relied heavily on cavalry patrols, combat air patrols, and scouts for intelligence. These units reconnoitered beyond flanks and front lines to observe enemy activities by line of sight and frequently engaged the enemy in firefights. The information they gathered gave commanders a limited and occasionally accurate picture of the battlefield. Interestingly, cavalry and reconnaissance were not typically associated with intelligence. The former were line commands, and the latter were academic endeavors, and so few strategic or tactical thinkers joined intelligence. Therefore, the U.S. military establishment never made a significant effort to integrate a capable intelligence service into the force structure. If it had, it would not have struck an intelligence vacuum at the beginning of World War II, when, according to the official Marine Corps record of the Pacific War, officers of low caliber, incompetent leaders, and "misfits" were funneled into intelligence services.[9] After the war, U.S. Army Gen. Omar Bradley said, "In some stations, G-2 became a dumping ground for officers ill suited to line command."[10] Although this was the unfortunate norm, there were exceptions.

One was Col. Edwin Schwien, USA, a 1932 graduate of the French military academy Ecole Supérieure de Guerre and an instructor at the Command and General Staff School at Fort Leavenworth, Kansas, from 1932 to 1936. His book, *Combat Intelligence: Its Acquisition and Transmission,* published by the *Infantry Journal,* discussed basics tenets of intelligence and supported them with case studies from World War I. It is a remarkable work of military science that exhibits the extraordinary usefulness of tactical intelligence in a warfighting support role.[11] It is apparent, however, that most of Schwien's cohorts tossed the book aside. Likewise, most of those who replaced the World War I officer generation never even heard of Colonel Schwien. The lessons of World War I stayed lost, and intelligence was never effectively integrated into operations planning.

Another post–World War I proponent of intelligence was Marine Corps Lt. Col. Earl H. Ellis, otherwise known as "Pete" Ellis. He hypothesized that the global naval arms race of the early 1920s would probably lead to a major war with Japan. He also believed that during such a war the United States would undertake a Pacific-wide amphibious campaign to secure bases and anchorages to support naval operations. Therefore, he lobbied senior Marine and ONI officers to allow him to conduct a clandestine intelligence operation aimed at collecting data on Japanese base and port construction activities throughout the Pacific's numerous island groups. With permission granted, in 1921, he began touring via ship around the Pacific, undercover, as a commercial trading agent for Manhattan-based Hughes Trading Company. After traveling through the Bonin, Caroline, and Marshall Island groups, he landed in the Palaus in 1923. Ellis had reportedly collected significant hydrographic information and data on some port facilities, but his apparent alcoholism severely impaired his mission. Besides, Japanese authorities, wary of foreign visitors to their mandated islands, suspected him of clandestine activities. By one account, Japanese administrators on Palau provided him with potent whiskey during one of his debilitating alcoholic stupors, and he died shortly thereafter. There is no evidence that the information he collected made it back to the United States.[12]

Nevertheless, it might have been highly valuable after 1941. Likewise, Colonel Schwien's analysis of the effectiveness of combat intelligence might have saved the United States considerable time and energy when World War II began, had senior officers in charge of force structuring realized the value of his thesis. None of these endeavors, however, came to fruition, and U.S. forces, especially those that would fight in the Pacific, remained without effective intelligence experience, doctrine, and infrastructure in the beginning stages of the war.

Indeed, the military's attitude toward the intelligence community remained negative well into the war. For example, it often passed over for selection competent and skilled intelligence personnel such as four of the seven officers who helped establish Pearl Harbor's famed radio intelligence unit that led to the Midway coup. Only when Japan became more threatening in the latter months of 1941 and radio intelligence became a valued commodity did the War Department promote three of them.[13] Ultimately, disdain for intelligence proved calamitous, because intelligence support for amphibious operations was vital.

Amphibious Assault

Numerous armies throughout history have relied on amphibious assaults, which are the movement of troops from naval ships at sea in tactical formation to seize land objectives. The Romans and Greeks relied on amphibious tactics for decades, as did several armies through the centuries into World War I. During World War I, however, the utility of the amphibious assault came under severe criticism after the disastrous British-run landing at Gallipoli. The real problem, however, was that no military had ever established an effective amphibious doctrine that dictated correct landing techniques, proper amphibious loading, and coordinated fire support procedures.

Enter the U.S. Marine Corps—the few, the proud, and the implementers of strong-arm U.S. foreign policy in the Caribbean during the years following World War I. Through this type of foreign policy, the Marines became involved in several low-intensity conflicts throughout the region. Most of their deployments involved ship-to-shore operations. In the Caribbean, the Marine Corps learned, among other war sciences, the littoral technicalities of ship-to-shore movement and combat loading, which is the logistical practice of embarking low-priority materials first in landing vessels and vital combat necessities last. This way, when the marines landed on the shores of an objective, they had ready access to the supplies that they needed the most: ammunition, medical stores, water, etc. The USMC stocked rear-echelon materials, such as administrative equipment, at the bottom of supply vessels because they would be needed last—only after they had secured a perimeter from which to erect a semipermanent head-quarters. In principle, combat loading sounds simple, but in reality, when combined with amphibious assault tactics and strategy, it can become complicated. Combat loading demands considerable forethought on the part of operations planners.

Because of their interest in establishing a meaningful mission with the fleet, in 1933 the Marines began developing a manual for amphibious land-ings. The U.S. Navy was also a significant force in developing this doctrine because it was responsible for transporting the Marine forces to the area of operations and for executing ship-to-shore operations. In 1934, the USMC published a landmark manual titled *Tentative Manual for Landing Opera-tions*. It specified the six elements of the amphibious landing: command relationships, naval fire support, tactical air support, ship-to-shore move-ment, securing the beachhead, and logistics.[14] By 1938, the USMC and USN had tested and refined the new doctrine. The U.S. Navy published the ver-sion it used in World War II in 1938, under the title *Fleet Training Publica-tion (FTP) Number 167: Landing Operations Doctrine, U.S. Navy, 1938*.[15] The work of the Marines and the Navy resulted in a specific landing doc-trine. It included the following steps: 1) cover operations to neutralize local enemy naval and air forces; 2) naval and aerial preliminary bombardment of the objective to prep the target for infantry attack; 3) ship-to-shore movement of assault forces; 4) establishment of the beachhead; 5) move-ment inland to secure objectives and ship-to-shore movement of follow-on forces and logistics.[16]

During the ship-to-shore phase, the Marines used tracked landing ve-hicles (LVTs) and landing craft to take the fight to land. LVTs were tracked amphibious armored personnel carriers that could negotiate reefs and swim, and landing craft were flat-bottomed boats with hinged ramps on their bows to land troops and supplies. This latter type of vessel varied in size and length according to payload. Some carried infantry (Landing Craft, Infantry—LCI), some carried vehicles and tanks (Landing Craft, Mech-anized—LCM), and some carried both vehicles and personnel (Landing Craft, Vehicle and Personnel—LCVP). Then there were much larger ver-sions, which were actually ships, such as Landing Ship, Tanks (LSTs) and Landing Ship, Mediums (LSMs), which carried large amounts of tanks, ve-hicles, and artillery. Usually, the tracked landing vehicles landed first, fol-lowed by successive waves of smaller landing craft, followed by larger land-ing craft.

Intelligence factored into each phase of an amphibious assault. Operations planners had to know where and in what strength to send their carrier task forces to successfully overwhelm the enemy and isolate an island designated for attack. Naval gunners had to know where to focus their bombardments to achieve maximum destruction of enemy positions on shore. The Marines had to know what type of beach they would be assaulting to insure an efficient landing and how much resistance to expect. The Navy also had to know beach conditions because they were the ones who planned and coordinated the amphibious movement of each Central Pacific island assault. And finally, the Marines needed to know the exact location of objectives to be secured and the whereabouts of enemy troop dispositions and strong points in order to plan an effective scheme of maneuver.

A Note about Researching Intelligence

People who write about intelligence operations well know that the theories that they publish today may crumble tomorrow when some hitherto secret document emerges into the open. In fact, the vast majority of intelligence documents germane to my subject have been declassified. However, because of a story I was told while in Southeast Asia, I have to acknowledge that there may be pertinent classified documents about my subject matter still in existence.

In the fall of 1996 in a bar in Saigon, I met an ex–U.S. Army officer and businessman whose father had claimed that he was part of a top secret Special Forces team sent to infiltrate a certain Pacific island months before the battle to capture it began. His mission was to conduct reconnaissance against Japanese military units and record their activities. On his deathbed, he told his son about the civilian islanders whom he had recruited to assist him in his spying. Curious, the son went to his father's former area of operations to check the story out. Upon his inquiry at one village, an old man told him to stop wandering around and asking questions and to meet him at a predesignated location later that night. Intrigued, the son agreed. At that meeting, the young officer met several elderly men who explained that the purpose of the midnight meeting was to maintain their "cover." Why? Because, they claimed, they had worked with his father against the Japanese, and they had been sworn to lifelong secrecy. The men further told him personal things about his father, not discussed with his first point of contact, that convinced him that the story was true.

To my knowledge, no documents that mention that particular island operation have been made public. Perhaps they were purposely buried in some vault or destroyed after the war. Perhaps they are still classified, or maybe they shed light on a facet of the Pacific War that remains unknown and will remain so until release or discovery. Until then, the top secret special operations that may have occurred on that island and perhaps on other islands as well will remain a "black bag job," otherwise known to the public as a mystery.

ACKNOWLEDGMENTS

I would first like to thank my mother, Patricia Moore, who is a freelance journalist, for editing several drafts for style and grammatical correctness. She also encouraged me to continue pushing this book forward, and without her support it might not have been published. (Thanks, Mom.)

Dr. Michael A. Palmer, Chair of the History Department at East Carolina University, Greenville, North Carolina, provided me with undaunted encouragement, technical support, and hours of editorial expertise while I wrote this book. I owe him many thanks for his tutelage and professional advice.

Thanks also to Michael C. Ramsdell for his editing services and feedback on issues put forth in this work. His assistance proved very helpful.

Three former JICPOA officers granted me personal interviews during the research phase. Rear Adm. Donald M. Showers talked to me about the history of JICPOA, how it operated in conjunction with strategic and tactical planning, and about intelligence issues in general. John A. Harrison described the Pacific intelligence community's information flow, clarified the duties of the JICPOA's operational intelligence personnel, and described the vital working relationship between JICPOA and the Pacific's military radio intelligence units. Frank Gibney, former JICPOA interrogator, discussed with me the details of the JICPOA's linguistic intelligence capabilities.

I would also like to thank Mr. Benis M. Frank, former Chief Historian of the U.S. Marine Corps Historical Center and World War II veteran of the First Marine Division, for introducing me to the existence of the little-known but historically significant JICPOA. Mr. Frank also edited a draft of this book, lending his extensive knowledge of the amphibious campaigns carried out under Admiral Nimitz. In addition, Mr. Mike Walker of the Naval Historical Center helped me track down elusive intelligence material contained within hundreds of U.S. naval intelligence and operations documents.

Much appreciation goes to several unnamed current and former combat veterans and career intelligence officers who helped professionalize concepts put forth in this book. Their insights and advice were invaluable.

Thanks also to Brig. Gen. Mike Ennis, Head of Marine Corps Intelligence Activity and former commander of the Joint Intelligence Center, Pacific, for editing this book for content, for providing insight into intelligence issues, and for writing the Foreword. He has my deepest gratitude.

Special thanks to 9th Insight, a graphics company based in Milan and Alexandria, Va., and their brightest graphics technician, Jag. They provided outstanding graphics services with regard to converting World War II intelligence maps to electronic form and cleaning them up for publication. Their professionalism is to be commended.

Finally, I would like to thank my friends, and especially my father and brother, who remained supportive of me throughout the writing of this book.

SPIES FOR NIMITZ

1

GENESIS

Long before the advent of JICPOA, the United Sates had a wide array of small, decentralized intelligence units trying to keep tabs on the rise of Japanese militancy during the late 1930s and early 1940s. Among the most prominent were the Office of Naval Intelligence (ONI), U.S. military attachés stationed throughout Asia, and OP-20-G, which belonged to the chief of naval operations (CNO). Routinely neglected, they were none too effective.

ONI conducted military intelligence analyses and covert operations. Its analyses included assessments of Japan's military capabilities and its intentions toward other Asian nations and the United States. For its covert operations, ONI placed spies in Asian ports to report on Japanese naval activity, had agents hunt for official documents in Japanese consulate and embassy trash containers, and conducted surveillance of Japanese living in the United States, many of them U.S. citizens. Occasionally, ONI operators would attempt an embassy break-in to try to steal codebooks or other secret documents.

U.S. military attachés served in U.S. embassies and collected information on everything they saw that might provide information on Japanese capabilities and intentions. They observed military training areas, commercial ports, and rail yards. They even listened in on the conversations of Japanese citizens on the street to see if the national mood supported war with the United States or Asia.[1] However, as the Japanese neared war with the United States, they placed severe restrictions on foreign attaché activity. For example, they stated that military attachés were not allowed to travel more than fifteen miles from Tokyo without advising the defense ministry. The advisory had to include a detailed description of the traveler's itinerary—departure time, destination, arrival time, number of people in the party, etc.[2] On the other hand, many military attachés were

1

simply language officers assigned to intelligence duty and had never received proper intelligence training. Moreover, many of these officers were not interested in intelligence, and it showed in their work.[3]

Finally, OP-20-G, the U.S. Navy's communications intelligence unit, eavesdropped on Japanese radio communiqués to gather information on Japanese Fleet activity and order of battle and Japanese intentions. This involved painstaking code-breaking work. To gain its information, OP-20-G had radio intercept towers, otherwise known as listening posts, scattered throughout the Pacific—Hawaii, Guam, Seattle, the Philippines, China. After collecting and analyzing information, each listening post passed its final assessment to Washington, D.C., where analysts often scrutinized the information a second time. OP-20-G sent most of its crucial intelligence directly to the War Department, the State Department, and the White House in raw form.[4]

The intelligence these units produced was important because Japan's growing militancy threatened the vital interests and national security of the United States. Since 1930, the Imperial Japanese Army (IJA) had become a power in Japanese domestic politics and foreign policy. Led by fascists and supported by a populace disaffected by corrupt politicians and economic depression and infused with xenophobia, the IJA had assassinated and intimidated its way into power.[5] The IJA's main goal was to assert control over the Asia-Pacific to gain access to its natural resources. Its leaders believed that this would alleviate Japan's economic woes and free it from dependence on Western imports and foreign influence. In accordance with this goal, IJA units deployed to protect Japanese business interests in Manchuria took over their host country in the fall of 1931. Executed without authorization from the Japanese government, the operation resulted in the acquisition of 440,000 square miles of foreign territory, renamed Manchukuo by the IJA.[6] In the months that followed, the IJA took control of Japan's government and society, preparing it for war by increasing military industrial output, enlarging the ranks of the military, and drawing war plans against its largest neighbor, China. On 28 July 1937, six years after the Manchuria takeover, Japan invaded China.[7] Japan joined forces with Nazi Germany three years later, in a formal alliance made on 27 September 1940.[8] Furthermore, as it pushed its war machine through China, Japan also made inroads into Southeast Asia, specifically Vietnam, in preparation to seize the rest of Indochina, Thailand, Burma, Malaysia, the Philippines, Brunei, and Indonesia.

Alarmed at Japan's growing military expansion, U.S. President Franklin D. Roosevelt relocated the Pacific Fleet from San Diego, California, to Pearl

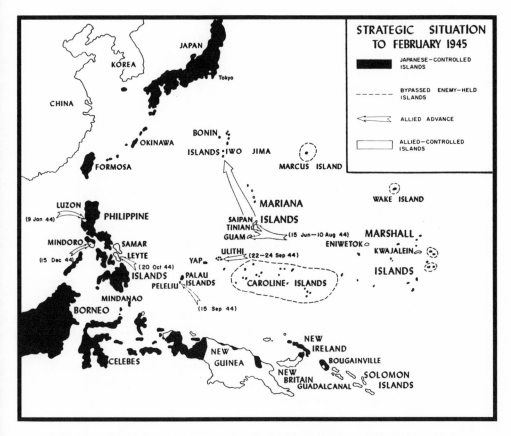

The Pacific Area of Operations, U.S. advances as of 1945. Garand and Strobridge, *Western Pacific Operations*

Harbor, Hawaii, to prevent possible Japanese moves against U.S. interests in the Pacific and the West Coast. Then, in July 1940, the United States placed an embargo on Japan that restricted the sale of aviation fuel—a vital war material[9]—and various nonlethal goods, such as cotton. With this collision of U.S. and Japanese interests, the possibility of military confrontation became a reality. Amid such tension, intelligence became a vital commodity to the White House. Naturally, OP-20-G's unit in Hawaii, code-named "Hypo" for its radio intercept tower at Heeia Island, grew in importance to the Commander in Chief, Pacific (CINCPAC), who at that time was Adm. Husband E. Kimmel.

Like his superiors in Washington, Kimmel needed to know what the Japanese were up to in the Pacific in case they decided to attack U.S. interests or the United States itself. Kimmel came to rely on Hypo to keep him abreast of Japanese activities; as result, the organization grew semiautonomous and became just as important as its parent office in D.C. As Hypo grew, it shouldered responsibilities in addition to code-breaking, such as trying to piece together the Japanese naval order of battle and assessing the abilities of platforms like Japan's new A-6M Zero fighter aircraft. With Hypo's new duties came a new name, the Combat Intelligence Unit (CIU), which it adopted in the summer of 1941.[10] Cdr. Joseph J. Rochefort, USN, served as the CIU's first commander.[11] However, the CIU's autonomy did not sit well with D.C.-based OP-20-G, so it began to keep to itself certain radio intercepts it gained from other listening posts. This withholding of information denied the CIU and Kimmel the larger picture of Japanese activity in the Pacific and proved especially unfortunate because Japan's military readiness was increasing as a result of its goals in Southeast Asia and President Roosevelt's embargo.[12]

Japan viewed the embargo as a direct attack on its interests because it relied on U.S. imports for national survival. Tensions in the Pacific increased, and both countries committed diplomats to try to solve their problems peacefully, but the initiatives fell apart. Then, on 24 July 1941, Japan took the whole of French-run Vietnam, claiming that its colonial masters invited the occupation, but the United States had Japanese radio transcripts that proved otherwise. (Vietnam was then part of Indochina, which included present-day Laos and Cambodia, and remained so until 1954.) The Japanese had threatened their way into Vietnam with military force,[13] and the French government, in reluctant cahoots with the Germans, capitulated to the Japanese Empire's demands. In other words, Japan had yet again taken a country by force, and Roosevelt was wise to it.

Enraged at the underhanded diplomatic smoke screen that had for so long been covering the aggressiveness of the IJA, Roosevelt ceased all trade with Japan, including oil shipments, and froze Japanese assets invested in the United States. Angered in turn, the IJA called for decisive military action against the United States. While executing this decisive action, the Japanese intended also to seize Southeast Asia and the Pacific, sooner rather than later.

The IJA persuaded the Imperial Japanese Navy (IJN) to help prepare a series of lightning strikes against key European and U.S. centers of gravity throughout Asia, including Singapore, Indonesia, and the Philippines. Senior naval commanders assigned Adm. Isoroku Yamamoto, commander in chief of the Combined Fleet, to plan and supervise an attack against the U.S. Fleet. Yamamoto wanted to eliminate U.S. naval power in the Pacific in one campaign, so he decided to attack it at its home base at Pearl Harbor, Hawaii. Victory there, he hypothesized, would keep the United States from hindering Japan's conquests in the near term.

Ironically, the United States was helping the Japanese with that very goal through a conflict between the CIU and OP-20-G. Technically, however, the struggle began in the summer of 1940, when two new intelligence entities came to the fore. They were the Fleet Intelligence Officer, Lt. Cdr. Edwin T. Layton, and the Director Of War Plans, Adm. Richmond Kelly Turner. As Fleet Intelligence Officer—technically the Chief of Staff of Intelligence—Layton was to coordinate all Pacific intelligence activities, collate significant intelligence, and disseminate it to specific end-users. Before the war began, his main intelligence provider was Hypo and, later, the CIU. His primary end users were Adm. Harold R. Stark, Chief of Naval Operations (CNO), ONI in Washington, D.C., and CINCPAC at Pearl Harbor.[14] He also had exclusive jurisdiction over the dissemination of ULTRA,[15] intelligence that came from Japanese military communications. MAGIC, another well-known type of communications intelligence, came from Japanese diplomatic cables and rarely factored into operational intelligence or support to the warfighter.[16]

Although Turner's job was to draw hypothetical war plans against the Japanese, he inserted himself and his staff into the Pacific intelligence community. Stationed in Washington, D.C., close to his powerful allies in the CNO's office and OP-20-G, he claimed that none of the existing intelligence units had the aptitude to analyze Japanese intentions and that his staff did.[17] The resulting fight over intelligence responsibilities and resources impaired U.S. intelligence capabilities prior to the attack on Pearl Harbor and even beyond to the operation against Guadalcanal in 1942.

According to Layton, Turner and his staff did not share with him most of the communications intelligence they received from OP-20-G. Layton further stated that many of Turner's estimates were erroneous. For example, Turner and his staff predicted in 1941 that Japan had no plans to attack Pearl Harbor and that, instead, it was planning to attack Russia.[18] Overall, none of the Pacific's intelligence activities were centralized, and as a consequence, there was very little effective intelligence work being done in the Pacific on 6 December 1941. Therefore, when Japanese fighters and dive-bombers attacked on the seventh, no one was prepared, and the United States suffered a crippling blow to its naval capabilities.

Adm. Chester Nimitz emerged in the aftermath of Pearl Harbor to take over as the new CINCPAC. Nimitz told Lieutenant Commander Layton that intelligence would be pivotal in the fight against the Japanese and that he wanted him to provide unique insight into Japanese capabilities and intentions.[19] This required a concentrated effort from all Pacific intelligence units under CINCPAC's command. However, the Japanese onslaught through the Asian Pacific after the attack on Pearl Harbor forced most U.S. military attachés to return home. Similarly, ONI had few resources in the Pacific, and CIU and OP-20-G did not get along. The unfortunate turn of events left Nimitz without effective intelligence support and blind to enemy activities in the midst of a world war.

Meanwhile, the Commandant of the U.S. Marine Corps, Lt. Gen. Thomas Holcomb,[20] realized that the war against Japan would require extensive amphibious operations supported by concentrated naval surface and air power. Like Pete Ellis before him, he further realized that intelligence would be vital to the success of such operations and that the United States did not have the intelligence capability to support them. Therefore, on 24 March 1942, Commandant Holcomb wrote a letter to the commander in chief of the U.S. Fleet (COMINCH), Adm. Ernest J. King, proposing the creation of a joint intelligence center (JIC) to be stationed at Pearl Harbor, Hawaii. The commandant suggested that the center's joint designation consist of U.S. Marine, Navy, and Army personnel and be supported by four miniature field JICs positioned throughout the Pacific as the war progressed.[21]

King, who was also serving as chief of naval operations (CNO), endorsed the idea and advised the commandant to prepare a plan for its implementation. (President Roosevelt authorized merging COMINCH and CNO into one job when the war began.) Lt. Gen. Holcomb submitted his plan, dated 11 April 1942, to both King and Nimitz, since it would undoubtedly operate under the latter's command. Admiral Nimitz also endorsed the plan and said that he sorely needed such an organization because a lack of intelligence had hindered planning military operations against the Japanese. Taking things a step further to insure that the plan was implemented, Nimitz wrote a letter to King dated 28 May 1942 endorsing the JIC proposal. He also made suggestions for its organization. Specifically, Nimitz suggested that the new organization absorb the intelligence agencies already working for him and that the four smaller intelligence centers not be established until the main one at Pearl was up and running. He further said that the new center should contain the following offices or "sections":[22]

An estimates section for estimating enemy intentions and capabilities
A database for reference and for cross-checking information for authenticity and accuracy

A photographic interpretation section for analyzing photos of enemy bases, ships, shorelines, beaches, etc.

A topographic office to make maps of enemy-held land masses and islands

A tracking unit for plotting the movement of Japanese naval traffic

A radio eavesdropping section for each of the Army and the Navy

An administrative section for JIC coordination

Admiral Nimitz requested that a naval officer with the rank of captain or commander be put in charge of the unit and that he have three assistants: one officer each from the Army, the Navy, and the Marines, plus a contingent of five yeomen.[23] Such an organization would provide the basic ability to assess Japanese capabilities and intentions. However, while this organization would provide insight on the location of Japanese forces and what they might be planning, it was not structured to provide comprehensive intelligence for planning offensive campaigns. That capability would have to come from a much larger unit, with a wider-ranging focus and more assets.

Time, however, was pressing, and the Japanese would not call a "time out" to let the United States regroup to build an effective intelligence unit to support killing the emperor's servicemen. Essentially what King, Nimitz, and Holcomb had done was to lay the skeletal foundation of an organization that would operate ad hoc until they could obtain more resources.

Meanwhile, the CIU, numbering about fifty personnel, was all Nimitz had.[24] Nevertheless, despite the debilitating rivalry between OP-20-G and the CIU, it was still able to produce a mass of intelligence. Under a dedicated and D.C.-defiant Commander Rochefort, the CIU had assumed additional tasks, including plotting the location of Japanese ships and analyzing Japanese military charts and maps. Each officer in the unit specialized in a particular area of expertise, such as analyzing Japanese ground forces, naval forces, merchant fleets, or air forces.[25] The CIU passed its information to Nimitz through Layton, a channel that would remain in effect for the duration of the war. Most of the CIU's intelligence came from enemy radio transmissions, because it lacked significant aerial photographic resources. Moreover, the CIU had few enemy documents to analyze and no prisoners of war to interrogate.

Nevertheless, the CIU is most renowned for orchestrating the Midway intelligence coup—one of history's most dramatic and effective intelligence operations. The coup took place during May 1942 when the Japanese launched an operation to destroy the U.S. carrier fleet that was absent during the Pearl Harbor attack. They also wanted to position themselves to invade Hawaii at a later date. Both could be accomplished, hypothesized Admiral Yamamoto, with an attack on Midway Island, a U.S. air base located 1,200 miles west-northwest of Pearl Harbor.

Rochefort had a hunch, based on recent Japanese naval activity, that the Japanese planned to strike Midway Island, but he could not be sure because the enemy's radio transmissions discussed target objectives only by using letter designations. From analyzing Japanese radio traffic about a large upcoming offensive, Rochefort hypothesized that the Japanese had assigned Midway the letters "AF," so he devised a plan to trick the Japanese into revealing if this in fact was the case. With considerable foresight, he petitioned Nimitz to openly transmit a false radio message reporting that the U.S. base at Midway had lost its water desalination capabilities. This was an important piece of information to the Japanese if their troops were going to occupy the island. Accordingly, Nimitz acquiesced and ordered the false transmission. Predictably, forward Japanese units overheard the transmission and radioed to their superiors that "AF" had lost desalination capabilities. Hearing this, Rochefort informed his superiors that the Japanese definitely planned to seize Midway. In June, Nimitz assembled a carrier strike force and ambushed Yamamoto's carriers just after his aircraft had conducted preparatory air strikes against the island base. The Japanese lost four carriers and squadrons of planes.[26] Unknown to Nimitz at the time, with such heavy losses the Japanese had also lost the momentum of the war in the Pacific, and they would constantly be on the defensive from that point on. Surprisingly, so would Rochefort. The Washington clique would eventually sack his command.

In the meantime, however, Layton saw that the Combat Intelligence Unit did not produce adequate strategic intelligence needed for large-scale offensive operations.[27] Radio intelligence provided by the unit did account for the victory at Midway, but for the long run, it alone was not enough. The CIU did not have the personnel, material, or workspace to handle the awesome responsibility of producing the high volume of intelligence needed to support naval offensives and amphibious assaults. Nimitz agreed and recommended that a larger intelligence organization be established to solve the problem.[28] But Nimitz did not want to expand Layton's staff,[29] and he still was anticipating the JIC that he wanted, so on 24 June 1942 he ordered that a new intelligence organization be built around the existing CIU.[30] They called it the Intelligence Center, Pacific Ocean Area, or ICPOA, and it absorbed the Combat Intelligence Unit. Rochefort served as ICPOA's first commander. The CIU continued its radio intelligence duties and kept its name as a section within ICPOA.[31]

Official military documents that discuss the history of the U.S. Pacific intelligence community indicate that Nimitz might have been trying to mold ICPOA into his joint intelligence center. However, the vice chief of naval operations (VCNO), Vice Adm. Frederick J. Horne,[32] had not wholly agreed with all of CINCPAC's March recommendations for the proposed joint agency. In a letter dated 26 June 1942, Horne asserted that a joint program hindered expedient implementation. In other words, there was a war on, and, in the short run, time would be better spent producing intelligence rather than spending time laboring over the joint structure of the agency. Therefore, Admiral Horne said, any new Pacific intelligence agency should remain a Navy-run operation.[33] Besides, the Navy was already running most Pacific intelligence operations. Nevertheless, both Nimitz and Horne agreed that hasty implementation of ICPOA did not necessarily preclude a joint intelligence center. It merely delayed one for immediate convenience. ICPOA began functioning on 19 July 1942, implementing all CINCPAC's original structural suggestions intended for the JIC along with additional ones offered by the VCNO. They included the following:

An enemy documents section comprised of Japanese linguists who would translate and analyze captured enemy literature

A prisoner of war (POW) interrogation section

A dissemination section designed to distribute ICPOA's information to the fleet

The VCNO assessed that it would take 81 officers and 121 enlisted men to adequately staff the unit, which was close to the actual number that staffed ICPOA. From its inception, ICPOA employed 190 personnel, including officers and enlisted. It operated in the basement of the Navy Yard's administration building at Pearl Harbor.[34] However, ICPOA did not function as a self-sufficient organization. It had to borrow services from other intelligence units within the U.S. military, such as the Photographic Reconnaissance and Interpretation Intelligence Center (PRISIC) on Ford Island, Honolulu.[35] PRISIC coordinated aerial photographic reconnaissance missions over enemy-held territory, developed film, and analyzed photographs for intelligence concerning the capabilities and intentions of enemy naval, air, and land forces. It also analyzed photographs of Japanese industrial centers. However, PRISIC did not have its own photo-equipped aircraft and pilots. Instead, it relied on the U.S. Army Air Force and the Pacific Fleet's carrier aircraft to fly aerial reconnaissance missions, as they did throughout the war.

For the next several months, ICPOA expanded rapidly. In September

1942, ICPOA received twenty-one officers and moved into Navy Yard Supply Building Number 167. Then in November 1942, it received fifty-seven enlisted men. It also added three new sections:

An enemy equipment evaluation section
A liaison office to the U.S. Army and Marine Corps
An enemy air forces section

The Air Forces Section took over and expanded the CIU's responsibility for analyzing Japanese air forces, and it provided technical specifications of Japanese air units and aircraft. Thereafter, the CIU efforts regarding air forces were limited to tracking Japanese air units.

The expansion of ICPOA meant that entire sections of analysts were now doing what individuals had been doing for months. At the same time, ICPOA continued to process information into intelligence for naval operations, but Nimitz had not yet planned a major offensive operation toward Tokyo. Most U.S. military activity involved blocking further Japanese expansion and stabilizing lines of communication between Hawaii and Australia.[36]

The Japanese threatened those lines of communication in July 1942 with the construction of a Japanese air base on an island in the Solomons called Guadalcanal. Another base nearby, Tulagi, supported Japanese activities in the Solomons. If the Japanese could effectively operate a military airstrip in the Solomons, then the United States might be cut off from Australia, the strategic point at which to divide and conquer. So Nimitz decided to attack. However, he did not have enough resources in theater to conduct a campaign at maximum efficiency and was forced to scrape up supplies, men, and vessels for the operation from all over the U.S. West Coast and Hawaii. Accordingly, it became semiofficially known as Operation Shoestring. Unfortunately, this lack of resources also included intelligence. In fact, the nature of intelligence for Guadalcanal caused one historian to note that "from an intelligence point of view, the Guadalcanal-Tulagi landings can hardly be called more than a stab in the dark."[37]

Interestingly, ICPOA did not have jurisdiction over the Guadalcanal landings. The Allied Intelligence Bureau (AIB) did, because the Solomons were initially in MacArthur's area of operations.[38] Based in Australia, the AIB had all-source intelligence assets, including aerial reconnaissance platforms, access to Allied personnel who had lived in Japanese-seized territory, radio intelligence specialists, translators, and stay-behind agents scattered throughout the South Pacific islands.[39] Unique to Southwest Pacific intelligence operations, stay-behind agents, otherwise known as coast watchers, were mostly British, Australian, and New Zealand citizens or military personnel who had fled to the interiors of the islands where they lived when the Japanese invaded. Many native islanders friendly to the Allied cause also served as coast watchers. Through their clandestine reconnaissance activities, the coast watchers provided pivotal military intelligence on Japanese military units for Allied South Pacific island campaigns.[40] (Today's U.S. reconnaissance units conduct the same type of mission by fulfilling the information requirements set by the acronym SALUTE, which stands for size, activity, location, unit, time, and equipment.)

Yet, typical of the chaotic nature of Pacific intelligence activities before the advent of JICPOA, the AIB was not up and running at full capacity when CINCPAC decided to seize Guadalcanal. Therefore, the ground force designated to attack the island, the First Marine Division, relied on its own intelligence officer to coordinate intelligence for the operation. Throughout the war in the Central Pacific, divisional intelligence staffs served as distribution points for intelligence passed down to them from JICPOA. These units often provided crucial and lifesaving support to supplement JICPOA's work, but they were not supposed to serve as the primary intelligence coordinators for Pacific campaigns.

For the Guadalcanal operation, though, the First Division intelligence officer was the only man on the case. This officer, Lt. Col. Frank Goettge,[41] interviewed former inhabitants of Guadalcanal, assessed coast-watcher intelligence, analyzed aerial photographs, and drew two freehand intelligence maps of the target's landing beaches and the terrain beyond—all in about four weeks. Although he did rely on the AIB for coast-watcher reports and aerial photos,[42] he completed most of the collection, analysis, assessment, and dissemination himself. OP-20-G, and to a lesser extent ICPOA,[43] supported his work by supplying radio intelligence on Japanese naval traffic in the area and by trying to assess the number of enemy troops on both Guadalcanal and Tulagi.[44] Despite the fact that Turner had left D.C. at this point to command amphibious forces at Guadalcanal, his cohorts in Washington controlled all Pacific radio intelligence activities except for those at Pearl Harbor.[45] The entire Pacific intelligence system remained awkward and ineffectual, and the results showed in the Guadalcanal campaign.

For example, except for estimates of enemy forces on Tulagi, the intelligence operation against Guadalcanal proved inefficient. Radio intelligence provided scant information on the enemy, and Goettge's terrain maps were little more than rough estimates. Aerial photographs that would have provided better information somehow got lost in the system.[46] When the Marines hit the beaches on Guadalcanal, they had only a slight idea of what to expect from the enemy and from the island's terrain.[47] Intelligence did not improve much for the next six months as Japanese and U.S. forces maneuvered to destroy one another. Ultimately, Marine patrols and coast watchers on Guadalcanal and throughout the Solomons provided the operation's most accurate and timely intelligence.[48]

While the infantry battle for Guadalcanal raged inland, the U.S. and Japanese navies fought each other for sea control around the objective. Again, U.S. intelligence did not improve on an efficient scale, and most of the victories were hard won. Layton complained to Nimitz that the turf war with Turner and his cohorts stifled his and ICPOA's efforts for Guadalcanal,[49] a situation that had to improve if the war were to be waged in an efficient manner.

Surprisingly, Rochefort was a casualty of that turf war. In the months after Midway, senior personnel at OP-20-G realized that Rochefort and the CIU had demonstrated considerable intelligence prowess. Since they did not want to lose control of Pacific intelligence activities, they convinced Admiral King that D.C. analysts had in fact engineered the intelligence coup that foiled Japanese plans at Midway and that Rochefort's contributions were at best minimal. Furthermore, they began a malicious rumor campaign that accused Rochefort of leaking top secret communications intelligence methodologies to the press and blamed him for failing to detect the attack on Pearl Harbor. Although quite astute, by fall 1942, King had succumbed to the side of the petty, and he sacked Rochefort's command on 25 October 1942 by recalling him to Washington for obscure duties.[50] Later, the Navy rerouted his posting to California, where he commanded a floating dock.

Nimitz fought the injustice, but his arguments fell on deaf ears. His attempts after the war to have Congress award Rochefort the Distinguished Service Medal did not succeed, either. Toward the end of the war, operations planners in D.C. did rely on Rochefort's services to assist in strategic assessments of Japanese forces for the invasion of the home islands, but the invasion never took place. Eventually, the behind-the-scenes hero of Midway did in fact receive the Distinguished Service Medal, but after his death, in the 1980s, during the Reagan administration.[51]

Rochefort's subordinates were shocked at the turn of events but could do nothing to correct the injustice. Capt. Roscoe Hillenkoetter, an intelligence officer from the European theater, took over as the commanding officer of ICPOA.[52] Capt. William B. Goggins, a naval communications expert, took over as the unit's executive officer,[53] and Lt. Jasper Holmes assumed command of the CIU.[54] Simultaneously dismayed and driven by duty, ICPOA's analysts continued working without their former commander to provide the best intelligence they could to CINCPAC.

Nimitz would soon need their best intelligence products because he, MacArthur, and the Joint Chiefs of Staff had decided on a general offensive against Japan, scheduled to begin in fall 1943. In political terms, they designed the offensive to force the Japanese to accept unconditional Allied surrender terms. It would be no easy task. The original plan first consisted of a giant pincer movement that converged on the Philippines. MacArthur would take a southern axis of advance through the South Pacific toward Mindanao, and Nimitz would parallel him through the Central Pacific, presumably beginning in the Marshalls.[55] After taking the Philippines, U.S. forces would then advance north on Formosa (present-day Taiwan), and then on to Japan itself. (Admiral Nimitz would eventually alter this strategy by dropping the Philippines and Formosa from his axis and lunging north through Iwo Jima and Okinawa.) No one had yet proposed the final assault on Japan, but planning for it would begin on a small scale almost immediately and escalate to consume massive intelligence and planning resources in the following years.

Although the dual axis of advance divided their forces, U.S. operations planners estimated that they could produce more material and harness more manpower in the Pacific than the Japanese could. From intelligence reports, they knew that Japan's hundreds of thousands of troops were spread through Manchuria, Korea, China, and Southeast Asia, the latter two areas being constantly contested. Allied and local unconventional units such as the Office of Strategic Services (OSS), the British Special Operations Executive (SOE), and Burmese Kachins fought the enemy in the Southeast Asian tropics, while the offensively ineffective but colossal Chinese National Army kept the Japanese busy in China. Simply put, Japan had overextended its forces, and it could not pull too many troops out of Asia to fight the United States and its allies in the Pacific.

Although Nimitz wanted to seize the Marshalls immediately, for their excellent naval anchorages, he could not because he had little intelligence on the island group. Radio intelligence provided some information, but Nimitz lacked basic geographic and order-of-battle data that only prisoners of war, enemy documents, or aerial photographs could provide. Since his scant carrier forces could not reconnoiter the Marshalls and risk engaging Japanese carriers suspected of being nearby, Nimitz decided to rely on longer-range, land-based reconnaissance aircraft to obtain the necessary intelligence, but he needed airstrips close to the Marshalls to facilitate the mission. Airstrips in the Gilberts, especially the one on Betio Island in Tarawa Atoll, were ideal for the job,[56] so he decided to seize the Gilberts before moving on into the Marshalls. With the decision to attack Tarawa in fall 1943, he tasked ICPOA with providing specific intelligence on the atoll and the Japanese based there—the hydrography of its islands, piers and wharves that U.S. forces might utilize, enemy numbers, and their scheme of defense.

ICPOA had difficulty completing these tasks because of dramatic personnel shifts that had occurred in the year prior to the operation. The last group of officers assigned to ICPOA, twenty-one in all, had arrived in September 1942,[57] but ICPOA did not immediately have work for them to do, so it transferred seventeen of them to other locations. Then, in February 1943, ICPOA received several officers from the Navy's Japanese language school in Boulder, Colorado, but these men were not order-of-battle specialists.[58] They specialized in POW interrogation and document translation, and there was little work for them. Predictably, as the operation to seize Tarawa came nearer, work developed for many analysts, but because of past transfers, there were not enough experienced personnel on hand to do the job.

Such a helter-skelter personnel flow, combined with a fluctuating work schedule, caused ICPOA to continue its awkward practice of borrowing services of other intelligence units such as PRISIC and mapmakers from the U.S. Army's Sixty-fourth Topographic Engineer Company.[59] To make matters more complicated, ICPOA moved yet again in April 1943, this time into a new radio intelligence building on the low crater surrounding Pearl Harbor.[60] These administrative maneuvers interrupted the flow of information, and as time approached fall 1943, Nimitz needed more intelligence personnel. He requested twenty-three more officers in July 1943.[61]

In early fall 1943, twenty new officers arrived to relieve the pressures building up at ICPOA, and twenty-four of the forty-four officers destined for PRISIC were rerouted to the struggling intelligence center as well.[62] Suddenly, with their numbers increased, the members of ICPOA thought that they would finally start to produce effective intelligence products for continual offensive operations, but it never happened for that particular organization.

Out of the blue, in a CINCPAC directive dated 7 September 1943, ICPOA became joint, or JICPOA,[63] under Col. Joseph J. Twitty, commander of the U.S. Army's Sixty-fourth Topographic Company,[64] ICPOA's outsource mapmaking unit. With this move, Twitty's unit and others like it became sections of JICPOA overnight. Consequently, Twitty also became assistant chief of staff of intelligence to CINCPAC; making him Layton's number two.[65]

This merging process continued with other agencies, PRISIC for example, through May 1944.[66] Eventually, all of these new sections would be housed under one roof. JICPOA's official mission statement was to implement "the collection, collation, evaluation, and dissemination of strategic and tactical intelligence for the Commander in Chief, Pacific Ocean Areas, and as directed by him."[67] At peak capacity, JICPOA consisted of 544 officers and 1,223 enlisted personnel.[68]

As a matter of course, the establishment of JICPOA ended the dispute between D.C.-based intelligence activities and those at Pearl Harbor. Technically, JICPOA had been preordained back in 1942 with the approval of King, Horne, and Holcomb, so a D.C.-controlled or a Pearl-controlled Pacific intelligence unit had never really been in question. But it was hard for the players involved to see it at the time—hindsight is always 20/20. Turner and his cohorts had only delayed the creation of an effective organization with their lunge for power. Furthermore, the ineffectual intelligence support at Guadalcanal made it clear that wrangling over who would control intelligence had to stop, and effective intelligence operations had to start. It also had become obvious that a D.C.-based organization eight thousand miles from the Pacific area of operations could not collect and analyze Pacific source data effectively;[69] the process was difficult enough for intelligence agencies already in the Pacific.

The assault on Tarawa proved the point on the morning of 20 November 1943. Although a success, the operation encountered several drastic difficulties. In three days, marines from the Second Marine Division had secured Betio at a cost of 1,027 killed in action (KIA), including many Navy corpsmen. Over two thousand marines fell wounded in action (WIA), while the enemy lost 4,700 KIA, almost the entire garrison.[70] The casualties shocked Nimitz and the U.S. public. Aside from the tenacity of the Japanese, numerous mishaps had driven up the casualty rate.

First, tactical radios, vulnerable to the elements, gave out as a direct result of contact with salt water. Second, the Marines did not attack Tarawa with enough demolition equipment or flamethrowers, clearly the ideal weapons for pillbox and bunker reduction.[71] Third, there were not enough amphibian tractors to support the landing. Fourth, the preliminary bombardment did not target specific enemy bunkers and weapons installations but instead saturated the island with ordnance—a tactic that did not bring about the destruction of enough enemy gun emplacements. Fifth, most naval shells that hit concrete bunkers did not destroy them, because the

Navy had used high-explosive (HE) shells instead of armor-piercing (AP) shells. HE rounds had the effect of slapping targets rather than punching through them as AP rounds would have done.

The naval preliminary bombardment problems should not have occurred, because intelligence had correctly gauged the number of defenders on Betio and had pinpointed every building and nearly every fortification on the island. On the other hand, ICPOA was not successful in analyzing Betio's hydrography. Intelligence analysts had encountered significant trouble in attempting to predict the tidal patterns at Tarawa Atoll. Therefore, they consulted several former inhabitants of the atoll, among them officers of the Royal Australian and New Zealand navies, to try and shed some light on the dilemma.

Through interviews, ICPOA's analysts learned that a coral reef as wide as a thousand yards surrounded Betio like a massive apron. U.S. intelligence officers wanted to know at what times during the day flat-bottomed landing craft could pass over the reef and get to the beaches. After intense debate, the analysts concluded that up to five feet of water would cover the reef, give or take one foot, a sufficient amount to allow a fully loaded landing craft to pass over during the assault, but just barely. Unfortunately, during the actual assault, an apogean neap tide occurred that stranded the landing craft on the fringes of the reef. An apogean neap tide results when the moon reaches its peak during a neap tide, and in this case, it caused the water level to be lower than hypothesized. As a consequence, the marines were forced to wade ashore from a thousand yards out instead of attacking from the beaches, where shock effect would have provided them with speed and concentrated mass—key tactical elements of successful amphibious assaults, especially in the face of such stiff resistance. Wading in, the marines made easy targets for the Japanese, and many others drowned in reef holes.[72]

Even though both ICPOA and JICPOA had contributed intelligence for the operation during a period of immaturity and fluctuation, JICPOA was the last agency to handle intelligence for that battle. In effect, Twitty began his intelligence career with a black mark on his record, but the war was moving too fast for anyone to lay blame at his feet. Time, on the other hand, would give him a chance to improve his new unit's image, and he soon demonstrated a capacity for solid intelligence work. After all, he did have the background for it. Twitty spoke Japanese and had served as the liaison between the U.S. Army and ICPOA.[73] In addition, his second in command, Cdr. W. Jasper Holmes, knew the intelligence business well, having served both in the CIU and ICPOA with Rochefort.

Things finally had come together, and the CINCPAC's intelligence unit became a mutual operation of U.S. Navy, Marine, and Army personnel after a year and ten months of trial and error. Its final form closely resembled the original concept submitted by the commandant of the Marine Corps in March 1942.[74] On the other hand, one major change did occur—the removal of radio intelligence from the Pacific intelligence community. Radio intelligence assets were technically part of standard USN communications activities, and the Navy did not want to separate them. While this was an administrative move designed to keep from clogging the intelligence cycle, radio intelligence continued to support JICPOA, and the two worked closely throughout the war.

Responsibility for radio intelligence collection fell to the organization that evolved from Hypo and the CIU. In 1943, it changed to FRUPAC, which stood for Fleet Radio Unit Pacific. While JICPOA and FRUPAC were technically separate, the former kept analytical personnel in the FRUPAC building because it depended on radio intelligence, namely ULTRA.[75] But since a cloak of secrecy surrounded FRUPAC, JICPOA's personnel were forbidden ever to mention the organization's real name and managed to keep Nimitz's most secret weapon hidden for the entire war.[76] Similarly, no member of JICPOA wore insignia to designate their military occupational specialty or unit. As far as Nimitz was concerned, the organization did not exist to the outside world that had no "need to know" about JICPOA's activities. Likewise, while most U.S. Pacific forces benefited from its intelligence, they were not allowed near the JICPOA building.

JICPOA's staff was enthusiastic about its achievements thus far. It had established the foundation of a major all-source intelligence organization based on strategic necessity, hard work, and common sense. Now it stood before the threshold of a major task, the offensive campaign against Japan, in which JICPOA would play a pivotal role. However, no one on the outside could know what JICPOA's intelligence specialists did. No one in the press could interview them and make them famous, as would be the several marines and one Navy corpsman who would raise the U.S. flag over Iwo Jima in 1945. No relative, wife, or girlfriend could visit them at work or discuss their job over a quiet meal. On occasion, journalists would catch tidbits of information about how intelligence performed in this campaign or that, but they never wrote an article exposing the sensitive activities of the organization. Otherwise, JICPOA's work remained secret, its gates guarded by Marine security guards with weapons locked and loaded.

JICPOA's influential role in the war would remain behind the scenes, influencing the strategic direction of the conflict and combat as well. In fact,

JICPOA stayed shrouded in mystery for the next twenty-five years, until most of its documents were declassified by the U.S. Government. Therefore, with its final consolidation and without fanfare, JICPOA moved into its own complex located on Makalapa Crater overlooking Pearl Harbor in the spring of 1944 and began its watch over the Pacific.

Operational Procedures

Every intelligence organization in history has followed similar procedures—direction, collection, processing, and dissemination. JICPOA was no exception. Its entire existence revolved around these four basic concepts. First (direction), it would coordinate with operations planners to design an intelligence plan to support a particular campaign. An intelligence plan outlined what operations planners needed to know, who would participate in the intelligence cycle, how and when it would be executed, and when it would be completed. Then (collection), JICPOA would implement that plan by collecting raw data on the Japanese military. If JICPOA was suffering from information overload and there was an upcoming operation just months away, it would prioritize all recently collected data to separate the irrelevant from the relevant. Afterward, it analyzed the data for its relevance and usefulness (processing). This included making assessments on Japanese capabilities, vulnerabilities, and intentions. After that, a production shop would format the intelligence in a usable, readable format. Last (dissemination), JICPOA disseminated the intelligence to operations planners who used it to plan and fight campaigns.

But how did JICPOA accomplish these tasks? Who were its analysts, and how were they trained? How did JICPOA coordinate its activities with the fleet, and what products did it produce for the Central Pacific Island assaults? Finally, how was JICPOA structured to accomplish these tasks? The answers require a detailed look at the inner workings of this remarkable organization.

Personnel and Training

JICPOA's analysts came from all over the United States, just as its combat soldiers did. However, most analysts were recruited from legal, journalistic, academic, or other research and logic-based vocations. When possible, JICPOA recruited individuals who had lived in target area countries—China, Taiwan, the Caroline Islands, and especially Japan.[77] JICPOA's recruits attended the Advanced Naval Intelligence School located at the Henry Hudson Hotel in New York City.[78] The school offered two courses: Operational Intelligence and Commerce and Travel. Each course lasted eight weeks. Toward the latter stages of the war, the Navy lengthened each course to ten weeks. Students learned about the universal intelligence procedures and a little about the organization and equipment of the Japanese military.[79] The school also familiarized students with the types of intelligence used by the U.S. military at that time: photographic, document, human, and radio signals. Professors taught courses on how the information would be used and who would be using it. Interestingly, the school did not teach the students how to analyze. That, figured the Navy, came from the innate ability of the individual intelligence student.

Recruits with specialties like photographic or radio intelligence completed further training in specialized schools. For example, photographic analysts attended the U.S. Naval Photo Interpretation School at the Naval Air Station in Anacostia, Washington, D.C.[80] Language specialists attended language schools, most of which taught Japanese, although some taught Chinese and other Asian languages. The U.S. Government contracted out the first language schools to the University of California, Berkeley, and to Harvard University. In January 1942, the government assessed the Harvard classes as not up to par, so it terminated the school's contract and diverted all language students to Berkeley. In summer 1942, the government decided to move its language students to yet another school, which remained in use until the end of the war: the U.S. Navy's Japanese language school at Boulder, Colorado. By 1944, its curriculum included Chinese and Malay as well.[81]

After completing their studies, intelligence graduates reported to JIC-POA or fleet intelligence units, where they received intense on-the-job training. JICPOA called it "earn while they learn."[82] Although the intelligence schools produced excellent graduates, they could not prepare their students for the incredible stress of the job, nor could they hone the skills of each analyst. Furthermore, professors were unable to teach their students everything they needed to know about the Japanese military. It was a vast and complex organization, and besides, the U.S. military was in the dark regarding much of Japan's capability. That is why senior operations planners and combat echelons needed JICPOA. Accordingly, intelligence personnel learned most of their trade not in the classroom but at JICPOA. This meant that the organization had a high percentage of inexperienced personnel, impairing its proficiency in analytical areas like advanced aerial photographic interpretation using stereoscopes. (A stereoscope was a type of magnifying-glass apparatus that, when paired with several photographs, allowed the user to see scenes in three dimensions and thereby more readily discern military structures, equipment, and terrain on the ground.)

JICPOA's intelligence specialists took on a wide array of tasks. Some researched, translated, analyzed, and wrote, while others interrogated POWs or explored seized islands for information on Japanese defensive tactics and fortifications. Monotony and boredom often plagued their work. Occasionally, an exhilarating intelligence coup made their efforts worthwhile. A select number joined battles to process combat intelligence for campaign commanders. Combat deployment was dangerous, because the analysts had to go into battle with infantry forces; several of these men were wounded while performing their duties in combat.

Within the JICPOA compound, intelligence specialists averaged fifteen to seventeen hours per day, seven days a week, although most paid no attention to what day it was. JICPOA printed almost two million sheets of intelligence material weekly and developed two million intelligence photographs quarterly.[83] All told, JICPOA produced hundreds of tons of intelligence material.[84]

JICPOA personnel took the war just as seriously as did combat personnel. According to one intelligence officer, Donald "Mac" Showers, most of them did not have time to enjoy the fruits of local Hawaiian life. Aside from being swamped with vital and time-sensitive work, they were literally within the enemy's area of operations. After all, Japan had attacked both Hawaii and Alaska. And despite the Midway victory, the powerful Japanese fleet still had the capability to threaten the U.S. West Coast and strike deep into its waters with significant naval force. Therefore, JICPOA's staff did not believe themselves beyond the reach of the Japanese. More importantly, if the Japanese found out about JICPOA, they would certainly attack it. Showers also asserted that the Japanese meant to control the entire Pacific. To accomplish this, the enemy had to defeat U.S. Pacific-based forces and dictate surrender terms from the White House, a possibility not fully appreciated in the United States today.[85]

Intelligence Coordination with the Fleet

JICPOA supported the Pacific Fleet by coordinating with operations planners to provide them with specific intelligence on enemy bases, fleet movements, and tactics. Such intelligence gave operations planners a good idea of how much force to apply to defeat their opponents. If, for example, JICPOA reported that ten thousand Japanese occupied a particular island base, then operations planners knew to send at least thirty thousand marines and soldiers to seize the island. (This practice accords with the theory that an attacker needs at least a three-to-one ratio to successfully defeat an entrenched defender. During the Pacific War, U.S. Navy expeditionary forces preferred a four-to-one ratio. In today's U.S. Marine Corps, operations personnel prefer a six-to-one advantage for amphibious assaults.)[86] Similarly, if JICPOA reported that the Japanese had a massive battery of model 89 150-mm howitzers in the center of that same island, operations planners ideally would have the battery strafed and shelled before the marines and soldiers landed. Collecting this type of information was not always easy, but it was essential for operations planning.

Nimitz and his USN and USMC commanders supervised operations planning. During the early phases of the war, the U.S. Navy consisted of the Third and Fifth Fleets. Adm. William Halsey commanded the Third, and Adm. Raymond Spruance commanded the Fifth. The ships and equipment of the Third and Fifth Fleets remained one and the same, but overall control of the platforms changed with each rotation of fleet commands. Toward the end of the war, however, the United States was producing enough ships for each fleet to be at sea at the same time.

Under the Third and Fifth Fleets were the III and V Amphibious Corps, commanded by Marine Generals Roy Geiger and Holland Smith, respectively. Fleet Marine Force, Pacific, served as the coordinating administrative command for all Marine forces in theater. For manpower, each corps drew from the many Marine divisions in the Pacific, which at the height of organization (September 1944) consisted of the First, Second, Third, Fourth, Fifth, and Sixth Marine Divisions. At full strength, a Marine division numbered about nineteen thousand, each with three regimental combat teams and supporting regiments. Unlike the Navy, the amphibious corps always kept their own equipment. A host of units supported the divisions, including five aircraft wings, eleven 155-mm gun battalions, sixteen antiaircraft battalions, and numerous LVT, engineer, and service units.[87]

U.S. Army units and their commanders also made a major contribution to many of Nimitz's campaigns, both in planning and in manpower. In fact, the Army provided battalion-, regiment-, and division-sized formations to all but one of the amphibious campaigns executed under CINCPAC, and it was in charge of the invasion of Okinawa. Army divisions that fought alongside the III and V Amphibious Corps included the Seventh, Twenty-seventh, Eighty-first, and Ninety-sixth Infantry Divisions.

Strategic war planning took place at several levels, the highest of which was the Combined Chiefs of Staff (CCS), a joint U.S. and British command. The CCS oversaw the general direction of both the European and Pacific theaters. The Joint Chiefs of Staff (JCS), the highest U.S. planning level, oversaw the United States' role in each theater. Typically, both of these senior groups were responsible for designating what island groups to attack.

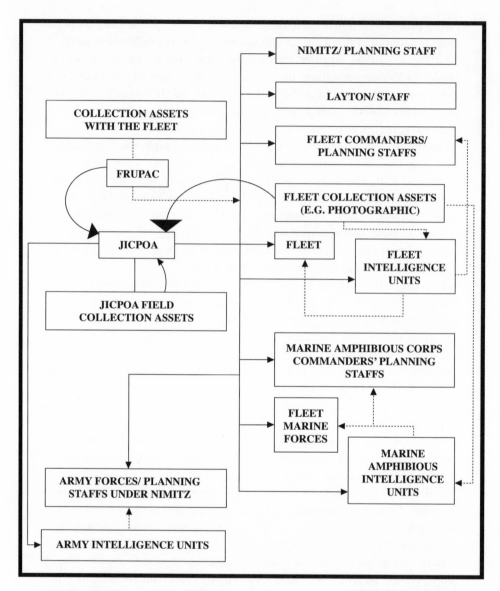

JICPOA's Intelligence Flow. The solid lines demonstrate JICPOA's dissemination; dotted lines represent fleet intelligence dissemination; curved lines represent the flow of information into JICPOA.

Theater-level commanders such as Nimitz were responsible for overseeing operations planning for the axis of advance through the Pacific.

Nimitz and his lieutenants each had planning staffs that helped them design naval and amphibious operations, the latter also referred to as campaigns. Fleet rotations set campaign schedules. For example, while one fleet command operated out in the Pacific, the other stayed in at Pearl Harbor and planned the next offensive. For naval battles and raids, CINCPAC and his staff coordinated with fleet commanders and the various carrier group commanders and their staffs. Designing island campaigns required the input of both fleet and USMC commanders, because each would be exercising command of different parts of the battle. The Iwo Jima campaign, for example, involved numerous planning staffs—among them were the VAC and the Third Marine Division, as well as Admiral Turner's Joint Expeditionary Task Force and that of Admiral Nimitz. After planning at the highest level, divisional and regimental commanders conducted more detailed planning on how their infantry forces would move inland to destroy enemy positions and seize key terrain.

When a fleet command came to Pearl Harbor to plan amphibious operations, its planners and intelligence staffs coordinated with JICPOA for the direction or tasking phase of the intelligence cycle. This took place between five and three months before the Marines stormed the beaches of the next target. They met at the Visiting Fleet Staff Office Building next to CINCPAC's headquarters. There, they specified the information requirements pertinent to the operation at hand and requested that JICPOA satisfy these requirements by providing intelligence on the proposed island objective and the surrounding enemy area of operations, which was often an island group.[88] On occasion, Nimitz and his lieutenants did not know exactly which island within a group to attack, so they tasked JICPOA with producing intelligence on several potential objectives. The commanders wanted to know everything about each island and the Japanese who occupied it— enemy troop strength, the location of fortifications, the island's hydrographic conditions, and the geography of the target. According to General Twitty, the intelligence plan that they agreed to was typically informal. In contrast, the intelligence deadline, which was when all compiled intelligence would be published for final review and utilization, was formal and definitive.[89]

Regrettably, JICPOA was unable to provide intelligence at what General Twitty referred to as "apple polishing perfection" because of the incredibly fast pace of the war. For example, JICPOA did not include biographies of Japanese commanders in its amphibious assault intelligence briefings because, despite its importance, such information was technically a luxury.[90] In another example, if JICPOA's analysts received mediocre reconnaissance photographs of a particular island, they analyzed the material as best as possible, disseminated the intelligence, and moved on to the next project. In such cases, JICPOA's analysts alerted the end user about the poor photographic situation but could do nothing to rectify the situation if operations officers denied their requests for additional photo reconnaissance. On the whole, General Twitty's analysts worked as hard as they could to provide basic, usable intelligence but were allowed very little lead time before each campaign. As a consequence, JICPOA sometimes was able to provide only a limited picture of the enemy situation.

JICPOA's Intelligence Products and Dissemination Policy

JICPOA produced five regular intelligence products: *Weekly Intelligence, Know Your Enemy, Translations and Interrogations,* information bulletins, and *Estimates of Enemy Forces and Capabilities.* It also generated intelligence for special projects at the direction of Admiral Nimitz or General Twitty, but these were sporadic. In contrast, *Weekly Intelligence* was a regular periodical that contained intelligence on enemy activities, habits, new developments, and after-action reports. *Know Your Enemy,* another regular periodical, discussed specific Japanese order-of-battle information such as antitank tactics, the organization of Japanese army units, and weapons capabilities. It occasionally included silhouette charts of Japanese military platforms. *Translations and Interrogations* made pertinent translated documents and POW interrogations available to the fleet when such intelligence became available but did not appear on a regular basis. JICPOA liberally disseminated these products to all U.S. forces in theater no matter the occupational specialty. Information bulletins, on the other hand, were tailor-made to help operations planners and combat forces design and execute island campaigns. Although information bulletins were less widely distibuted than the periodicals, they still circulated into the thousands. Finally, *Estimates of Enemy Forces and Capabilities,* a weekly product, kept key commanders and planners abreast of the enemy situation with the most current intelligence available, usually with a heavy slant on radio intelligence as a source. Unlike its other products, JICPOA kept estimates dissemination to a minimum because of its sensitive nature. Overall, however, JICPOA prided itself on its extensive dissemination channels and its ability to keep its end users informed.[91] It was, after all, one of its primary jobs. JICPOA also embraced integration with operations planners and endeavored to provide its customers with crucial information, another aspect lost in many intelligence circles today.

Regardless, of all JICPOA's intelligence products, information bulletins had the greatest impact on island-hopping campaigns. Operations planners called them "yellow books" because of their yellow security covers. Information bulletins were vital to campaign planning, and according to General Twitty, they were used "in all phases of planning and operations for all operations."[92]

For dissemination purposes and to protect sources and methods, JICPOA adhered to specific classification levels. Information bulletins typically did not reach above the secret level, and intelligence officers would sometimes lower the classification of a bulletin as a campaign progressed. Nevertheless, the classifications were:[93]

restricted: the lowest classification (kept to U.S. forces and select foreign forces)

confidential: the second security rating (typically kept within the ranks of a particular operation)

secret: the highest security rating for a bulletin (kept within the highest officer ranks under CINCPAC and planning and intelligence personnel at corps, division, and regimental levels)

top secret: reserved for intelligence products that included data from highly sensitive operations and sources such as ULTRA, and typically not associated with information bulletins

top secret ULTRA: intelligence derived only from ULTRA, and typically associated with memos that went directly to Layton or Nimitz or processed information contained in *Estimates of Enemy Forces and Capabilities.*

Planners usually had the same information requirements for each campaign, so they and JICPOA developed an information template for island assaults that specified essential elements of information. Once filled, the template became a profile of a designated target. Each information bulletin adhered to a particular format, though there were exceptions, and the information bulletin evolved as the war progressed.

The format of each bulletin was simple. The title page listed the subject, date, bulletin number, and classification. Next was a general map of the target area. An executive summary followed the map. The final sections, which comprised the bulk of the information bulletin, reported on the target in detail.

The key sections varied somewhat from target to target. For example, the

Kyushu information bulletin contained chapters on prisoner of war camps, telecommunications, and health and sanitation in addition to standard defense and geographic data. In contrast, the Eniwetok information bulletin reflected the most common information template:

Summary	Fuel	Factors Limiting Beach
Physical Survey	Communications	Information
Distance Table	Health and Sanitation	Engebi Island
Population	Military Survey	North Coast
Climate	Fortifications	Southwest Coast
Physical Geography	Airfield	East Coast
Navigational	Seaplane Base	Parry Island
Information	Naval Base	West Coast
Anchorages	RDF (radio directional	East Coast
Wharves	finding equipment)	Eniwetok Island
Buildings	and Radar	Southeast Coast
Roads	Landings	Northwest Coast
Logistics	General Information	West Coast
Food	Reef Conditions	
Water	Surf Conditions	

Data in these sections ran from one small paragraph to several pages, depending on the complexity of the target. Maps and photographs appeared where appropriate. Topographical maps accompanied the bulletins, irregularly. Sometimes, JICPOA included topographical data on enemy defenses maps and sometimes on maps denoting anchorages. It published very little geographic map intelligence on occasions when collection and analytical personnel were not able to produce sufficient topographical data by the intelligence deadline. In these cases, JICPOA disseminated topographical maps as soon as they became available. Likewise, in conjunction with but separate from the information bulletins, JICPOA disseminated terrain maps of the objective to the fleet's combat echelons through their respective commands or intelligence staffs.

CINCPAC and his planning staff, Navy and Marine commanders, and the fleet's intelligence units such as the G-2 sections at the corps and division level—in short, everyone who gathered at the Visiting Fleet Staff Office Building[94]—were the first to receive JICPOA's information bulletins. Shortly thereafter, distribution spread to lower echelon fleet staffs and units involved with the campaign at hand. Sometimes, this list numbered well over fifty separate commands, and each often requested numerous copies. For example, 1,615 copies of the Iwo Jima information bulletin went to eighty-nine separate commands. A portion of the dissemination list follows:[95]

Iwo Jima Information Bulletin—Distribution (Partial List)

Unit	No. of Copies
(Army) Chief Signal Officer, War Department, Washington, D.C.	2
(Army) G-2 Western Defense Command, Presidio, San Francisco	2
(Army) Comdt, MIS Language School, Ft. Snolling, Minn.	2
(Army) G-2, USAF Burma-India, New Delhi, India	2
(Army, Pacific & SWPA) AAFPOA, (Inc: all Pacific AAF)	200
(Army, Pacific & SWPA) G-2, Tenth Army	25
(Navy) COMINCH, Washington, D.C.	2
(Navy) CNO, Washington, D.C., (Inc: DMI, MI2, Whitehall and DNI, Admiralty, Whitehall)	20
ComAirPac	720
(Navy) Cmdt, NavWarColl, Newport	1
(Navy, Pacific & SWPA) ComSubPac	1
(Navy, Pacific & SWPA) ComThird Fleet	10
(Navy, Pacific & SWPA) ComFifth Fleet	3
(Navy, Pacific & SWPA) D/ I, Royal Australian Ny	1
(Navy, Pacific & SWPA) ComAmphibForPac	50
(Marine Corps) G-2, FMF Pac	2
(Marine Corps) CG Third Phib Corps	8
(Marine Corps) Fifth Phib Corps	8
(Marine Corps) CG each MarDiv	15
Adv Intell Off, Guam	150

The Pacific Fleet's own intelligence officers served as indispensable conduits between JICPOA and the fleet. According to General Twitty, JICPOA had excellent relations with the fleet's intelligence staffs, and his analysts frequently augmented their staffs during combat operations. These small but valuable units supported their superiors during operational planning, and they also executed small-scale collection and analytical operations just before and during battles. Their products included final intelligence estimates of the enemy situation on an objective, typically a week or two before an amphibious campaign began. These reports sometimes demonstrated shifts in enemy defenses and increases in enemy troop numbers, but they never indicated a situation so different from JICPOA's estimates that commanders canceled or significantly altered a campaign. In fact, never once during the Pacific War did Nimitz recall an assault force en route to an objective because last-minute intelligence said that the enemy situation had changed from original estimates, nor did any fleet commanders urge him to do so.

Intelligence Sources

Most of JICPOA's information came from four sources: photographs, captured documents, prisoners of war, and enemy radio transmissions. Each source of information could prove invaluable or useless, depending on the circumstances. Similarly, each source was either easy or impossible to attain. When possible, JICPOA's analysts tried to achieve source corroboration (i.e., two or more sources agreeing with one another).

Photographs. Photo intelligence provided most of the raw data that intelligence personnel used to analyze Japanese-held bases. Under ideal circumstances, photographs could supply more data than any other source. For example, they could demonstrate hydrographic conditions, terrain features, enemy order of battle, and defensive plans. While photo intelligence had been used in World War I, operations planners never made full use of it, so photographic technology was not advanced. By World War II, however, photography had become more sophisticated, and resolution had improved. That meant analysts could see more in a photograph in 1943 than they could have in 1915.

In many cases, aerial photographs provided the only available information on enemy activities on a target. U.S. Navy Underwater Demolition Teams (UDTs) and Marine Reconnaissance units did surreptitiously reconnoiter most Japanese island bases to conduct hydrographic surveys, and occasionally they infiltrated beach defenses. But enemy bases were like fortresses with dense concentrations of troops. Reconnaissance of inner defenses under such circumstances was frowned upon by Pacific commanders because capture was likely, and capture meant the loss of surprise, not to mention tortured and interrogated U.S. servicemen. In today's military, U.S. Army Special Forces, Rangers, Navy Sea/Air/Land commandos (SEALs), Reconnaissance Marines, and like groups can and do conduct dangerous missions of this type, but in the absence of such capabilities in the 1940s, photography held the van.

Photographic squadrons belonging to the fleet and the Army carried out reconnaissance missions. For example, more than forty-four years before he became president of the United States, George Bush flew aerial reconnaissance missions for the U.S. Navy as well as combat missions. His photo-equipped TBF Avenger had cameras housed in its bomb-bay doors.

The cameras' lenses were aimed down, port, and starboard,[96] used lenses that ranged from 4.5 inch to 40-inch telephoto, and produced images that ranged from 4 x 5 to 9 x 18 inches.[97] This was typical of many photo reconnaissance platforms. Others flew dual missions and carried both bombs and cameras. Pilots also used hand-held cameras; they would actually turn the aircraft on an angle, lean out of the cockpit, and take pictures of defenses on the ground. They took pictures from high-oblique, low-oblique, and vertical angles, depending on what enemy antiaircraft fire would allow. Most of the time, vertical photographs demonstrated the most about enemy garrisons and defense installations. These pictures best revealed the outlines of manmade structures, which were given away by straight lines, right angles, and spherical shapes. Shadows cast by fortifications further revealed their purpose and location. However, natural defensive positions, such as caves, were much harder to spot.

Sometimes, photo analysts could spot fortifications by evidence of construction crews—manual labor equipment, trampled and cleared foliage, removed dirt (spoil), and concrete mixing and setting materials. Occasionally, high and low obliques produced better pictures because of the way light hit the object on the ground at certain times of the day.[98] Regardless, if pilots could not obtain verticals, obliques were better than no photographs at all.

Technical deficiencies inherent in aerial photographic work resulted in blurred photographs and made interpretation difficult.[99] Either tilt of the aircraft, engine vibrations, turbulence, or concussion from flak could impair the photographic results. Clouds, heavy vegetation, and thick tree canopies also made it hard for photo analysts to identify objects on the ground. During cloud cover, of course, aerial photography was useless. Moreover, the Japanese often employed expert camouflage techniques to hide their activities, and their skills improved dramatically as the war progressed. Ironically, after the war, the Navy hypothesized that the Japanese may have increased their camouflage efforts because they had read American press stories about U.S. photo-interpretation prowess.[100]

Accordingly, aerial photography was not a foolproof source of intelligence. All the same, experienced photo interpreters could learn much about the enemy from clear and well-timed photographs. This was truer if they used stereoscopes. Stereoscopes were bi-lens magnifying glasses that allowed the analyst to see a set of photographs in three dimensions, thereby revealing more distinct shapes and shadows than two-dimensional readings.[101] Stereoscope analysts had to have a high degree of photo analytical experience before taking on 3-D analyses, and it appears from the history of JICPOA and from studying its products that little such training took place. Senior analysts might have viewed stereoscopic analysis as "apple polishing" intelligence work and therefore did not develop it on a wide scale.

JICPOA also relied on submarines for photo reconnaissance. Navy photographers accompanied submarine crews on reconnaissance missions and photographed the coastlines of Japanese-held islands with German-made Primaflex cameras specially mounted on periscopes.[102] Submarine photographic reconnaissance showed enemy activities in coastal areas where the Japanese typically placed most of their defenses. Periscope-view photographs provided amphibious operations planners with outstanding views of designated landing beaches. These photographs sometimes revealed if a beach contained mines and other obstacles that needed to be destroyed by UDTs before assault waves landed.

Captured Documents and Prisoners of War. JICPOA's Japanese-language experts, all fluent or nearly so, conducted POW interrogations and translated captured documents. They operated in the field, at Pearl Harbor, and at POW camps on Hawaii. On several operations such as Eniwetok, Guam, and Tinian, linguists provided field commanders with tactical intelligence that helped carry the campaign to victory and kept casualties to a minimum. These personnel, however, mostly translated captured documents because so few Japanese soldiers surrendered; most fought to the death. On the other hand, the Japanese who did surrender usually answered the interrogators' questions with total compliance because the IJA and IJN never briefed its soldiers or sailors to resist questioning if caught. Japanese military doctrine stated that they were not supposed to get caught in the first place.

Radio Signals. JICPOA and FRUPAC collaborated in the use of ULTRA, top secret radio intelligence equipment, to intercept, decrypt, decode, and analyze Japanese military radio transmissions. During World War II, the military called it "radio intelligence." Today, it is known as "communications intelligence" or "signals intelligence." In any event, upon intercepting a message, cryptologists would decode it, and then translators would translate it. Afterward, analysts would read the message for information that might be valuable to ongoing or upcoming operations. Such intelligence was often critical and time-sensitive. Enemy radio traffic sometimes revealed what units occupied what islands and if they were going to be reinforced. On several occasions, radio intelligence revealed the exact order of battle of Japanese island bases. Consequently, communications intelligence was quite exotic for the 1940s and proved to be one of the most innovative and productive intelligence tools of the war. Toward the beginning of the Pacific War, radio intelligence was the only source of intelligence CINC-PAC had on the enemy.[103]

The Structure of JICPOA

JICPOA's massive effort to produce intelligence took place under a coordinated system of specialized sections that by the end of the war employed 1,767 intelligence analysts.[104] Each section evolved with the needs of the war, and several of the most active sections absorbed many of the smaller ones. Despite JICPOA's designated structure, General Twitty was flexible to the needs of the fleet, and he frequently created temporary intelligence cells using in-house personnel to process information for special projects. Once the operation had ended, he dissolved the cell, and its members returned to their respective sections.[105] Regardless, the description of the following sections reflects, with a few noted exceptions, JICPOA's architecture at the war's end in 1945, when there were four groups of sections with each group focused on a particular type of intelligence task.[106]

Group One

Group One consisted of eight sections that focused on enemy bases and "static information concerning enemy terrain, peoples, health, industries, and hydrography."[107] They were the Geographic, Photographic Interpretation, Terrain Model, Hydrographic, Cartographic, Target Analysis, Reference, and Medical Sections.

The Geographic Section. The Geographic Section analyzed and coordinated most of the intelligence that went into information bulletins. It received its name from the way it filed and produced intelligence—geographically. For example, JICPOA produced the information bulletin on Tarawa under the heading of its geographic region, the Gilbert Islands, not simply "Enemy Activities on Tarawa." Specialists in this section concentrated on analyzing military bases, such as the air base on Roi-Namur Island in Kwajalein Atoll. Furthermore, the Geographic Section analyzed information concerning Asian Pacific socioeconomics, agricultural output, infrastructure, military industries, hydrography, and to a certain extent, geography. However, other sections concentrated their full resources on Pacific geography.[108]

Since this section mainly produced information bulletins, it utilized every collection source in theater. Furthermore, all sections at JICPOA worked with the Geographic Section. For instance, the Cartographic Section supplied topographical maps and similar graphics, and the Estimates

```
                        ┌─────────────────────┐
                        │     CINCPAC,         │
                        │   Adm. C. Nimitz     │
                        └─────────────────────┘
                                  │
                   ┌────────────────────────────────┐
                   │ CHIEF OF STAFF, INTELLIGENCE,   │
                   │        Cdr.  E. Layton          │
                   └────────────────────────────────┘
                                  │
  ┌──────────────────┐  ┌──────────────────────────────────┐
  │  FRUPAC, USN      │  │ COMMANDER, JICPOA AND ASSIST.    │
  │  Communications   │  │ CHIEF OF STAFF, INTELLIGENCE,    │
  └──────────────────┘  │          BG. Twitty              │
                        └──────────────────────────────────┘
                                  │
                   ┌────────────────────────────────┐
                   │ SECOND IN COMMAND, JICPOA,      │
                   │       Capt. W.J. Holmes         │
                   └────────────────────────────────┘
```

GROUP I	GROUP II	GROUP III	GROUP IV
•Geographic Section •Photographic Section •Terrain Model Section •Reference Section •Medical Section •Hydrographic Section •Cartographic Section •Target Analysis Section	•Enemy Shipping Section •Enemy Air Section •Enemy Land Section •Enemy Flak Section •Estimates Section	• Psychological Warfare Section • Escape and Evasion Section	• Bulletin Section • Production Section • Administration Section • Translation Section • Interrogation Section • Operational Intelligence Section

FIELD TEAMS (Group I)

FIELD TEAMS (Group II)

FIELD TEAMS (Group IV)

Wire Diagram of JICPOA with FRUPAC. This configuration represents the final structure of JICPOA in late 1945. JICPOA documents and author

Section contributed to order of battle analyses. This is not to say, however, that the Geographic Section simply coordinated and assembled the work of other sections. Despite its agency-wide cooperation, the Geographic Section's analysts specialized in specific types of military intelligence and analyzed and produced most of their own material. They even had their own photographic interpreters to assess enemy defenses. In fact, 60 percent of JICPOA's photographic specialists worked for this section.[109] The Geographic Section's specialties were:[110]

Beaches and Terrain	Photogrammetry
Defenses	(stereoscopic analysis)
Ports, Anchorages,	Mapping
and Harbors	Airfields
Mosaics (special photographic	POW Camps
collages of targets or target	Special Assignments
areas)	

Many of these analysts carried out unique missions. For example, among other things, defense specialists reported on enemy defensive structures such as pillboxes and blockhouses. In doing so, they studied enemy building materials, the dimensions of specific bunkers, and any pattern of tactical defense unveiled through successive campaigns. To collect this type of information, defense analysts assembled into small teams and explored every inch of a Japanese base after it had been secured. They crawled into bunkers, examined artillery pieces, hiked through trench lines, and walked through rows of beach obstacles—meanwhile taking pictures, making sketches, and taking notes. The information provided an excellent picture of what Japanese defenses were like before the battle began. This, in turn, helped them understand Japanese defensive tactics. It also made them better photo interpreters, since they had been on the ground and had seen enemy defenses up close. Admiral Nimitz frequently accompanied them. He personally inspected nearly every seized island in his area of responsibility in order to gain insight into the enemy's defensive logic.

Analysts in the Geographic Section also worked on special assignments such as port studies and similar projects for the fleet's submarine command, SubPac.[111] Taken as a whole, this type of intelligence consisted of the core of JICPOA's work, therefore making the Geographic Section one of the most important. On the other hand, the Geographic Section would not have functioned effectively without the assistance of the rest of the organization. The whole process involved a massive team effort.

Generally, the Geographic Section published its reports in a three-volume set, the first two based mostly on research and the last one always supported by photographic reconnaissance. A full staff of graphic technicians provided technical illustrations and maps of enemy defensive positions, weapons emplacements, and buildings on each target.[112] By the end of the war, the Geographic Section employed fifty-six officers, twelve yeomen, and four Navy Waves (from the acronym for "Women Accepted for Volunteer Emergency Service"). It was by far the most diverse section in

JICPOA, and as the war progressed, General Twitty authorized its division into numerous subsections or "desks," which were divided by geographic areas of responsibility. They were as follows:[113]

The Nansei Shoto Desk
The Formosa (Taiwan) Desk
The Japan Desk (with six supporting desks)
The China Desk (with three supporting desks)
The Korea/Manchuria Desk
The Nanpo Shoto Desk
Specialty Desks (for special projects)

Areas that demanded more attention had several supporting desks. Japan had six because analysts needed to know everything about that country—its socioeconomic status, its weapons industries, its nonlethal industries, the location of naval and air bases, the density of population centers, etc. The China desk had three supporting desks; aside from its sheer size, continual large-scale combat operations were occurring in China. In point of fact, the Japanese put more troops into China than any other region. China also contained Allied airfields, and the CCS considered it a potential staging area for the amphibious invasion of Japan.

Given the importance and high profile of this section's work, its deficiencies did not go unnoticed. Because of the fast pace of the war, however, JICPOA did little to solve its problems. Some of the major difficulties the Geographic Section faced were a lack of personnel, a shortness of experienced personnel, a high turnover rate, insufficient working space, not enough access to photo interpretation personnel, and an incomplete understanding of the operational needs of the Pacific Fleet.[114] As evidenced by its intelligence products, however, the Geographic Section performed well enough to get the job done for Nimitz's amphibious campaigns.

The Photographic Interpretation Section. The Photographic Interpretation Section did as its name implied: It analyzed photographs. It began as PRISIC, CINCPAC's independent photographic interpretation center, only to be absorbed by ICPOA and later by JICPOA. In the beginning of the war, this section analyzed all intelligence photographs in Nimitz's area of responsibility, including pictures of Japanese bases, ships, and industrial centers. But eventually, the fleet's intelligence needs matured beyond the scope of the general capabilities of this one section. For that reason, the Photographic Interpretation Section eventually ceased analytical operations and simply served as a pool of specialists from which other sections drew. Many of them ended up in the Geographic Section, and JICPOA loaned others to the fleet to serve on ships. In the fleet, JICPOA's photo interpreters provided operations personnel with up-to-date photo intelligence as a task force neared and assaulted a given objective. To carry out such work, they served on aircraft carriers on a temporary basis and permanently in amphibious commands.[115] JICPOA also sent photo interpreters to two special autonomous field organizations that analyzed photographs that the fleet needed immediately: InterpRon One on Guadalcanal and InterpRon Two at Eniwetok Atoll.[116] Despite the Pacific's many photographic analytical units, on the other hand, there never seemed to be enough to handle the intelligence needs of all U.S. Pacific forces.[117]

The Terrain Model Section. The Terrain Model Section made large-scale topographical models of island objectives that displayed terrain, defenses, and roads. Model builders received intelligence from photo analysts, which helped them construct their target mock-ups. According to General Twitty, the models proved quite accurate. Nimitz and his Navy and Marine commanders used the models while planning operations to understand the full effect of a target's geography and defenses and to plan preliminary naval bombardments. In this latter regard, the Terrain Model Section produced excellent models for the Gilberts, Marshalls, and Marianas campaigns. Line officers used the models to show their troops a bird's-eye view of an objective's strong points, landing beaches, and the scheme of maneuver that would be utilized to seize the objective.[118]

The Hydrographic Section. The Hydrographic Section produced intelligence on the hydrographic conditions surrounding Allied bases in the Pacific, specifically secure and nonsecure sea lanes, except for those in the Hawaiian Islands. It had a massive database of texts, hydrographic charts, and nautical charts, which demonstrated depths, shoals, and general sea conditions in operational areas. U.S. Navy officers used the information to navigate to and from friendly bases, and operations officers relied on the data to issue classified navigational coordinates.[119] Oddly, the Hydrographic Section did not produce hydrographic intelligence on Japanese-held bases, a job left in part to the Geographic Section, which had subsections that focused on a beaches, terrain, anchorages, and harbors. But the latter did not have sole jurisdiction over hydrographic intelligence; the Hydrographic Office in Washington, D.C., did—a strange arrangement for an office thousands of miles from the Pacific. JICPOA complained that this arrangement denied effective support to U.S. amphibious forces, but history demonstrates that the Geographic Section and intelligence from the Hydrographic Office did in fact prove sufficient.[120] Undoubtedly, however, the process proved cumbersome.

The Cartographic Section. The Sixty-fourth Topographical Engineer Company, or elements of it, served as JICPOA's Cartographic Section. It produced intelligence for making topographical maps, hydrographic charts, gridded bombardment charts, and air target maps for island campaigns, but it printed few maps. Instead, the Cartographic Section relied on the U.S. Army's Sixty-fourth and Thirtieth Topographic Battalions to produce its maps, because they had established comprehensive production shops by 1943 and there was no reason to duplicate their work. (This was an unusual arrangement; JICPOA seldom relied on outside units to produce intelligence material.) Photographs, U.S. and Allied prewar maps, and captured enemy maps provided the Cartographic Section with most of its source material.[121]

One of this section's most notable accomplishments was the production of a standard grid map system adopted by all U.S. forces operating in the Pacific, including those under General MacArthur. JICPOA documents assert that Twitty himself developed the grid. His efforts centralized a previously ad hoc system whereby grid coordinates differed from service to service and theater to theater.[122] Under Twitty's system, any infantry unit in any Pacific area of operation using one of JICPOA's gridded maps could call in naval artillery, land-based artillery, or tactical air support from any branch of service. Until the advent of Twitty's system, this was an impossibility.

The Target Analysis Section. The Target Analysis Section designated high-value and high-payoff targets for naval air operations. Furthermore, it recommended the type of ordnance to use to achieve maximum destruction. To accomplish this end, target analysts studied the structural strengths and weaknesses of all types of Japanese buildings, weapons emplacements, bunkers, blockhouses, and pillboxes. They also researched what types of ordnance had and had not destroyed these structures in past campaigns. In addition, the Target Analysis Section participated in planning strategic bombing missions over Japan, but the Joint Target Group (JTG) in Washington, D.C., decided what factories and military bases to bomb in such cases. The JTG based its research on socioeconomic factors, with a view to grinding down not only Japan's war industries but its civilian infrastructure as well. JICPOA's target analysts, however, reviewed the JTG's recommendations and made adjustments according to the latest intelligence.[123]

The Reference Section. The Reference Section maintained JICPOA's all-source database, which consisted of a huge, hard-copy file system. Other sections, the Geographic Section for example, had similar file systems, but they were small and esoteric according to their data specialties. Centralized and much larger, the Reference Section's files contained information from every section in JICPOA. If intelligence or raw data had come to JICPOA on a piece of paper or had been transferred to a piece of paper, then the Reference Section retained a copy or a write-up of that data. Reference Section analysts filed photographs as well. All the other sections of JICPOA relied on the database to conduct research, to crosscheck information for authenticity, to attempt source corroboration, or to provide background data for information bulletins. By the end of the war, the Reference Section consisted of five subsections:[124]

The Library Division (including a hard-copy index, bound literature, and bulky material such as maps)

The Objective Files (a wing of the library that housed battle reports and bulletins from other intelligence services)

Photographic Files Division (copies of photographs, plot charts; was organized by its own hard-copy file system)

The Maps and Charts Division (U.S. and captured Japanese maps and charts of Pacific waters and land masses)

The Medical Section. The Medical Section rounded out Group One, but it never became fully functional. The officer chosen to jump-start the section had to finish a tour with the III Amphibious Corps, and he could not be pulled from his duties. By the time he arrived at Pearl Harbor on 23 July 1945, the end of the war was only a month away. This section, however, had an interesting number of tasks that JICPOA wanted to accomplish. Among them was to analyze intelligence concerning the future site of Allied field hospitals in targeted enemy territory; to study, assess, and test captured Japanese medical equipment; to evaluate the effect of enemy medical practices and health standards; and find out if the Japanese had been using chemical or biological weapons.[125]

There is evidence that the Japanese did engage in biological warfare and "human medical experiments" during World War II. On 16 November 2000, a Japanese war veteran said in an Associated Press interview that his unit—Unit 731—tried to spread diseases throughout the China-Mongolia area of operations. He also asserted that he supported experimental surgical procedures, without anesthesia, on Chinese citizens.

Yoshio Shinozuka, a seventy-seven-year-old veteran of Unit 731, said that he helped produce typhoid, dysentery, and cholera at his base of operations at Harbin City. Shinozuka said that in 1939, he and his unit created these diseases to support combat operations against the Russians at Nomonhan, Mongolia, and for various bombing missions against the Chinese.

Shoichi Matsumoto, a pilot for Unit 731, said that he helped drop plague-carrying fleas on Hangzhou in 1940 and Nanjing in 1941. He also carried bubonic plague–carrying rats to Java and Singapore.[126]

Luckily, the operations never produced significant results. Even luckier for Japan, JICPOA never discovered such operations; otherwise its intelligence might have influenced the U.S. president to authorize the use of similar weapons on the Japanese.

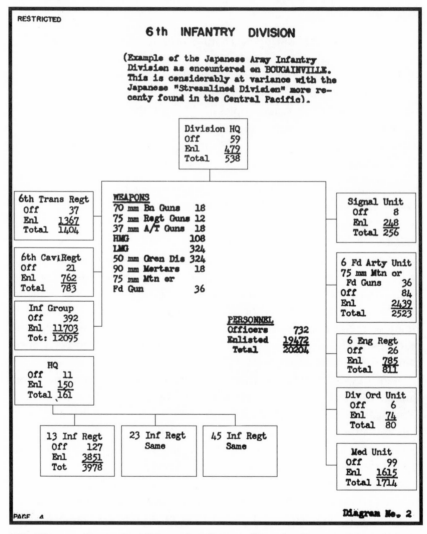

Wire Diagram, Enemy Land Forces Intelligence. The wire diagram shows weapons and personnel of an IJA infantry division. JICPOA Information Bulletin 151-44

STRENGTH AND WEAPONS OF VARIOUS JAPANESE ARMY UNITS

	BATTALIONS				REGIMENTS				DIVISIONS	
	Amph. Bn.	Regt. Bn.	6th Div.	Ind. Inf.	Amph.	RCT.	6th Div.	IMR.	Streamlined.	6th Div.
Personnel	1030	615	11400	579	3964	3165	3942	2688	13565	20204
Light Machine Gun	36	36	36	27	108	108	108	81	324	324
Heavy Machine Gun	6	6	12	12	18	18	36	36	54	108
A/T Guns 37mm	2	2		2	6	6	6	2	18	18
Type 98, 20 mm Auto Guns	3				6				6	
70 mm Howitzer	6	2	2	4	18	6	6	12	30	18
Mortars	12				36		6		36	18
75mm Mtn Guns	3				9	12			33	48
Grenade Dischargers	36	36	36	27	108	108	108	81	324	324
Tanks					9				26	12-15

Weapons Strength Diagram, Enemy Land Forces Intelligence. JICPOA Information Bulletin 151-44

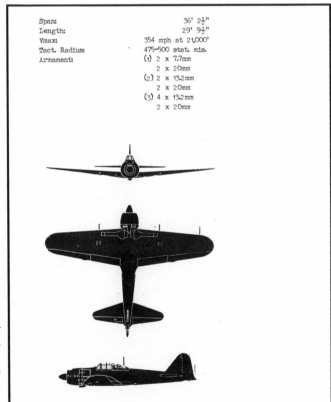

Span: 36' 2½"
Length: 29' 9½"
Vmax: 354 mph at 21,000'
Tact. Radius: 475–500 stat. mis.
Armament: (1) 2 x 7.7mm
2 x 20mm
(2) 2 x 13.2mm
2 x 20mm
(3) 4 x 13.2mm
2 x 20mm

Enemy Air Forces Intelligence. From a JICPOA recognition report on the ZEKE 52 navy fighter. JICPOA "Know Your Enemy" series, no. 105-45

SECRET

April 5, 1944

NOTES ON JAPANESE AIRCRAFT PRODUCTION- (NO.5)

JICPOA BULLETIN NO. 44-44

KASEI 11 AND 15 AIRCRAFT ENGINES

Cover Page, Report on Japanese Aircraft Engine Production. This report combined enemy air force and geographic (military industries) intelligence. Note the commentary on sources. JICPOA Information Bulletin 44-44

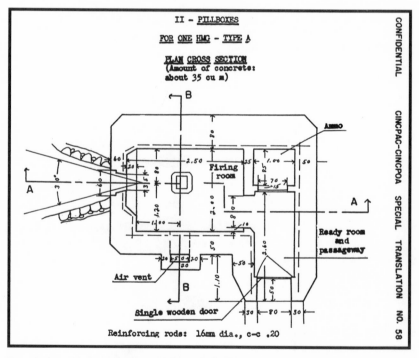

Translation, Technical Plan of Japanese Pillbox Schematics and Construction. A combination of enemy land forces, target analysis, and translation intelligence. JICPOA "Special Translation Number 58" series, no. 94-45

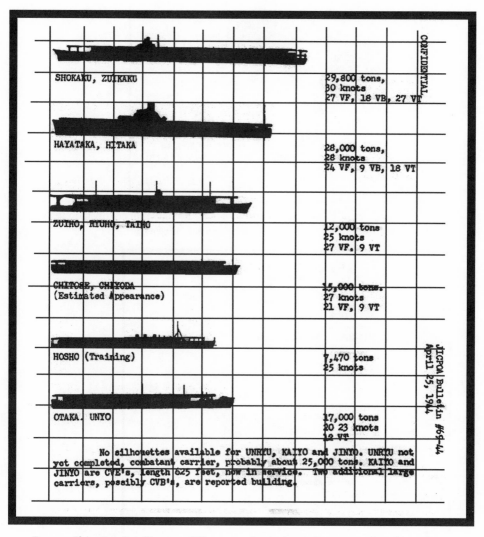

SHOKAKU, ZUIKAKU	29,800 tons, 30 knots 27 VF, 18 VB, 27 VT
HAYATAKA, HITAKA	28,000 tons, 28 knots 24 VF, 9 VB, 18 VT
ZUIHO, RYUHO, TAIHO	12,000 tons 25 knots 27 VF, 9 VT
CHITOSE, CHIYODA (Estimated Appearance)	15,000 tons, 27 knots 21 VF, 9 VT
HOSHO (Training)	7,470 tons 25 knots
OTAKA, UNYO	17,000 tons 20 23 knots 12 VT

No silhouettes available for UNRYU, KAIYO and JINYO. UNRYU not yet completed, combatant carrier, probably about 25,000 tons. KAIYO and JINYO are CVE's, length 625 feet, now in service. Two additional large carriers, possibly CVB's, are reported building.

JICPOA Bulletin #69-44 April 25, 1944

Enemy Shipping Intelligence. Silhouette chart shows Japanese aircraft carriers.
JICPOA Information Bulletin 69-44

Field Drawing, 15-cm Howitzer Emplacement. A combination of enemy land forces and target analysis intelligence. JICPOA Information Bulletin 68-44

EVASIVE ACTION
AGAINST
HEAVY FLAK
(A.A. GUNS)

1. ALTITUDE

As high as possible for Bombing Accuracy.

2. CHANGES IN ALTITUDE

Squadrons at different altitudes.

Gain height outside defended area.

Lose height inside defended area,

on approach and immediately "Bombs Away".

3. CHANGES IN COURSE

Squadrons on different headings.

Change Course every 20-40 seconds.

Turn at I.P. and at "Bombs Away".

Make changes IRREGULAR.

DO NOT REPEAT.

4. SURPRISE

Feint towards other targets.

I.P. close Bomb Run.

Use Sun and Cloud Cover.

5.

Avoid stepped-down formations.

In formation use planned maneuvers.

En route AVOID defended areas.

EVASIVE ACTION MUST BE
PLANNED
IRREGULAR
DELIBERATE
MAKE THE GUNNERS' JOB
TOUGH

JICPOA 42-45-13

TIDE TABLES

KWAJALEIN (KWAJALEIN ATOLL)

8° 44' N - 167° 44' E

Period February, 1944

Calculated on -11 Zone Time

		High Water				Low Water			
DATE 1944	HIGH -11 Z	FEET PLUS	HIGH -11 Z	FEET PLUS	LOW -11 Z	FEET PLUS	LOW -11 Z	FEET PLUS	
FEB. 1	0843	4.6	2102	4.3	0218	0.9	1450	1.4	Neap
2	0948	4.6	2216	3.8	0315	1.2	1611	1.6	
3	1055	4.6	2334	3.6	0419	1.4	1731	1.5	
4	1159	4.8	----	----	0518	1.5	1840	1.4	
5	0040	3.6	1254	5.0	0613	1.5	1934	1.2	
6	0135	3.7	1340	5.1	0702	1.5	2018	1.0	
7	0217	3.8	1420	5.3	0747	1.4	2056	0.9	
8	0254	3.9	1456	5.3	0827	1.3	2130	0.8	
9	0329	4.1	1531	5.4	0906	1.1	2203	0.7	Spring
10	0401	4.2	1605	5.4	0945	1.0	2235	0.6	
11	0435	4.3	1639	5.3	1020	1.0	2305	0.6	
12	0510	4.4	1711	5.2	1056	1.0	2337	0.8	
13	0546	4.4	1746	5.0	1133	1.2	----	----	
14	0622	4.4	1822	4.7	0008	0.9	1210	1.4	
15	0701	4.3	1901	4.4	0040	1.0	1252	1.5	
16	0744	4.3	1948	4.0	0116	1.3	1343	1.7	
17	0835	4.3	2047	3.8	0158	1.4	1448	1.8	Neap
18	0936	4.5	2159	3.6	0250	1.4	1604	1.8	
19	1043	4.7	2318	3.7	0353	1.5	1720	1.4	
20	1150	5.0	----	----	0500	1.4	1827	1.1	
21	0030	3.8	1250	5.4	0605	1.3	1925	0.8	
22	0130	4.1	1345	5.8	0705	0.9	2017	0.3	
23	0221	4.5	1435	6.0	0801	0.6	2105	0.0	
24	0309	4.8	1525	6.3	0856	0.4	2153	-0.1	Spring
25	0357	5.1	1611	6.2	0949	0.2	2238	-0.1	
26	0443	5.2	1700	6.1	1040	0.2	2321	0.1	
27	0530	5.4	1750	5.7	1131	0.5	----	----	
28	0620	5.3	1840	5.1	0006	0.5	1225	0.8	
29	0710	5.1	1936	4.6	0051	0.8	1322	1.0	
	0806	4.9	----	----	0140	1.2	----	----	

Hydrographic Intelligence. A February 1944 tide table estimate for Kwajalein Atoll, written in December 1943. JICPOA Information Bulletin 69-43

Facing page, bottom

Flak Intelligence: "Make the Gunners' Job Tough." Evasive maneuvering for pilots. JICPOA "Flak Intelligence Memorandum Number 3" series, no. 42-45

CHART 2

CHART OF THE STANDARD RATE OF FIRE OF FIELD ARTILLERY

Classi-fication Type of Gun	Rate of fire per gun per minut (rounds)			Average maximum number of shells fired per gun per hour (rounds)
	Very Rapid, for a time not over 2 minutes	Rapid, for a time not over 5 minutes	Normal, for a time not over 15 minutes	
Field Guns (improved model	10 - 12	6 - 8	4	100 - 120
Horse Artillery	10 - 12	6 - 8	4	100 - 120
Mountain Guns	10 - 12	6 - 8	4	100 - 120
10 cm Howitzer	6 - 8	4 - 5	3	60 - 70
10 cm Gun	6 - 8	3 - 5	2	50 - 60
15 cm Howitzer	3 - 4	2 - 3	1	30 - 40

NOTE:

1. In demolition fire while firing in preparation for an attack, the usual rate is "normal". In artillery neutralization firing, the usual rate is rapid.

2. In firing to support a break-through, the usual rate is rapid.

3. In defensive fire, the usual rate is very rapid, or rapid.

* Light Artillery in Cavalry Brigades

Enemy Land Forces Intelligence. The chart demonstrates the rate of fire of various Japanese artillery weapons for different types of operations. JICPOA Information Bulletin 167-44

Group Two

Group Two, essentially the former Combat Intelligence Unit, consisted of five sections that analyzed the force structure, logistics, and capabilities of each service of the Japanese military, which consisted of the Imperial Japanese Army (IJA), the Imperial Japanese Navy (IJN), and their air forces. Group Two also conducted tracking operations to keep tabs on the location of certain Japanese units.[127] Collectively, it consisted of the Enemy Air, Enemy Shipping, Enemy Land, Flak, and Estimates Sections.

The Enemy Air Section. The Enemy Air Section analyzed Japanese air forces of the IJA and IJN. Under the CIU and ICPOA, this section tracked the movements of Japanese air units with a plot, but plotting took up a considerable amount of the section's resources, so the War Department took over these duties in mid-1944. Afterward, the Enemy Air Section's sole function was to analyze the enemy's air order of battle, and its analysts became definitive experts in their field. Accordingly, the Enemy Air Section disseminated its intelligence not only to the fleet, but to Washington, D.C., as well. Its publications covered numerous subjects, including Japanese bombers, fighters, suicide aircraft, airfield schematics, engine technology, armaments, aircraft armor, the organization of air units, and the Japanese aircraft industry. The Enemy Air Section also published the silhouette charts of Japanese planes that were posted on nearly every U.S. ship in the Pacific. Furthermore, it produced models of these planes and wrote assessments concerning their strengths and weaknesses.[128]

The Enemy Air Section published some of its intelligence, such as airfield diagrams, in *Weekly Intelligence* because it was vital to tactical air raids and strategic bombing missions. The fleet wanted its pilots to have ready access to such intelligence to improve their mission results. To achieve such focus, JICPOA organized the Enemy Air Section into specialized subgroups organized along functional and geographic lines. Functional groups studied aircraft technicalities, tarmacs, apron space, fuel storage facilities, and similar subjects. Geographic groups studied airfields according to location—China or the Palau Islands, for example. Analysts who researched airfields in Japan worked at the Advance Intelligence Center, a field branch of JICPOA located on Guam (by 1945), which was also the home of the XXI Bomber Command. Those who focused on airfields elsewhere in the Pacific worked at Pearl Harbor.[129]

The Enemy Air Section relied on diverse sources. Field intelligence personnel collected Japanese aircraft parts and intact aircraft from crash sites and seized islands. They then sent those parts to JICPOA, where analysts with aeroengineering backgrounds spent months assessing their technologies and airframes. Enemy Air Section analysts also worked with captured documents, POW interrogations of pilots and air base personnel, intelligence reports from other units, and aerial photographs of airfields, aircraft industries, and aircraft.[130]

Aside from supporting bombing missions, intelligence from the Enemy Air Section helped bring to light deficiencies in Japanese aircraft. This helped U.S. engineers design combat aircraft that could exploit those deficiencies. For example, intelligence on the infamous A-6M Zero, or Zeke, fighter, the world's most advanced fighter at the beginning of the Pacific War, indicated that it had poor armor, light armaments, and fuel tanks that did not self-seal. Based on this information, U.S. aircraft manufacturers, at the behest of the War Department, built planes to counter the weaknesses of the Zero. The results? Legendary fighters such as Vought's F-4U Corsair, which was faster than the Zero and protected by heavy armor. Additionally, Vought armed it with several large-caliber machine guns that could saw the Zero in half. This plane and others like it helped tilt technology scales in favor of the United States and gave its pilots an edge in aerial combat maneuvering.

The Enemy Shipping Section. The Enemy Shipping Section analyzed Japanese maritime vessels, including battleships, submarines, aircraft carriers, barges, small attack craft, and merchant marine ships. Its analysts also studied Japanese shipping lanes, dock facilities, shipyard production capacity, and harbor layouts. Analysts who studied just the IJN focused on naval tactics, armaments, ordnance, and armor. Intelligence on Japanese naval weapons and armor helped the U.S. Navy understand Japanese naval capabilities, which in turn influenced U.S. fleet tactics and surface warfare. When U.S. Navy commanders understood their enemy, they were better able to defeat him. Source material on Japanese maritime forces came from photographs, POW interrogations, captured documents, radio intelligence, and after-action reports from naval battles.[131]

The Enemy Land Section. The Enemy Land Section analyzed Japanese land forces. It played a vital role in amphibious assault planning by providing, when possible, pertinent IJA order-of-battle data. It also provided intelligence on the IJN's Special Naval Landing Forces, which had been so difficult to defeat on Tarawa Atoll. Additionally, Land Section analysts drew valuable wire diagrams of Japanese ground units that demonstrated the manpower and armaments of each type of unit. They updated the intelligence as contact with the enemy increased. The Land Section consisted of two sections: Enemy Methods (Japanese weapons, defense fortifications, and tactics) and Enemy Dispositions (estimates of the number of Japanese soldiers on targeted bases). Both sections relied on all-source data, and Enemy Dispositions worked hand in hand with the Estimates Section and its radio intelligence because its information was time-sensitive to operations. The Enemy Land Section contributed volumes of intelligence to the Geographic Section, and their work overlapped on occasion.[132] Sometimes, duplication clogged JICPOA's information flow, but it helped when the Geographic Section could not concentrate on a particular project.

The Enemy Land Section had its own linguists and photo interpreters, but if it lacked sufficient personnel for an important project, it drew from JICPOA's comparable sections. Like the Geographic Section, the Land Section sent collection teams to seized enemy bases, but not to duplicate analyses of fortifications. Land Section field teams specialized in Japanese weaponry. This section probably had the greatest collection of Japanese infantry weapons outside the Japanese military. Its cache included pistols, grenades, bolt-action rifles, light and heavy machine guns, antitank weapons, machine cannon, and artillery pieces of medium and heavy caliber. They became experts in the use of all of these weapons, and they also experimented with them. After the Iwo Jima operation, for example, Land Section analysts conducted Japanese antitank gun penetration tests on U.S. Sherman tanks in order to assess why the Marines had lost so many during that battle.

At the request of the Marine Corps, JICPOA's Land Section established a training facility to teach marines how to use Japanese firearms and heavy weapons. Why? Because, in a few past operations, such as the 1942 raid on Makin Island, marines had to use captured Japanese weapons when they either ran out of ammunition for their own weapons or lost them in the confusion of combat.[133] If such circumstances arose again, the USMC wanted their men to be able to fight effectively with any weapon available. More important, reports on the capabilities of these armaments helped fleet personnel understand how their enemy functioned in battle. Weapons capabilities dictate tactics, so a combat commander who had read an enemy weapons report could, with a little analysis, understand enemy tactics associated with that particular weapon. Such intelligence helped in assault planning and clarified tactical options on the battlefield.

The Flak Intelligence Section. The Flak Intelligence Section analyzed Japanese antiaircraft (AA) capabilities. Similar to the Enemy Land Section's evaluations, flak analysts assessed the capabilities of Japanese AA weapons and therefore exposed their strengths and weaknesses. Using this type of intelligence, they produced flak maps for all U.S. pilots in the Pacific that pinpointed danger zones or "air envelopes." An air envelope is a dome of airspace surrounding an AA weapon on the ground that defined its firing range. For example, the Japanese Model 98 20-mm AA cannon had a maximum vertical range of twelve thousand feet. Its maximum horizontal range was 1,816.6 feet.[134] Correspondingly, its air envelope would enclose a "dome" 12,000 feet high and 1,816.6 feet wide at its base, in 360 degrees. Attack pilots tried to avoid air envelopes when bombing and strafing targets on the ground. This type of intelligence also revealed the safest entry and exit corridors for strike operations, and it helped pilots formulate evasive maneuvers to avoid being shot down when they had to attack within range of Japanese AA guns.[135] The Flak Section's analyses rose in importance as the war neared Japan's home islands, because strategic bombing missions increased and Japanese AA techniques improved. It was so specialized that other Pacific intelligence units solicited its information so they could produce their own flak maps. Source material included photographs, documents on Japanese AA weapons and capabilities, and POW interrogations.

The Estimates Section. While the other sections in Group Two concentrated on order-of-battle analyses, the Estimates Section focused its efforts on locating and tracking Japanese units. It was one of the most important sections at JICPOA and was originally the backbone of the Combat Intelligence Center. Housed outside JICPOA in the FRUPAC building, the Estimates Section relied almost exclusively on radio intercepts, and most of its intelligence received top secret classification or higher.

The Estimates Section contributed to all types of offensive operations. For example, it plotted enemy fleet movements for naval operations, and it supported amphibious assaults by analyzing enemy radio traffic to assess how many Japanese occupied an island objective. However, JICPOA did not print radio intelligence in information bulletins unless another source corroborated it. "Secret" was typically the highest classification that information bulletins achieved, and radio intelligence was always classified top secret or top secret ULTRA.[136] Instead, the Estimates Section published plot intelligence in a weekly report titled *Estimates of Enemy Forces and Capabilities.* Each report covered a branch of the Japanese military. For example, the report on enemy naval forces was called "Weekly Estimate of Location of Japanese Naval Vessels." Estimates produced similar reports on enemy activities in island groups or on islands targeted for invasion.[137] Other ULTRA intelligence that had to be disseminated immediately reached Lieutenant Commander Layton via special memo, who then personally informed Admiral Nimitz. This back channel evolved out of the strict security precautions surrounding radio intelligence. If senior Japanese officers ever suspected that U.S. forces had cracked their codes, they would have changed them immediately and closed off a highly valuable source of information. The JICPOA-FRUPAC team, therefore, kept its "need to know" circle as small as possible.

The Estimates Section also kept a plot of Japanese fleet movements. A plot was an overlay, similar to tracing paper, which lay on top of a large map of the Pacific theater. To generate the plot, JICPOA and FRUPAC used sophisticated signals intelligence equipment to monitor enemy radio transmissions. When a Japanese ship sent a radio message, radio intercept specialists would zero in on where the signal came from and pinpoint the location of the vessel that sent the transmission. Interceptors would then send the message to cryptologists who would decrypt and decode it. Afterward, translators would transform the communiqué from Japanese to En-

glish. Translators subsequently sent the messages to analysts who documented the time of the interception and then scoured the transmission
for key words such as the name, location, or sailing direction of an enemy
ship. At the same time, other analysts marked or "plotted" the vessel's location and sailing direction on the large map overlay, thereby earning the
term "plot." By the end of a twenty-four-hour period, the plot displayed the
location of numerous Japanese ships and submarines. The end result
yielded a picture of enemy naval mass and direction, or probable direction,
in a given area.[138] Taken as a whole, senior analysts would use the data to
estimate enemy intentions, such as whether the Japanese were launching
an offensive against a U.S. base or carrier group.

Estimates stored all of its data in a hard-copy file system that complemented current intelligence operations. Hypothetically, if an enemy transmission discussed a particular Japanese carrier, the *Zuikaku,* for example,
and its proximity to the Marianas Islands, then analysts would have made
two copies of the transmission with each important word or phrase high-
lighted. In this case, it would have been "Zuikaku" and "Marianas Islands."
Analysts would have then filed each copy in the appropriate index for later
use by operational planners.[139] Later, if U.S. forces intended to operate near
the Marianas, intelligence analysts would have retrieved all information
concerning that island group from the Estimates Section's files. In this hypothetical case, they would have discovered that the *Zuikaku* had recently
been in the area, which would have caused two reactions. First, it would
have prompted the retrieval of all information concerning *Zuikaku,* its
battle group, and its most recent location to see if it was still in the area.
Second, it would give planners a good reason to make a hasty request of
JICPOA to look into the possibility of strong enemy naval activity in the vicinity of the Marianas.

Group Three

Group Three contained the Psychological Warfare and Escape and Evasion
Sections, the latter known in military jargon as E&E. Although different in
scope of purpose, both sections dealt with enemy contact. Psychological
warfare required contacting Japanese citizens and soldiers. E&E activities
were aimed at avoiding it.

The Psychological Warfare Section. The Psychological Warfare Section
published propaganda leaflets, distributed misinformation, and broadcast
radio messages designed to demoralize and confuse Japanese soldiers and
civilians alike. In theory, demoralization and confusion would have caused
the Japanese to abandon their war effort. Sometimes the Psychological

Warfare Section dropped leaflets from aircraft on Japanese bases, urging soldiers to surrender before U.S. forces attacked. But JICPOA's propaganda never influenced many to give up; most Japanese servicemen were fanatically loyal. On the other hand, some of the Psychological Warfare Section's leaflets did influence Japanese civilians to evacuate war industrial centers and surrounding towns before being bombed. In fact, many cities attempted mass evacuations before being hit by air raids.[140] Psychological Warfare consisted of three specialty areas:[141] Strategic Propaganda (aimed at Japan—to cause civilian mistrust of the government and to weaken the will of the populace); Tactical Propaganda (aimed at soldiers and civilians on targeted islands); and Propaganda for Bypassed Islands (aimed at Japanese soldiers belonging to neutralized garrisons on bypassed islands such as those in the Carolines).

The Psychological Warfare Section experienced most of its success with air raid warning leaflets. Postwar analyses indicated that the second most successful effort was disseminating news from the outside world to Japanese citizens and telling them how their military was mistreating foreign POWs. (Since the Japanese lived in a closed, martial society, the government censored all news sources. Such a system allowed the government to control the thoughts of the people. Even in 1944, Japanese citizens believed that they were winning the war.) Leaflets defining the Potsdam Declaration, the decree that demanded the unconditional surrender of Japan, came in third. Fake yen, especially the "Ten-Yen" bill, equivalent to an faux U.S. three-dollar bill, had the fourth highest success rate and impact, the goal being to invoke a lack of confidence in the government. Leaflets that attempted to make the imperial military look bad to civilians had the least impact.[142]

The Escape and Evasion Section. The Escape and Evasion Section helped downed pilots survive and escape enemy territory through training and publications. E&E analysts published survival manuals and established Pacific-wide networks of Allied military units and indigenous peoples designed to funnel missing soldiers back to friendly lines. They relied on numerous esoteric sources for their unique intelligence products, including Allied soldiers who had escaped or evaded capture in hostile areas, Allied intelligence officers working behind enemy lines in countries such as China, Japanese POWs who had hunted downed pilots, captured documents that demonstrated dense Japanese troop concentrations (and hence areas to avoid), and aerial photographs that demonstrated civilian areas and terrain variation.[143]

Group Four

Group Four included six sections. They were the Bulletin, Production, Administration, Interrogation, Translation, and Operational Intelligence Sections. The first three dealt with publication and management, and the last three engaged in collection and analysis.

The Bulletin Section. The Bulletin Section published *Weekly Intelligence.* Classified confidential, circulation reached fourteen thousand copies. It contained updated information regarding enemy aircraft capabilities, the status of large Japanese bases of operations and staging areas, Japanese defensive tactics encountered during recent campaigns, analyses of specific enemy units, and similar topics. All sections at JICPOA contributed to the report, as did the fleet by providing useful battle action reports. However, the Enemy Air, Shipping, and Land Sections provided the majority of the information in *Weekly Intelligence* because it dealt primarily with order-of-battle information. In addition, the Translation Section frequently contributed translated order-of-battle documents for fleet officers to study. JICPOA published the last issue of *Weekly Intelligence,* volume 2, number 5, on 13 August 1945.[144]

The Production Section. The Production Section finished, edited, and published all of JICPOA's intelligence reports, including *Weekly Intelligence, Know Your Enemy,* and the Geographic Section's information bulletins. The Production Section had several teams of specialists who worked in shifts because of their heavy workload. They included draft artists, who worked on maps and charts, lithograph experts who produced photographic materials, and an editorial board that proofread some of JICPOA's publications. The editorial board, however, was small and edited only interrogation reports and document translations. By June 1945, a sufficient number of editors joined the board to edit all of JICPOA's publications, but the war ended two months later and so did their duties.[145]

The Administration Section. The Administration Section managed JICPOA's operations infrastructure and kept it in functioning order. It consisted of essential bureaucrats whose countless responsibilities included intelligence dissemination, mail distribution, equipment procurement (such as photo interpretation equipment), personnel file maintenance, and payroll management. The Administration Section also handled security for key JICPOA personnel, the JICPOA building, and for the dissemination of vital intelligence maps and bulletins.

Compared to the other sections at JICPOA, the Administration Section's work might seem boring; however, security and dissemination are two vital aspects of intelligence work. Security was important because JICPOA had to protect itself against attack and infiltration. A physical blow to JICPOA would have curtailed its intelligence production, thereby temporarily blinding the fleet and giving the Japanese time to regroup and effect better defenses. Dissemination is the last phase of the intelligence cycle and how JICPOA communicated with its customers. It was pivotal that JICPOA deliver its products to the right people in a timely fashion. Otherwise, its intelligence was useless.[146]

The Translation Section. The Translation Section translated Japanese military documents into English and produced the *Translations and Interrogations* series of publications. It conducted its work both in the field for immediate tactical exploitation and at Pearl Harbor for use in future operations.[147] Translators provided JICPOA with an invaluable intelligence edge: the ability to understand the enemy's capabilities and intentions through the written word, known in today's intelligence community as "document exploitation." Most armies record in writing their operational procedures and force structure, whether they are mess hall menus, schematics of combat units, or top secret battle plans. The Japanese military was no exception. Each Japanese command and control center kept multitudes of military documents and, curiously, did not often destroy them even when being overrun, so each combat operation yielded a wealth of enemy literature.

Officially, the Translation Section began functioning as a component of ICPOA on 16 February 1943, although CINCPAC had language officers at his disposal as early as 1939. ICPOA had twenty language officers who had completed eleven months of intensive language training at the U.S. Navy Language School in Boulder, Colorado. They conducted both document translations and POW interrogations; however, as the war progressed, the increase in POWs and especially Japanese documents dictated a more focused approach to language-based intelligence activities. Therefore, they divided into two organizations—the Translation Section and the Interrogation Section.

Unlike most other sections at JICPOA that focused on singular Japanese military issues, analysts of the Translation Section covered almost all of them. In order to gain a fuller understanding of military operations across the board, they spent time with numerous fleet commands, learning a wide array of military occupational specialties. This included attending naval gunnery practice, visiting radar installations, participating in amphibious landing exercises, and flying on air combat missions. Being familiar with most military subjects helped the Translation Section's analysts write an extensive Japanese dictionary of military terms and place names,[148] a document so comprehensive that the Japanese themselves could have used it.

The Translation Section was so vital to JICPOA's operations that it expanded its personnel base several times. In late 1943 when the Translation Section became a part of JICPOA, it increased from twenty to forty-six officers, just in time to accommodate documents coming in from the Gilberts. In January 1944, it expanded again by twenty officers just before the Marshalls operations began. By the end of the war, the Translation Section consisted of 240 personnel.

With so many specialists handling such a vital intelligence source, the Translation Section followed a highly organized and specific set of standard operating procedures. When a document fell into the hands of U.S. forces in the field, a JICPOA or a fleet translation officer analyzed the importance of the document on the spot and designated it either useful to the combat operation at hand or not. If it was useful, the translator analyzed it and disseminated the intelligence to operational commanders. If it was not, the analyst sent the document to JICPOA. At JICPOA, sorting room analysts, otherwise known as "scanners," categorized newly arrived documents according to subject and then stamped them accordingly. They also wrote short summations of each document on scanning slips. Scanners then sent the slips to all of JICPOA's sections to see if any analyst needed the information immediately. If they did, translators translated the needed documents and forwarded the data to whoever needed it. If not, the documents went into a large file organized by a subject-based hard-copy system containing over sixty thousand documents. From this file, analysts could retrieve documents as needed.[149]

Like other sections, the Translation Section divided its work by subsections because the massive number of documents it possessed covered a mind-boggling scope of subject material. By the close of hostilities in the Pacific, the section contained fifteen different subsections and covered the following Japanese military subjects:[150]

Air (air forces)
Land Forces (ground troop order of battle, tactics, etc.)
Bases (bases, fortifications, air bases, war industries)
Geography (topographic and hydrographic maps, charts)
Weather (enemy meteorological research)
Radar, Sonar, and Command & Control (related documents)
Ships (merchant and naval)

Ordnance (army and navy shells, bombs, mines, bullets, etc.)

Order of Battle (related documents)

Medical Data (army and navy medical services, capabilities)

Chemical Warfare (related documents)

Military Government (civil affairs/military government structure and procedures)

Manuals (a library of captured manuals)

Files & Publications (clerical work, file maintenance, captured document publications)

Annex (Japanese-Americans, translating nonsensitive intelligence material such as diaries and notebooks)

Unlike translators who worked at Pearl Harbor, field translators had to be able to assess all of these subjects during combat. In the process, they frequently exposed themselves to grave danger. During the course of the war, one translator earned a Bronze Star and two others earned Purple Hearts. Combat translators worked at regimental, corps, and command ship levels. They were always in high demand. During the invasion of Okinawa, for example, JICPOA sent eighty-four translators into combat. In two cases in the Marianas, they provided field commanders with vital intelligence that helped achieve efficient victories, and on one occasion in the Marshalls, they helped prevent a potential blood bath (see chapter 2).

Strategically, the Translation Section provided exceptional warfighting support. General Twitty, in his report of intelligence activities at the end of the war noted the following:[151] "Thanks to information discovered in a memorandum book, for example, it became clear that the Japanese were using 10-centimeter radar. An immediate change in the Radar Counter Measures setup at CINCPAC was effected and the jamming of 10-centimeter radar inaugurated."

Such information told U.S. forces exactly what kind of radar the Japanese used to detect incoming aircraft. Armed with this intelligence, U.S. forces had the ability to jam Japanese radar and help hide the size and flight paths of their air attacks. In another case, General Twitty noted:[152]

The document Digest of Japanese Naval Air Bases, captured on Saipan, contained sketches of all the principal naval air bases in Japan and her various possessions. As it was received prior to the time when adequate photo coverage of the Empire was available, it proved to be of considerable value in surveying installations, etc. In addition, information on complements or planned complements of these fields made it possible to make estimates of their relative importance in the Japanese war effort.

Knowing the location of nearly every Japanese air base in the Pacific, plus their technical specifications, put the United States far ahead of the Japanese with regard to strategic planning. Armed with this information, Nimitz did not have to grope around in the Pacific from island to island hoping that aerial reconnaissance and radio intelligence would detect Japanese air bases. Because of JICPOA's intelligence, he knew where they were and therefore knew Japanese land-based air capabilities. This allowed him to plan effective attacks on these bases, forcing the Japanese to react to his actions, further keeping them off balance.

Although the Translation Section did excellent intelligence work, it did have its fair share of problems. Very few of its officers were intimately familiar with the Japanese language, mastery of which takes years of practice and cultural immersion. An occasional slip-up or linguistic misunderstanding from time to time caused the loss of intelligence. Furthermore, Japanese is a compartmentalized language that consists of different types of linguistics for different types of speaking situations. Language used with children, for example, is not used with adults. Likewise, the military and government used numerous specialized words that further complicated the work of translators. Last, even though Translation Section analysts had gone through some infantry training, it was not enough to make them universally effective under fire.[153] In fact, translators at times added unnecessary risk to themselves and those around them but were kept in the field anyway because of their valuable skills.

The Interrogation Section. The Interrogation Section consisted of linguists who interrogated POWs for information on Japanese defense tactics, the whereabouts of various enemy units, the garrison strength of Japanese bases, and the defense plans of targeted islands. Some linguists spoke Korean, which was beneficial in interrogating the hundreds, and sometimes thousands, of Korean laborers captured on seized islands. Like the Translation Section, the Interrogation Section fielded teams of linguists during combat operations to collect and process tactical intelligence from captured Japanese servicemen. In the field, interrogators interviewed POWs for information such as the name of the captive's unit, the number of personnel in his unit when captured, and related information such as the location of artillery units.[154] Operations commanders used the intelligence to piece together a picture of the enemy situation and then exploit it. If, for example, a POW told his captors where his unit's artillery sectors were, his interrogators would forward that intelligence to the commander, who would then probably have his artillery units shell those positions.[155]

For less urgent interrogations, the section had a stockade at Iroquois

Point located sixteen miles from JICPOA. Complete with a recreation pen, five interrogation cells, five solitary confinement cells, bathrooms, showers, a Propaganda Section liaison hut, and six sixteen-foot tents to serve as auxiliary interrogation cells, the stockade could handle 250 POWs at one time. But even this proved to be too small a capacity, so the U.S. Army built its own facility to pick up JICPOA's overflow. Overall, 3,615 POWs from all over the Pacific passed through the Iroquois Point stockade,[156] a small number compared to the large number of Japanese soldiers encountered from 1941 to 1945.

POW interrogators attended the same schools that translators did, and no background experience steered them into one specialty or the other. They were simply picked either for interrogation duty or translation duty. With no formal interrogation training, they learned from experience how to approach Japanese servicemen for questioning.[157] However, they did not use torture to elicit information from POWs because that sort of thing simply was not done at JICPOA. Besides, most Japanese soldiers, airmen, and sailors coughed up information rather quickly. As noted above, their superiors never told them not to because capture was never discussed as a possibility. One POW actually threatened suicide if his JICPOA captors did not interrogate him. Interrogation specialists reasoned that he wanted to be seen as important enough to be questioned by the enemy.[158]

Tactically, POWs did not provide pivotal intelligence on the battlefield in the manner that captured documents occasionally did. Instead, it generally supported small unit actions like the artillery scenario previously discussed. But small accomplishments added up and saved hundreds and possibly thousands of U.S. servicemen's lives in the long run. Based on JICPOA's records, it appears that the Interrogation Section's efforts also supported strategic intelligence. For example, marines on Saipan captured the special aide to Vice Adm. Chuichi Nagumo, commander of the First Air Fleet that raided Pearl Harbor and responsible for the defense of Saipan. The aide provided a wealth of intelligence on Japanese naval tactics, including carrier order of battle and air capabilities, all vital to the overall prosecution of the war.[159]

The Operational Intelligence Section. The Operational Intelligence Section provided a continuing education course for graduates of the Advanced Naval Intelligence School destined for intelligence units belonging to the U.S. fleet, such as the Second Marine Division's G-2 section. Specifically, the Operational Intelligence Section oriented operational intelligence officers to the U.S. intelligence infrastructure in the Pacific theater. In doing so, it rotated officers through JICPOA's various sections and fleet units in order to demonstrate how the entire operational-intelligence flow worked. The process took about two months. Once trained, these officers transferred to their particular billets but maintained close contact with JICPOA, which provided them with most of their intelligence. In turn, they disseminated it to the fleet command that they supported.[160] They also worked side by side with JICPOA's personnel assigned to the fleet and collected and processed photographic, signals, document, and POW intelligence.

The latter arrangement worked well because JICPOA published each information bulletin a month or two before an assault began, and the enemy situation on a target could change within that time frame. Therefore, JICPOA personnel worked with operational intelligence officers to keep field commanders abreast of the changing situation. Most operational officers were trained to analyze the Japanese order of battle, so they were familiar with enemy naval, infantry, and air forces. JICPOA trained some of these personnel to be photographic interpreters, and others became radio intelligence specialists. Many radio intelligence personnel served on flagships and kept key commanders, such as Admiral Spruance, aware of any last-minute information gained from the Estimates Section and FRUPAC.

Advanced Intelligence Center, Guam

The Commandant of the Marine Corps had originally suggested having advanced intelligence centers stationed throughout the Pacific. Accordingly, JICPOA expanded in January 1945 and placed a forward JIC at Guam: the Advanced Intelligence Center (AIC). Nimitz used the AIC to keep his forward headquarters on Guam updated with the most current intelligence. The AIC also helped disseminate JICPOA's intelligence to the fleet.[161] However, the war ended shortly after the AIC was established, and it never realized its potential.[162] The AIC consisted of the following sections:

Operational Intelligence Section (collected, processed, and disseminated photo and combat report intelligence and ran intelligence reproduction and liaison between JICPOA and the fleet)

Photographic Reconnaissance Section (made requests for aerial reconnaissance missions, distributed film and negatives to the fleet, and assisted with photo interpretation)

Geographic Section (same duties as sister section at JICPOA)

Reference Section (same duties as sister section at JICPOA)

Weekly Intelligence Section (worked for JICPOA's *Weekly Intelligence*)

Interrogation and Translation Section (same duties as sister section at JICPOA)

Escape and Evasion Section (lectured to bomber groups on Guam about E&E procedures)

Psychological Warfare Section (represented JICPOA)

Flak Intelligence Section (same duties as sister section at JICPOA)

Aviation Charts Section (produced charts and maps for carrier operations)

Photographic Laboratory Section (photo lab)

Distribution Section (assembly, packaging and dissemination of intelligence products)

Administrative Section (same duties as sister section at JICPOA)

Unlike the AIC, JICPOA did realize its potential—a monumental task because its personnel had to learn the intelligence business, build the organization, and produce usable intelligence all at the same time. Furthermore, JICPOA did not have an organization to mimic, as the Office of Strategic Services (OSS) did in Europe. The OSS based its organization on, and received assistance from, Britain's Special Operations Executive (SOE). Besides, their missions differed from JICPOA's in many respects. These organizations functioned much like the modern CIA and Britain's MI-6. The OSS and SOE ran agents, conducted clandestine operations, directed paramilitary operations, and produced certain types of military intelligence but were unable to plot German fleet movements and analyze the Wehrmacht's order of battle. JICPOA exclusively conducted military intelligence operations and evolved into an organization similar to the modern Defense Intelligence Agency (DIA). In essence, JICPOA built itself and educated its personnel on the job under wartime conditions. The fact that JICPOA accomplished all it did under such conditions is remarkable.

JICPOA performed its duties well, primarily because of its joint designation. Brigadier General Twitty remarked highly of this characteristic. He claimed that intelligence was a "joint function"[163] and that having members of the various services working together in the same building greatly enhanced JICPOA's final intelligence products. Each service pooled its assets and drew from each other's different perspectives of military science.[164] Additionally, having members of each branch of service in JICPOA meant that its analysts had a good understanding of how the military worked and what it needed.

The U.S. Navy enhanced JICPOA's performance because the Pacific War was primarily a naval conflict. Carrier warfare, undersea warfare, and enemy shipping all fell under the expertise of the Navy. Naval personnel dissected and studied Japanese naval capabilities and tracked the IJN's movements in order to detect offensive actions or to lay submarine ambushes for Japanese convoys. Through the Navy, JICPOA had access to submarine reconnaissance platforms stationed throughout the fleet to facilitate Marine Corps needs for surf-level photographs of potential landing beaches. Furthermore, USN language officers intercepted and translated Japanese radio communiqués and served as POW interrogators.[165]

The Marine Corps also sent JICPOA Japanese linguists and proved especially helpful in analyzing information on Japanese Naval Special Landing Forces. In addition, a marine who worked for the Estimates Section on special projects headed the Enemy Land Section.[166] JICPOA's marines also studied and evaluated captured Japanese rifles, pistols, machine guns, and other weapons. Most importantly, however, marines helped analyze the beach defenses of islands scheduled for invasion and therefore supported one of the most pivotal types of military operations of the war. The marines understood the mechanics of amphibious warfare better than anyone else at JICPOA and looked for defensive measures and terrain features that might impede amphibious landings.

The U.S. Army offered much to JICPOA's already diverse capabilities. It, like the Navy and the USMC, provided Japanese language officers for interrogation and translation duties.[167] In fact, an Army officer, Maj. Lachlan M. Sinclair, served as second in command of the Translation Section.[168] Likewise, Army personnel were especially useful for analyzing Japanese infantry order of battle and their tactics. For example, Army officers supervised the Estimates Section's efforts to analyze enemy ground force strength for the Guam and Saipan campaigns.[169] The Army perspective on Japanese infantry forces, coupled with that of the Marine Corps, provided JICPOA with effective order-of-battle intelligence.

The U.S. Army had a superior system of distributing top secret ULTRA intelligence. JICPOA came to rely heavily on the Army's distribution system through its Estimates Section, which included fifteen Army personnel. The Estimates Section worked closely with the Army's Signal Intelligence Service (SIS) and utilized its ULTRA distribution system because it was secure and effective.[170] SIS attached a well-trained intelligence officer to major commands that needed access to ULTRA intelligence. That officer and that officer alone was responsible for collecting, receiving, analyzing, and disseminating ULTRA to the particular command he served. He was also responsible for keeping his lines of communication secure and reported any violations of procedure to the War Department.[171]

JICPOA disbanded at the war's end because the fleet ceased offensive operations and no longer needed strategic, operational, or tactical intelligence to support planners or the warfighter. It closed down quickly, burned most of its printed intelligence at Honolulu's thermal power generator,[172] and cut 80 percent of its personnel within thirty days after the Japanese surrendered.[173] CINCPAC sent many of JICPOA's best analysts to comparable units such as the U.S. Strategic Bombing Survey and the Naval Technical Mission to Japan.[174] The Strategic Bombing Survey assessed the effects of bombing campaigns on Japanese war-making industries and high-value targets. Established on 14 August 1945, the Naval Technical Mission to Japan collected, examined, and analyzed Japanese war technologies and equipment of importance to the U.S. Navy and Marine Corps. It operated in Japan, China, South Korea and other areas where the Japanese operated. The mission sent teams of engineers, scientists, and linguists into military compounds to conduct their work. For example, Team 29, consisting mostly of former JICPOA personnel, entered Sasebo Harbor on 23 September 1945 and set about analyzing the entire facility, from its wharves and armories to its mess halls.[175] Other JICPOA personnel were sent home after the war. More importantly, some JICPOA personnel stayed in government service and helped the United States create a professional intelligence community.

After World War II, U.S. national security policymakers did not want to get caught in another conflict without having a standing intelligence service. Furthermore, World War II had demonstrated that effective intelligence could help prevent war or detect one in time to prepare for it. JICPOA demonstrated that intelligence was vital to win a war. Accordingly, the U.S. Government began building professional intelligence services in 1947. Ultimately, these efforts produced the Central Intelligence Agency, the National Security Agency, and the Defense Intelligence Agency—the backbone of the U.S. intelligence community in 2002. Consequently, JICPOA had a tremendous impact on the U.S. national security infrastructure far beyond the bloody Pacific War.

2

THE MARSHALLS

Flintlock and Catchpole

Strategic Background

By the fall of 1943, Nimitz was ready to put his Central Pacific drive into gear. MacArthur had already begun his drive into enemy territory on an axis of advance that contained large and bountiful landmasses that afforded him considerable attack options. He often landed in lightly contested areas where he could apply his genius for maneuver warfare and outflank or isolate areas of heavy enemy concentration. The land on Nimitz's axis of advance, on the other hand, had no opportunistic terrain, and the Marine and Army troops who fought there had little room for creative maneuvering. Their attacks would often entail head-on, bloody assaults, but such attacks were imperative. The tempo of the Allied advance had to be increased to keep the Japanese off balance and to prevent them from consolidating strong defensive positions.

Strategically, Australian campaigns in New Guinea had stopped Japanese expansion in the Southwestern Pacific, while U.S. campaigns in the Solomons and Gilberts had reversed Japanese advances in the Southern and lower part of the Central Pacific. Therefore, Japanese territory in mid-1943 included Manchuria, most of Southeast Asia, roughly half of China, and numerous island groups throughout the Pacific, including the Marshalls, Carolines, Marianas, Bonins, and the Palaus.[1]

But Japanese could expand no farther. Unknown to the Allies, the Japanese had used up most of their offensive resources in their attempt to seize the Pacific, including the blow to Pearl Harbor that was supposed to eliminate the bulk of U.S. Pacific naval forces, especially aircraft carriers. When Yamamoto designed the Pearl Harbor attack plan, he sought to inflict enough damage on the U.S. Navy to buy time to build up indomitable defenses in the Pacific. By the time the United States had rebuilt its fleet, Yamamoto believed, Japanese defenses would be too strong, and then Washington would have to accept the situation. However, as the battle of Midway demonstrated, the raid on Pearl Harbor failed to accomplish its true Mahanian goal of complete destruction of the enemy's fleet.[2] Furthermore, the Japanese did not have the ability to attack U.S. war industrial centers scattered throughout the forty-eight states, where production ran unhindered. The Japanese strategy of severely injuring and disarming their opponent, which were limited warfare goals, did not take into account a total warfare reaction on behalf of the United States. They had gambled and lost.

Now, U.S. forces were preparing to attack Japan from two directions in the Pacific: the south and the east. With the sudden realization that their war had taken a defensive turn, the Imperial General Headquarters held an emergency meeting on 15 September 1943 to discuss their alternatives, which were few. Negotiation and cease-fire were out of the question and dishonorable to even entertain. On the other hand, Japan could not take the offensive because the enemy had put them on the defensive.

Thereafter, the Japanese drafted a plan called the "New General Outline of the Future War-Direction Policy." It established a wide defensive perimeter around Asia that enclosed most of their seized territory.[3] Within that wide sphere sat a tighter defensive zone that arced through the Marianas down through the Palaus. Within that sphere sat yet another that ran through the Bonins and Ryukus. Beyond that sat Japan itself. The Japanese planned to defend these zones with rigor, and they did not believe that U.S. forces could penetrate deep into their territory.

By implementing this plan, the Japanese tightened their defensive zones and shortened their interior lines of communication. In doing so, they also deserted three hundred thousand troops in the contested part of the South Pacific with the stroke of a pen.[4] Although this demonstrated considerable shortsightedness on the part of the Japanese—they would desperately need the men in the coming months[5]—it also demonstrated the degree to which they were willing to fight and sacrifice life. In theory, the new defensive zones made it easier to transport infantry, defense construction materials, and heavy weaponry to bases that needed defending. Similarly, the Imperial Japanese Navy could more quickly aid besieged island garrisons or attack U.S. forces that attempted ship-to-shore operations. In fact, Japan's Pacific defense plan depended on an agile navy for shipping and defense. It organized 360 ships and two thousand aircraft to execute this new plan, but three problems hindered its successful implementation.[6]

First, although having the benefit of interior lines of communication, the Japanese were still overextended throughout Asia, and their resources were spread thin. This resulted in the inability of the Japanese to concentrate significant mass to defend their island holdings. Second, the IJA and the IJN had begun to fight over precious and dwindling oil supplies. Both services suffered from an intense historical rivalry, and each struggled to outdo the other, often at the expense of the empire's war goals. Oil, in part, dictated how far a military offensive could go and how much power the offensive could amass. The IJA had more influence over military affairs and ended up controlling most of Japan's oil, leaving the IJN to languish, unable to operate at maximum range and full capacity. Third, the United States had struck back more suddenly and more forcefully than the Japanese had anticipated. It also had thrown itself into war industry production, building numerous new battleships, cruisers, destroyers, submarines, several different types of aircraft carriers, and thousands of warplanes.[7] The draft and volunteers had increased the ranks of the U.S. Marine Corps, the U.S. Navy, and the U.S. Army by the tens of thousands. The Japanese needed time to build up their defensive zones, but because of Pearl Harbor, the United States had the will, and because of their industrial strength, the material, to deny time to the Japanese.

Did all of this mean that the Japanese had lost the war already? Certainly not. There was no guarantee that the United States had the will and the means to push their war machine all the way to Tokyo. Moreover, the Japanese still possessed considerable war material in the Pacific area of operations, including more than one million active-duty ground combatants, at least twelve aircraft carriers, and hundreds of surface ships and submarines. Two of its battleships, the *Musashi* and the *Yamato,* were the largest ever to put to sea.[8] The fight for the Pacific would be difficult indeed, and Admiral Nimitz had no illusions about an easy fight for the Marshalls, the second objective of the Central Pacific drive and the outer arc of the Japanese defensive zone.

Operation Flintlock: Kwajalein Atoll
Campaign Background

On 1 February 1944, the U.S. Marine Corps' Fourth Division and the Army's Seventh Infantry Division stormed Kwajalein Atoll in a well-orchestrated amphibious assault.[9] It was the key element in Operation Flintlock, the U.S. thrust into the Japanese-held Marshall Islands. The fall of Kwajalein provided U.S. forces with a foothold from which to conquer the rest of the Marshalls. Control of the island group accomplished three vital objectives. First, it heightened the security of Allied lines of communication in the Pacific. Second, it upset Tokyo's strategic plans by breaking through its outer defensive ring. Third, it provided Admiral Nimitz with valuable anchorages and airstrips to mount offensive operations against other Japanese bases in the Pacific along the road to Tokyo.[10]

The U.S. Marine Corps and Army troops who carried out the campaign neutralized enemy resistance on Kwajalein with skill and speed, effectively securing the main objectives in the atoll, Roi-Namur and Kwajalein Islands, in a mere four days.[11] In addition, the assault forces sustained low casualties: 1,295 WIA and 486 KIA.[12] This was in part due to excellent intelligence. Accurate intelligence on enemy strength in the Marshalls, the military importance of Kwajalein Atoll, Japanese order of battle, and the location of weapons positions on the principal island objectives enabled Nimitz to strike at the heart of the Marshalls with maximum effectiveness and economy of force,[13] all in a minimum amount of time. Good intelligence also allowed Spruance to formulate a devastatingly accurate preliminary naval bombardment that ensured minimal ground combat.

Except for the preliminary bombardment, this good intelligence mattered less in the tactical sense. In fact, detailed intelligence on Japanese weapons positions only reached assault teams the day before D-Day. Fortunately, the lack of advanced tactical intelligence did not have a negative impact on the overall attack. The targeted islands were small, and the USMC and U.S. Army planners who knew the basic layout of each objective finalized their schemes of maneuver at the last minute with little difficulty.

Target Location

Kwajalein Atoll holds the largest lagoon in the world and is part of the vast Marshall Island group. It is approximately 2,500 miles west-southwest of Pearl Harbor, Hawaii,[14] and 540 miles northwest of Tarawa Atoll.[15] The Marshalls consist of thirty-two atolls[16] that span nearly four hundred nautical miles northwest to southeast.[17] Kwajalein contains 655 square miles of water and ninety-three islands.[18]

Why Kwajalein?

Nimitz targeted Kwajalein because he needed to control the Marshalls. Under the JCS's original Pacific war plan, the Marshalls would provide Nimitz a primary staging area for his axis of advance on the Philippines. MacArthur would advance on the left, parallel and south of Nimitz.[19] Ultimately, however, Nimitz would divert his axis of advance north toward Okinawa. Regardless, the Marshalls were full of atolls that the Japanese had used for attacking the southern and eastern Pacific. Specifically, they contained valuable airstrips, air service facilities, lagoon anchorages, and logistical storage warehouses. Therefore, Nimitz knew that the Marshalls

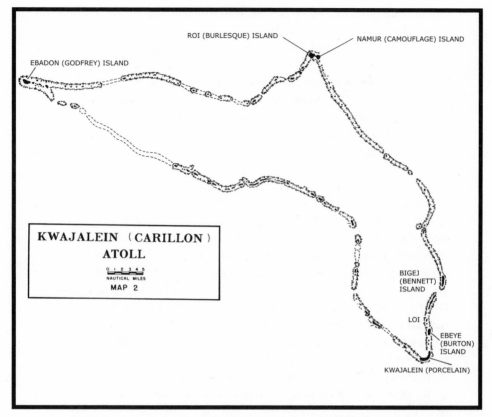

KWAJALEIN (CARILLON) ATOLL

MAP 2

Kwajalein Atoll. Roi-Namur is the farthest north, Kwajalein Island the farthest south.
Heinel and Crown, *The Marshalls: Increasing the Tempo*

could provide the same assets to him, only in the opposite direction—toward Tokyo. So in the early scheme of the war, the Marshalls held tremendous strategic importance. However, Nimitz did not know that he would be seizing Kwajalein in the beginning; he only knew that he had to seize several atolls within the Marshall group.

The Marshalls Intelligence Operation

The JCS issued Nimitz a formal order to seize the Marshalls in September 1943.[20] Additionally, they solicited his strategic thinking on which atolls to attack, how much force to apply to achieve victory, and when to execute the attack. While Nimitz and his staff had formulated several options for the Marshalls campaign, they could not plan definite assaults on specific atolls because they knew little about Japanese forces in the area. CINCPAC therefore directed JICPOA to provide him with intelligence on Japanese activities throughout the island group.

Originally, Nimitz and his staff drew hypothetical attack plans for five atolls—Maloelap, Wotje, Kwajalein, Jaluit, and Mille. While ground troops would attack the first three, U.S. aircraft would neutralize enemy air power on the last two.[21] The operation required complicated planning, synchronized attacks, and a significant amount of time. For that reason, Nimitz expressed discontent with the Marshalls plan. He preferred to remain flexible to alternate attack schemes in case the strategic picture of the Marshalls changed. Eventually, it did, but it took an extensive intelligence operation on behalf of JICPOA to alert him of that change.

Aerial photographic reconnaissance over the target area began more than a year before Flintlock took place under cover of a January 1942 surface and air raid on the Marshalls.[22] Unfortunately, this information provided only general background data on Japanese activities in the Marshalls. Land-based reconnaissance aircraft began reconnoitering the Marshalls after construction engineers had repaired Tarawa's main airstrip on Betio. What's more, the capture of Tarawa allowed Adm. Charles Pownall, commander of carrier Task Force 50, to approach the Marshalls and launch his aircraft for quick strikes and photo reconnaissance missions. The Japanese retaliated from time to time but lost twenty-nine fighters during attacks on U.S. ships.[23] Enemy attempts to push the U.S. Navy away from the Marshalls failed, and photographic data on their island bases poured into JICPOA.

As usual in the Pacific War, air strikes and photo reconnaissance missions coincided with one another. Some intelligence experts and operations planners at Pearl Harbor believed that if reconnaissance aircraft photographed enemy bases without a "cover," then the Japanese would know that they were being photographed. Their reasoning was that only two types of aircraft flew over enemy bases: the destructive type and the reconnaissance type. If the Japanese recognized that intelligence aircraft were photographing them, they would probably have taken steps to change their defensive posture. This might have included increasing camouflage discipline, hardening fortifications, calling for reinforcements, or even destroying their airfields and anchorages and then abandoning the island. Furthermore, obvious photographic missions might have given away the element of surprise—a major benefit in amphibious assaults—so reconnaissance aircraft followed the bombers. Dual-purpose missions flew over the Marshalls through March[24] and December 1943,[25] and into January 1944. Such missions against Kwajalein Atoll actually continued up to two days before D-Day.[26] Photographs from 4 December contributed to the main Kwajalein Atoll information bulletin.

Submarines on photo reconnaissance missions infiltrated the Marshalls as well. The submarine USS *Seal* reconnoitered the area in December 1943, and the USS *Tarpon* reconnoitered it a month later in January 1944. Both took periscope photographs of Japanese bases in the Marshalls and collected data on the hydrographic conditions surrounding each atoll.[27] However, the final hydrographic survey of the invasion beaches on Roi-Namur and Kwajalein took place the night before D-Day in a daring probe by UDTs and Marine Reconnaissance personnel.[28] But because of the late timing of such risky operations, their information did not see publication in JICPOA information bulletins. Instead, tactical beach reconnaissance intelligence went directly to amphibious assault planners.

Nevertheless, photographs of the Marshall Islands disclosed an enormous amount of information on geography, hydrography, and order of battle. Granted, as already noted, photographic intelligence did not always perform to its end users' complete satisfaction, but its benefits proved extremely useful in cases such as Operation Flintlock. For example, pictures of Roi-Namur Island distinctly showed nearly all of the enemy's weapons positions, buildings, and defensive networks. Pictures of Kwajalein Island showed about half of the defenses and structures on that island, because the reconnaissance planes captured only half of Kwajalein Island in vertical photographs, the most revealing type. Oblique photographs, which only partially revealed gun positions, made up the rest.[29] Despite such minor setbacks, JICPOA's analysts were able to use the photographs to effectively gauge enemy strength for the various targeted islands in the Marshalls attack plan.

Furthermore, the Marshalls intelligence operation benefited from defense documents and surveys of Japanese fortifications captured on Betio Island by field intelligence personnel.[30] Like most militaries, the Japanese had standardized their defensive doctrine, and JICPOA's analysts expected that many of the same type of gun emplacements, defensive structures, and tactics from Betio probably could be expected in the Marshalls. They were right.

JICPOA and FRUPAC supported the Marshalls intelligence operation by intercepting and analyzing Japanese radio transmissions.[31] They listened to combat units communicating with each other in the target area, with command and control centers, and with supply echelons. From this, radio intelligence analysts were able to locate most of the Japanese units that occupied the Marshalls. Once they discovered the specific units, they were able to estimate what kind of opposition U.S. forces were facing. If they did not know a specific unit, they would compare it to a similar unit—information perhaps contained in the Reference Section—and estimate its force structure and capabilities.[32] Radio intelligence analysts reaped other pertinent data by pinpointing sources of radio transmissions in the Marshalls whether they originated from ships, aircraft, or command posts.

As the intelligence deadline approached, JICPOA analyzed and combined all of the important bits and pieces of the Marshall Islands intelligence and produced useful information bulletins on the various targeted atolls. The resulting intelligence gave Nimitz an excellent picture of the strategic situation in the Marshalls. Armed with a breadth of intelligence, he and his staff began weighing their options.

How Intelligence Influenced Nimitz's Strategic Decision Making

Of the several information bulletins JICPOA produced on the Marshalls, the Kwajalein information bulletin, number 53-43, caught Admiral Nimitz's attention. Dated 1 December 1943,[33] it provided detailed intelligence on the location of Kwajalein Atoll, its size, its military infrastructure, and the number and type of troops based there.

The report's summary stated that the Japanese had established two important bases in the atoll: Roi-Namur in the extreme north, and Kwajalein in the extreme south. Roi-Namur encompassed two islands joined by a 430-yard-long causeway and a 160-yard-wide, triangular piece of beach partially covered with vegetation.[34] Several small islets closely surrounded both islands. Roi, the westernmost of the two islands, contained an area of land 1,250 yards long, north to south, and 1,170 yards long, east to west. An airfield and its service buildings covered most of the island.[35] Namur embodied an area of land 890 yards long, north to south, and 800 yards wide, east to west.[36] Brush and trees covered its eastern and northern quadrants. Buildings covered the rest of the island, including seven hardened structures toward the east beach, presumably used for ammunition storage. A command and control center occupied Namur's southwestern corner.[37] Turbulent surf conditions racked the seaward shore of both islands, but the lagoon was calm.[38]

Kwajalein consisted of a crescent-shaped landmass 2.5 nautical miles long and 2,500 feet wide at its greatest width. Thick jungle covered the south side of the island.[39] While photographs had revealed only part of the island,[40] they clearly demonstrated the calm nature of Kwajalein's lagoonside beach, thirty to fifty feet wide, compared to its rough seaside beach.[41]

A partially completed airfield was located in a clearing in the middle of Kwajalein accompanied by 120 buildings scattered throughout the island's interior.[42]

This information indicated to Admiral Nimitz that, geographically, the islands contained few physical obstacles that the Japanese might use to impede an assault. Regarding hydrography, the calm nature of the lagoon shores on both prospective targets presented viable landing beaches. But Nimitz needed more than just hospitable terrain and decent landing beaches to convince him to alter his five-atoll attack plan. The admiral needed to know, for example, how much importance the Japanese placed on Kwajalein Atoll.

Early intelligence reports from ICPOA corroborated JICPOA's intelligence and maintained that the Japanese used Kwajalein as a naval and air base and possibly as a submarine base.[43] While the island had no port facilities to speak of, the Japanese navy used the island's lagoon as an anchorage. Surveillance aircraft revealed that the atoll could accommodate at least thirty ships of various types, including submarines, gunboats, patrol boats, subchasers, tankers, supply ships, repair ships, and flagships.[44] One of the most active air bases in the area, Kwajalein Atoll accommodated both fighters and bombers. Roi-Namur boasted an airstrip that consisted of three runways and four turning circles that allowed aircraft to launch in almost any direction. In addition, the base contained a wide array of aircraft service facilities, including a large number of aviation fuel storage tanks.[45] Likewise, an unfinished airstrip, located in the lower half of Kwajalein, threatened to complement that island's impressive high-capacity military storage facilities.[46] JICPOA also confirmed an issue of major importance about Kwajalein Atoll—it served as Japan's command and control center for the entire Marshall and Gilbert Island area.[47] Obviously, the Japanese placed a great deal of importance in Kwajalein Atoll and its military infrastructure, and this had a major impact on Nimitz's strategic thinking for the Marshalls campaign. The chance to knock out the Japanese "brain center" for the whole region undoubtedly appealed to Nimitz. But he also needed to know if the Japanese had heavily fortified the atoll.

Surprisingly, for all of Kwajalein's worth, the Japanese had not heavily fortified it. JICPOA produced excellent intelligence on how many and what kind of heavy weapons the Japanese possessed throughout the atoll. It also pinpointed the location of most of these weapons. Additionally, radio intelligence had indicated how many Japanese soldiers were in the Marshalls, atoll by atoll. Because of this, Admiral Nimitz knew approximately how strong the garrisons were. JICPOA estimated that approximately seven thousand soldiers occupied Kwajalein Atoll: about three thousand on Roi-Namur and four thousand on Kwajalein.[48] When the battle ended, the number of Japanese KIA validated these estimates: 3,563 on Roi-Namur and 4,823 on Kwajalein Island.[49] Information Bulletin 53-43 also predicted with a relative degree of accuracy the numbers, and in some cases the types, of weapons found on the islands as indicated by the following table.

Estimated vs. Actual Number of Japanese Weapons on Kwajalein

Type	Estimated Number of Weapons[i]	Actual Number of Weapons[ii]
Roi-Namur Island		
Coastal Defense Gun	1	0
Twin Mount Dual Purpose Guns	4	4
Machine Guns and Medium AA	24–36	28
Mobile Artillery Positions	6	0
Blockhouses	7	3
Pillboxes	31	17
(Not estimated) covered artillery positions	—	2
Kwajalein Island		
Dual Purpose Guns	6–7	6
Twin Mount Dual-Purpose Guns	2	4
Heavy AA	12–17	0
Machine Guns and Medium AA	30–48	29
(Not estimated) artillery guns of varying size	—	12
Total Number of Guns:	124–59	105

[i] Source: JICPOA Information Bulletin 53-43, "Roi and Namur Islands" map and the "Kwajalein Islands" map.
[ii] Source: JICPOA Information Bulletin 48-44, *Japanese Defenses: Kwajalein Atoll* (Pearl Harbor, Hawaii, 10 April 1944), maps 1 and 4.

In the table, blockhouses and pillboxes represent variable amounts of weaponry. The former were large concrete and steel buildings, usually one story high with walls up to several feet thick and a small observation tower on top. These structures typically contained a large gun—75-mm for example—with smaller portholes for support weaponry such as machine guns and machine cannon. Pillboxes were smaller, low-silhouette steel and concrete or coconut log fortifications that usually housed a machine gun or two.

Although the figures do not represent a perfect estimation, they do represent accuracy within the realm of military intelligence and operations planning. At the time, Nimitz believed that this intelligence was correct, and he was right: JICPOA's intelligence indicated with accuracy the Japanese capability to defend Roi-Namur and Kwajalein Islands.

More important, JICPOA's intelligence demonstrated to Nimitz the vulnerability of Kwajalein compared to that of the other two prospective targets marked for amphibious invasion, Maloelap and Wotje. The Japanese garrisons on Maloelap and Wotje possessed heavier weapons, entrenched in more hardened and sophisticated defensive positions, than did the Japanese on Kwajalein.[50] They were more heavily defended because the Japanese Naval General Staff thought that U.S. forces would attack these atolls first. They were closer to Pearl Harbor and had more airstrips than did Kwajalein.

Because of the intelligence JICPOA had presented, Nimitz made a command decision regarding Operation Flintlock. On 14 December 1943, he ordered his staff to draw attack plans for Kwajalein Atoll and several other lesser-defended islets nearby.[51] Nimitz surely saw that Kwajalein presented an ideal target—a weak center of gravity with a good military infrastructure—so he dropped Maloelap and Wotje from his scheme. A few of his cohorts, especially amphibious task force commander Rear Adm. Richmond K. Turner, disagreed and aggressively insisted that they attack Maloelap and Wotje because those islands possessed larger airfields. But Nimitz believed in his intelligence and had confidence in his strategy, so after repeated attempts by Turner to adhere to the original plan, Nimitz suggested that the admiral could resign if he continued with his line of argument. Realizing his predicament, Turner ceased and accepted his superior's line of reasoning.[52]

Chain of Command

Having formulated a plan, CINCPAC appointed a chain of command for the task force and designated troops for the assault.[53] Nimitz assigned Vice Admiral Spruance to command the operation. Admiral Turner retained command of the Joint Expeditionary Force and the Southern Attack Force—respectively the amphibious transport group and the naval bombardment group for Kwajalein Island. Rear Adm. Richard Conolly served as the Northern Attack Force commander of the Roi-Namur preliminary naval bombardment. Marine Maj. Gen. Holland M. Smith, V Amphibious Corps commander, would control the ground troops, which were the Fourth Marine Division, the U.S. Army's Seventh Infantry Division, and the 106th Infantry.[54]

Plan of Attack

The attack plan for Kwajalein Atoll consisted of three phases. The first involved a three-day naval preliminary bombardment of Roi-Namur and Kwajalein Islands in order to soften the Japanese up for the amphibious invasion.[55] The second phase required the storming of the smaller islets surrounding both objectives for use by artillery units that would assemble firebases and support the attack. The third phase, scheduled to begin on 1 February 1945, consisted of an amphibious attack against the objectives themselves. Two regimental combat teams of the Fourth Marine Division would land on Roi-Namur, and two from the Army's Seventh Infantry Division would attack Kwajalein Island. In conjunction with Flintlock, Nimitz made plans to seize Majuro, an island three hundred miles southeast of Kwajalein, to use as a temporary forward fleet command.[56]

The overall plan proved highly successful. A 297-ship flotilla, naval aviators from twelve carriers, and 350 land-based aircraft attacked the Marshalls at various intervals for seven weeks before the landings took place. Nimitz had the objective localized just two days before D-Day with the destruction of 150 Japanese aircraft scattered throughout the island group.[57] Japanese forces based in Rabaul and Truk could not respond to the Marshalls with air or naval surface power in light of continuous localization raids. In other words, they had their hands full defending themselves and could spare nothing for the Marshalls.

How Intelligence Influenced the Campaign

Good intelligence influenced all phases of the Flintlock campaign and most heavily influenced phase one. JICPOA had pinpointed with a high degree of accuracy most Japanese defenses on Roi-Namur and most of those on Kwajalein. This is evident by comparing JICPOA's pre-action and after-action intelligence maps concerning Japanese defensive positions.[58] On both islands, JICPOA's maps demonstrated that, for the most part, the Japanese had enacted a so-called crust defense. A crust defense consisted of strongpoints connected by infantry positions that ringed the perimeter of an island, usually close to the shoreline. The goal of the crust defense was to defeat the enemy at the water's edge. Strongpoint defenses typically incorporated large, concrete-encased weapons supported by heavy machine guns and infantry positions. The infantry positions that connected strong-points consisted of trenches, foxholes, spider holes, and small bunkers such as pillboxes. Although the crust defense was not as deep as a tradi-tional layered defense, it did compose a mutually supportive defense.

Vice Admiral Spruance used this intelligence to plan the naval and islet-based preliminary bombardment.[59] Since he knew where most of the en-emy fortifications were, he knew where to bombard with maximum effec-tiveness. In past campaigns such as the one at Tarawa, naval gunners simply blanketed an area with shells through a technique not unlike car-pet-bombing. The inadequacy of this procedure, along with using the wrong type of ordnance, resulted in the destruction of few fortifications on Tarawa.[60] At Kwajalein Atoll, naval gunners picked their targets ahead of time and used appropriate ordnance—armor-piercing for concrete de-fenses and high-explosive for softer targets.[61]

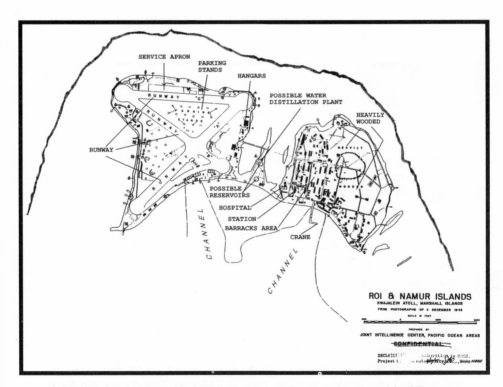

JICPOA Prebattle Map of Roi-Namur. Crust defense positions and buildings are shown on each island. The Marines landed on the lagoon side of both islands and swept north. JICPOA Information Bulletin 53-44

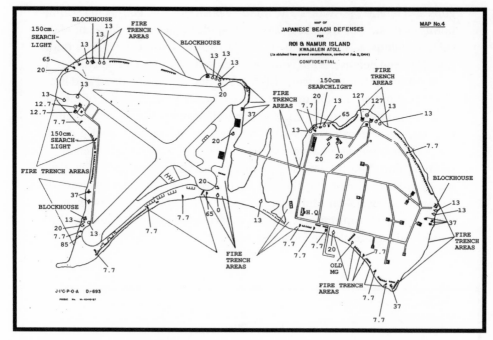

JICPOA Postbattle Map of Roi-Namur. This map confirms the accuracy of prebattle intelligence. JICPOA Information Bulletin 48-44

Spruance's bombardment planning staff was also able to estimate the location of defenses not shown on the Kwajalein Island map. JICPOA's analysts and most Central Pacific operations planners had by that point in the war recognized the Japanese crust defense. It was easy to spot, and they had seen it before in the Gilberts. Furthermore, they recognized it on numerous islands in the Marshalls. Therefore, all JICPOA's analysts had to do was pinpoint several defensive positions on an island to demonstrate the Japanese defensive scheme for the rest of the island. One pinpointed strongpoint on a given stretch of beach, for example, indicated the location of probable adjoining defensive positions. Based on this information, naval gunners bombarded areas where enemy gun positions probably existed, and they frequently were correct. Such was the case with the islands of Roi-Namur and, especially, Kwajalein.

At Roi-Namur,[62] the preliminary bombardment destroyed all of the most menacing Japanese gun emplacements, blockhouses,[63] and the majority of the smaller defensive positions. The surviving Japanese were forced to fight from the ruins of their once fortified island.[64] At one point during the as-

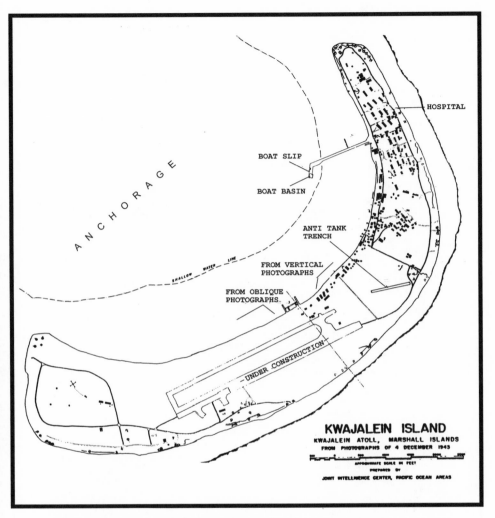

KWAJALEIN ISLAND
KWAJALEIN ATOLL, MARSHALL ISLANDS
FROM PHOTOGRAPHS OF 4 DECEMBER 1943

APPROXIMATE SCALE IN FEET
PREPARED BY
JOINT INTELLIGENCE CENTER, PACIFIC OCEAN AREAS

HOSPITAL

BOAT SLIP

BOAT BASIN

ANTI TANK TRENCH

FROM VERTICAL PHOTOGRAPHS

FROM OBLIQUE PHOTOGRAPHS

UNDER CONSTRUCTION

ANCHORAGE

SHALLOW WATER LINE

JICPOA Prebattle Map of Kwajalein Island Showing Crust Defense Positions. Photo reconnaissance did not locate defenses on the west lagoon side and some beach areas in the south, but not to the detriment of the assault. Army troops landed on west beach and advanced east and then north. JICPOA Information Bulletin 53-43

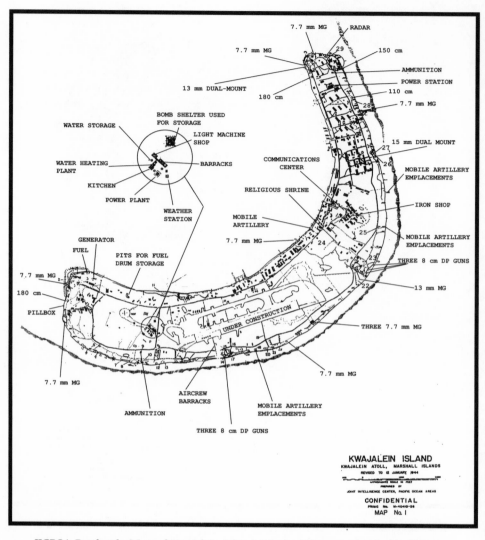

JICPOA Postbattle Map of Kwajalein Island. Map confirms prebattle intelligence.
JICPOA Information Bulletin 48-44

sault on Roi, marines, elated at the meager resistance they encountered, went berserk and ran clear across the island on a mad shooting spree.[65]

It is estimated that perhaps only three hundred Japanese survived the shelling of Roi.[66] On Namur, according to the official Marine Corps record of the operation, the preliminary bombardment disorganized the Japanese to such an extent that they "were no longer capable of launching a coordinated counterattack against the rapidly expanding beachhead."[67] The same source states that much the same occurred on Kwajalein Island. Although many fortifications there escaped destruction as a result of the incomplete photographic coverage, elements of the Seventh Infantry Division landed on Kwajalein with "comparative ease."[68] The official record went on to say that the U.S. Army troops encountered an enemy who fought mainly "from ruined buildings, shattered pillboxes, and piles of debris"[69] instead of intact concrete defensive positions.

JICPOA's linguist teams provided valuable intelligence to Marine artillery units through POW interrogations and by translating captured documents. In one such case, JICPOA interrogators interviewed a Japanese soldier for information about remaining units on Roi-Namur. He told his captors about a command post nearby, and within ten minutes the linguists had forwarded the intelligence to Marine artillery units that promptly shelled the site and therefore helped destroy Japanese command and control capabilities for that sector. In a similar case, a JICPOA team translated captured documents that disclosed the location of Japanese troops and numerous supporting strongpoints on Kwajalein Island. The information was valuable to infantry and artillery units and helped isolate and destroy pockets of enemy resistance at a low cost of life to Army units.[70]

While JICPOA forwarded the spontaneous field intelligence to its customers with speed, it remains unclear why JICPOA's excellent prebattle intelligence did not reach the ground element in a timelier manner. The V Amphibious Corps intelligence officer held the responsibility of disseminating intelligence to the assault force. According to Isely and Crowl's *The U.S. Marines and Amphibious War,* that officer did not receive reconnaissance photographs that pinpointed Japanese defensive positions until 29 January, the day before the assault.[71] Such a lapse is hard to explain, given that JICPOA obviously had this information as early as 4 December.

There are several possible reasons for the delay. First, JICPOA's dissemination channels might not have been completely set up at that point. Even though JICPOA had taken over ICPOA's dissemination channels, the new management might have ordered an overhaul of the existing flow of information. Second, Nimitz might have decided that JICPOA's secret intelligence should remain at the higher echelons for security reasons and that fleet units should bear the responsibility of providing the combat echelons with tactical intelligence. These two reasons are supported by the fact that the Kwajalein information bulletin was classified "secret," a designation that did not allow wide distribution. (Later in the war, secret intelligence did in fact reach battalion- and company-level infantry units.) Nevertheless, the Kwajalein bulletin eventually did see a reduction in classification to "confidential," but that occurred on D-Day.[72]

In any event, the intelligence could have saved lives if assault troops had received it in time for close study. An unforeseen tragedy during the first day's fighting on Namur exemplifies this point. JICPOA's analysts located seven buildings on Namur designated as ammunition storehouses.[73] The marines were probably not aware of this because, during an attack on a unit of Japanese hiding in one of the buildings, they tossed a high-explosive satchel charge into the structure to clear it. Upon detonation, the charge set off a number of torpedo warheads stored inside, and the ensuing explosion killed twenty U.S. servicemen and wounded a hundred.[74]

Conclusion

Such mishaps notwithstanding, in the greater scheme of the operation, JICPOA's intelligence had a positive impact on the campaign and helped keep casualties to a minimum. But intelligence is a tricky business, and the Kwajalein model was not always the norm in the Pacific. Why, then, was JICPOA able to produce accurate intelligence for this particular operation? There are three reasons. First, aerial reconnaissance efficiently covered the islands, especially Roi-Namur. The numerous and clear photographs taken by reconnaissance pilots provided intelligence analysts with media that they could well utilize. Second, geography played against Japanese counterintelligence efforts. The flat nature of these small atolls made it difficult for the Japanese to hide themselves and their equipment. Japanese utilization of camouflage netting and natural foliage proved inefficient. Moreover, an atoll's proximity to sea level negated deep burrowing, a common and effective Japanese defensive tactic used later in the war. As a result, exposure plagued defenses on most Japanese-held atolls. (There were exceptions, however. See the next section, on Eniwetok.) Third, photo analysts understood and recognized Japanese defensive doctrine at that period during the war: the crust defense. Certain weapons, strongpoints, and infantry defenses predictably fell into place and revealed the defensive plan for the atoll.

However, JICPOA's analysts did make a few numerical mistakes regarding weaponry on the objectives. Those stemmed from miscalculations in photo analyses. More than likely, the photo analysts mistook the twelve artillery guns of varying size on Kwajalein for twelve heavy AA guns—not a terrible oversight because the Japanese used these weapons against both aircraft and enemy infantry. Pillboxes on Roi-Namur might have resembled blockhouses, and buildings close to the beaches undoubtedly looked like pillboxes. In the end, however, these miscalculations did not matter. Analysts located most of the structures on each of the islands, and the naval bombardment destroyed them.

Of course, the Kwajalein campaign demonstrates that good intelligence can have a positive impact on a battle by increasing the effectiveness of lethal force application and by keeping casualties to a minimum. But it also demonstrates that an adept commander can make multiple uses of intelligence that might seem to fit only a strategic, operational, or tactical format. For instance, in the case of Kwajalein, Nimitz compiled tactical order-of-battle and airfield intelligence on five individual atolls and used it as operational intelligence to shape the Marshalls campaign. His cohorts used the same intelligence in a tactical sense to conduct amphibious assaults or air strikes on bypassed islands.

Unfortunately for JICPOA, the Marshalls campaign represented the last that involved atoll warfare. In the future, combat took place on larger islands—Peleliu and Okinawa, for example. In contrast to atolls, these islands contained difficult terrain and increasing numbers of Japanese, who gradually upgraded their defensive tactics. Consequently, photo reconnaissance personnel had to work twice as hard to analyze terrain and pinpoint enemy defenses. Similarly, in future campaigns, it would become increasingly difficult to understand the changing Japanese defensive doctrine.

But these events should not detract from the tremendous intelligence success in Operation Flintlock. Accurate intelligence on the Marshalls provided operations planners with the following information: where to strike the enemy to achieve maximum effectiveness, where to avoid the enemy where well defended, and how much force to apply to win. Essentially, intelligence provided Admiral Nimitz with a strategic force multiplier that helped achieve victory.

Operation Catchpole: Eniwetok Atoll
Campaign Background

Operation Catchpole was the last major amphibious campaign in the Marshalls. By its conclusion, the United States controlled the entire island group.[75] The objective of Catchpole was to seize Eniwetok Atoll. A hastily planned but efficient operation, it began on 17 February 1944 and ended a mere five days later. The Twenty-second Marines and the 106th Infantry of the U.S. Army's Twenty-seventh Infantry Division constituted the main assault force.[76] They achieved their objectives expeditiously, the one exception being several units of the 106th, whose soldiers had not been thoroughly trained in amphibious assault tactics.[77]

Nevertheless, Catchpole was a major success. Admirals Nimitz and Spruance and their planning staffs drew up an outstanding blueprint for the seizure of Eniwetok. JICPOA's intelligence helped them in three areas. First, it helped them strike the atoll while it was weak and void of stout enemy defenses. Second, it contributed to a proficient preliminary bombardment. Third, it aided effective ship-to-shore landings on three island objectives. Good intelligence also positively influenced the campaign while in progress by furnishing commanders with secret Japanese defensive plans that sped the operation along and probably saved the lives of several hundred U.S. servicemen.

Target Location

Eniwetok Atoll is located 1,200 nautical miles west-southwest of Pearl Harbor and seven hundred nautical miles north of Guadalcanal.[78] The atoll, consisting of thirty tiny islands, forms a rough circle that encloses a lagoon with an area of seventeen by twenty-one miles.[79] The Japanese occupied the three largest islands in the atoll—Engebi to the north, Eniwetok to the south, and Parry to the southeast.

Why Eniwetok?

Operations planners targeted Eniwetok Atoll for one major reason: to complete the conquest of the Marshalls. Nimitz knew that he did not have to invade each atoll to control the entire island group. Seizure of a few key atolls would suffice to simultaneously provide bases from which to neutralize the remaining atolls and to launch further advances into the Japanese-held Pacific. Since the Japanese had most heavily fortified the eastern portion of the Marshalls, CINCPAC attacked the western portion. The first thrust into the western portion of the Marshalls was Operation Flintlock, executed earlier in February.

Eniwetok, strategically located in the most northwestern corner of the Marshalls,[80] had been discussed as a possible target since May 1943 by the CCS, but only in passing. In September 1943, when the JCS told Nimitz to seize the Marshalls, his staff began planning for a possible assault against the isolated atoll. However, CINCPAC scheduled the assault for May, well

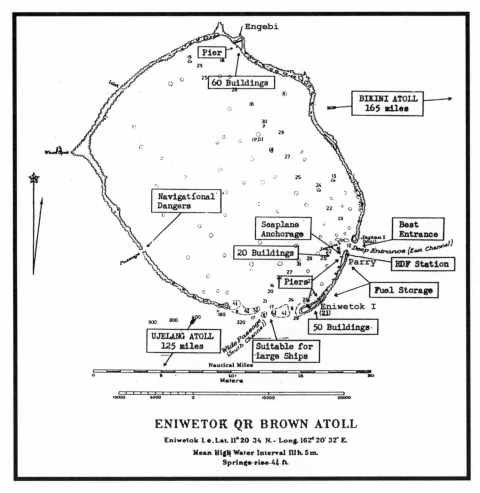

JICPOA Map of Eniwetok Atoll. Engebi is at the far north, and Eniwetok and Parry Islands are in the southeast. JICPOA Information Bulletin 3-44

after operations had ended against Kwajalein and New Ireland in the Solomons. He had no intention of attacking Eniwetok in winter 1944, but the rapid seizure of Kwajalein changed the strategic situation in his area of responsibility, and Eniwetok became a target of opportunity that Nimitz could not resist.[81]

The Eniwetok Intelligence Operation

The first intelligence on Eniwetok Atoll came from ICPOA. Its intelligence specialists had prepared drawings of the atoll based on photographs taken by a submarine in July 1943.[82] The drawings pointed out three towers in the atoll, including one lookout post on Engebi.[83] Aerial photo reconnaissance flights first overflew Eniwetok on 28 December 1943.[84] According to JIC-POA's intelligence maps, reconnaissance pilots photographed their objectives from oblique and vertical angles, but only "from single, high level" flyovers.[85] Photographs were the primary source for the Eniwetok information bulletin, number 3-44, published on 20 January 1944. The report described the location, geography, hydrography, navigational information, and defenses of each island in the atoll. Meanwhile, the JICPOA-FRUPAC team worked overtime to keep Nimitz abreast of the size of the Japanese garrison on Eniwetok.[86]

The Eniwetok information bulletin stated that the Japanese had been using Eniwetok as a radio directional finding (RDF) station, a radar platform, an air base, a seaplane base, and a naval anchorage.[87] The RDF post and radar station provided the Japanese with an early warning station and radio intercept post. JICPOA specifically stated that the Japanese used the airstrip on Engebi "probably as a staging point on the Truk-Wake and Truk–Northern Marshalls air routes."[88] Additionally, it observed that Parry and Eniwetok Islands, if captured, could both facilitate Allied-built airstrips up to seven thousand feet long.[89] The Japanese also used Eniwetok's sheltered lagoon as a seaplane base and as a naval base. For example, close to the time of the publication of Information Bulletin 3-44, four enemy cruisers and six destroyers had used Eniwetok's lagoon as an anchorage.[90] Quite obviously, the report demonstrated the usefulness of the atoll if captured by the Allies.

While bulletin 3-44 contained vital information, it did not clearly establish Japanese capabilities or intentions for the defense of the atoll. Photographs from the December reconnaissance missions simply did not show a multitude of enemy weapons or weapons positions on the atoll's main islands. This meant either that the Japanese had effectively camouflaged their defensive positions or that the atoll was lightly defended. JICPOA, in continuing its Eniwetok intelligence operation, ascertained that the atoll was poorly defended. Why? Because in late January 1944, radio intelligence discovered a Japanese naval convoy transporting an estimated four thousand troops from Truk to reinforce Eniwetok Atoll, which was occupied by an estimated seven hundred Japanese.[91] Carrier photographic sorties flown later on 30 January confirmed what JICPOA's photo interpreters had already discovered about defenses throughout the atoll—that they remained weak.[92]

At about the same time, U.S. Navy divers dove on a sunken ship in Kwajalein Atoll to explore its interior for intelligence material. Sunk on 28 January 1944, the *Eiko Maru* was a 3,500-ton merchant ship, and while it did not contain secret order-of-battle documents, it did contain naval charts of numerous Japanese-held bases in the Pacific.[93] Translated by intelligence personnel on Kwajalein and then sent to JICPOA for filing, the documents provided valuable hydrographic intelligence on Eniwetok's lagoon and added to that which had already been collected.[94]

How Intelligence Influenced Nimitz's Strategic Decision Making

With the rapid seizure of Kwajalein Atoll on 4 February 1944, intelligence concerning Eniwetok suddenly became vital to the immediate strategic direction of the war. The Japanese were weak in the western Marshalls, and Nimitz now wanted to skip the New Ireland operation and seize Eniwetok immediately. This would secure the Marshalls for rapid exploitation by the U.S. Navy. Rear Admiral Turner[95] and General Smith[96] had earlier submitted hypothetical proposals for the Eniwetok assault. However, Nimitz withheld from implementing any of the submitted schemes until he was sure that he could seize the atoll with the men and material at hand in the Marshalls. Accordingly, CINCPAC directed JICPOA to provide intelligence that would help him answer a decisive question: Should he attack Eniwetok immediately and capitalize on the Kwajalein initiative, or wait and attack at a later date?

JICPOA's intelligence up to early February indicated to Nimitz that he should seize Eniwetok as soon as possible. There were three reasons. First, Eniwetok's main three islands were small enough for two U.S. infantry regiments to operate on, and two infantry regiments is what Nimitz had immediately available to him. Specifically, JICPOA described Engebi Island as "an equilateral triangle, with each side a little more than a mile long."[97] Eniwetok Island was three miles long, shaped like boomerang,[98] and varied in width from two thousand to five hundred feet. Parry resembled a two-mile-long teardrop running north with the head over two thousand feet wide.[99] Any more than two regiments and the attack might become bogged down because of overcrowding.

Second, the sea area around Eniwetok was small enough for naval forces already in the Marshalls to effectively cover and isolate. The lagoon of the atoll was modest as well. JICPOA's analysts said that it stretched about twenty miles north to south and seventeen miles east to west,[100] quite diminutive compared to Kwajalein's, which encompassed 655 square miles.[101]

Third, on 10 February, just seven days before the attack was to commence, JICPOA interrogators elicited information from Japanese POWs on

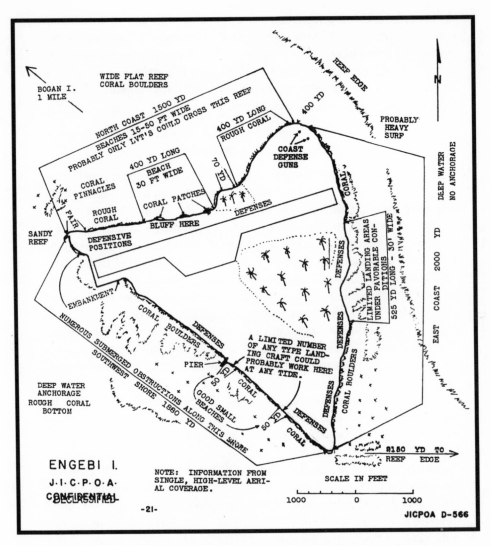

JICPOA Prebattle Map of Engebi Island. The Marines landed on the southwest coast.

JICPOA Information Bulletin 3-44

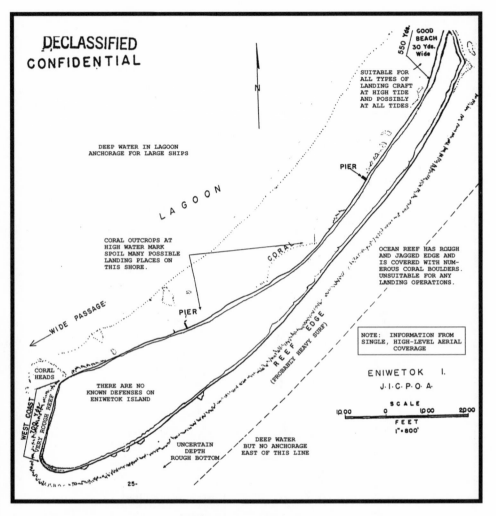

JICPOA Prebattle Map of Eniwetok Island. Army troops landed on the western portion of the lagoon side. JICPOA Information Bulletin 3-44.

Kwajalein indicating that two to three thousand enemy combatants occupied the objective. Combined with the January radio intelligence on the Japanese transport ship sailing from Truk to reinforce Eniwetok, analysts estimated that U.S. forces faced between 2,900 and 4,000 defenders.[102] Nimitz probably believed that the intelligence was accurate and further figured that if U.S. forces attacked Eniwetok immediately, they could catch the Japanese in a moment of weakness before they had a chance to harden

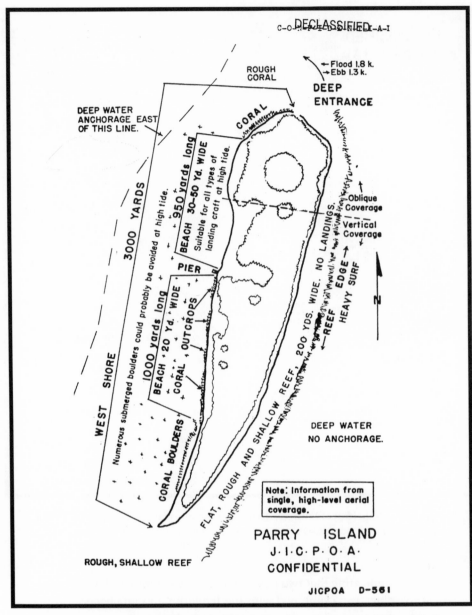

JICPOA Prebattle Map of Parry Island. The Marines landed in the middle of the lagoon side of the island. JICPOA Information Bulletin 3-44

the atoll with concrete fortifications as they had on Tarawa. As of late January, Engebi Island possessed the only defenses detected on the atoll. Engebi's arsenal included two coast defense gun emplacements under construction on the northern tip of the island, up to ten heavy and medium AA guns surrounding the airstrip, up to eight pillboxes, and ten machine gun positions along the island's three coastlines. Approximately 1,350 feet of trenches connected the various gun emplacements. Submarine reconnaissance conducted in July 1944 claimed to have spotted weapons positions on the northeast end of Eniwetok Island, a supposition unsubstantiated by air surveillance.[103]

Admirals Spruance and Turner and General Smith reviewed the intelligence and recommended to Nimitz that he strike Eniwetok immediately.[104] By 5 February, Nimitz had agreed and made a command decision to execute an immediate attack against the atoll. In doing so, Nimitz decided to execute a good plan immediately without the benefit of more precise intelligence, thereby attacking the Japanese while they were weak instead of executing a perfect plan later when the Japanese would be stronger.[105] CINCPAC tasked Rear Adm. Harry Hill to lead the attack. He had seen action earlier in support of the Kwajalein and Tawara operations. Nimitz wanted to move as soon as possible and gave Hill only seven days to plan the operation.[106]

Hill quickly set to work by first directing that additional aerial reconnaissance flights be flown over Eniwetok to photograph the atoll during its high and low tide phases. High-altitude flyovers mostly contributed to the photographic intelligence contained within bulletin 3-44,[107] and Hill ordered that the renewed flights cover the atoll from multiple altitudes.[108] Using equipment on Turner's amphibious force command ship, analysts on site conducted stereoscopic analyses of the photographs to update intelligence maps of the three main objectives. The photos showed new trench lines and foxholes throughout Engebi, Parry, and Eniwetok Islands, but nothing more substantial.[109] Hill then disseminated the new intelligence data throughout the task group.[110] However, order-of-battle intelligence was for some unknown reason not included in the tactical maps distributed to the infantry echelons.[111] This is similar to what had happened on Kwajalein.

Interestingly, as D-Day approached, JICPOA and Pacific Fleet intelligence personnel discovered new but sketchy details about the Japanese troops assumed to be on Eniwetok Atoll. Captured documents and a POW from Kwajalein indicated that the troops in question belonged to the First Amphibious Brigade and that they occupied Engebi Island. Parry and Eniwetok Islands were supposedly lightly defended.[112]

Chain of Command

Under normal circumstances, the planners of Flintlock would have planned Catchpole, but they had to attend to pressing business elsewhere in the Pacific, so replacements filled their positions. Admiral Hill personally commanded the overall operation, including the amphibious landing phase and the naval strike force responsible for the preliminary bombardment. The task force organization stated that Marine Brig. Gen. Thomas E. Watson would assume control of all combat troops once they landed on their objectives.[113] For the actual attack, Nimitz gave Hill and Watson the reserve forces from Flintlock, which consisted of the Twenty-second Marine Regiment and the 106th Regiment of the Army's Twenty-seventh Infantry Division. For all intents and purposes, the entire assault force, including the ships and the Marines, had already been assembled.[114]

Plan of Attack

Plans for the seizure of Eniwetok fell into four phases. Phase one, set to begin on 17 February, consisted of Marine reconnaissance units commandeering three islets off the coast of Engebi to use as artillery support bases. In phase two, set to begin on 18 February, the Twenty-second Marine Regiment would assault Engebi. Phase three, set to begin after the fall of Engebi, consisted of simultaneous attacks against Parry by the Twenty-second Marines, and Eniwetok by the Army's 106th Infantry Regiment. In phase four, Hill's task force would secure the remaining small islets in the atoll. Naval gunfire missions would begin on the seventeenth and continue until each objective had fallen.[115] In conjunction with this plan, Adm. Marc A. Mitscher would conduct thirty carrier raids within two days on Truk to keep Eniwetok localized.[116] JICPOA's intelligence heavily influenced the first three phases of the operation.

How Intelligence Influenced the Campaign

JICPOA provided excellent navigational and hydrographic intelligence on Eniwetok Atoll for the naval preliminary bombardment task force. The Eniwetok information bulletin stated that the Japanese had exclusively used Wide Passage and Deep Entrance to enter and exit the lagoon. Wide Passage, it reported, was over five miles wide and bordered by Eniwetok Island. The channel's center and possibly right side (as entering the lagoon) were the only approaches that could accept deep draft ships. Information from 1923 when the USS *Milwaukee* had traveled to Eniwetok stated that Wide Passage had a maximum depth of thirteen fathoms (78 feet).[117]

Analysts wrote that Deep Entrance, bordered by Parry Island, was narrower than Wide Passage but suitable for deep-draft vessels. Japanese ships passing through this channel had given nearby Jeroru Island a five-hundred-yard berth to the southwest, indicating shallow water or a reef. Most importantly, however, JICPOA stated that the Japanese had recently used Deep Entrance almost exclusively, leading them to believe that the other entrances, Wide Passage included, were obstructed or mined. Using reports of Japanese and U.S. (the USS *Milwaukee*) ship traffic in and out of the lagoon, JICPOA added navigational coordinates that operational planners might use in negotiating their way into Eniwetok.[118] The Eniwetok information bulletin also said that "a submarine reported that sound conditions in the vicinity [were] good," meaning depths surrounding the atoll, as deep as 250 feet, were suitable for naval traffic.[119] Consequently, the excellent hydrographic intelligence allowed U.S. ships to enter Eniwetok Atoll with ease. A U.S. Navy officer remarked: "In my study of naval history I do not recall any other instance where a naval force of this size and composition has steamed up into an enemy held harbor, formed column and entered in much the same manner as it would enter its home port."[120]

Admiral Hill used JICPOA's excellent hydrographic intelligence to navigate his preliminary bombardment task force throughout the atoll and bombard each island objective from their lagoon and sea sides, a highly effective tactic that allowed naval gunners to fire on their targets from multiple angles.[121] Specifically, Hill knew that he could send part of his force into the lagoon via Deep Passage and that his other ships could navigate around the outside of the lagoon, thus positioning themselves to accomplish their missions with maximum efficiency.[122] Consequently, the bombardment proved devastating to the Japanese.

Even though naval gunners did not have a specific layout of Japanese defenses on each island, JICPOA pinpointed, through text and maps, multitudes of manmade structures throughout the atoll that undoubtedly included defensive positions. Analysts stated that reconnaissance from 28 December 1943 indicated that most Japanese defenses were on Engebi Island. They included the weapons discovered earlier that told Nimitz that the enemy position was weak: two coast defense guns, nine to ten AA weapons (medium and heavy), three to eight pillboxes, and nine to ten machine-gun positions. Approximately 1,350 feet of zigzagged infantry trench lines and barbed wire connected many of these positions. Submarine reconnaissance in 1943 claimed that there were gun emplacements being constructed on Eniwetok Island, but 1944 photographic intelligence did not show the supposed positions. Analysts remarked: "Present aerial coverage shows no such emplacements, and installations, if they exist, are well camouflaged."[123] The last-minute reconnaissance ordered by Hill reinforced the defense intelligence contained within the Eniwetok information bulletin.

In addition, JICPOA's photo interpreters discovered sixty hardened structures on Engebi, fifty on Eniwetok and approximately twenty on Parry, notably near or on the lagoon shores of those islands.[124] Since Nimitz was attacking the Japanese before they had a chance to establish an intricate defense system, they probably would be using all available cover to defend their islands. Therefore, naval gunners probably targeted these buildings to deny them to the Japanese to use as cover and concealment. Furthermore, the layout of defenses and some buildings on the three main islands resembled a crust defense. Therefore, as with Kwajalein, the Navy shelled specific targets as well as areas of probable defenses along the beaches.

Accordingly, the air target and naval gunnery maps used for Catchpole proved highly valuable to their respective end users.[125] In most cases, the bombardment shattered resistance ashore. On Engebi, it destroyed all aboveground buildings and structures, and a POW from that island believed that preparatory gunfire had killed half of his garrison.[126] The official Marine Corps record of the assault stated that it was observed upon landing that "the enemy remained too dazed from the effects of the preliminary bombardment to contain the Marines."[127] On Eniwetok, the bombardment did not possess the destructive power that it did on Engebi because of the smaller-caliber projectiles used. However, it was sufficiently violent to keep the Japanese from offering stiff resistance during the vulnerable landing phase of the attack.[128] For Parry, naval gunners increased the tonnage of their shells in light of the Eniwetok scenario, and the lagoon and seaside bombardment again proved its deadly effectiveness in a repeat of the devastation inflicted on Engebi.[129]

The intelligence that helped Hill navigate his preliminary bombardment force into Eniwetok's lagoon also helped the amphibious force plan an effective ship-to-shore movement. First, details on all of Eniwetok's entrances informed operations planners that Wide Passage provided the most desirable avenue of approach into the lagoon. It was deep enough to accept amphibious transports. (Once in the lagoon, the ground combatants moved from their transports into landing vehicles and landing craft and assaulted the first objective.) Second, the old navigational coordinates from the USS *Milwaukee* told assault planners exactly what approach to take when entering Wide Passage. Analysts also stated that Japanese patrol craft had been spotted off Wide Passage, indicating safe use by smaller vessels. Third, before entering Wide Passage on D-Day, the Navy sent mine-sweepers into the channel because of the mine and obstruction warning issued by JICPOA. They found twenty-eight mines and quickly removed them so that the landing craft and ships could enter the lagoon without further delay.[130] The intelligence helped planners prevent a major catastrophe in which the boat-laden landing teams might have suffered as many as one thousand casualties, a majority of which would have likely been KIA.

Most of the amphibious landings experienced successes as well. JICPOA's Eniwetok information bulletin contained three and a half detailed pages on the hydrography of Engebi, Eniwetok, and Parry Islands. Descriptive maps of each island accompanied the text. Intelligence on Engebi Island stated that its seaside beaches contained rough surf, typical of most atoll islands. However, this mattered little since U.S. landing forces usually used lagoon-side landing beaches, which were typically calmer. Engebi's lagoon-side beach, located on its southwest side, did not contain many favorable landing areas because coral boulders covered the beaches, but two landing areas did exist on the lower portion of that shore. These beaches were small and therefore could not facilitate a wide frontal assault. They were, however, accessible to all types of landing craft.[131] Armed with this intelligence and that which had come from the reconnaissance ordered by Hill, Navy and Marine planners decided to land on these small beaches. On 18 February 1944, D-Day for Engebi, all three assaulting battalions completed flawless landings.[132]

Similarly, at Eniwetok, JICPOA's intelligence indicated that the best place to land existed on the northern end of the lagoon shore. However, operations planners wanted to attack at the wider part of the island where their assault teams could branch out and have more room to maneuver than if they landed on the thin, restricting northern end of Eniwetok. In addition, intelligence analysts stated that Eniwetok's western lagoon shore had accessible landing beaches that were free of impending terrain and well suited for LVTs and tanks.[133] In the end, the intelligence proved correct, and the amphibious landings on Eniwetok Island occurred without incident.[134]

The only glitch in the landings occurred on Parry, where, although JICPOA pinpointed an excellent beach on the island's northwest coast,[135] harsh currents pushed many of the marine-filled LVTs three hundred yards down shore from their assigned landing beaches.[136] Fortunately, 650 yards of favorable beach conditions joined the designated landing beaches,[137] and the marines made it ashore safely. It is not clear why JICPOA did not know about the swift current that caused this problem. It is possible that it was a freak of nature similar to the apogean neap tide that caused problems for the landing forces at Tarawa Atoll. Nevertheless, if defenses on Parry had been like those on Tarawa, disaster might have occurred.

In any case, JICPOA's intelligence also helped shape the scheme of attack once the battle had started. As the fight for the atoll progressed into phase two (prior to the landings on Parry and Eniwetok Islands), a JICPOA field intelligence officer accomplished an astounding intelligence coup that changed the landing schedule for the rest of the campaign. A Japanese linguist, Ens. Donald M. Allen, captured enemy documents of high importance—the Japanese order of battle for the entire atoll. When Allen found the documents amidst the ruins of what he assumed to be the Japanese command post for the island, he did not know what they were. But as he read through them, he saw the information shown in the table below:[138]

Contents of Japanese Documents (Personnel) Captured on Engebi

Engebi	
1st Amphibious Brigade	692
Civilian employees of the brigade	24
Naval garrison detachment	44
Air Force	70
Japanese construction workers	53
Korean construction workers	228
Sankyu Coolies	165
Total	1,276
Eniwetok	
1st Amphibious Brigade	779
Civilian employees of the brigade	24
Naval personnel (lookout station)	5
Total	808
Parry	
1st Amphibious Brigade	1,115
Civilian employees of the brigade	47
Air Force	80
Japanese construction workers	20
Sankyu coolies	35
Survey party (civilian under naval officers)	50
Total	1,347

The documents demonstrated that many more Japanese than expected occupied Eniwetok and Parry Islands;[139] 808 on the former, and 1,347 on the latter.[140] It appeared that their primary opponents were as originally thought—the Japanese First Amphibious Brigade.[141] In continuing his quick scan of the document, Ensign Allen also read the following (as translated from the Japanese and published in Information Bulletin 89-44, pages 6 and 7):

Contents of Japanese Documents (Weapons) Captured on Engebi

Weapons of the Engebi Garrison

Small arms (bolt action rifles and pistols); 13 heavy grenade dischargers; 16 machine guns (light and heavy); 12 mortars; one 20-mm automatic gun; two flame throwers; two 37-mm rapid fire guns; two 75-mm mountain guns; two 12-cm naval guns; two 20-mm machine cannon (AA); two twin-mount 13-mm AA machine guns; and three light tanks.

Weapons of the Eniwetok Garrison

Small arms; 13 heavy grenade dischargers; 14 machine guns (light and heavy); 12 mortars; one 20-mm automatic gun; two flame throwers; two 37-mm rapid fire guns; two 75-mm mountain guns; three 20-mm machine cannon (AA); and three light tanks.

Weapons of the Parry Garrison:

Small arms; 36 heavy grenade dischargers; 42 machine guns (light and heavy); 10 mortars; three 20-mm automatic guns; two 75-mm mountain guns; one 20-mm machine cannon (AA); three light tanks.

After reading this, Allen forwarded the information to General Watson who, upon receiving the news, altered phase three of Catchpole on the spot. The weapons information did not cause him great concern. It merely reassured him that he had more firepower than did the Japanese. But the distribution of forces throughout the atoll gave him pause. The captured documents indicated that the Japanese had concentrated their mass on the three main islands more than anticipated. Accordingly, Watson reorganized his assault forces to attack Eniwetok and Parry one at a time in order to have a reserve force ready in case something went wrong—and something did.[142] The poorly trained Army troops of the 106th Infantry Regiment who attacked Eniwetok Island lost momentum during their initial assault and did not strike inland in accordance with amphibious shock tactics. It did not help matters that their objective received the lightest preliminary bombardment, and the fact that they were unable to properly utilize naval fire support to suppress the enemy just made the situation worse. As a result, General Watson sent in a unit of marines to bolster the attack and reestablish the offensive.[143] Had it not been for the intelligence captured on Engebi, the 106th would likely have been left on Eniwetok to fend for itself, and casualties would likely have mounted.[144]

As the campaign continued, U.S. Navy seaplanes and ships easily provided assault echelons with a steady supply of logistics due to JICPOA's excellent intelligence on Eniwetok's lagoon anchorages. The Eniwetok information bulletin demonstrated numerous anchorages off Eniwetok and Parry Islands that ran as deep as thirty fathoms (80 feet). Engebi Island contained an anchorage that could facilitate at least three freighters of medium size.[145] Similarly, since JICPOA had stated that the Japanese had used the lagoon as a seaplane base, operations planners knew that they could do the same. Navy seaplanes transported vital supplies not only to combatants ashore but also to ships assisting the operation from within the lagoon.[146]

JICPOA's simple yet vital geographic intelligence contributed to the Catchpole operation in two ways. First, it helped operations planners designate islet fire support bases for the assaults against Engebi and Parry. Second, it demonstrated that tanks and self-propelled artillery could operate on the flat and stable terrain of each island objective.

Regarding artillery support, JICPOA had pinpointed numerous islets off Engebi.[147] Although tiny, the islets were stable enough to support artillery batteries. Accordingly, operations planners picked three to serve as firebases and assigned them code names: Zinna to the north and Camellia and Canna to the south. For the assault against Parry, operations planners designated Japtan Islet, just north of the objective,[148] as a fire support base.[149] As a result, the marines who assaulted Engebi and Parry were able to call on land-based artillery as well as naval artillery in support of their operations onshore.

JICPOA's geographic intelligence indicated that each island had flat and stable terrain, which was ideal for tank and self-propelled gun (SP) traffic. While mangroves and thick clusters of coconut trees dominated many of the coastal areas of the main objectives, they would not restrict armored support in the way that swamps might have.[150] Excellent maps of Engebi, Eniwetok, and Parry accompanied text descriptions of each and clearly showed where tanks and other tracked vehicles could maneuver.[151] With this intelligence, operations planners sent assault teams ashore with a full array of tank and SP support, a measure that greatly accelerated the collapse of Japanese resistance on the atoll. For example, on Engebi, Marine tanks destroyed Japanese armor masquerading as pillboxes near the airfield. On the opposite side of the island, tank-infantry teams aided by powerful 105-mm SPs quickly demolished an enemy stronghold of pillboxes and infantry trenches nicknamed Skunk Point.[152] Tanks and artillery systematically smashed enemy emplacements made of logs and earth on Eniwetok and Parry, where infantry alone would have been less effective.[153] Timewise, the armor and SPs helped the Marines eliminate Japanese resistance on Engebi and Parry in less than one day,[154] and it helped neutralize the most difficult resistance on Eniwetok in twenty-four hours.[155]

Only two instances of incomplete intelligence adversely affected the campaign. First, in their efforts to fortify Eniwetok Atoll, the Japanese constructed numerous shallow subsurface defense networks called "spiderwebs" because of their spindle-like design. Spiderwebs were fortified foxholes connected by trenches covered with iron sheets and camouflaged with sand. The Japanese thereby blunted some of the tactical thrusts made by advancing platoons of marines and Army troops, who did not expect to face defenses of this type. It was an excellent use of cover and concealment.[156] Aerial reconnaissance did not discover the spiderwebs because of the effective camouflage discipline of the Japanese soldier, expertise that plagued photographic analysts for the duration of the war.[157] These positions were flush with the ground, and photo analysts could not see them,[158] but a Marine after-action report on Catchpole stated that low-altitude vertical aerial photography might have revealed these particular defenses.[159] More than likely, however, aerial reconnaissance missions would have had to catch the Japanese either building them or coming or going from them to understand this defensive tactic. Interestingly, the Eniwetok information bulletin did note that submarine reconnaissance in 1943 saw "installations resembling gun emplacements being constructed" on the island, but aerial reconnaissance could not confirm the information.[160] On the surface, it would seem that the report is referring to a gun platform, such as for a coast defense weapon. But it could have been referring to infantry defenses such as a spiderweb. Disappointingly, the submarine reconnaissance report is short and lends no further evidence to postanalyses.

The second surprise was a nine-foot embankment on Eniwetok Island not noted in intelligence reports, which contributed to the chaos that halted the 106th's advance inland. Its LVTs did not have the power to traverse the obstacle. The embankment added to the confusion the 106th faced because of its insufficient training and weak naval preliminary bombardment. Interestingly enough, JICPOA's map of Eniwetok did show a single line that could be a contour line that spanned the circumference of the island. However, analysts made no written reference to it, and the map did not note the height of the possible topographic line.[161]

Conclusion

By and large, JICPOA produced excellent intelligence for Operation Catch-pole, a result of efficient photographic reconnaissance, adept analyses, and excellent radio intelligence. Furthermore, JICPOA contributed to the success of the operation by providing linguists to support the Marines. Just as important, commanders put the intelligence to good use in a timely manner.

Air reconnaissance squadrons conducted enough surveillance so that analysts could accurately assess the atoll's terrain and hydrography. Surveillance reports from surface vessels and historical accounts of U.S. ships that visited Eniwetok in 1923 also contributed to effective analytical work.[162] Radio intelligence personnel, by intercepting and analyzing the enemy's communications, provided Nimitz with near real-time intelligence on the ever-changing enemy situation on Eniwetok. Having skilled linguists attached to the operations provided pivotal combat intelligence to General Watson that improved the effectiveness of the last two assaults of the campaign.

Comprehensively, the Catchpole Operation offers a prime example of the positive results that can be accomplished when operations planners and intelligence personnel work together to achieve specific goals.[163] Nimitz did not direct JICPOA to collect intelligence on Eniwetok because he planned to seize the atoll. Rather, he directed JICPOA to collect intelligence on Eniwetok because he had *considered seizing* the atoll. Nimitz was not sure he could succeed until he knew what he faced. JICPOA, by supplying constant intelligence on the target, furnished Nimitz with a clear picture of the enemy situation. With that information, Nimitz planned appropriately. In a like manner, the combat intelligence that Ensign Allen produced during the assault on Engebi influenced General Watson to alter his attack sequence for the assaults on the remaining objectives. Consequently, intelligence influenced every level of the Catchpole operation, and most intelligence operations within the Eniwetok campaign were conducted hand in hand with operational planning and execution. Historical examples such as the Eniwetok campaign have provided the U.S. military intelligence community with the precedents to establish their principal axiom—"the commander drives intelligence."[164]

The Strategic Implications of Flintlock and Catchpole

Strategically, the Marshalls provided Nimitz with exactly what he wanted: a staging area for his axis of advance through the Pacific. By the end of February 1944, he had captured Kwajalein and Eniwetok Atolls, plus nearby undefended Majuro Island, and U.S. Navy SeaBees set to work immediately to develop these small land masses into multipurpose military bases.[165]

The SeaBees were U.S. Navy construction battalions, technically known as "C.B.s." A witty sailor along the way decided that "C.B.s" sounded like "sea bees," and the name stuck—acknowledging the unit's ability to descend like a swarm of bees on a captured island and transform it into a sprawling naval or air base. As a unit, they could build entire airports, wharf and docking facilities, barracks, administrative buildings, and railroads, as well as bomb and bullet resistant structures. Nimitz used the SeaBee-transformed Marshalls, specifically Kwajalein and Eniwetok, as bases for the new Central Pacific Air Command, as a base for air strikes against Truk and regional targets of opportunity, and as an advance headquarters and staging area for the next stop on the Central Pacific drive: the Marianas Islands.

First and foremost, however, he used the captured islands as a base to localize the rest of the Marshalls. Central Pacific Air Command pilots flew harassing raids over atolls such as Mille, Wotje, and Maleolap for months after Flintlock and Catchpole to pound local Japanese garrisons into submission.[166] The raids worked. After a short time, these troops could not put up enough AA fire to defend themselves against U.S. aircraft. Furthermore, the Marshalls had been localized to such an extent that no Japanese aircraft or ship could slip in and resupply or evacuate the stranded garrisons. They were completely isolated and left to fend for themselves for the duration of the war.[167] Nimitz called this leaving the enemy to "wither on the vine," and he used this strategy throughout the war.

Land-based bombers and photo reconnaissance planes flew out of the Marshalls in March to bomb Truk and to bomb and collect intelligence on the Marianas farther to the northwest. In addition, planes on the same missions based on other distant islands such as Guadalcanal used the Marshalls as a rallying point to refuel and replenish before executing their missions.[168] Without the Marshalls, these bombing and intelligence missions would have been impossible, because bombers at Guadalcanal and Pearl Harbor did not have the range to make it to distant target areas without refueling. Similarly, Marshalls-based bombers destroyed enough enemy aircraft in Central Pacific so that carrier task forces could probe deeper into enemy waters without being ambushed by superior numbers of enemy planes.

Just as important was the role the Marshalls would play in the next major island offensive: the invasion of the Marianas. Over 127,000 assault troops would participate in the Marianas operation backed by 112 combat ships, including carriers, battleships, cruisers, and destroyers.[169] Their support ships numbered even higher. Nimitz's first target was Saipan, one of the largest islands in the Marianas chain. It would have been difficult, dangerous, and perhaps impossible to attack Saipan straight from Hawaii, some 3,500 miles away.[170] Refueling and replenishing at sea would have been extraordinarily complex, and transporting so many combatants and their beach landing control personnel to their landing ships in the middle of the Pacific might have been impossible.

U.S. control of the Marshalls helped make all of these tasks possible. Although atolls such as Eniwetok were too small for large-scale, shipyard-type activities, they did provide adequate logistics bases. For example, more than twenty fleet oilers used the Marshall's anchorages and provided an astronomical 158,800,000 gallons of fuel to the Marianas attack forces, all in just the beginning stages of the operation.[171] All troop transports destined for the Marianas replenished their supplies in the Marshalls as well.[172] These islands also provided a safe rendezvous point before the invasion took place.

Administratively, this served to assure that all sections of the Pacific Fleet were synchronized with one another, and it allowed for last-minute changes in operational plans. Furthermore, the Marshalls facilitated a safe anchorage for transferring the Saipan amphibious forces from their transports to their landing ships[173] and provided harbor for six floating naval hospitals.[174] In the end, JICPOA's intelligence had an indirect but substantial impact on the next offensive before it ever happened. But it would happen soon enough, and JICPOA would have to work harder to reap the sparkling results of Flintlock and Catchpole.

3

THE MARIANAS

Forager

Strategic Background

The U.S. advance into the Marshalls had forced the Japanese to retreat over five hundred nautical miles west to the Philippines, where they established a new headquarters for the Combined Fleet.[1] Out of strategic necessity, the Japanese began to build up their defenses in the Palaus, Marianas, and the Philippines to consolidate the next line of defense mandated in the "New General Outline for the Future War Direction" policy. More than just a standard defensive line, the Marianas formed part of the Japan's "Absolute National Defense Sphere," a defensive line over which the IJA had vowed to the emperor that no Allied force would cross.[2]

This westward movement demonstrated considerable foresight on the part of the Japanese, because U.S. forces were about to sweep north-northwest from the Marshalls into the Marianas, a move that Nimitz and the Joint Chiefs of Staff had discussed as a possibility before 1944. Unfortunately for the Japanese, the U.S. advance came quickly. As a result, the Japanese did not have enough time to build defensive fortifications to accommodate all the soldiers sent to defend the Marianas. Furthermore, U.S. submarines had nearly isolated the entire area by sinking most Marianas-bound troop transports and supply ships laden with fortification construction materials.[3] Still, the Japanese had enough power to inflict defeat on U.S. forces or at the very least serious casualties.

Operation Forager: Saipan
Campaign Background

"Our war was lost with the loss of Saipan," exclaimed Vice Adm. Shigeyoshi Miwa, Submarine Department Director of the IJN and former chief of the Sixth Fleet.[4] Indeed, the attack on Saipan on 16 June 1944 had cracked the empire's inner Pacific defensive perimeter, after which the Allies systematically defeated each Japanese bastion they encountered. Accordingly, the battle for Saipan set the stage for unconditional surrender. Bombers flying out of Saipan and neighboring Tinian and Guam pummeled the heart of Japan's war-making industries, weakening its military might and demoralizing its people. The loss of the island caused an unprecedented scandal within the Imperial Government that forced the resignation of Premier Hideki Tojo and his entire cabinet. Battle casualties on both sides reflected the strategic and political fallout. The United States suffered 3,225 KIA and 13,387 WIA and MIA. The Japanese lost about thirty thousand men—nearly the entire garrison.[5] The high casualties also reflected the intense nature of the campaign.

U.S. forces faced three major difficulties in wrestling the island from the Japanese. First, as usual, Japanese soldiers offered tenacious resistance and most fought unyieldingly to the death. Second, Saipan's large landmass required that a massive number of U.S. troops—three divisions—be landed, coordinated, and then maneuvered over a vast area of operations. This encompassed a complex sequence of planning, synchronization, and execution. Third, operations planners had to design a Herculean amphibious logistical operation[6] to supply the large number of combatants and their support echelons.[7] Neither of the two latter tasks had been attempted in the most common form of smaller Pacific operations, atoll warfare.[8] Inadequate intelligence, however, imposed even greater difficulties on the campaign. JICPOA and Pacific Fleet intelligence echelons underestimated the number of troops defending the island, could not locate Japanese main-battery artillery sectors, and were unable to assess the total extent of Saipan's terrain.

Target Location

The Marianas run north to south for about five hundred miles. Saipan, Guam and Tinian, the islands chosen for the Forager attack plan, are located at the bottom of this great chain. Saipan sits approximately 1,250 miles north of New Guinea and 1,500 miles east of Manila Bay.[9] The island is about fourteen miles long, and five and a half miles wide at its widest point.[10] Saipan's shape is odd. It has a short, stubby peninsula halfway down the west coast, and on its southeast coast it has two wider and longer peninsulas that form a bay three miles wide.[11]

Why Saipan and the Marianas?

After the Marshalls fell, the Marianas became highly significant. On 12 March 1944, the JCS formally adopted a proposal of the U.S.–British Com-

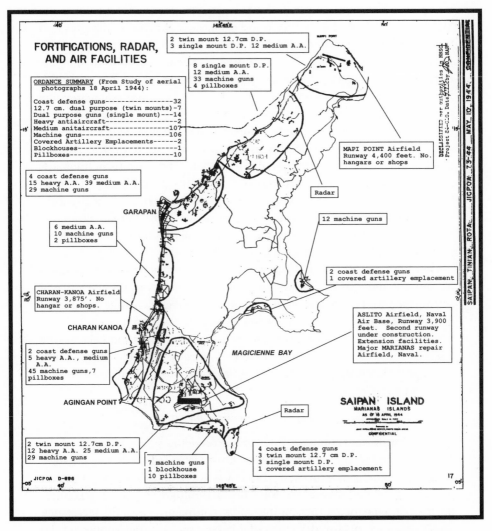

FORTIFICATIONS, RADAR, AND AIR FACILITIES

ORDANCE SUMMARY (From Study of aerial photographs 18 April 1944):

Coast defense guns----------------32
12.7 cm. dual purpose (twin mounts)-7
Dual purpose guns (single mount)---14
Heavy antiaircraft-----------------2
Medium anitaircraft----------------107
Machine guns-----------------------106
Covered Artillery Emplacements------2
Blockhouses------------------------1
Pillboxes--------------------------10

2 twin mount 12.7cm D.P.
3 single mount D.P. 12 medium A.A.

8 single mount D.P.
12 medium A.A.
33 machine guns
4 pillboxes

MAPI POINT Airfield
Runway 4,400 feet. No.
hangars or shops

4 coast defense guns
15 heavy A.A. 39 medium A.A.
29 machine guns

GARAPAN

Radar

6 medium A.A.
10 machine guns
2 pillboxes

12 machine guns

2 coast defense guns
1 covered artillery emplacement

CHARAN-KANOA Airfield
Runway 3,875'. No
hangar or shops.

ASLITO Airfield, Naval
Air Base, Runway 3,900
feet. Second runway
under construction.
Extension facilities.
Major MARIANAS repair
Airfield, Naval.

CHARAN KANOA

MAGICIENNE BAY

2 coast defense guns
5 heavy A.A., medium
A.A.
45 machine guns,7
pillboxes

AGINGAN POINT

Radar

SAIPAN ISLAND
MARIANAS ISLANDS
AS OF 18 APRIL 1944
CONFIDENTIAL

2 twin mount 12.7cm D.P.
12 heavy A.A. 25 medium A.A.
29 machine guns

7 machine guns
1 blockhouse
10 pillboxes

4 coast defense guns
3 twin mount 12.7 cm D.P.
3 single mount D.P.
1 covered artillery emplacement

JICPOA D-896

17

JICPOA Prebattle Map of Saipan. The map shows only some of the Japanese defenses. The Marines landed on the island's southwest side, drove southeast to seize the airfield, and then swept north to secure the remainder of the island. JICPOA Information Bulletin 73-44 bined Chiefs of Staff to attack the Marianas for three reasons. First, the Marianas had several anchorages and numerous airfields, and it provided the Japanese with an opportunity to place considerable air and sea power on Nimitz's axis of advance. Accordingly, it became important that the United States seize the island group to deny the Japanese this capability. Second, the same anchorages and airfields in the Marianas that helped the Japanese defend the Pacific would also help U.S. forces conduct amphibious and naval operations to penetrate it.[12] Third, Admiral King and the JCS wanted to conduct strategic bombing raids over Japan to destroy its war-making industries and to demoralize its people. The airstrips in the Marianas, specifically those on Saipan, Tinian, and Guam, would provide excellent bases for the new, long-range B-29 Superfortress bomber, the platform chosen to achieve King's and the JCS's bombing goals. Saipan alone had three major airstrips.[13] Furthermore, the Marianas provided airstrips closer to Japan than those in China, for launching air raids.[14]

Therefore, on 20 March 1944, acting on orders from the JCS, Admiral Nimitz ordered that Operation Forager be prepared with the objective of seizing Saipan, Tinian, and Guam. Of the three islands, Nimitz designated Saipan as the first target for invasion, primarily because it contained the Japanese command and control center for the Marianas and Palaus—the Japanese Thirty-first Army headquarters. The early capture of Saipan also could provide a staging area and fire support base to facilitate the invasion of Tinian just a few miles to the south.[15]

The Saipan Intelligence Operation

Admiral Nimitz had complete intelligence on neither the geography of the Marianas nor the strength of Japanese units stationed there. (He did have volumes of intelligence on Guam, but it was not detailed enough for proper planning.) For that reason, the Navy began photographic reconnaissance, the main intelligence source for the Saipan campaign,[16] over the target area on 23 February 1944 under cover of a carrier air raid that supported the Eniwetok campaign.[17] These were the first reconnaissance missions to penetrate the Marianas, and they did not produce adequate results.[18] Knowing this, and aside from JICPOA's requests, the Marines asked USN aerial reconnaissance units to photograph the objective ninety, sixty, thirty, and fifteen days prior to D-Day.[19] However, Admiral Spruance, commander of the Marianas campaign, denied the request for two reasons that marked the beginning of a series of photo intelligence difficulties. First, he said that, since combat operations in neighboring island groups had tied down his aircraft, he had none to spare for intelligence collection missions. Second, Spruance believed that continuous carrier raids might disclose the Pacific Fleet's plans to attack Saipan and therefore ruin the element of surprise. Spruance stuck by his decision with steadfast determination, despite the fact that his reconnaissance missions had not produced photos of significant military value.[20] His decisions came back to haunt the campaign in the end.

In April and May, however, a few land-based Army Air Corps and Navy planes flew out of the Marshalls to reconnoiter Saipan.[21] Photographs from these missions provided JICPOA's analysts with their main data source for assessing the Japanese situation on the objective.[22] Unfortunately, none of the aerial reconnaissance gained significant photographic data concerning terrain or defenses on Saipan. In another operation, the submarine USS *Greenling* tried to photograph Saipan's shores where the Marines planned to land.[23] But the USS *Greenling* photographed the wrong beaches. The collective result was that photographic information was lacking, and neither JICPOA nor the Marine G-2 was able to accurately discern Japanese capabilities and intentions. Clouds in particular hindered photographic efforts, and there was no way around that problem. During the spring and early summer of each year, low cumulus clouds hovered above the Marianas, obscuring targets on the ground from U.S. cameras.[24] Additionally, heavy foliage canopy in certain spots around the island inhibited effective photography. Bad photographic angles also prevented the gathering of more accurate photographic coverage.[25] And because aerial reconnaissance over Saipan took place during air raids, photographic aircraft had to fly where the raids focused, not necessarily over the areas where intelligence officers wanted photographs taken. Furthermore, carrier raid planners perceived photo intelligence missions as a secondary priority at best.[26] Therefore, the true strength of the Japanese on Saipan remained a mystery, and terrain maps based on the photographs proved inadequate.[27]

Documents captured in the Marshalls[28] and intercepts of Japanese radio communications[29] provided additional information on the target but did not reveal the enemy's defensive plans or vital details about Saipan's geography. The intelligence contained within JICPOA's Saipan information bulletin, number 73-44, published on 10 May 1944, lacked pertinent information, and the Corps G-2 knew it.[30] Undoubtedly, operations planners knew it as well. In a desperate attempt to rectify the poor intelligence picture, aerial reconnaissance aircraft flew missions over Saipan as late as 6 June, just nine days before D-Day. The last-minute intelligence, included in a Corps G-2 study, indicated significant increases in AA weaponry, the construction of numerous additional defensive fortifications, and the possibil-

ity that a tank regiment would be on Saipan. However, the report also indicated that the new intelligence did not demonstrate a force significantly
more powerful than had been originally estimated, so the attack proceeded
as planned. Unfortunately, the last-minute estimates, according to the official U.S. Army history of the assault, were "well under the mark."[31] JICPOA's
were, too.

Reconnaissance photographs that showed the newly discovered fortifications were not disseminated to the initial assault waves. They had already left for Saipan by the time the photos were ready for dissemination.[32]
More than likely, there were senior officers who believed that this did not
matter too much, since the new intelligence did not indicate a significant
upgrade in the enemy situation. However, if the photographs had captured
the actual situation, operations planners would have adjusted their attack
plans for the large and hostile Japanese force they were about to attack.

Chain of Command

While JICPOA struggled with its Saipan intelligence operation, Nimitz organized a familiar command structure to oversee the battle. Forager would
involve assaults on three islands, a massive undertaking. The overall landing force for Saipan, including immediate reserves, consisted of about forty
thousand combat troops backed by 535 naval vessels just off the coast.[33]
Nimitz retained overall control of the entire operation but assigned Vice
Admiral Spruance as commander of the campaign.[34] Vice Admiral Turner
again commanded the joint expeditionary task force and held the responsibility of getting all the marines and soldiers and their equipment to each
of their beachheads. Nimitz assigned Vice Adm. Marc A. Mitscher and his
fifteen aircraft carriers to cover the assault.[35] Once ashore, command of
combat personnel would revert to VAC commander Lt. Gen. Holland M.
Smith. The Second and Fourth Marine Divisions were designated to land
and seize the island with the U.S. Army's Twenty-seventh Infantry Division
in reserve.[36]

Plan of Attack

The U.S. plan to seize Saipan fell into four phases. Phase one consisted of
the naval preliminary bombardment. In phase two, the Saipan reserve
force would feign a landing north of Tanapag Town on the island's west
coast. At the same time—phase three—the real landing force would assault
the beaches at the southwest side of Saipan and secure the southern half of
the island, including Aslito Airfield. Phase four consisted of sweeping
through the northern portion of Saipan.[37]

Simultaneously, the Navy set up an ambush of surface ships, submarines, and carriers to counter a major Japanese naval attack on the Saipan invasion forces.[38] A separate intelligence operation that involved both ATIS and JICPOA alerted Nimitz to Japanese plans. This marked the second time during the war that the Japanese attempted to defeat an amphibious landing with naval power.[39] Lacking surprise, however, their naval attack was doomed to fail. During the battle for Saipan, the U.S. Navy pulverized the Japanese task force in a lopsided engagement that came to be known as the "Great Marianas Turkey Shoot." Unfortunately, the land forces did not have it as easy and encountered more Japanese, more artillery, and rougher terrain than had been anticipated by JICPOA. Although the intelligence inadequacies overlap, it is possible to provide distinct examples of how each one influenced the operation.

How Intelligence Influenced the Campaign

JICPOA did not print enemy manpower estimates in the Saipan information bulletin because the source of the information came from ULTRA. Regardless, in his book *Double Edged Secrets*, W. J. Holmes, former second in command at JICPOA, says that from his "undocumented recollection" twenty-five thousand Japanese defended Saipan.[40] The official Marine Corps record of the assault stated that prebattle intelligence estimates placed 15,000 or 17,600 Japanese on the island.[41] In reality, the Japanese had 29,662 to 30,000 troops ready to fight to their deaths to keep Saipan from falling into the hands of their enemy. Their order of battle consisted of the following units:[42]

Japanese Units on Saipan

Army Units	"Straggler" Units
42d Division (3 regiments) 47th Mixed Brigade (3 infantry battalions, 3 battalions of artillery, 1 engineering company)	14th Independent Mortar Battalion
	17th Independent Mortar Battalion
	9th Expeditionary Force
9th Tank Regiment	Portions of the 3d and 4th Independent Tank Companies mixed (118 personnel)
1st Infantry Battalion of the 18th Regiment	
25th AA Regiment minus 4 batteries	
7th Independent Engineering Regiments	Portions of two regiments: 11th Engineers and the 150th Infantry (500 personnel)
16th Shipping Engineering Regiments	
278th Transportation Company	Various supply and maintenance units
Navy Units	
55th Naval Guard Force	
1st Yokosuka Special Naval Landing Force	

However, none of the intelligence estimations concerning enemy manpower occurred early enough in the countdown to D-Day to influence planners to add more assault troops to the fray. Unfortunately, the Second and Fourth Marine Divisions totaled only about forty thousand personnel—hardly the three-to-one ratio required to defeat a determined foe in a defensive posture. Furthermore, this was the first time in the Central Pacific that U.S. amphibious forces faced a division-sized unit of the Imperial Japanese Army supported by artillery.

Clearly, combat on Saipan required more than the two Marine divisions originally assigned. For example, on D-Day, General Smith landed all Marine reserves to commit to the battle. Furthermore, the day after D-Day, he landed his campaign reserve component, the Twenty-seventh Division.[43] General Smith did this for two reasons, the first of which had nothing to do with combat ashore.

First, Spruance wanted the reserves landed because the Japanese navy was on its way to try to stop the landings, and he did not want a division of infantry at sea in transports where they would be sitting ducks to enemy air attacks. Smith agreed, commenting that it was better to have ground combatants ashore than on ships offshore.

The second reason for landing the reserves directly related to the land battle. Shortly after landing the initial waves, General Smith said that "a long and vicious fight was in prospect, and it was already apparent that more troops would be required."[44] In other words, the initial attack waves had encountered more fierce resistance than expected.[45] In fact, it took three days to secure the beachhead.[46] At first, the resistance seemed due to overwhelming enemy artillery fire, but continued combat also made it obvious that the Japanese had so many men on Saipan that U.S. commanders would need more than two divisions to seize the island.

As the battle for Saipan raged, it became evident that the Japanese had enough personnel to enact not only a crust defense but a delaying action and interior defense as well.[47] They positioned the bulk of their troops and weaponry in static defenses around the beaches to stop the U.S. assault at the water's edge. Then they placed reserve forces—consisting of tanks and infantry units—well inland but ready to reinforce any defensive zone that was having trouble containing the enemy.[48] If U.S forces managed to breach shore defenses, then the Japanese planned to enact a protracted delaying action from scores of makeshift pillboxes and bunkers scattered throughout the interior. Although U.S. forces had destroyed the main defensive line in three days,[49] they unknowingly faced thousands of Japanese soldiers beyond the landing beaches ready to continue the defense of Saipan.

After their primary defense failed, the remaining Saipan defenders frustrated each major U.S. advance inland with a solid front. After the battle for the coast, it took an another four days for the Marines to clear Japanese troops from the southern portion of Saipan.[50] Then the three U.S. divisions pivoted abreast along a north-facing front that extended from one side of the island to the other. According to Isely and Crowl, when the infantry advanced to clear the rest of the island they met "the fiercest fighting encountered since the initial assault."[51] Three different POWs estimated that on about D+9 their comrades numbered twenty thousand.[52] Large numbers of Japanese and the jagged terrain they occupied, another intelligence problem, set the stage for difficult and painstaking offensive operations from regimental down to platoon levels. In the center of Saipan, where some of the most harrowing combat took place, it took some units as many as seven days to move between a thousand and three thousand yards.[53]

This difficulty contributed to an infamous altercation between the U.S. Army and Marine Corps. It seems that Maj. Gen. Ralph Smith's Twenty-seventh Division in the center of the island had not advanced evenly with the marines on either flank. It had not trained in the USMC's deep-penetration island assault tactics, and according to various Pacific commanders, the unit in question, a National Guard division, lacked an aggressive spirit. The predicament caused a concavity in the U.S. line that put the entire ground element at risk. If the Japanese could exploit the bulge by inserting troops into it, then they could pivot and slice into one of the Marine flanks, or drive deeper into the center and cut the attackers in half. Any such maneuver probably would have halted the attack, increased casualties, and merged the two opposing armies to a point where no lines existed, thereby negating the use of supporting arms. This might have reduced the battle for Saipan to the equivalent of a gigantic barroom brawl. Gen. Holland Smith, therefore, relieved the commander of the Twenty-seventh of his post and replaced him with another. The new commander, with the help of supporting arms, rectified the tactical error and pushed the attack forward.[54] Nonetheless, casualties still mounted.

The Japanese had so many soldiers on Saipan that, even after the main battles for the island had ended, they managed to muster around three thousand men for a massive surprise banzai attack on the Twenty-seventh Division. It is the largest such attack on U.S. forces on record.[55] The attack rolled through U.S. front lines and command areas, weakening with every step but still continuing. It did not stop until it met Marine Corps artillery units that held their ground with small arms and point-blank canister fire while using their massive guns as cover and concealment.[56]

In a larger sense, intelligence problems concerning the number of Japanese affected the overall strategy for all of Operation Forager. The Twenty-seventh Division was supposed to be the reserve force slated for Guam as well as Saipan, but the heavier-than-anticipated resistance and the attack by the Japanese fleet forced Nimitz to delay invasion plans for Guam from 18 June to 22 July. This altered the entire timetable for the conquest of the Marianas.[57] Furthermore, a slower attack tempo allowed the Japanese on Guam to dig in deeper and plan a more effective defense.

JICPOA also underestimated the extent of Japanese artillery and heavy weapons on Saipan. To its credit, JICPOA accurately pinpointed some beach defenses at the water's edge and slightly to the rear of the water's edge between Garapan Town and Agingan point, where the marines landed. In these areas, JICPOA's "Fortifications, Radar, and Air Facilities" map shows six coast defense gun emplacements, nine pillboxes, seventy-eight AA gun positions, and eighty-four machine-gun nests.[58] Battle accounts of D-Day and documents from Nimitz's office cited in the official Marine Corps record of the campaign corroborate JICPOA's findings that many of these weapons did in fact exist on Saipan's east coast.[59] This intelligence proved valuable to both the amphibious and naval preliminary bombardment task forces. The first assault waves had a good idea of what to expect from shore defenses, and the Navy was able to bombard marked enemy positions and reduce resistance to the landings. Regrettably, however, reconnaissance photographs revealed only a portion of the artillery weapons present on the coast. The Japanese were able to move most of their artillery off the beaches to reverse-slope positions on the hills behind the beaches during the preliminary bombardment.[60] They could not have done so if intelligence had accurately pinpointed these weapons in the first place.

The Japanese artillery that had thus escaped destruction rained down fire on marines as they landed on Saipan's shores.[61] Worse, the lack of reconnaissance photographs kept JICPOA from discovering the forty-six artillery pieces[62] in south central Saipan behind Mt. Fina Susu.[63] The upshot was that, despite the usable shore defenses intelligence, resistance to the landings proved stiff.[64] The Mt. Fina Susu artillery sector in particular served as the main artillery support base for all Japanese defense sectors on Saipan.[65] These artillery units belonged to the Forty-seventh Mixed Brigade and consisted of the Third Independent Mountain Artillery Regiment, less a battalion, and the Third Battalion, Tenth Field Artillery Regiment.[66] Spotters hidden along the ridge beyond the landing beaches[67] directed fire onto the beachhead with a high degree of accuracy. In addition, Japanese artillery positions on Tinian fired on the Saipan invasion forces and added to the effectiveness of those on the primary objective.[68] Enemy artillery accounted in part for the first days' appalling two thousand U.S. casualties and continued to pound U.S. forces until the campaign was half over.[69]

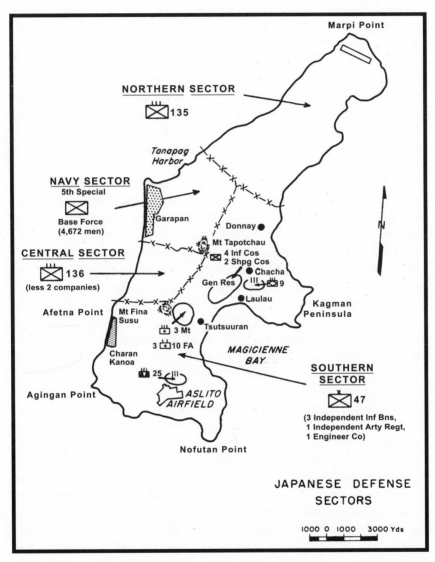

Actual Japanese Defenses on Saipan. Note the Mt. Fina Susu artillery battery.
Hoffman, *Saipan: The Beginning of the End*

Consequently, the inability of JICPOA to discover coast defense and dual-purpose weaponry and the Mt. Fina Susu artillery base contributed to an inadequate preliminary naval and air bombardment of Saipan. An accurate preliminary bombardment requires that intelligence pinpoint enemy positions so that pilots and naval gunners will know where and what to strafe and bombard. Such was not the case at Saipan. The two-day preparatory bombardment left much to be desired. It did not eliminate a sufficient amount of Japanese heavy weaponry to maintain an efficient operational tempo or keep casualties to a minimum.[70] Fire from artillery, mortars, machine cannon, and anti-boat weaponry poured into the marines as they landed.[71] Many Japanese positions were so well hidden that they remained operational for four days after D-Day.[72] And a 15 May 1944 JICPOA target survey for pilots assigned to strafe and bomb the area well behind the landing zones mistakenly pointed out only a sparse number of gun emplacements in the disputed area.[73]

As fate would have it, inexperienced gunners on ships ineffectively located ten thousand yards from shore botched the first day's bombardment, compounding the impact of the lacking intelligence. Furthermore, the gunners were on fast battleships and had trained for surface warfare, not land bombardment. When more experienced naval gunners of the Joint Expeditionary Force (the landing force) arrived on 14 June, they could not execute an effective preliminary bombardment, either, because of the inadequate intelligence.[74]

In one instance, however, a JICPOA field team helped make up in a small way for the overall incomplete order-of-battle intelligence. On D+1, they discovered, in a vacated Japanese command post in a schoolhouse at Charan Kanoa, a significant quantity of high-value documents containing information such as the location of Japanese tanks on the island and the enemy's plan of defense.[75] According to Rear Adm. Edwin T. Layton's book *And I Was There,* this helped the V Amphibious Corps plan for and defeat a major Japanese counterattack that occurred during the campaign,[76] probably in the early stages. However, his book did not shed any light on how those documents impacted the rest of the campaign, and neither do the Marine Corps and U.S. Army official histories of the battle for Saipan.

JICPOA's lacking geographic intelligence also had a negative impact on combat operations ashore. Information Bulletin 73-44 demonstrated Saipan's general terrain features, such as the large lake and swampy area behind the Charan Kanoa area (the center of the landing beaches) and the high ground behind Garapan (the northern end of the landing beaches). It also described some of Saipan's more difficult terrain:[77]

Mt. TAPOTCHAU, in the center of the island, rises to an elevation of 1,554 feet and is the dominating physical feature. Between MT. TAPOTCHAU and MT. MARPI, with an elevation of 832 feet at the end of the north end of the island, there is a ridge 7 1/2 miles long with an elevation of over 600 feet and four peaks between 720 and 947 feet. The slopes on the sides of the ridge average about one in six.

However, it is evident from the complaints of combatants that JICPOA did not provide sufficient geographic intelligence necessary for effective campaign planning and execution. Descriptions such as this were probably too general to give operations planners an accurate idea of the terrain that lay ahead of their troops.

The maps JICPOA sent to the combat echelons did not accurately illustrate Saipan's terrain, either.[78] Their topographic maps, for example, showed gradual inclines where there were sheer cliffs, and gorges where there were canyons.[79] Without specific topographic information and accurate maps, the assault forces did not know what type of terrain to expect. This slowed the marines' advance across the island and provided the Japanese with natural fortresses that commanded mutually supportive fields of fire.

For example, initial assault plans called for LVTs to drive inland from the beaches, lance through enemy defenses, and discharge marines behind Japanese lines. This was supposed to induce shock effect, clear beach congestion, and reduce the effectiveness of Japanese resistance. Swampy ground, ditches, and bombardment refuse slowed the LVTs,[80] but a four-to-five-foot embankment undetected by photo analysts and not shown on maps halted the advance dead cold.[81] (JICPOA's analysts stated that gentle slopes were behind the west coast beaches for five hundred to five thousand yards.)[82] Therefore, the attempt to bypass enemy shore defenses failed, and the marines had to consolidate the beachhead while exposed to Japanese artillery and infantry fire.

Additionally, Saipan's harsh terrain slowed infantry traffic and delayed supply lines as the marines and soldiers trudged their way over rocky terrain, gullies, and elevations not shown on JICPOA's maps.[83] The same terrain, coupled with untold numbers of natural and man-made caves,[84] provided the Japanese with intrinsic defensive positions that assault forces had to eliminate slowly and methodically.[85] But since intelligence had not forewarned of the naturally defendable terrain, assault forces attacked Saipan without a sufficient number of combat engineers, men who were specially trained to destroy positions such as fortified caves.[86] Consequently,

JICPOA Map, AA and Coast Defense Guns, Saipan. The map shows a topographic estimation of the island's terrain. JICPOA Information Bulletin 66A-44

U.S. infantrymen suffered higher casualties and spent an extended amount of time fighting the campaign.

On a positive note, JICPOA did produce accurate hydrographic data for the assault. Information Bulletin 73-44 accurately described the coral reefs, surf conditions, and landable shores on Saipan's west coast as compared to the island's less hospitable "north, south and east coasts [that were] dominated by rocky cliffs."[87] With this type of information, along with tactical hydrographic intelligence gained from UDTs, operations planners chose to land on accessible beaches and staged an effective ship-to-shore landing.[88]

JICPOA also warned of the swampy ground behind the landing beaches that slowed the advance inland. In text, analysts noted that this "poorly drained coastal plain" extended from Garapan down to Agingan Point with a width of five hundred to five thousand yards.[89] Strangely though, JICPOA's information bulletin maps were not as detailed. In fact, the Charan Kanoa map area showed only a small swamp behind the town that was about a thousand feet square in a diamond pattern. Off to the right of the town analysts had written "Charan-Kanoa Swamp" but did not demonstrate its actual size. The other map in the Saipan information bulletin that did represent the terrain features of this particular area, the "Navigational Information" map, showed foliage in this area instead of swamps.[90] Another JIC-POA map of this specific area, a topographical air target chart,[91] did not accurately show disputed terrain contours or the swamp in question. Ultimately, U.S. servicemen had to rely on captured Japanese maps to facilitate geographic intelligence on Saipan.[92]

USMC Historical Map, Central Saipan. This map shows the actual topography of the island. Shaw, Nalty, and Turnbladh, *Central Pacific Drive*

Regarding captured documents, Saipan proved to be a gold mine of intelligence that would impact the next four island campaigns. As marines and soldiers fought their way inland, they came across the abandoned command post of the Thirty-first Army headquarters in Garapan Town that contained a wealth of secret Japanese military documents.[93] The Thirty-first Army headquarters was the command and control center for all Japanese land forces assigned to defend the Marianas, the Bonins, and the Palaus.[94] Fortunately for JICPOA, this particular command also housed the headquarters for two additional Japanese units: the Fifth Base Force and the Central Pacific Fleet.[95] Each held valuable intelligence material on order of battle for numerous Japanese-held islands in the Pacific, including Guam and Tinian.

U.S. servicemen recovered tons of documents from Saipan and the rest of the Marianas, and JICPOA never was able to translate all of it. JICPOA and fleet intelligence personnel spent weeks conducting preliminary assessments of these documents in the field, looking for information on Guam and Tinian—the next two objectives. Analysts found excellent order-of-battle information on these two islands, and they would eventually find information on Peleliu and Iwo Jima, two future targets yet to be officially designated. Translators sent other important documents to JICPOA for immediate dissemination, and most background information of lesser value was sent to the Washington Document Center.[96]

Conclusion

There are five interconnected reasons for the many intelligence problems that arose during the Saipan campaign. First, there is evidence to suggest that Admiral Spruance might have rushed preparations and planning in order to maintain a high operational tempo and keep pressure on Japanese forces. Joseph Alexander writes in *Storm Landings* that "Several units in fact complained that the whole schedule seemed too frenetic for adequate planning, training, and combat loading."[97] This concerted rush to prepare for the attack probably had a negative impact on the Saipan intelligence operation.

Second, and in keeping with the above theory, Spruance did not order enough surveillance over the target area. The photographic reconnaissance missions conducted by aircraft and the USS *Greenling* did not produce a sufficient volume of quality photographs that analysts could have used to locate more concentrations of enemy troops and heavy weapons. Likewise, JICPOA's cartographers did not have enough raw data to accurately assess defensively advantageous terrain features on Saipan. Therefore, the Cartographic Section was reduced to disseminating incomplete topographical data to JICPOA's subcontracting tactical mapmakers.

Third, JICPOA had to conduct intelligence operations against four targets in the Marianas scheduled for attack in the summer months of 1944: Rota, Saipan, Tinian, and Guam, the last three of which were attacked amphibiously (Nimitz had Rota strafed and bombed). Such a large and widespread intelligence operation might have strained JICPOA's collection resources and analytical capability. In the end, it appears that the restrictions may have affected the quality of its work—a prime example being that JICPOA's analysts noted the swampy land behind the landing beaches in the text but not on the maps in Information Bulletin 73-44.

Fourth, as previously mentioned, bad weather and a dense foliage canopy impaired the photo analytical process. One way to penetrate it would have been by heavily bombarding areas of suspected fortifications, a tactic that could have sheared away enough camouflage to expose enemy defenses to photographic reconnaissance pilots. Although this idea was proposed in the aftermath of the Peleliu campaign (fall 1944) as a possible remedy for Japanese camouflage, it was never implemented during the Pacific War. As far as cloud cover was concerned, there was no solution. In time, the adverse weather front that hovered over Saipan would have moved off, but it was important to Nimitz to keep constant pressure on the Japanese, so time was of the essence.

Fifth, numerous units used Saipan as a staging area for deployment to other regions, and many just happened to be there when the Marines landed.[98] As a result of so many units coming and going, radio intelligence analysts probably had a difficult time attempting to decipher who and what units were actually going to defend the objective[99]—a problem that would plague the Okinawa campaign as well. Fortunately, though, the long battle on Saipan bought time for data collection and analyses of Tinian and Guam, the next targets in the Marianas, and as a result, intelligence for Operation Forager improved.

Nevertheless, the battle for Saipan demonstrates that without proper and thorough surveillance of an objective, the resulting analysis will suffer. Correspondingly, planning against the objective will suffer as well, leading to high casualties, botched fire missions, and other operational problems. For Saipan, intelligence analysts had to make do with the scant data that arrived from collection missions, and as a consequence they were unable to provide advantageous intelligence comparable to that produced for Kwajalein and Eniwetok. Ultimately, Spruance, in forbidding further carrier sorties over the target, sacrificed thorough surveillance for the element of surprise. Although the Japanese were caught by surprise by the swift U.S. attack on Saipan, better intelligence probably would have contributed to a more efficient campaign, especially if it had pinpointed Japanese artillery units well inland from the beaches. In fact, the after-action intelligence report from Headquarters, Task Force 56 (the expeditionary task force), stated that the denial of more photo reconnaissance missions by "higher authorities" resulted in "the consequential loss of intelligence information that would have proved useful both in the planning and assault phases of the operation."[100] Spruance's decision remains problematic, given that two of his biographers, Vice Adm. E. D. Forrestal and Thomas Buell, both commented that he placed a high value on intelligence and discussed how vital it was to attain accurate information on Japanese forces in the Marianas.[101] In any event, based on the evidence provided and the Marine after-action report, this particular facet of the Saipan intelligence operation can be categorized as a failure.

Operation Forager: Guam
Campaign Background

On 22 July 1944, the U.S. Marine Corps attacked the island of Guam to retake it from the Japanese and to seize strategic control of the Central Pacific. By 10 August, Admiral Spruance had declared the island secure and raised the Stars and Stripes over the recaptured U.S. Navy base at Apra Harbor.[102] The victory cost 1,744 U.S. servicemen KIA and 5,308 WIA,[103] and 18,377 Japanese KIA.[104]

The Japanese fought hard from well-defended positions and wicked terrain. These elements, coupled with Guam's large size, made the battle tactically difficult for the marines and soldiers who assaulted the island. All things considered, however, the campaign went well, in part due to good intelligence. JICPOA and the fleet's intelligence units had a positive impact on the campaign by providing accurate intelligence on Guam's hydrography, basic geography, road systems, and Japanese order of battle. On the other hand, in some cases there occurred an odd operational or logistical snafu that counterbalanced the positive intelligence but not to an extent that threatened victory. From a historical viewpoint, this made Guam one of the more interesting Pacific battles.

Target Location

Located 1,100 miles north of New Guinea and 4,000 miles west-southwest of Pearl Harbor, Guam sits at the bottom of the Marianas. It is the third island from Saipan, 120 miles to the south. Guam is 34 miles long, averages 7 miles in width, and resembles the shape of a figure eight.[105]

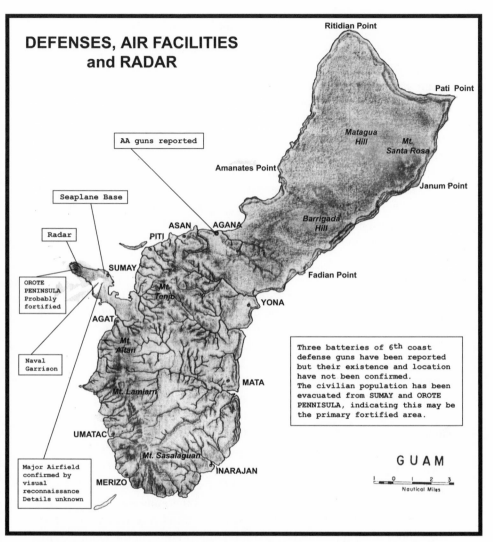

DEFENSES, AIR FACILITIES and RADAR

AA guns reported

Seaplane Base

Radar

OROTE PENINSULA Probably fortified

Naval Garrison

Major Airfield confirmed by visual reconnaissance Details unknown

Ritidian Point

Pati Point

Matagua Hill

Mt. Santa Rosa

Amanates Point

Janum Point

ASAN   AGANA

PITI

SUMAY

Mt. Tenjo

AGAT

Mt. Alifan

Mt. Lamlam

UMATAC

Mt. Sasalaguan

MERIZO

Barrigada Hill

Fadian Point

YONA

MATA

INARAJAN

Three batteries of 6th coast defense guns have been reported but their existence and location have not been confirmed.
The civilian population has been evacuated from SUMAY and OROTE PENNISULA, indicating this may be the primary fortified area.

GUAM

1   0   1   2   3
Nautical Miles

JICPOA Shaded Relief Prebattle Map of Guam. The map shows only a few defenses. The Marines landed on two west coast beaches: Asan (north) and Agat (south). Army troops helped secure Orote Peninsula and other areas. Clearing the rest of Guam took months. JICPOA Information Bulletin 52-44

Why Guam?

The JCS and Nimitz targeted Guam for five reasons. First, capture of the island would finalize control of the Marianas. Second, Admiral Nimitz needed Guam and its military base as an advanced command and control center from which to direct the war. This was necessary because, as the war moved closer to Japan and farther from Pearl Harbor, it became increasingly difficult and time-consuming to direct operations and plan offensives from the rear. Third, the Army Air Corps wanted Guam as a B-29 base to carry out strategic bombing raids on Japan. Fourth, Guam possessed the best harbor in the region, and the Navy needed that to maintain sea control of the Central Pacific. Last, for purposes of raising the nation's morale, war planners targeted Guam in order to take back a U.S. possession that had been seized by the Japanese just three days after the attack on Pearl Harbor.[106]

The Guam Intelligence Operation

At that time, intelligence operations aimed at Guam were the most extensive of the war. In fact, after-action intelligence reports stated that there was so much information collected on Guam that analysts could not process all of it.[107] Still, aside from the usual intelligence sources, JICPOA cited seventeen secondary sources in its Guam information bulletin.[108] Several were open sources and came from books such as Laura Thompson's *Guam and Its People*. Most sources were classified—for example, a 345-page essay produced by the Office of Naval Intelligence called "Strategic Study of Guam." JICPOA's analysts also consulted an official U.S. war plan called "A Military Study of Guam," and they requisitioned data from U.S. Marine Corps Schools at Quantico, Virginia.[109] As mentioned earlier in this chapter, air reconnaissance over the Marianas began on 23 February 1944.[110] These missions included Guam. The first sets of photographs were not good for the same reasons that plagued the Saipan photos, and cloud cover was especially a hindrance.[111] So while photo interpreters planned requests for additional reconnaissance flights, JICPOA and FRUPAC's radio intelligence specialists intercepted and analyzed local Japanese radio communications in attempts to discover the size of the garrison on Guam and if it was being reinforced or not.

JICPOA used its many sources to compile a fifty-four-page Guam information bulletin accompanied by a second volume of maps. Published on 15 April 1944, the bulletin covered important subjects such as Guam's location, history, water supply, anchorages, climatology, roads, communications, harbor facilities, and possible beach landing sites. However, JICPOA had collected little information on the Japanese order of battle, so the report said next to nothing about Japanese defenses.

The III Amphibious Corps, the lead ground element for the assault, liked JICPOA's road map of Guam except for the fact that it did not include recently built Japanese roads. On the other hand, the III Amphibious Corps G-2 did not like JICPOA's terrain maps and claimed that they were inaccurate.[112] While the USMC did not have much intelligence on Guam, they did have knowledge of its topography because they used to station personnel there. Therefore, the Marines spoke with some authority when they did not fully agree with JICPOA's analysis.

JICPOA applied several solutions in attempts to remedy the criticism. First, aerial reconnaissance pilots flew additional missions over the big island from late April through July to try to gain more accurate geographic data. These photos were better than the first set and provided analysts with good media to work with. In addition, photo interpreters received color photographs of Guam's littoral areas, which were especially helpful in assessing hydrographic conditions such as water depths around the landing beaches.[113] Second, JICPOA interviewed a former public works officer on Guam, Naval Commander Richard F. Armknecht, to gain firsthand information about the island's terrain to help produce a relief map. Rear Adm. Richard Conolly, commander of the landing phase of the Guam campaign, used one of these maps to plan the preliminary naval bombardment and said that it was useful. However, the map did not provide intricate terrain details and neither did the late April reconnaissance flights because of continuing cloud cover. Further reconnaissance flights learned nothing more, and the details of Guam's geography remained a mystery for the meantime.[114]

As D-Day approached, JICPOA continued to collect and process intelligence for the upcoming assault. Fleet intelligence echelons, augmented as usual by JICPOA personnel, also continued their Guam intelligence operations from the USS *Appalachian,* an amphibious flagship. On board, intelligence specialists had established a collection and processing office complete with a photo lab, a photo interpretation office, and a map reproduction room.[115] On 29 April, the submarine USS *Greenling* returned from its reconnaissance of the Marianas with beach photos of Guam's landable beaches. Photographic interpreters analyzed the photographs and from them made detailed drawings of the proposed landing beaches, shore defenses (few were discovered), and the terrain lying behind the shores. The illustrations went into the operational plans for the assault.[116]

Then in late June, photo reconnaissance discovered something vital that had for the most part eluded JICPOA up to that point—Japanese weapons positions. Intelligence analysts used these photos to plot hundreds of enemy gun emplacements all over Guam. Unfortunately, most of the newly discovered positions sat on top of the proposed landing beaches on the central west side of the island.[117]

Additional intelligence came from natives of Guam who were serving in the U.S. Navy,[118] and as the battle for Saipan raged, JICPOA's field intelligence personnel learned more about Guam's defenses from Japanese POWs.[119] However, the Guamanians were in the Navy and absent from their home island when the Japanese attacked, so they could not provide any effective intelligence on the Japanese order of battle. Nor could they provide technical topographic information on Guam's interior. More than likely, they provided general background information that allowed intelligence personnel to verify some of the information they had collected.

As Saipan fell, more precise information on Japanese defenses became available and the intelligence picture of Guam continued to improve. This was a godsend because, in the early stages of the Guam intelligence operation, it was beginning to look like a repeat of Saipan. Interestingly, the new information came from the Japanese themselves, specifically the headquarters of the Thirty-first Army, which moved several times during the battle for Saipan. With each move, however, the Japanese left important secret documents behind. U.S. combatants found some of these documents in a safe in Garapan. Why the Japanese did not destroy them is not clear. In all, there were fourteen instances on Saipan of infantry or intelligence personnel discovering documents directly relating to Guam. These documents included a Japanese handbook on Guam, a list of all imperial forces in the Marianas, maps and photos of the objective, an order-of-battle document that listed Japanese units stationed there, and documents detailing their defense installations.[120]

On a final note regarding the Guam operation, JICPOA had a difficult time disseminating intelligence to its end users. This occurred because, at this stage in the war, U.S. forces were scattered wide instead of in one concentrated area. The amphibious and naval forces were strewn throughout Guadalcanal, Purvis Bay, Efate, Hawthorne Sound, New Georgia, and Espíritu Santo.[121] Despite these problems, JICPOA did manage to disseminate its intelligence on time, and the fleet intelligence echelons located in the Marianas distributed information to the combatants as they arrived.

Chain of Command

While the intelligence operation against Guam continued, Nimitz designated a command structure for the assault. He assigned Vice Admiral

Spruance to command the operation, Vice Admiral Turner as commander of the expeditionary forces, and Rear Adm. Richard Conolly as commander of the amphibious task force. Unlike most Central Pacific campaigns where the Fifth Fleet and V Amphibious Corps worked together, for Guam, the Fifth Fleet provided the naval contingent of the operation, but the III Amphibious Corps provided the infantry forces. Therefore, Maj. Gen. Roy Geiger, IIIAC commander, directed the ground element that consisted of the Third Marine Division and the First Provisional Marine Brigade—the Fourth and Twenty-first Marine Regiments, reinforced. The 305th Regiment of the U.S. Army's Seventy-seventh Infantry Division was selected to support the First Provisional Brigade just after the landings, while the remainder of the Seventy-seventh was to remain in reserve.[122]

Plan of Attack

The attack plan for Guam fell into four phases. In phase one, Conolly's ships were to bombard enemy positions beginning on 8 July and continue for 13 days, the longest preliminary naval bombardment in World War II to that point. In phase two, the Marines were to land five miles apart on either side of Orote Peninsula on 22 July. The Third Division would land on the northern landing zones at Asan Point, and the First Provisional Brigade would land in the south at Agat Bay. Afterward, they were to move inland and secure the high ground behind their beachheads. In phase three, the 305th was to land behind the First Brigade, link with Marine units to the north, and help seize Orote Peninsula, which contained the important deep-water harbor and airfield that Nimitz wanted. In the last phase of the operation, all forces were to sweep north and secure the rest of the island.[123]

On the whole, the Guam operation went according to plan. Operations planners designed a good scheme of attack, and U.S. combatants fought hard and successfully completed each phase of the campaign. Marines landed on their designated beaches without one serious setback and pushed inland where resistance stiffened, but not to an insurmountable magnitude. U.S. Army troops followed on accordingly and linked the northern and southern ground elements. Units from both services then collaborated in seizing Orote Peninsula. With the most difficult part of the battle over, the attackers then turned their attention to sweeping and clearing the northern portion of the island.[124] Accurate intelligence concerning Guam's hydrography, basic geography, road system, and Japanese order of battle greatly contributed to their success.

How Intelligence Influenced the Campaign

Isely and Crowl stated that the ship-to-shore movement at Guam "was not especially remarkable except that it went more smoothly than usual,"[125] an obvious result of the long naval bombardment but also of JICPOA's excellent hydrographic data. JICPOA's analysts accurately described the tidal conditions, surf conditions, and the location of reefs off potential and actual landing beaches in text and on a landings map. The information was clear, concise, and well illustrated.

Analysts stated that tides for Guam only varied 1.2 to 1.9 feet, and water levels remained close to the reef. Reefs of two types, coral and nullipore, surrounded the island. Coral reefs, which were flat and broad, mostly covered the western beaches. Nullipore reefs, which were narrow and extended above water level like boulders in the surf, covered the east coast. The latter type precluded LVT and most landing craft traffic. Coral reefs around Guam allowed LVT traffic, but not that of landing craft.[126]

As with most beaches all over the world, surf conditions at Guam in part depended on wind conditions. (Other influential phenomena included lunar cycles and tides.) High winds meant a rough surf, and light wind meant an easy surf—the latter being the most ideal condition for an amphibious assault. Although winds had nothing to do with the timing of the campaign, JICPOA said that during June and August the wind blew over Guam primarily from the east, making the sheltered west coast the better landing option.[127]

So, with a few exceptions, LVTs could land over west coast reefs during all tidal phases and average weather conditions, while landing craft could not pass over any of Guam's reefs. Troops and vehicles in landing craft would have to stop at the edge of the reef and disembark into LVTs or rafts.[128] Overall, JICPOA's intelligence influenced amphibious planners to land on the west coast nearest their primary objective, Orote Peninsula.

However, JICPOA said that Orote Peninsula had no beaches—only sheer cliffs—so IIIAC's infantry element could not attack it directly.[129] Therefore, they chose indirect landing beaches at Agat and Asan, which flanked the right and left of Orote. But because of reef conditions, the assault forces would be able to land on the beaches only in LVTs. This reduced the flexibility of landing operations. Equipment, provisions, and perhaps even follow-on forces would have to transfer at the outer edge of the reef from landing craft to LVTs, depending on their availability.[130]

JICPOA's analysts described the specific landing zones in greater detail with text, maps, and photographs. For the southern landing beaches, the report stated:[131]

> The reef is broad (800 yards) in the center of this stretch but narrower at each end. All craft drawing more than two feet, except amphibious tanks, would have to unload at the reef edge. The southern part, near POINT FACPI, is not very favorable but DADI beach, at the northern end, is somewhat better. The sand beach is about five to ten yards wide and gives access to the main military area.

For the northern landing beaches, JICPOA declared:[132]

> Reef is 300 to 700 yards wide and could not be crossed by landing craft except through narrow channels. LVT's could reach beach but there are forbidding hills and cliffs inland. Road communications to other parts of the island from AGANA, north of POINT ADELUP, are good.

The accurate intelligence contributed to a successful assault at both beachheads. Unfortunately, bad luck kept it from having the same effect for follow-on ship-to-shore operations on the southern landing beach. In a tactical combat snafu, a lone Japanese 75-mm gun and its crew miraculously survived the naval preliminary bombardment and caused the loss of about two dozen LVTs, the prime mover of men and supplies from ships to the beach. This, in turn, resulted in combat shortages of important logistics such as ammunition and fuel, which decreased U.S. firepower and mobility. Eventually, the Marines enveloped the position from the rear and destroyed it, but the resulting damage it inflicted to logistics operations continued to impair the campaign.[133]

Nonetheless, marines and naval landing teams alleviated some of this pressure with unique logistical procedures. They installed about twenty-five cranes at the edge of each landing area's reef to speed up offloading from ships into LVTs and trains of rubber rafts. These improvised operations contributed to the movement of logistics from forty-two transports and twenty-eight tank landing ships (LSTs) during the first phases of the campaign.[134] Good intelligence on the reef surrounding Guam helped commanders solve this serious problem.

Although JICPOA and the fleet's intelligence staffs were never able to collect and process better information on the intricacies of Guam's terrain, they were able to produce elementary geographic intelligence sufficient to design an effective plan of attack. Their intelligence told operations planners that the northern portion of Guam consisted of a wide, vegetation-covered plateau with three small mountains. The rest of Guam contained jagged, mountainous terrain with steep peaks and rivers that gradually subsided into softer, steep rolling hills farther south. A long, looming ridgeline about a thousand feet high paralleled the west coast. Coastal areas contained marshes, swamps, and crop fields.[135]

JICPOA's Guam information bulletin also provided a detailed written description of the island's difficult terrain, especially in the interior. The report stated that this information came from the "Guam Reconnaissance Officer" who in 1914 hiked all over the island and filed a brief on his findings. He discussed the difficulty of travel throughout Guam because of its scraggly terrain—steep cliffs, high mountains, deep gorges, and thick jungle.[136] But this was only a written description and did not contain topographical maps. Still, the assault troops had a good idea of the terrain they would be fighting on and that the Japanese would exploit it militarily. As a result of the basic terrain intelligence, operations planners steered infantry assault units into advantageous avenues of approach to seize their objectives. Furthermore, although the attack echelons did not have intricately accurate topographical maps, marines and soldiers knew that they faced tough terrain. Therefore, when they landed on the island, the impositions imposed by the rough ground did not shock them, a welcome contrast to the experiences of the Saipan invasion forces.

In another case involving geographic intelligence, drawings of the landing beaches made from submarine reconnaissance photos showed wide, flat, concave coastal plains behind the landing beaches where marines could assemble before striking inland.[137] From this type of intelligence, operations planners understood the basics of Guam's terrain at the landing beaches. This enabled them to direct assault troops to utilize the natural wedges at each beachhead to first attack the high ground, a vital strategic necessity, and then proceed with taking the rest of the island.

Yet the absence of detailed topographical intelligence eventually took its toll. Because infantrymen did not know the exact terrain features they faced, tactical maneuvers were arduous. They knew Guam's general elevations and depressions, but for infantry assaults, this was not enough. For example, when the Third Division penetrated the heights behind the northern beachhead, its infantry commanders became confused as to their exact location. As a consequence, none of its regimental combat teams linked to one another on a horizontal front. Dangerous gaps developed in the division line, and the Japanese fought hard to exploit them, racking up Marine casualties. The enemy poured troops into these gaps and attacked the regiments on their flanks, constantly probing for weak points.[138] Only

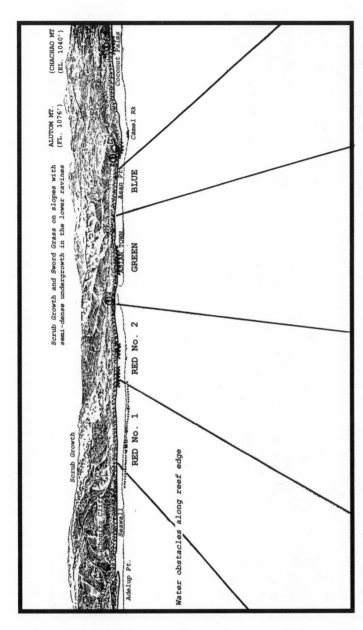

Northern Landing Beaches, Guam. Drawing, from submarine reconnaissance photos. This one shows the northern landing beaches on Guam. Commander, Task Force 53, Op. Plan A162-44, 7 June 1944, Guam; Appendix 30 June 1944

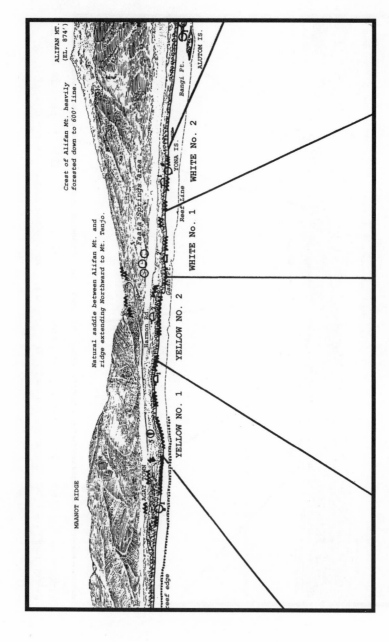

Southern Landing Beaches, Guam. Drawing, from submarine reconnaissance photos. Commander, Task Force 53, Op. Plan A162-44, 7 June 1944, Guam; Appendix 30 June 1944

adept forward fire controllers who directed artillery into the gaps saved the Marines from continued Japanese onslaughts.

Fortunately, U.S. combatants were not universally restricted by Guam's difficult terrain because the island had an excellent road system. JICPOA knew that the majority of military operations on Guam would revolve around road trafficability,[139] and it produced excellent intelligence on the island's road system. Information Bulletin 52-44 described Guam's road network as containing three different types of roads. Class "A" roads were two-lane, all-weather, and surfaced. Class "B" roads were one-lane, dry-weather, and nonsurfaced. The third type consisted of small trails or "bull cart" roads. JICPOA also described which roads could handle heavy and light traffic.[140] Most importantly, it pinpointed the location of these roads on a Guam road map.[141] Intelligence analysts discovered that a good system of class "B" roads twisted through the mountainous area east of Agana, the northern landing zone.[142]

Once ashore, the Marines used these roads to transport infantry on trucks to where the Japanese were entrenched—the high ground behind the landing beaches.[143] When they arrived near their destinations, they disembarked and closed in on the enemy. Tanks used these same roads to support them with 75-mm cannon and .50-caliber machine-gun fire. The mobility and tank support helped the marines and army troops attack Japanese positions with speed, concentrated mass, and heavy firepower, which was more effective than lone infantry navigating by foot over long distances and up Guam's jungle-covered slopes. Similarly, marines put tanks on the roads that paralleled the landing beaches as roving artillery to blast fortified cave positions on the cliffs that overlooked the sea.[144]

In another case, JICPOA's road intelligence helped operations planners design and execute the last assault on organized resistance on Guam on Orote Peninsula. Interestingly, in a unique case for Guam, JICPOA also provided detailed topographical intelligence on the marshes and swamps that flanked roads leading into Orote. Combined, the intelligence provided an excellent picture of natural barriers and avenues of approach—in other words, where assault forces could go, and where they could not go. JICPOA's analysts probably collected this information from U.S. Navy and Marine Corps sources that undoubtedly included maps of the Apra Harbor base and airfield. Armed with this intelligence, in the last week of July 1944, the ground assault force massed tank-infantry teams on the roads leading into Orote and, supported by heavy artillery fire, drove into fanatical and well-constructed Japanese resistance. By 29 July, U.S. forces had overcome the enemy and secured the peninsula.[145]

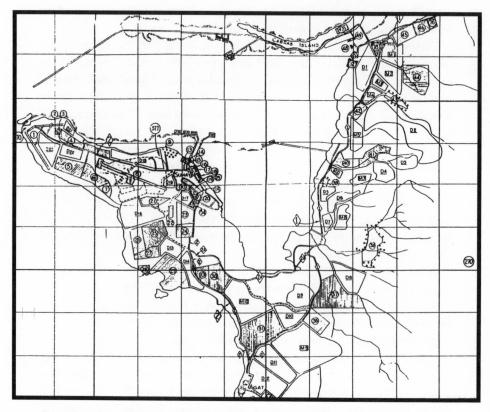

Operations Map Showing Roads on Orote Peninsula. This is an example of road intelligence for Guam. The author found no road map for Guam in any of several JICPOA information bulletins about Guam. Commander, Task Force 53, Op. Plan 1-44, 11 May 1944, Guam; Appendix 30 June 1944

The above scenarios played out repeatedly during the operation to seize Guam. Roads provided the key to victory, so whenever possible, infantry commanders directed convoys of tanks and infantry throughout the island and systematically destroyed enemy-infested areas. Vital supply trains followed suit, and U.S. logisticians were able to ship supplies into combat zones, rear service areas, and command and control centers as the operation matured.[146]

Unfortunately, a tactical problem marred the results of the good road intelligence. Trucks and other wheeled vehicles were not readily available to the combat troops, and they never received as many as requested. Only 50 percent of the Third Division's trucks landed in the first days of the campaign. The rest never arrived. III Amphibious Corps suffered from a truck shortage, and V Amphibious Corps had none to spare. Mechanical problems and rain-soaked roads further impeded vehicle movement—not to an extent that they threatened the campaign, but they did impede the tempo of the attack.[147]

Regarding enemy order of battle, initial estimates from radio intelligence in May estimated as many as 6,900 Japanese occupied Guam. Fortunately, JICPOA and fleet linguists had numerous Guam order-of-battle documents from the Thirty-first Army headquarters on Saipan, which stated that 18,657 Japanese troops occupied the objective. Marine Corps postwar records list the defenders as numbering 18,500.[148] Captured documents also disclosed that the Japanese occupied terrain that overlooked potential landing beaches on the west coast and the high ground beyond,[149] but official sources say that photographs still provided the bulk of intelligence for the campaign.[150] Apparently, the captured documents focused mainly on Japanese naval units and did not include every unit on Guam. Furthermore, they did not reveal the exact location of each of these units. Still, documents did reveal the exact location of coastal defense guns, a major benefit to preliminary bombardment planners.[151]

Although the number of troops chosen for the assault, fifty-six thousand, fell short of the three-to-one ratio required to conquer a defender, intelligence had indicated that a little more than half of the Japanese on Guam defended coastal areas. The rest had positioned themselves well behind the landing beaches and throughout the northern end of the island. So the fifty-six thousand U.S. servicemen essentially faced around ten thousand Japanese during the initial assault, an acceptable ratio. Shortsightedly, the Japanese did not concentrate their mass on the high ground of Guam's west coast, the most ideal defensive area on the island. If they had, Marine Corps and Army casualties would have been much higher, and the campaign would have taken longer.

Nevertheless, at the end of the battle for the beaches and Orote Peninsula, U.S. forces had killed more than half of the Japanese on the island. But from that point to 15 August 1945, patrols of infantrymen and U.S.–trained locals engaged and killed over eight thousand Japanese holdouts.[152] None of these operations, however, were in doubt. The Japanese did not consolidate or execute significant attacks. On the other hand, despite the obvious U.S. victory, the Japanese never actually surrendered the island. Some remained alive and hid for years after the war's end. Cpl. Yokoi Shoichi held out on Guam until January 1972, his uniform long gone, his rifle still in working order.[153]

Perhaps the most successful facet of intelligence and the Guam campaign deals with the naval preliminary bombardment. Intelligence from the captured Thirty-first Army documents, combined with the late June photographs, enabled Admiral Conolly to establish a special preliminary bombardment intelligence section to target Japanese shore defenses. Intelligence Section, Group 3, Amphibious Forces, Pacific, prepared the map. This special intelligence group appears to have been assembled in the field from fleet intelligence and JICPOA personnel. Part of the intelligence that contributed to the bombardment map came from JICPOA-interpreted documents, most likely IJN documents captured on Saipan. These told the exact or approximate location of shore defenses and many weapons positions on the high ground behind the landing beaches. Specifically, the IJN documents discussed defense construction activity through May 1944.[154] Aerial photographs from before and up to June 1944 also contributed to the preliminary bombardment intelligence map, although cloud cover hindered complete interpretation for the entire area of landing operations.[155] Their efforts produced a document titled "Defense Installations—Island of Guam," which was a top secret gridded bombardment map that was downgraded to "restricted" once the battle began.[156] Even with the cloud cover, the intelligence proved accurate enough for Conolly to accomplish his mission with outstanding results.

To achieve such ends, intelligence analysts and bombardment planners divided the island up onto zones that overlaid the gridded bombardment map. Analysts labeled each zone with a common American first name. For example, the northern landing beaches included zones "Ralph," "Dick," "Bob," "Bill," "Bert," and "Jake." The high ground behind the beaches included "Sal" and "Ann." Analysts pinpointed weapons positions in these zones with specific circular symbols, as they had for every intelligence map in past campaigns. For example, half-black and half-white circles indicated AA guns. Black circles with a white line running through them indicated coast defense guns. Various types of zigzagged or dotted lines indicated trenches and barbed wire. If analysts saw what they thought was defense activity in a photograph but were unable to tell exactly what it was, they indicated the area with a dotted circle and labeled it "Activity."[157] The defenses map also demonstrated that all types of weapons—machine guns, covered artillery, AA weapons, coast defense guns, and anti-boat weapons—covered the landing beaches from barbed wire-protected trench lines, pillboxes, and similar concrete fortifications. When the intelligence analysts and operational planners finished their work, they had produced an accurate picture of enemy shore defenses and a semiaccurate one of the area behind the beaches. Afterward, they disseminated their map to Admiral Conolly's naval preliminary bombardment task force, which used the information to target each Japanese defensive position.

The information helped Conolly execute a careful and destructive naval preliminary bombardment that devastated shore-based opposition to the landings.[158] Admiral Conolly claimed that his goal was to "get the troops ashore standing up,"[159] and this he did. Almost all the Japanese shore defenses were destroyed, and most of those that were not had been vacated out of fear of the harsh thirteen-day rain of naval artillery. While several

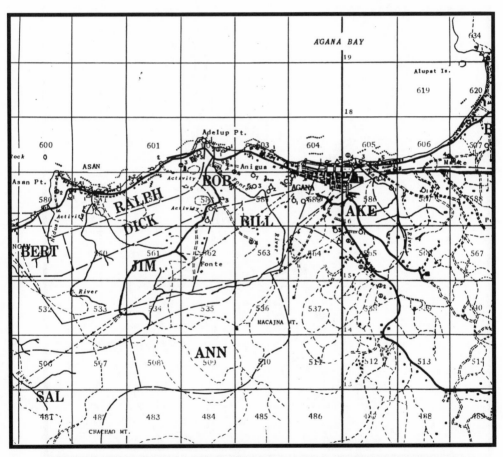

Operations Map, Defenses around Northern Landing Beaches, Guam (Zone "Ralph"). A temporary field intelligence unit that included JICPOA personnel created the map. Various circle designs indicate defenses. "Activity" indicates enemy actions of an undetermined sort. Commander, Task Force 53, Op. Plan A162-44, 7 June 1944, Guam

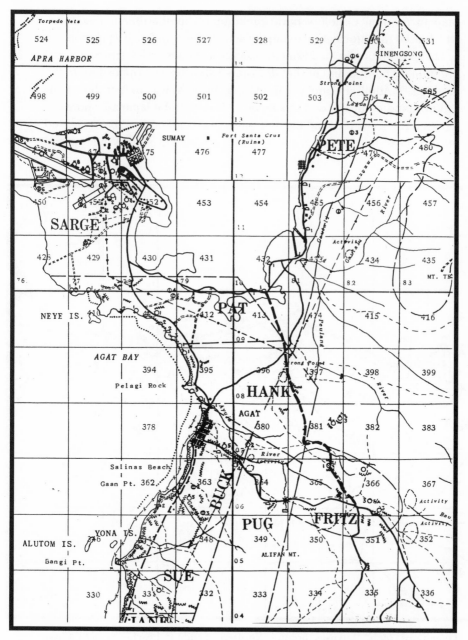

Operations Map, Southern Landing Beaches (Zone "Buck" and Orote Peninsula). A temporary field intelligence unit that included JICPOA personnel created the map. Various circle designs indicate defenses. "Activity" indicates enemy actions of an undetermined sort. Commander, Task Force 53, Op. Plan A162-44, 7 June 1944, Guam brave and lucky Japanese did survive the incredible bombardment, in most cases, they offered feeble resistance. During the amphibious phase of the attack, the marines did not receive any serious return fire until they had consolidated their beachheads. For example, in the Third Marine Division's area of operations, casualties on W-Day numbered 697. Most of the fire that the marines did receive came from high ground behind the beaches.[160]

Conolly's bombardment stands as one of the principal reasons that the U.S. troops did so well on the island. Casualties suffered during the landing phase, usually the bloodiest phase of an assault, were astoundingly light, especially if compared to Saipan. This meant that the United States had thousands of fresh troops with which to advance inland instead of a force battered and depleted by deadly shore fire. More important, the bombardment allowed the first few waves of landing teams to mass their war material on the beachhead without being pummeled, effectively sealing the fate of the Japanese defending Guam.

Enemy resistance increased as the marines moved inland, but the preliminary naval bombardment still showed its successful effects. The pounding had ruined the organization of Japanese defensive sectors. Each sector had served as an independent cell with its own defense, logistics, medical, and command and control units. The turmoil wrought by the bombardment forced Japanese field hospitals, for example, to evacuate their positions and move inland to escape destruction. Other rear service echelons, such as logistics units, followed suit. This overextended and disorganized the defensive sectors, rendering them less effective. Injured Japanese troops had to travel at least twice as far to receive medical attention. Supply trains had to travel twice as far to transport ammunition and water. Command and control units had to strike their posts and communications equipment and relocate. All of these actions clogged interior lines of communication and dispersed the enemy over a wide area. In addition, the U.S. forces noticed that the Japanese fought as if dazed and confused from the intense bombardment, a beating that undoubtedly upset the equilibriums of each surviving soldier. By and large, the preliminary naval bombardment, based on accurate intelligence, ensured that the Japanese could not effectively resist the landings.[161]

Regrettably, intelligence efforts did not locate as many Japanese defenses on the mountains behind the landing beaches as it did on the landing beaches. In addition, mountain defenses that analysts did manage to locate were nearly impervious to the naval preliminary bombardment because they occupied reverse slope positions.[162] In contrast, the Japanese could elevate their weapons and fire on U.S. forces on the beaches below.

To overcome these defenses, marines and army troops attacked them via infantry assault with tactical air support. Thousands of enemy troops protecting the guns made this more difficult.[163]

The battle for Guam closed with a moving ceremony on Apra Harbor's parade ground at the old Marine barracks. Admiral Spruance and his two infantry counterparts, Generals Smith and Geiger, both attended. Local inhabitants also attended the ceremony, thankful to be rid of the Japanese who had promised liberation but had given only racist grief. Nimitz and the JCS welcomed the recapture of Guam for its great symbolic importance. It signified the first piece of U.S. territory wrestled back from the Japanese since the war began.[164] Most important, now Nimitz had his forward naval base and command control center to push his offensive farther into enemy territory on the final leg of the "Road to Tokyo."

Conclusion

JICPOA produced good intelligence for the Guam campaign based on hard work and luck. Aerial reconnaissance conducted at regular intervals generated a mass of raw data that analysts used to produce an excellent analysis of Guam's hydrography, a rudimentary but useful analysis of its terrain, and an effective assessment of the enemy's order of battle. Documents from Saipan, captured by chance and exploited with skill, greatly bolstered U.S. intelligence efforts, especially with regard to the devastatingly efficient naval preliminary bombardment. U.S. military data, open source documents, and POWs complemented JICPOA's classified material and ensured efficient collection and processing phases.

But intelligence could have been better. In fact, it should have been superb. Nimitz, Geiger, and Spruance had all of May, June, and July to order more thorough aerial surveillance of the target. This might have revealed more Japanese troops and the heavy weapons positions hidden in the mouths of caves and on the reverse slopes of the mountains behind the beaches in the enemy's intense effort to fortify the area. Aircraft specifically designated to reconnoiter Guam's coastal mountain range could have spotted construction of such a large defensive line. Yet, it is obvious that operations planners were more concerned about Guam's shore defenses,[165] possibly because captured documents from Saipan did not emphasize defense of the high ground. This possibility poses serious questions concerning overreliance on enemy documents versus basic military common sense. Naturally, the Japanese would defend the high ground, so why did U.S. forces neglect to thoroughly reconnoiter the area? Was it simply because of the documents captured on Saipan? Official records do not shed light on this question.

Finally, the fact that more detailed information did not exist on Guam's terrain is a travesty. The island had been a U.S. possession since 1898,[166] yet no serious effort had ever been undertaken to accurately map it. The U.S. Navy used Guam as coaling station and a port, and it understood all too well the overwhelming danger imposed on Guam by the Japanese. In fact, in 1936, some of its officers unsuccessfully begged Congress to authorize placing heavy defenses on the island.[167] It is strange then, that the U.S. Navy did not realize the value of collecting intelligence on its own base before disaster hit in December 1941. Similarly, the Marine Corps had been studying the possibility of retaking Guam from the Japanese in the event of war since 1936, yet it never collected enough geographic intelligence on the island to support such an effort.[168] With all that time and diligent study, why did the U.S. military fail to acquire easily attainable, effective intelligence on their own island to use in the event of war? The reason undoubtedly resides in the historically negative attitude of the military toward intelligence, a phenomenon that came to haunt the United States during the Pacific War and resulted in unnecessary loss of life, war material, and time.

Nevertheless, Guam demonstrates the value of broad-based collection and stands as a model for all-source intelligence operations. JICPOA drew from as many sources as possible, including open sources, photo intelligence, captured enemy documents, and human intelligence. Broad collection can result in a wide variety of data providing a comprehensive perspective of the objective. It also allows analysts to cross-check pertinent subjects for authenticity. This process requires diligence but can reap valuable returns for operations planners and combatants alike.

Guam also makes evident that effective direction and proper use can turn intelligence into a force multiplier. Admiral Conolly directed a unique, makeshift cell of JICPOA and fleet intelligence units to process collected data on Japanese defenses solely for the purposes of the naval preliminary bombardment. Conolly's foresight and the hard work of the men under him resulted in extremely accurate targeting. Then he correctly applied the intelligence, which neutralized Japanese beach defenses. The bombardment also destroyed the enemy plan of defense and made them easier to defeat. Combined, these factors made the marines and army troops on the ground more formidable than their physical force structure, which helped achieve victory.

Operation Forager: Tinian

Campaign Background

During one week in August 1945, U.S. B-29 bombers took off from a tiny island in the Pacific called Tinian, dropped two atomic bombs on Japan, and put an end to World War II. The story of the bombings is well known, but, oddly, the story of the assault on Tinian on 24 July 1944 is not.[169] The Tinian campaign set the standard for successful amphibious operations. In fact, Gen. Holland M. Smith claimed that Tinian was "the perfect amphibious operation in the Pacific War."[170]

The Marines secured the island with astonishing speed and sustained relatively few casualties. The campaign took only nine days and cost 328 Americans KIA,[171] and 1,571 WIA, light casualties compared to other campaigns in the Pacific. The Japanese, in contrast, suffered about eight thousand KIA, practically their entire garrison.[172] Admiral Spruance praised the assault as "brilliantly conceived and executed."[173] The success of the campaign in part resulted from near-perfect intelligence on Tinian's hydrography, geography, and Japanese order of battle.

Target Location

Located in the bottom half the Marianas Islands and just three miles below Saipan, Tinian is 1,250 miles north of New Guinea and 1,500 miles east of Manila Bay.[174] The island is about eleven miles long and five miles wide at its greatest width, and it encompasses forty-eight square miles of land.[175]

Why Tinian?

Nimitz and the JCS included Tinian within Operation Forager for two simple reasons. First, the island sat just three miles south of Saipan and contained a sizable Japanese garrison that posed a security threat to U.S. forces in the vicinity. Air base personnel on nearby Saipan did not need Japanese on Tinian launching amphibious raids to hamper Allied base construction and B-29 traffic. Second, Tinian contained more flat land than the other Marianas Islands, and, therefore, could facilitate more vital B-29 airstrips—one of the main reasons for seizing the Marianas.[176]

The Tinian Intelligence Operation

The JCS had discussed Tinian as a potential target in 1943 when Nimitz hypothesized seizing the Marianas. Fleet photographic reconnaissance of the objective on 23 February began at the same time that surveillance aircraft over flew Saipan and Guam. U.S. pilots flew additional reconnaissance

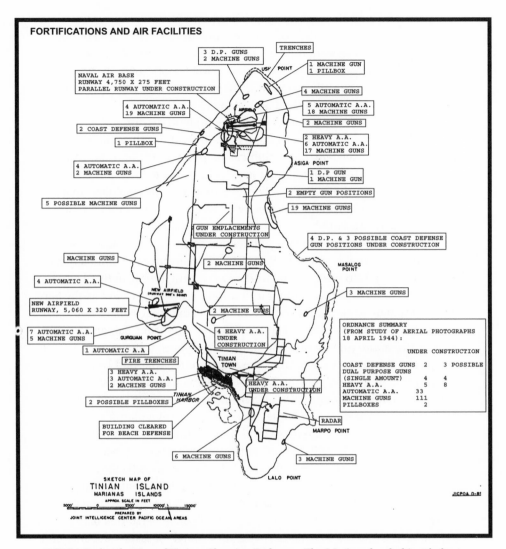

FORTIFICATIONS AND AIR FACILITIES

JICPOA Prebattle Map of Tinian, Showing Defenses. The Marines landed just below Ushi Point on the northwest coast, established a defensive perimeter inland, and then swept south to seize the remainder of the island. JICPOA Information Bulletin 73-44 (with graphics enhancement) missions on 18 April, and as usual, JICPOA and FRUPAC concentrated on intercepting Japanese radio communications in the Tinian area of operations. Initially, these were the only collection operations aimed at Tinian, but more would follow. In the meantime, however, photographs and reference information contributed to JICPOA's primary Tinian information bulletin—number 73-44, published on 10 May 1944.

Despite the lack of multiple sources, the bulletin disclosed the basics of Tinian's hydrography, geography, and order of battle with accuracy.[177] JICPOA produced excellent topographical maps of the island, and photographic analysts had pinpointed a large number of enemy gun emplacements, shown on the bulletin's "Fortifications and Air Facilities" map. In this regard, JICPOA's analysts correctly revealed the basic Japanese defensive scheme for Tinian.[178]

But two months separated the publication of the Tinian information bulletin and the actual assault, so JICPOA field intelligence personnel, mostly linguists and photo interpreters, worked in conjunction with the fleet's intelligence staffs to gather more information on the target. And as the Saipan campaign wrapped up, information became increasingly bountiful. Language officers translated captured documents from Saipan that disclosed the entire enemy order of battle for Tinian—a major intelligence coup. The documents came from the same source that had been helpful with the Guam campaign—the Thirty-first Army Headquarters. Interrogators interviewed Japanese POWs from Saipan, who contributed still more information. Prisoners helped decipher the defensive plan for Tinian regarding the location of Japanese infantry positions.[179] Overall, there were three major instances of POWs on Saipan supplying intelligence for Tinian. A captured Japanese pilot gave details on Tinian's air base facilities and garrison, an infantryman added to what the pilot said, and natives on Saipan provided details on Tinian's reefs and elevations.[180] There were twelve occasions on Saipan when infantry forces or intelligence personnel discovered Japanese documents that discussed a wide range of issues dealing with Tinian. They included map collections and individual documents that discussed the size of the garrison, how many weapons it had, what type of weapons it had, and the hydrographic conditions that surrounded the island.[181]

Furthermore, one week after landing on Saipan on 16 June, U.S. forces had secured the lower half of that island and had begun to use it as an aerial reconnaissance base for intelligence operations against Tinian. Air reconnaissance continued through June and up to 24 July, so photo analysts had plenty of data to work with.[182] A combination of JICPOA, fleet, and InterpRon Two photo interpreters on Eniwetok analyzed this material.[183] Astoundingly, photographs, along with document intelligence, revealed all but three main weapons positions on Tinian.[184]

Operations planners in charge of the Tinian assault ordered that a special intelligence operation be conducted to find suitable landing beaches. The Japanese had heavily fortified the widest and most obvious landing beaches at Tinian Town. Therefore, during the first week of the Saipan invasion, aerial reconnaissance took oblique photographs of other possible landing sites, including two small beaches on Tinian's extreme northwest coast, designated White One and White Two. The excellent photographs showed the width of each beach: sixty yards for White One and 120 yards for White Two. The photos also showed the terrain beyond the beaches.[185] In July, Navy UDTs and Marine Reconnaissance units infiltrated these and several other potential if obscure landing beaches. They conducted full hydrographic surveys and reconnoitered Japanese beach defenses on each insertion, which resulted in top-grade hydrographic data on White One and White Two. The photographic intelligence and tactical reconnaissance influenced planners to choose these beaches as the landing beaches in spite of their small width and length.[186]

Chain of Command

The invasion took place under the aegis of Admiral Spruance. Rear Admiral Hill commanded the amphibious task force, and Vice Admiral Turner supervised the amphibious phase of the assault. Marine Maj. Gen. Harry Schmidt, who had recently replaced Gen. Holland Smith, commanded the V Amphibious Corps, which consisted of the Second and Fourth Marine Divisions with the U.S. Army's Twenty-seventh Infantry Division, minus one regiment, in reserve. These units had attacked and defeated the Japanese garrison on Saipan, and although they were salty combat veterans, their ranks were depleted from high casualty rates.[187]

Plan of Attack

The plan for seizing Tinian fell into five phases. First, artillery on Saipan and naval ships were to bombard enemy gun positions throughout the island. Second, the Second Marine Division would conduct a feint, landing off the coast of Tinian Town where intelligence had found the heaviest concentration of enemy fortifications and the best beaches on the island. In the third phase, Fourth Division marines were to land on White One and White Two and establish a beachhead for follow-on forces. However, as he had in the Marshalls, Turner wanted to land at Tinian Town despite its innumerable defenses.[188] It is unclear why Turner often lobbied to land on the most heavily defended beaches or on the most staunchly fortified islands. Regardless of his organizational prowess, this particular facet of his military thinking demonstrated an unimaginative approach to amphibious assaults. Fortunately, Smith did not share his vision of attack, and he successfully lobbied to land at White One and White Two. Phase four included penetration inland for three thousand yards and the establishment of a logistics base. In phase five, assault troops were to sweep south and seize the rest of the island.[189]

The Marines attacked Tinian on 24 July and routed the enemy in nine days. The feint succeeded in tricking the Japanese into thinking that Tinian Town would bear the U.S. landing, so the landings on White One and Two proceeded without a hitch. Nowhere on the island did the attackers experience one serious setback. Excellent intelligence on Tinian's hydrography, geography, and Japanese order of battle greatly contributed to the astounding victory. Pacific War historians Isely and Crowl stated that for Tinian, U.S. intelligence produced "the most accurate and detailed intelligence data to be made available to Marines in the war."[190]

How Intelligence Influenced the Campaign

The Japanese commander on Tinian, Col. Keishi Ogata, never thought that U.S. forces would try to land a major assault force over Tinian's northwest beaches because of their small size and depth.[191] But they did, and quite successfully. The Marines initially landed only two hundred men on White One in order to avoid cramming an entire regiment of a few thousand men onto such a minuscule shoreline, a maneuver that would have stalled the attack. The first wave secured the beach under little return fire and were reinforced immediately by a second company. Only then did the Marines land an entire battalion.

Since White Two commanded a wider shore, the Marines landed two battalions to secure a foothold, again under scant enemy fire.[192] After these two landing forces consolidated their beachheads, the bulk of assault units landed behind them. In addition, because intelligence had indicated that cliffs three to ten feet high flanked the landing beaches,[193] the USMC created an artificial landing zone over the beaches with specially designed ramps carried to the cliffs on LVTs. Shortly after, the man-made landing beach was augmented with pontoon causeways. Tanks, jeeps, and vehicles loaded with heavy equipment easily negotiated the steel bridges and kept the marines supplied with vital war machines and materials.[194]

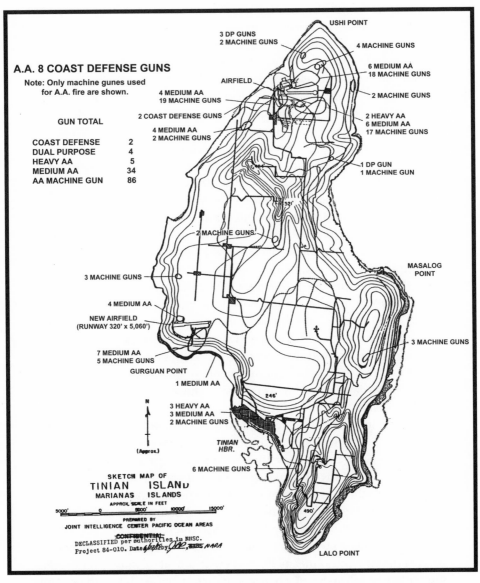

A.A. 8 COAST DEFENSE GUNS

Note: Only machine gunes used
for A.A. fire are shown.

GUN TOTAL

COAST DEFENSE	2
DUAL PURPOSE	4
HEAVY AA	5
MEDIUM AA	34
AA MACHINE GUN	86

3 DP GUNS
2 MACHINE GUNS

USHI POINT

4 MACHINE GUNS

6 MEDIUM AA
18 MACHINE GUNS

AIRFIELD

4 MEDIUM AA
19 MACHINE GUNS

2 MACHINE GUNS

2 COAST DEFENSE GUNS

2 HEAVY AA
6 MEDIUM AA
17 MACHINE GUNS

4 MEDIUM AA
2 MACHINE GUNS

1 DP GUN
1 MACHINE GUN

2 MACHINE GUNS

3 MACHINE GUNS

4 MEDIUM AA

NEW AIRFIELD
(RUNWAY 320' x 5,060')

MASALOG
POINT

7 MEDIUM AA
5 MACHINE GUNS

GURGUAN POINT

3 MACHINE GUNS

1 MEDIUM AA

246'

N

(Approx.)

3 HEAVY AA
3 MEDIUM AA
2 MACHINE GUNS

TINIAN
HBR.

6 MACHINE GUNS

SKETCH MAP OF
TINIAN ISLAND
MARIANAS ISLANDS
APPROX. SCALE IN FEET

5000'   0   5000'   10000'   15000'

PREPARED BY
JOINT INTELLIGENCE CENTER PACIFIC OCEAN AREAS

490'

LALO POINT

JICPOA Prebattle AA and Coast Defense Guns Map. The topographic estimate of Tinian's terrain is accurate. JICPOA Information Bulletin 67-44

Regarding geography, JICPOA described Tinian as "a broad, elevated limestone plateau" with vegetation-covered slopes and hills as high as five hundred feet in the north and south. Sugar cane fields covered 90 percent of the rest of the island.[195] JICPOA's excellent topographical intelligence specifically noted three elevations on the island: two steep hills located below the northern airfield—one 424 feet high and the other 521 feet high—and a 490-foot plateau on Tinian's southern tip. Cliffs bracketed the southeast coast, but flat land dominated the whole of Tinian.[196] While this intelligence proved valuable, many Marine commanders scheduled to participate in the assault personally scouted the island's terrain in light reconnaissance aircraft based out of Saipan. They included officers from the General Staff, regimental combat teams, and battalion landing teams.[197] Combined, JICPOA's intelligence and the several personal reconnaissance missions told operations planners that no impeding terrain would hamper their assault, and that the flat nature of the island would lend itself well to tank support and high mobility.

On the first day of the assault after the establishment of a secure beachhead, a few Marine tanks landed, crushed feeble pockets of resistance, and moved 1,400 yards inland.[198] Later that day, U.S. forces landed still more tanks and vehicles to add punch and speed to the attack. In fact, the marines on Tinian enjoyed more effective tank support than had been employed on any island assault in the Pacific to date, including Saipan and Guam.[199] Two days later, with the top half of the island secured, the Marines set up a logistics base and an artillery base on predesignated terrain east of the landing beaches.[200] After fending off a moderately heavy counterattack, on 28 July, the Marines split into two columns, one on the east coast and one on the west coast. They then mounted tanks and half-tracks and launched a two-pronged blitzkrieg that thrust with impunity over Tinian's flat terrain to the bottom tip of the island. The elevations near the north airfield caused them no delay. Intelligence had indicated that the Japanese had fortified these areas, so the Navy shelled them. Naval aviators complemented the shelling with napalm bombs; the first time this ordnance was used in the war. By no means did this eradicate all resistance on the hills, but it did neutralize the effectiveness of their defenses. When the marines arrived at the hills, they dispatched assault teams to secure the elevations and kept driving the main bodies of their two columns on a southerly avenue of approach. Some units penetrated through 7,300 yards of enemy-held territory on the day of the blitzkrieg.[201] In the process, the Marine troops eliminated all enemy resistance encountered.

Similarly, and again because of good intelligence, the marines put their knowledge of the island's terrain to use and trapped the remaining Japanese on a giant elevated terrace at the bottom of Tinian. First, the attackers blocked all avenues of escape that the Japanese might use to break out. Then they attacked the terrace. Combat included close-in fighting with small arms and grenades from cave to cave and foxhole to foxhole. In several instances, marines blew up cave entrances and sealed Japanese troops inside, a tactic they would have to use more often in future campaigns such as Iwo Jima.[202]

Such maneuvering, however, could not have been achieved on geographic intelligence alone. Near-perfect intelligence on the Japanese order of battle and the location of enemy weapons emplacements ensured a devastating preliminary bombardment that minimized ground combat. The order-of-battle information came from documents captured from Saipan, which stated that 8,900 Japanese defended Tinian. The documents further stated that their mobile artillery force consisted of the following weapons:[203]

Japanese Mobile Artillery Force on Tinian

Weapons	Number
70-mm guns	6
75-mm guns	12
37-mm high velocity cannon	6
Tanks	12
140-mm coast defense guns	10
120-mm dual purpose guns	10

Aerial reconnaissance from February and April 1944 had pinpointed main concentrations of Japanese defensive installations on Tinian's northeast coast, the northern airfield, the southwest airfield, Tinian Town, and Asiga Bay. Weapons in those areas included the following:[204]

Japanese Main Defense Guns—First Estimate

Weapons	Number
Coast defense guns	up to 5
Coast defense guns	4 plus 4 more under construction
Heavy AA guns	13
Automatic antiaircraft guns	33–35
Machine guns	111
Pillboxes	2

The additional aerial reconnaissance flown from Saipan discovered a remarkable number of additions to fortifications photographed earlier. For example, by the time J-Day had arrived, the Japanese had constructed twenty-three pillboxes along Asiga Bay on the west coast of the island. But the additions did not give the attackers pause because JICPOA and fleet intelligence were able to pinpoint every major Japanese weapon position and most machine-gun positions on Tinian. This intelligence helped Navy and Marine planners design a thorough preliminary bombardment that began on 13 June. It destroyed most Japanese support weaponry before the Marines ever set foot on the island.

Similarly, as J-Day neared, marines and army troops erected an artillery base on southern Saipan and joined the preliminary bombardment. Their weaponry included huge 155-mm "Long Tom" artillery that had a far reach and massive destructive power. Focusing on northern Tinian, the Saipan artillery base conducted 1,509 fire missions before J-Day. Saipan gunners increased the tempo of the bombardment on 16 July in preparation for the landing, and by 23 July, the entire preliminary bombardment had reached full force. Light reconnaissance aircraft flew over Tinian to locate fortifications that had escaped destruction so that gunners could eliminate them, and some targets were hit as many as three times to ensure their destruction.[205] By the time the Marines landed, the Japanese on Tinian had been subjected to the most accurate and destructive preliminary bombardment of the war.[206] Almost every Japanese defense installation on Tinian had been destroyed. For example, all twenty-three pillboxes that had been pinpointed on Asiga bay, the heavy defenses at Tinian Town, and most defenses around the airfields had been demolished. Except for the moderate counterattack on the night of J-Day, marines encountered little organized resistance.[207] Overall, the accuracy of the bombardment ruined Japanese defense capabilities and set the enemy up for a rout.

Granted that the preliminary bombardment helped insure victory on Tinian, it must be remembered that in land warfare the ground troops guarantee victory by physically gaining control of the area of operations. In this regard, the marines who invaded Tinian deserve credit for forcefully taking the island away from the Japanese. Since planners knew that there were about eight thousand Japanese on Tinian, they used two Marine divisions for the assault. Although the Second and Fourth Marine Divisions had just fought a severe battle on Saipan and were therefore somewhat weary and numerically depleted, they still retained effective combat readiness with a force of about thirty thousand, plus extra artillery and tank support. This figure satisfied the ideal three-to-one ratio desired for assaults against entrenched defenders. Knowing the Japanese order of battle beforehand also helped the first assault waves prepare for the Japanese counterattack that came the first night of the landing. Technically, operations planners utilized a more powerful order of battle to defeat that of the enemy, a tactic made possible by outstanding intelligence.

Furthermore, the location of Japanese troop concentrations and gun positions heavily influenced the excellent scheme of maneuver utilized by the Marines in securing Tinian. A basic point of amphibious warfare is to land, if possible, where the enemy is weakest to reduce exposure to enemy fire during both the vulnerable ship-to-shore movement and the establishment of the beachhead. In other words, it is more prudent to land where the enemy is not, consolidate a tactical hold on the objective, and then attack the enemy's main defenses instead of attempting the same maneuver directly in the face of heavy resistance. Since operations planners knew that the Japanese placed most of their heavy defenses at Tinian Town, Asiga Bay, and the airstrips, operations planners directed the initial attack against the enemy's weakest point—the northwest portion of the island. The planned scheme of maneuver also directed marines to the flanks and to the rear of Japanese defenses, the most advantageous avenues of approach for assaults against defensive fortifications.

JICPOA and the fleet's intelligence units made only minor mistakes in the Tinian operation. Photographs did not reveal, nor could UDTs and Marine Reconnaissance units discover and destroy, all of the mines on beaches White One and White Two. Many of them were horned mines. On White One, rust rendered the mines useless, but on White Two, operable mines delayed vehicle movement inland until engineers landed and blew them up.[208] In addition, aerial reconnaissance and photographic analysts did not recognize two six-inch coast defense guns near Tinian Town. Naval bombardment ships received heavy fire from the position, especially the battleship USS *Colorado* and destroyer USS *Norman Scott*. As a result of the gun battle, their casualties totaled sixty-two dead and 123 wounded. Four days later, the battleship USS *Tennessee* closed in and destroyed the enemy emplacement.[209]

Conclusion

In the major scheme of the assault on Tinian, intelligence miscues proved trivial. Tinian stands out as a model for outstanding intelligence operations for three rudimentary reasons. First, thorough and constant surveillance produced a vast amount of data that analysts used to draw a near-complete picture of the enemy situation,[210] a task accomplished because of the close

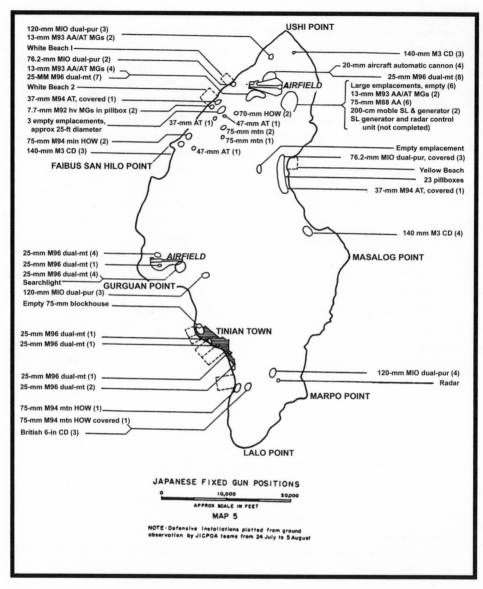

120-mm MIO dual-pur (3)
13-mm M93 AA/AT MGs (2)
White Beach I
76.2-mm MIO dual-pur (2)
13-mm M93 AA/AT MGs (4)
25-MM M96 dual-mt (7)
White Beach 2
37-mm M94 AT, covered (1)
7.7-mm M92 hv MGs in pillbox (2)
3 empty emplacements,
approx 25-ft diameter
75-mm M94 min HOW (2)
140-mm M3 CD (3)

FAIBUS SAN HILO POINT

37-mm AT (1)
70-mm HOW (2)
47-mm AT (1)
75-mm mtn (2)
75-mm mtn (1)
47-mm AT (1)

USHI POINT

AIRFIELD

140-mm M3 CD (3)
20-mm aircraft automatic cannon (4)
25-mm M96 dual-mt (8)
Large emplacements, empty (6)
13-mm M93 AA/AT MGs (2)
75-mm M88 AA (6)
200-cm mobile SL & generator (2)
SL generator and radar control
unit (not completed)

Empty emplacement
76.2-mm MIO dual-pur, covered (3)
Yellow Beach
23 pillboxes
37-mm M94 AT, covered (1)

140 mm M3 CD (4)

MASALOG POINT

25-mm M96 dual-mt (4)
25-mm M96 dual-mt (1)
25-mm M96 dual-mt (4)
Searchlight
120-mm MIO dual-pur (3)
Empty 75-mm blockhouse

AIRFIELD
GURGUAN POINT

25-mm M96 dual-mt (1)
25-mm M96 dual-mt (1)

TINIAN TOWN

25-mm M96 dual-mt (1)
25-mm M96 dual-mt (2)

75-mm M94 mtn HOW (1)
75-mm M94 mtn HOW covered (1)
British 6-in CD (3)

120-mm MIO dual-pur (4)
Radar

MARPO POINT

LALO POINT

JAPANESE FIXED GUN POSITIONS

0   10,000   20,000
APPROX SCALE IN FEET
MAP 5

NOTE: Defensive installations plotted from ground
observation by JICPOA teams from 24 July to 5 August

JICPOA Postbattle Map of Tinian. This map confirms the accuracy of prebattle intelligence. Hoffman, *The Seizure of Tinian* proximity of U.S–held Saipan to the target and the number of surveillance missions conducted against Japanese defenses. If Tinian had been off to itself, this might not have been possible.

Second, luck played a role in intelligence gathering, with the discovery of Japanese order-of-battle documents on Saipan. The documents just happened to be on Saipan, which the United States had attacked first in the Marianas. And the documents, amid the carnage of the attack, just happened to survive destruction to be discovered by servicemen who, upon recognizing the importance of their find, alerted their superiors to what they had discovered. Luck, however, played no role in the skillful and rapid exploitation of the documents. As on Eniwetok and Guam, JICPOA's long arm into enemy-held territory through its field intelligence personnel proved invaluable to campaign commanders. It also demonstrated the value of the policy that deployed linguists with combat echelons.

Third, the pooling of intelligence resources in the field played a major role in the Tinian intelligence operation, but JICPOA did not hold center stage. This was a team effort. Success came from the cooperation of JICPOA and the Pacific Fleet's intelligence units such as V Amphibious Corps's G-2 section, the Marine divisional intelligence sections, and InterpRon Two. All of these groups pooled their resources and analytical capacities to produce excellent intelligence. Their efforts exemplify two important ingredients for success in intelligence operations: flexibility and diversity—in collection, sources of data, and intelligence personnel.

What else does the Tinian operation say about intelligence? Of course, it says that thorough and accurate intelligence can have a positive impact on the planning and execution phases of combat operations, but it also says something more. The Tinian operation demonstrates that war planners do not have to sacrifice intelligence collection for the element of surprise if the situation can be exploited. Surprise is a vital element of warfighting, but some commanders through history have forgone thorough intelligence, settling for substandard intelligence to avoid warning the enemy. For example, during several campaigns in the Pacific such as Saipan, the commander denied thorough aerial reconnaissance, fearing that numerous reconnaissance flights would tip off to the enemy what island might be attacked and where U.S. forces might attempt an amphibious landing. The trade-off contributed to inadequate intelligence coverage of the island. In contrast, Tinian demonstrates an alternate strategy. With hard work and creativity under favorable circumstances (the proximity of Saipan), the Tinian task force achieved both tactical surprise and complete intelligence coverage. The results paid off handsomely and reaped the most efficient amphibious assault in the history of modern warfare.

The Strategic Implications of Forager

With the Marianas under U.S control, once again the SeaBees plunged into action and transformed the captured islands into major military installations and bomber bases for B-29s. Saipan was first.[211] Construction efforts there produced the temporary field headquarters of the XXI Bomber command,[212] the unit that would spearhead bombing efforts against military industrial targets in Japan. (Eventually, this command moved to Guam.) Although the SeaBees had not completed Saipan's runways by the time the first bomber arrived on 12 October 1944, the base was operational.[213] This bomber, named "Joltin' Josie," sported racy nose art—a sexy, scantily clad blonde woman toting a muzzle-loading rifle and wearing a raccoon hat.[214] To the novel entertainment of the servicemen and pilots on Saipan, other similarly painted aircraft followed, but the fanfare did not detract from the serious nature of their missions. On 1 November, a B-29 flew a photo reconnaissance mission over Tokyo. A few fighters flew up to intercept it but disengaged, uncharacteristically, after dueling with the aircraft's numerous .50-caliber machine guns; in future raids, the Japanese would try hard to crack the bombers' defenses. This time, though, at thirty-two thousand feet, the plane flew too high for flak to hit it. Therefore, for thirty-five minutes, its cameras took seven thousand intelligence photos of the ground below for the Joint Target Group in Washington to analyze for strategic bombing targets.[215] JICPOA and the other intelligence agencies likely analyzed the photographs for evidence of POW camps and Japanese military activity. By mid-November, Saipan had more than a hundred bombers lined up on its runways prepared to take the war to Japan.[216] By December, these aircraft were doing just that.

Meanwhile, the SeaBees excavated eleven million cubic yards of earth on Tinian to build the world's largest bomber base, which consisted of six runways, each one over a mile long.[217] With the advent of atomic weaponry, these strips would soon be the most important in the entire Pacific. Guam, however, proved to be the largest U.S. Central Pacific base during the war. A monument to SeaBee construction efforts, Guam had approximately eight million square feet of runways and six hundred thousand square feet of foundation for buildings,[218] including Nimitz's new command and control center, barracks, administrative offices, airplane hangars, two airports, and harbor edifices. Modern roads, including a four-lane highway, connected the base's facilities. Guam turned out to be comparable to similar facilities on the U.S. mainland regarding size, sophistication, and infrastructure.[219] The base housed over two hundred thousand personnel and boasted two colossal airfields,[220] the focal point of most of Guam's activities. The North Field began operating in February 1945, and the Northwest Field began operations in June.[221] At peak construction efforts, the SeaBees ran a thousand bulldozers around the clock to transform the island into CINCPAC's forward headquarters in the Pacific.[222] Guam was also important to the strategic bombing campaign. In just the last six months of the war, the Army Air Corps flew 6,339 bombing missions off of Guam's North Field alone.[223] Japan's factories and their immediately surrounding neighborhoods shook and burned from their destruction, under a massive 34,494 tons of bombs.[224]

It was these island bomber bases that placed the Japanese into a strategic form of check. Checkmate would occur only at "bayonet-point" upon invasion of Japan by ground troops or by the untested and controversial "atomic equation." Nevertheless, the U.S. Army Air Corps put the empire's war-making potential in grave danger. The bombing reduced the numbers of rifles, planes, tanks, and munitions the Japanese could make for their armed forces, therefore lessening their offensive and defensive capabilities—something the United States had not been able to do until this stage of the war. Indirectly, JICPOA helped U.S. forces achieve that end with its intelligence for Forager. It directly contributed to the strategic bombing campaign through its Target Analysis Section.

But the bombing campaign did not produce the immediate, dramatic results that air power proponents wanted. The missions hit several snags, among them a small island on the bombing route northwest of the Marianas called Iwo Jima. Harassment by fighters from Iwo, combined with other difficulties, led to less effective bombing. Furthermore, the bombing campaign against Japan's factories did not have a significant effect on the next island campaign under Nimitz—the horrific assault on Peleliu, a tough nut to crack for the First Marine Division, the U.S. Army's Eighty-first Infantry Division, and JICPOA as well.

4

PELELIU

Stalemate II

Strategic Background

During planning for the Marianas, the Combined Chiefs of Staff recognized that the Palau Islands might become part of a new Japanese line of defense after the Marshalls fell. The Palaus, including a large enemy air base on Peleliu, constituted the far southwestern reaches of the Caroline Islands, which were packed full of Japanese air bases, naval bases, and fortified islands. The CCS suggested that Nimitz seize the Palaus in coordination with the Marianas because control of both chains would seal the western and eastern sides of the Carolines. Additionally, General MacArthur had drafted the Palaus into his plan to retake the Philippines. Regardless of which strategy mattered more, the campaign commenced and finished under bloody conditions.

Campaign Background

The assault on Peleliu on 15 September 1944 is one of the least studied amphibious operations of the Pacific War, despite the fact that it was one of the most difficult ever attempted in U.S. Marine Corps history. While this assault did not inspire movies or high drama as did the assault on Iwo Jima, Peleliu did teach the U.S. military valuable lessons about logistics[1] and new Japanese defensive tactics. Perhaps the most interesting elements of this comparatively understudied campaign relate to insufficient intelligence.[2] In the end, U.S. Marine and Army casualties totaled 9,740, including 1,790 KIA.[3] Japanese casualties totaled 10,695,[4] most of whom were KIA.

In particular, the one Marine division and one Army regiment that seized Peleliu sustained about the same number of casualties as had the Guam assault force, which consisted of one Marine division, one Army regiment, and a Marine brigade. Needless to say, the battle did not unfold according to plan, and misconceptions concerning the operation occurred throughout the ranks. Based on the assumptions of operations planners and from prebattle intelligence estimates, Maj. Gen. William Rupertus, the First Marine Division commander, thought the operation would last only three days.[5] The operation actually lasted two months and six days.[6] Rear Adm. Jesse B. Oldendorf, commander of the preliminary naval bombardment task force, believed that his ships had destroyed most Japanese defensive positions on Peleliu. Oldendorf even called off the three-day preliminary bombardment early, believing he had run out of targets. In reality, hundreds of Japanese defenses had escaped destruction, and the preliminary bombardment proved inadequate.[7] Less optimistic participants of the operation, such as the legendary Col. Lewis B. "Chesty" Puller, First Regimental Commander, had anticipated stiff resistance despite assurances from the planners. The ensuing days proved him tragically correct.[8] Unfortunately, incomplete intelligence on terrain, caves, enemy fortifications, and order of battle was a primary reason that the campaign did not proceed according to plan.

Target Location

Peleliu is located in the Palau Island chain, a subchain of the Caroline Islands in the Central Pacific. The second to the last island in the Palaus, Peleliu is five hundred miles north of New Guinea and 450 miles east of the Philippines. Slightly smaller than Peleliu, Anguar Island sits five nautical miles to the south.[9] Babelthuap, the largest island in the Palaus, sits approximately thirty miles to the north. Peleliu is nearly six miles long and just over two miles wide at its widest point.[10] The official Marine record of the campaign states that the shape of the island resembles a lobster claw.[11]

Why Peleliu?

The Peleliu operation, code-named Stalemate II, evolved out of perceived strategic necessity. The two-pronged offensive toward Japan through the central and southwest Pacific was well under way by the summer of 1944. Admiral Nimitz had overseen the steady advance through the Gilbert, Marshall, and Marianas Island groups. Gen. Douglas MacArthur had fought his way from New Britain to the island of New Guinea, where he controlled its eastern and extreme western sides. From the western side of New Guinea, MacArthur was poised to strike at the Philippines and severely damage the lines of communication between Japan and its natural resources in Southeast Asia.[12] In between the two-pronged offensive sat the Carolines, a vast island chain filled with Japanese bases already bypassed and neutralized by the Allies. The Japanese in the Carolines posed little threat to the Central

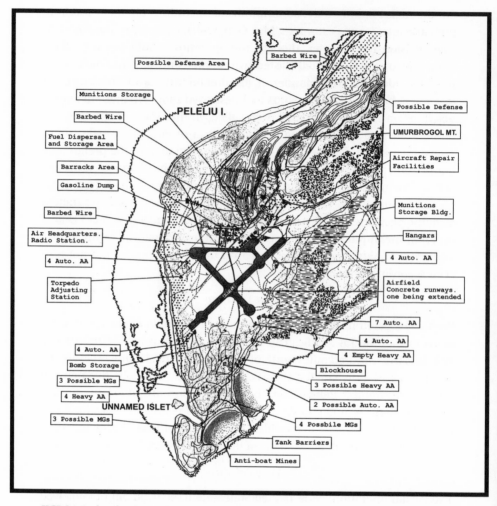

JICPOA Prebattle Map of Peleliu. The airbase is located in the center, and the Umurbrogol Mountains are just north. The Marines landed on the lower portion of the west coast, drove inland to the airbase, and then turned north to seize the mountains, where the Army joined the battle. JICPOA Information Bulletin 124-44

Pacific campaign, but the Palaus threatened MacArthur's northwest avenue of approach to the Philippines.[13] Strategically, MacArthur suffered from an unsecured right flank—a problem that both Nimitz and MacArthur believed had to be rectified.[14]

After meticulous study that began in the spring of 1944, planners targeted for attack the two extreme southern islands of the Palau chain, Peleliu and Anguar.[15] Originally, Nimitz and his planning staff had targeted several more islands in the Palaus through a massive operation named Stalemate. This had included an attack on the large and heavily fortified Babelthuap. Upon further analysis, they decided Peleliu and Anguar would suffice and called the new operation Stalemate II. Peleliu contained the largest air base in the area and boasted heavy defenses. Anguar, with its flat terrain, offered excellent potential for an additional airfield.[16]

The Peleliu Intelligence Operation

The Peleliu intelligence operation took seven months to complete, and it did not go smoothly. Collection operations produced data of varying accuracy on a sporadic basis, and analysts ended up processing three estimates of the enemy situation—the first differing tremendously from the last. Overall, JICPOA was not able to produce a high degree of advantageous intelligence in a timely manner for Stalemate II.

Photographs provided the majority of intelligence for the Peleliu operation.[17] Aerial reconnaissance missions over the objective began in March 1944 under cover of air attacks throughout the Palau chain, but these missions did not produce satisfactory data.[18] Therefore, reconnaissance continued with additional missions on 2–3 July, 26–27 July, 2 August, and 25 August, but none of these missions produced sufficient data, either.[19] Additional photographic intelligence came from the submarine USS *Seawolf,* which reconnoitered Peleliu from 23–28 June, followed by the USS *Burrfish* in July.[20]

The USS *Burrfish* spent two weeks circling the island trying to launch a five-man UDT for a reconnaissance of Peleliu's beaches. It eventually launched a team but collected little worthy hydrographic and beach defense information. UDTs completed their most effective missions on D-Day under cover of the preliminary naval bombardment.[21] Still, they were unable to penetrate shore defenses as they had on Tinian, and so the full extent of Japanese shore fortifications went unchecked by human reconnaissance.

Although radio intelligence collected information on Japanese troops on Peleliu, most order-of-battle information on the garrison came from Japanese documents captured during the Saipan campaign. These documents came from the Japanese Thirty-first Army headquarters[22]—the same source that had proved advantageous for the Guam and Tinian campaigns. Interestingly, historical accounts of the Peleliu operation report that U.S. forces captured a Japanese intelligence officer from the Thirty-first Army headquarters as well. Interrogators solicited his assistance in interpreting order-of-battle documents for Operation Stalemate II and for other

Japanese units throughout the Pacific. However, intelligence documents do not shed light on whether he was helpful or not.[23]

The primary difficulty in the Peleliu intelligence operation probably dealt with source corroboration. The most comprehensive Peleliu photographic mission, flown on 2 July 1944, did not produce clear photographs,[24] causing a serious dilemma. Without more readable photographs, JICPOA's analysts could not accurately analyze Japanese defenses. Furthermore, although they did manage to analyze some photos of the island, they could not truthfully assert that they had corroborated photographic intelligence with radio and document intelligence. In other words, the documents and radio intercepts indicated a particular situation on Peleliu, but photographs did not necessarily support the data.

This situation reveals how much stock JICPOA placed in photographs, because the radio and document intelligence appeared to corroborate one another. In past campaigns, such as Saipan, analysts relied almost entirely on photographs. Looking back over JICPOA's past intelligence operations, it seems that if analysts could not see it, they were less likely to trust it. It is no surprise, then, that analysts stated in writing that the Peleliu information bulletin, number 124-44, did not reflect the actual enemy situation.[25]

Nevertheless, the late August photographic reconnaissance revealed a more accurate picture of Japanese coast defenses than prior missions,[26] and some analysts had discovered additional ground forces in the target area by studying photos of naval personnel engaged in construction activity on Ngesebus Island, an islet attached to Peleliu.[27] However, intelligence personnel received and processed the photographs about two weeks before the Marines landed on Peleliu's beaches, and the assault forces never saw them. Instead, commanders passed the resulting intelligence to the Marine forces already en route to the objective by visual signal from the assault task force flagship, a hasty and inefficient method of relaying important photographic intelligence material.[28]

But there was more late intelligence to come. Analysts discovered new and valuable order-of-battle information on Peleliu after they disseminated the August photographic intelligence. The new intelligence came from recently discovered documents from Saipan—Imperial Japanese Navy documents, to be specific.[29] In contrast, document intelligence in information bulletin 124-44 had come from IJA documents. Apparently, the new information indicated that the garrison on Peleliu was twice as large as previously thought, a disparity of major importance. But no one halted the operation, and assault forces continued into harm's way.[30]

The Peleliu Campaign
Chain of Command

Even though General MacArthur included Peleliu in his plans to retake the Philippines, the island sat within Nimitz's area of operations. He assigned the III Amphibious Corps to direct the assault. But IIIAC had unfinished business on Guam, so Nimitz created a temporary command and control echelon, X-Ray Provisional Amphibious Corps, to temporarily take its place during planning.[31] Nimitz assigned Admiral Halsey and the Third Fleet the responsibility for conducting the attack, but Halsey thought the operation was a waste of time. Through carrier raids in the Palaus and the Philippines, he discovered that Japanese air strength in the Philippines was not as great as previously thought and so recommended advancing the Philippines schedule and skipping the Palaus.[32] In hindsight, he was probably right, but Nimitz suspected that the unexpected could happen and that Japanese air strength in and around Peleliu might upset MacArthur's plans. Furthermore, JICPOA did not indicate that the Japanese had stiff defenses on Peleliu, and Nimitz had no reason to think that the battle would be a bitter one. So he took Halsey's remarks under advisement by advancing the schedule for the attack on the Philippines, but he continued assigning command positions for Stalemate II.

With that, he appointed Adm. Theodore S. Wilkinson to command the amphibious task force but not the actual Peleliu landing, a job left to his subordinate, Rear Adm. George H. Fort.[33] Rear Adm. Jesse Oldendorf conducted the preliminary bombardment. Maj. Gen. Roy Geiger, freshly arrived from Guam, commanded the III Amphibious Corps, the amphibious assault corps. His units consisted of the First Marine Division and the Army's Eighty-first Infantry Division.[34]

Plan of Attack

The Stalemate II attack plan consisted of three phases. Phase one, as usual, was the preliminary bombardment. During phase two, all three regiments of the First Marine Division, less one battalion in reserve, were to land on Peleliu and advance inland to seize the airstrip and ground adjacent to it. In addition, the Eighty-first Division would seize Anguar after the Marines had landed on Peleliu. In phase three, the Marines were to clear the northern portion of the island, the Umurbrogol Mountains.[35] Major General Rupertus, commanding general of the First Marine Division, estimated a three-day campaign.

When the Marines landed, phases two and three did not go according to plan, and as combat on Peleliu grew more intense, it became apparent that phase one had not, either. The Marines did manage to advance inland and seize the airstrip, but at a slow and costly rate. By the time they made it to the Umurbrogols, their ranks were so badly depleted that the 321st Regimental Combat Team of the Eighty-first Infantry Division on Anguar had to ship over to Peleliu on 22 September (D+7) and assist the Marines with phase three.[36] Inadequate intelligence on Peleliu's geography, enemy defenses, and order of battle contributed to the incredible hardships that U.S. forces had to face.

How Intelligence Influenced the Campaign

JICPOA's hydrographic intelligence proved correct. Its assessment of Peleliu's coastline included the island's east, west, and south shores. The Peleliu information bulletin stated that rocks and difficult surf conditions beset the south coast but that landing craft could operate there. The east coast presented similar surf conditions from the fall to the spring, and its reef varied. In the southeast, the reef was simply a few flat coral formations. The central part of the eastern reef was steep and narrow, and the northeastern portion extended 1,200 to 5,000 yards offshore. Analysts said that landing craft could pass over the reef at high tide. On the other hand, at low tide, landing craft would probably have to stop at the reef and disembark marines far offshore, possibly under fire, as had occurred at Tarawa.[37] In contrast to the southern and eastern coasts, the western coast had calm surf conditions. The west coast reef extended into the sea for over fourteen hundred yards in the northeast and up to five hundred yards in the southeast. Parts of the reef were segmented, which allowed for passage of landing craft.[38] In short, the hydrographic survey clearly indicated that the southern half of the west coast provided a more inviting landing beach than Peleliu's other shores. This intelligence undoubtedly convinced operations planners to choose the west shore opposite the airfield as the primary landing beach. Furthermore, the Peleliu information bulletin's "Defenses" map, which included defenses and topographic features in a single format, showed the west beach as flat and free of adjoining high ground that the Japanese might fortify.[39]

The Peleliu information bulletin's topographic analysis contained some accurate information but mostly mistakes regarding terrain features. It stated that Peleliu's northern peninsula contained the Umurbrogol Mountains, a four-thousand-yard ridge that had "many steep slopes and ledges."[40] It also declared that hills blanketed the area behind the southern portion of the west beach, and that the remainder of the island contained flat ground. The "Defenses" map showed that dense vegetation covered most of Peleliu, except for the nonmountainous regions of the extreme northern peninsula. This map, consequently, was the first of its kind that combined detailed topographic intelligence and enemy defenses in a single format in an information bulletin.[41]

The bulletin correctly presumed that the island's vegetation afforded the Japanese superb cover and concealment and that it would also hinder traffic inland. It further established that open areas and coconut groves blanketed the nonmountainous regions of the northern peninsula in picturesque tropical fashion. Maps showed that Peleliu's airfield, located at the central southern end of the island, was separated from the east coast by a strip of thick jungle and a mangrove swamp. Supporting text noted that the swamp would hinder movement on the southeast side of the island.[42]

Peleliu contained two small islets off its northwest peninsula—Ngesebus and Kongaru. A short footbridge connected Kongaru to Ngesebus, and a causeway, eight feet wide and two thousand feet long, connected Ngesebus to Peleliu. Neither islet offered formidable defenses, but Ngesebus contained a lightly defended, supplementary airstrip under construction.[43]

Regrettably, the terrain analysis suffered from three discrepancies. First, JICPOA's "Defenses" map did not accurately reveal a large coral outcropping three hundred yards long, a hundred and fifty yards wide, and about a hundred yards off the beach on the Marines' left flank. The outcropping stood about thirty feet high.[44] Japanese soldiers had fortified this natural castle with heavy armaments and machine guns. The outcropping surprised the First Division's landing teams because they had not been told that it was there. Chesty Puller had seen it and requested that naval gunfire destroy it, but it is apparent that the lower combat echelons were not privy to Puller's information.

After the battle, a Marine captain said of the outcropping that "[it] surpassed by far anything we had conceived of when we studied the aerial photographs,"[45] indicating that intelligence did not know it was there. As a consequence, the Japanese split the Marines' left flank and created a hole through which they could have poured troops, pivoted south, and charged down the shore, possibly destroying the beachhead. Fortunately, because of the "fog of war" or intense naval fire support, the Japanese were unable to exploit the gap, and the beachhead remained intact.[46]

Second, the "Defenses" map, with one exception later noted, did not accurately display terrain in most areas just off the beaches in the center of the Marine front. Assault forces relied on JICPOA's terrain intelligence, as

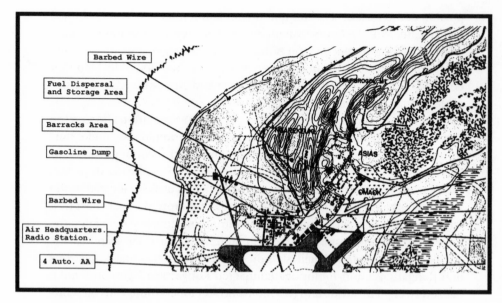

Barbed Wire

Fuel Dispersal
and Storage Area

Barracks Area

Gasoline Dump

Barbed Wire

Air Headquarters.
Radio Station.

4 Auto. AA

JICPOA Prebattle Map, Peleliu. It does not show the coral outcropping just northwest of the west corner of the air base. JICPOA Information Bulletin 124-44

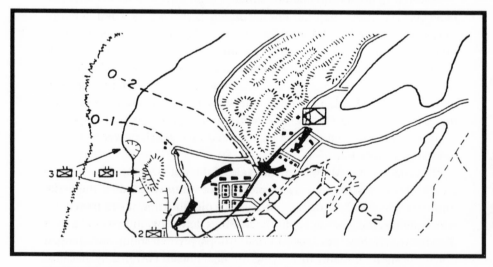

USMC Historical Map (Detail). This map shows the coral outcropping and the Marine units that assaulted it. Garand and Strobridge, *Western Pacific Operations*

demonstrated in the "Defenses" map, to negotiate the island.[47] To make matters worse, the ground element did not receive terrain maps in a timely manner because of the delay in achieving satisfactory photographic coverage.[48]

At any rate, JICPOA warned that the terrain off the beaches consisted of dense vegetation that would make an assault difficult. However, it also said that this ground was flat when most of it (with one exception) was not.[49] As a result, the marines encountered unanticipated terrain features that hampered their attack. Even the official Marine Corps record of the operation stated, "[R]iflemen were guided by maps that only sketchily portrayed the terrain."[50] This impeded tactical command and control and produced gaps in the front lines, as had happened on Guam.[51] But, again as in Guam, the Japanese never exploited their tactical opportunity on the Peleliu beachhead, and the marines pushed inland once they had secured their lines.

Third, JICPOA's assertion that the Umurbrogol Mountains had "many steep slopes and ledges" was an understatement. So, in effect, was JICPOA's terrain display on the "Defenses" map, which showed approximately fifteen Umurbrogol elevations as simple steep peaks[52]—not as menacing military obstacles, as was the case. A more accurate postbattle description in the official Marine Corps record described the Umurbrogols as "literally honeycombed with natural caves, a nightmare of crags, pinnacles, and coral rubble," and that "this type of terrain [lent] itself well to defensive tactics."[53] Over three thousand yards long and about four hundred yards at its greatest width, the Umurbrogols consisted of tightly knit coral elevations and depressions, sheer cliffs, unassailable ravines, and deep crevices. Much of the area did not allow effective infantry traffic, but the Japanese had infested it, and they had to be rooted out one by one.

Tragically, Marine commanders assumed that the Japanese occupied a thin horizontal front in these mountains, when in fact they had layered their positions in successive foxholes and caves throughout.[54] Not knowing any better, the commanders ordered their infantry to lance through what they thought was a single defensive line. When the marines advanced, the Japanese fired at them from all angles—flanks, fronts, from up high and down low, and even from behind. This is where the casualties mounted up for the Peleliu campaign and subsequently reduced the combat effectiveness of the First Division.[55] One battalion lost 70 percent of its manpower. Consequently, the 321st Regimental Combat Team of the Eighty-first Division had to be called in to relieve a Marine regiment. By mid-October, the entire Eighty-first Division had replaced most of the shot-up marines. Then began a dangerous, close-in war of attrition that began on 24 September and ended approximately two months later.[56]

But the Japanese did more than simply occupy this ideally defensive terrain. They complemented it with hundreds of manmade caves and weapons emplacements.[57] JICPOA infrequently mentioned caves in its analysis of the Umurbrogol Mountains.[58] To make matters worse for the attackers, Japanese cover and concealment techniques in the mountains made them nearly impervious to tactical air support and naval gunfire. The marines and army troops had no alternative but to root them out with small arms and light weapons.

It is obvious that combat in the Umurbrogols required teams of combat engineers and special weapons such as bazookas and flamethrowers to reduce enemy pockets. And although the entire First Engineer Battalion landed in support of the First Marine Division, combat reports made it obvious that this was not enough. Likewise, First Division had only a standard supply of special weapons, which made combat more tedious. The soldiers of the Eighty-first fared the same. Major General Geiger probably would have requested additional combat engineers and special weapons had intelligence accurately disclosed the nature of the terrain and Japanese defenses in the area.

When the campaign concluded, after-action reports lambasted prebattle terrain intelligence. A III Amphibious Corps report stated the following: "Unfortunately, the maps of PELELIU and ANGAUR were found to be extremely inaccurate in their representation of the configuration of the terrain." The same report asserted that hill masses displayed on maps were nothing like the actual terrain and that better photographs would have averted that misdirection. IIIAC analysts closed by saying that it was vital that combat troops receive the best and most accurate maps available to carry out their missions effectively.[59]

Similarly, the military survey in Information Bulletin 124-44 did not accurately demonstrate the enemy's capability to resist invasion, but JICPOA knew that, and so did its target audience. The Peleliu information bulletin began with a note to the reader stating: "Photographs of 2 July 1944 are not sufficiently clear to permit a thorough survey of enemy defenses on Peleliu."[60] This resulted in an indefinite guesstimation of enemy defenses and order of battle, and analysts did their best with the data at hand to describe weapons positions and also to pinpoint them on the "Defenses" map.

The bulletin indicated that the Japanese concentrated their main defensive positions, which were few in number, in the western and southeastern regions of Peleliu and toward the beaches in those areas. According to

JICPOA, the west beaches were covered with barbed wire but contained "few permanent defenses." In contrast, analysts believed that the area behind the beaches contained foxholes, trenches, tank obstacles, and pillboxes, which were all well concealed by the island's thick foliage.[61]

Further, Information Bulletin 124-44 affirmed that aerial photographs had revealed coast defense guns around Peleliu's shores but did not list how many or pinpoint their locations on the "Defenses" map. The map did show, on the other hand, twelve antiaircraft guns and six possible machine-gun nests on the west coast. It also pinpointed numerous positions on the east coast: four possible machine-gun nests, fifteen AA guns, four empty heavy AA emplacements, five possible AA guns, tank barriers, a small collection of boat mines, and one blockhouse.[62] Because of the swampy, uneven nature of portions of the east coast, most of these latter gun emplacements sat well inland at the eastern edge of the airstrip but were capable of defending the tarmac from attackers from the west. The map demonstrated one possible defensive area far north in the Umurbrogols but said nothing about caves in this area. Defenses there simply had not been spotted.[63] A separate topographic map listed several caves but did not show if they were fortified or not.[64] Lastly, the Peleliu information bulletin stated "mobile artillery is present on the island and is to be expected in the hills behind this area" (the east shore).[65]

Main Japanese defensive positions did in fact cover the western and southeastern portions of Peleliu, just as the bulletin stated, but in much greater numbers than first predicted. There were pillboxes, blockhouses, and coast defense positions all along the coast and in depth toward the airfield.[66] Sturdily built weapons emplacements containing 37-mm and 47-mm guns poured fire on the assault forces throughout D-Day.[67] Over half of First Division's thirty tanks received heavy coast defense fire upon ship-to-shore movement, but luckily, most survived. LVTs, however, did not fare as well. The Marines lost twenty-six the first day and at least forty more were seriously damaged.[68] By the sixth day of fighting on Peleliu, the Marines had encountered a multitude of defensive positions including three large blockhouses, ten fortified coral ridges, thirteen antitank guns, twenty-two pillboxes, and 144 reinforced caves.[69] Japanese defensive fortifications were well designed, constructed of concrete, coral, and limestone, and expertly camouflaged.[70] In summary, an after-action report of the campaign stated that while combat forces had enough intelligence to fight with, photographs prior to D-Day were not clear enough for analysts to discern vital aspects of the enemy situation on Peleliu—especially defensive installations.[71]

Neither did JICPOA or UDTs produce effective intelligence on mine-fields. The Peleliu information bulletin revealed antitank trenches, barbed wire, and beach obstacles along the island's west coast. Specifically, the bulletin said that there were 1,240 yards of boat obstacles, between 1,800 and 2,150 yards of barbed wire under water, and 1,200 yards of barbed wire on the beaches.[72] It said nothing, however, of the large number of mines found on Peleliu, and neither did the UDTs that destroyed Peleliu's boat obstacles shortly before the landings took place. Apparently, the Japanese had sown single- and double-horned mines along the west beaches. To these, they added conventional mines and aerial bombs rigged to explode as mines. After-action reports testified that the minefield ran a hundred yards inland in various places. Luckily for the marines, the majority of the horned mines did not detonate, and analysts were not sure why. It may have been because of rust corrosion—the same reason that horned mines on Tinian did not explode. One after-action report maintained that the Japanese did not correctly improvise triggering devices for the aerial bomb mines.[73] A Marine historian said that the preliminary bombardment had cut the detonation wires on many of the improvised mines and destroyed nearly all of the buried mines.[74] Fortunately, as with the fortified coral outcropping, mines did not impede the marines' advance inland to a serious extent, but they exemplified how dangerously lacking intelligence was for the campaign.

JICPOA had similar problems assessing Japanese order of battle on Peleliu. Analysts based their earliest order-of-battle intelligence on captured Japanese documents from the Thirty-first Army headquarters on Saipan.[75] Unfortunately, these documents discussed only what Japanese army units occupied the island. JICPOA suspected that IJN units also occupied Peleliu because, as previously mentioned, some photographs showed IJN personnel manning AA guns. Furthermore, although aerial photographs did show the location of some defenses, captured documents demonstrated that the Japanese had more weapons than had been spotted. JICPOA therefore was unable to corroborate photo intelligence with other sources. This probably led JICPOA's analysts to believe they were not seeing the actual enemy situation on Peleliu.

Nevertheless, JICPOA still managed to put together estimates of Japanese manpower and firepower for operations planners. Actually, as mentioned above, it made three estimates of the situation because documents kept trickling in from Saipan, and the fleet continued to fly photo reconnaissance missions over the objective. JICPOA's first enemy order-of-battle assessment came from documents that arrived at Pearl on 5 August 1944 and was included in Information Bulletin 124-44. Analysts estimated that 4,350 Japanese troops occupied Peleliu, with the possibility that a battalion of the Fifteenth Infantry Regiment accompanied them.[76] That put the total at approximately five thousand, as the following table indicates:[77]

Prebattle Estimate of Japanese Manpower and Weaponry on Peleliu

Unit	Number of Personnel
Second Infantry Regiment	3,200
First Infantry Battalion	900
1 battalion of the 15th Regiment*	Approx. 650
Part of the 14th Division's Field Hospital	250
Total	Approx. 5,000

* JICPOA Information Bulletin 124-44 stated that one battalion of the Fifteenth Infantry Regiment on Babelthuap might be on Peleliu.

Analysts advised that the Japanese probably had a great many weapons at their disposal, but they were not as specific as they had been in other campaigns such as Eniwetok. This was because the captured documents discussed only what Japanese units occupied Peleliu, not their firepower. Therefore, analysts consulted the Reference Section to find out what type of weapons these Japanese units had.

Among its many functions, the Reference Section kept a hard-copy database of every type of Japanese unit known to exist. Data on enemy units included wire diagrams that explained force structure and how many and what type of weapons they possessed. Since analysts working on the Peleliu campaign knew what units were on the objective, they looked up the wire diagrams of the respective units to analyze the size and firepower of the enemy garrison.[78]

Order-of-Battle Intelligence, Peleliu Information Bulletin 124-44*

Inf. Regiment:
   3 Ind Bns (36–40 LMG; 30–32 Grenade Dischargers; 6 HMG; 2 Inf Guns; 2–4 37mm AT guns each)
   1 Arty Bn (8 75-mm Mortar Field Guns and 4 75 or 105mm howitzers or guns.)
Inf Battalion:
   HQ (rifles and LMGs)

3 Rifle Cos: each has three rifle platoons (4 LMG and 3–4 Grenade Dischargers each) and one HMG platoon (2 HMG)
12 LMG; 9–12 Grenade Dischargers (2 HMG per Co.)
Inf Gun Co: 1 platoon of 70mm Battalion guns and 1 platoon of 37mm
AT guns. (2 70mm Inf guns; 2–4 37mm AT guns).
Arty Battalion
3 Batteries: (4 guns each). (8 75mm Mtn or Field guns; 4 75mm or
105mm howitzers or guns).

* This is exactly the way the information appeared in Information Bulletin 124-44,
in the section entitled "Strength of Enemy Ground Forces."

The bulletin assumed, moreover, that an Imperial Japanese Navy unit,
possibly the Thirtieth Base Force, manned Peleliu's air defenses, but captured documents had not confirmed this hypothesis. Analysts estimated
that Japanese AA guns would include 7.7-mm, 25-mm, 8-, 12- and 12.7-cm,
and possibly 15-cm guns. Correspondingly, they said that units comparable to the Thirtieth Base Force on other islands had used a wide array of
dual-purpose guns, so the Japanese on Peleliu might have the following
types of dual-purpose weapons: 8-cm and 20-cm mortars; and 12-, 14-,
and 15-cm guns.[79] Finally, analysts were not sure, but they thought that
there might be up to nine tanks on either Peleliu or Babelthuap; however,
none had been spotted.[80]

Just before the Peleliu information bulletin went to press, analysts made
their second revision of the enemy situation on Peleliu. JICPOA did not
mention the source, but it is evident that the revision came from the late
August photographs, because analysts used specific language in describing
the way certain defenses looked. For example: "An 'S'-shaped series of boat
obstacles located 100 yards offshore from the northern end of the beach
and extending southward for 300 yards." And "Entire bay obstructed by a
single line of anti-boat obstacles, pyramidal in shape, apparently of coral
construction."[81]

However, the second estimate consisted of only a slight revision of Japanese defenses and in a few cases a mere confirmation of what had already
been analyzed. JICPOA included the new information as an addendum at
the end of the bulletin: one blockhouse, eight heavy AA, 31–38 auto AA, and
5–15 machine guns. Unfortunately, the addendum must have been a rush
job because it did not state the location of these weapons.[82]

Despite the long listings of possible weapons on Peleliu, the final report
proved thin, but, as discussed in "The Peleliu Intelligence Operation,"
above, an interesting development regarding the problem evolved in late

August as the assault forces rehearsed landing procedures on Guadal-canal.[83] New intelligence from Saipan—more accurate information from the captured Thirty-first Army documents—became available. This initi-ated a third estimate of the enemy situation on Peleliu, one by both JICPOA and fleet intelligence echelons. The new documents, dated 28 August, claimed that there were between twelve and nineteen tanks on the island, along with an extra artillery battery and a mortar company.[84] Moreover, in-stead of five thousand Japanese on Peleliu, the new intelligence indicated that there were 10,700.[85] Japanese navy units comprised most of the addi-tions in manpower, as the following table demonstrates.[86]

Late Intelligence Estimates of Japanese Manpower on Peleliu

Units	Number of Personnel
2d Infantry Regiment	3,283
1 battalion of the 15th Infantry Regiment plus 1 artillery battery and 1 mortar company	1,030
1 tank unit	100
Signal, intendance, and hospital personnel	290
1 battalion of the 53d Brigade	685
45th Naval Guard Force	between 200–400
114th and 126th Naval AA units	600
204th and 214th Naval Construction Battalions plus parts of the 43d and 235th Construction Battalions	2,200
Air base personnel (Navy)	2,200
Total	Approx. 10,700

Higher numbers of Japanese defenders meant higher numbers of weap-ons and defensive fortifications, at least twice as much, and the fact that many of them were construction or air base personnel did not mean that they would not fight. Combined, they constituted a force larger than the Second Infantry Regiment. Fleet intelligence indicated that these units might man 2,200 rifles, thirty-six grenade dischargers, fifty light machine guns, one 75-mm gun, ninety-nine 20- or 40-mm AA guns, four 105–127-mm dual-purpose guns, five 3–5-inch coast defense guns, and two 20- or 40-mm anti-boat guns.[87] No matter what specific weapons these troops manned, however, it was obvious that the Japanese had more manpower and firepower than previously estimated, and seizing the island would be more difficult than expected.

Unfortunately, by the time JICPOA and fleet intelligence had analyzed the new information, the attack plans had already been laid, and the assault troops had left Guadalcanal for Peleliu.[88] Halting the campaign to redesign the attack would have thrown off the tempo of the drive to the Philippines, and pressure had to be kept on the Japanese. So the attack proceeded as scheduled, and JICPOA sent the new intelligence to the X-Ray Staff, who disseminated it from ship to ship by visual signal.

The new intelligence helped the Marines prepare for certain tactical threats. For example, it warned that there were nineteen Japanese tanks on the island. This information, coupled with the JICPOA's accurate analysis of flat portions of terrain between the airfield and the beaches, gave Marine commanders an idea of where the Japanese might send their tanks to thwart the U.S. landing. Consequently, the Fifth Marine Regiment commander ordered his marines to mass antitank guns and bazookas on the beachhead as early as possible on D-Day.[89] In support of this effort, the Marines also succeeded in putting all of the First Division's tanks ashore on the first day of the assault, "a record unsurpassed in any previous Marine landing in the Central Pacific, except for the Marshalls," according to the official Marine Corps history.[90] The Fifth Marines received several of these tanks to bolster its firepower, so when the Japanese launched a tank attack at sundown, they were able to hold their ground,[91] although two tanks broke through Marine lines and limped to the beach, where they were destroyed. On the whole, however, the intelligence helped the Marines neutralize a major threat to the beachhead and, significantly, robbed the Japanese of their armored capabilities.[92]

Operationally, the new intelligence mattered little. It had no effect on the overall attack plans for Peleliu.[93] The intelligence had not reached operations planners early enough to permit them to alter their plans and add extra troops to the attack. As a result, the Marines did not enjoy a numerical three-to-one ratio of superiority on Peleliu. The fortified nature of the Japanese defenses on Peleliu acted as a force-multiplier and required additional manpower and firepower to defeat. On Peleliu, the official Marine Corps record states that the Marines battled the Japanese "toe-to-toe." Col. "Chesty" Puller claimed the combat ratio was little better than one-to-one.[94] A more efficient assault on the island would have required extra personnel, an opinion shared by the III Amphibious Corps commander, Maj. Gen. Roy S. Geiger. Even the Japanese commander of the Palau Islands, Lt.

Gen. Sadae Inoue, thought that Nimitz would attack with more than just one division.[95]

But even if order-of-battle intelligence had been perfect, there was no way short of having a mole in the Japanese Palau command structure—an improbable scenario at best—to discover the defensive strategy for Peleliu. In retrospect, JICPOA could have spotted more defensive positions through aerial photography, but it could not have known Lieutenant General Inoue's tactical thoughts. His plans radically departed from past campaigns, in which the Japanese attempted to halt U.S. invasions at the water's edge by massing troops and weapons on and around the beaches.

By the time the Marianas fell, the Japanese had decided that their usual defensive tactics did not work.[96] An enemy garrison on Biak in the South Pacific, however, did have some success, if not in defeating the U.S. Army unit sent to seize the island, in seriously mauling it . On Biak, the Japanese made their fortifications in the mountains that overlooked the airstrip, which was the obvious objective. On the high ground, they fortified caves and dug well-covered and concealed foxholes that commanded overlapping fields of fire from which they fought to their deaths. No Japanese soldier died defending pillboxes or trench lines on landing beaches that would be destroyed by naval artillery and air strikes. Most importantly, their new tactics kept U.S. troops engaged for twice as long as Army commanders had expected. The Japanese word for these tactics was *fukkaku*.[97] In one case, JICPOA's analysts referred to them as the "cornered rat" defense, but they did not seem to fully understand this revolution in Japanese defense. It took a captured document titled "The Hypothetical Defense of Kyushu" to alert JICPOA to this change in enemy tactics, but analysts translated the document in July 1945, and by then the war was nearly over.[98]

Regardless, Imperial Headquarters made note of the innovative tactics used on Biak and so did Lieutenant General Inoue and his staff, who had begun to apply them to Peleliu when Tokyo sent word sanctioning such actions. The Japanese high command furthermore sent guidelines outlining its ideas. First, it said that Inoue should design defenses without expecting Japanese naval and air support. Second, U.S. preliminary bombardments of landing beaches were awesome in destructive power and would continue to grow more devastating. Third, U.S. forces had consistently landed on beaches near airfields from which they could move inland with the most haste and seize and then utilize those airfields.[99]

With all of this in mind, Inoue ordered the field commander on Peleliu, Colonel Nakagawa, to place some weapons positions on the landing beaches but to layer the majority of his defenses behind the beaches toward the airfield. This created an in-depth defense. Inoue also told the Peleliu garrison to fortify the Umurbroguls as Biak had been defended, and Nakagawa stationed counterattack forces in strategic locations to thwart U.S. advances from multiple angles.[100]

Inoue strictly forbade reckless and suicidal banzai charges in favor of well-coordinated counterattacks. If U.S. forces managed to push through and secure the airfield, he directed that each surviving Japanese soldier retreat to the Umurbrogol Mountain defensive zone, where there were hundreds of prebuilt defenses. Inoue hoped that, even in defeat, he might blunt the U.S. advance through Japan's Pacific territory by severely injuring a Marine or Army combat division.[101] This "bleed the Americans" defensive tactic had more success than had previous defenses, and it subsequently became the hallmark of Japanese island defenses for the rest of the war.

Conclusion

It is clear then, that Stalemate II suffered from inadequate intelligence. Why did this happen? The answer is a circumstance that plagued several campaigns during the Pacific War: Collection operations did not obtain enough accurate data on the objective.[102] The shortfall of information occurred as a result of four major problems. First, thick vegetation covered the contours of the island and concealed the difficult terrain in numerous areas bordering the landing beaches and in the Umurbrogol Mountain range. This clearly demonstrated the limitations of World War II photographic technology.[103] Second—and again—heavy foliage, combined with expert Japanese concealment techniques, hid defensive positions such as pillboxes, blockhouses, and fortified coral ridges. Only a dense, protracted preliminary naval bombardment would have destroyed the island's thick foliage and exposed Japanese defenses, a tactic suggested after the fact and never carried out during the Central Pacific drive.[104] Third, according to an Army Air Corps report, more frequent photo reconnaissance flights might have revealed Japanese defensive positions by photographing construction crews at work or by photographing evidence of their work, such as piles of earth from excavations and construction paths. Of course, the Japanese camouflaged their construction activities, so this was not a simple solution to the problem.[105]

The fourth reason deals with the disposition of the Thirty-first Army documents that provided the Japanese order of battle for Peleliu. Historical records do not state why the important information from these documents reached Peleliu planners so late, but it is probable that their importance was obscured by the huge volume of documents from Saipan—literally tons of them. Additionally, at the time U.S. forces discovered the documents, it is likely that finding intelligence about Peleliu was not as important as finding intelligence about Saipan, Tinian, and Guam. After all, the Marines and Army were engaged in combat on Saipan, and the fleet would be attacking the other two islands in a matter of weeks. In fact, JICPOA's field intelligence teams and the fleet's intelligence staffs spent June, July, and early August processing the Thirty-first Army documents for ongoing combat in the Marianas. Finding documents regarding Peleliu was probably a low priority. It is also possible that the linguists were not privy to the fact that Peleliu was the next objective. In such a case, they would not have even looked for Peleliu-related material. Another likelihood is that there were too few Japanese linguists in theater to exploit the Saipan intelligence bonanza. Even though the government had established language schools at the outbreak of the war, it is seems that the schools did not produce enough personnel to meet the heavy demands of the Pacific intelligence community. Then there is the question of the captured Japanese intelligence officer whom JICPOA interrogated regarding Peleliu. He may have been stalling to prevent the U.S. forces from gaining effective intelligence on his brothers in arms, or he may not have known about Japanese defenses on Peleliu because of compartmentalization.

JICPOA produced an after-action report on the enemy use of caves for defensive fortifications after the assault ended. Unfortunately, the report was not published until the end of the war and was unavailable to the planners of the next major assaults in the Pacific—Iwo Jima and Okinawa—where it would have been put to good use.[106] But, looking at the long-term goals of the Pacific War, it is most probable that intelligence analysts had written the report to influence the operations planners working on the invasion of Japan scheduled for the fall of 1945.

The fleet, in its after-action report of the Peleliu campaign, provided suggestions on how intelligence might be improved for future operations. (After-action reports were not always prepared, and suggestions for improvement were not always forthcoming.) This particular report offers telling evidence of the peculiar events relating to intelligence and Peleliu. Regarding the late documents, it suggested that JICPOA translators be briefed on upcoming operations so they would be able to assess captured documents for intelligence vital to the next campaign. This would, in the future, increase the timeliness of processing and dissemination, which lends credence to the theory that field teams sorting through captured documents did not know to look for data on Peleliu. The report also stated that photographic coverage of the objective should be more frequent than it had been for the Peleliu campaign. It added that bad coverage should be rectified immediately with more reconnaissance missions.[107]

Peleliu provides an educational case study because it demonstrates the unpredictable nature of intelligence operations. Countless factors influence direction, collection, processing, and dissemination. Anything can happen along the way to support, impair, begin, or halt the intelligence cycle. The last-minute discovery of the Thirty-first Army documents triggered a short, spontaneous cycle, which included the translation and dissemination of vital order-of-battle intelligence that likely saved many Marine lives during the Japanese armored counterattack. On the other hand, the infrequent photo reconnaissance flights, thick vegetation, and Japanese camouflage continually impaired collection and processing like an infection that would not go away. And it indirectly contributed to the casualty rate. In short, intelligence operations are subject to the same unpredictables as combat operations are. But while obtaining accurate intelligence under adverse circumstances is difficult, the Peleliu campaign demonstrates that it is paramount in importance.

The Strategic Implications of Stalemate II

While the Peleliu campaign provides valuable insight into the mechanics of the intelligence cycle, the campaign itself, tragically, produced few significant results. The Joint Chiefs of Staff and MacArthur decided to skip the attack on Mindanao, the original objective in the Philippines, in favor of Leyte, a more convenient and valuable target. By doing so, MacArthur diminished the value of Peleliu as a bomber base, fighter base, or any other type of base that would have supported the original plan. He did, on the other hand, put Anguar to use as a bomber base to support the invasion of the Philippines, but no U.S. forces used Peleliu for any significant purpose until one month after the invasion began. After that, U.S. air forces used the hard-won island as a stopover and refueling point for flights traveling from East and South Pacific islands to the Philippines.[108]

The base at Peleliu did have a role in one of the Pacific War's more bizarre occurrences, the USS *Indianapolis* disaster. The USS *Indianapolis* transported the atomic bomb bound for Hiroshima to Tinian. In early August , a Japanese submarine torpedoed and sank the ship as it made its way back to port. The surviving crew abandoned her, leaping into shark-infested waters where, over a period of several days, hundreds of U.S. sailors were eaten alive. No rescue vessel came to their aid, and in fact, no one knew the ship had sunk.[109] By happenstance, a Ventura PV-1 patrol aircraft based out of Peleliu spotted the survivors and radioed for help.[110] Rescue vessels picked up the remaining men and transported them to a thousand-bed hospital on Peleliu,[111] where they recovered from shock and dehydration.

Another drama concerns a gang of Japanese holdouts on Peleliu who occupied the wilder parts of the island until 1947. They were discovered after a slew of strange incidents. One day, two island natives on their way home from their work shifts at the U.S. Navy compound were ambushed in a stretch of jungle. Troops stationed on Peleliu began to notice stolen supplies, and a marine fired on a group of thieves one night only to be answered with grenades and rifle fire. Area commanders responded by sending in twenty-six well-armed marines equipped with mortars, flamethrowers, and machine guns to bolster security. Eventually, the marines captured the survivors—twenty-nine Japanese soldiers and four Okinawan laborers, to be exact—most in complete disbelief that Japan had surrendered to the United States. All of them were astonished to hear about the destructive capacity of the atomic bomb.[112] Ironically, it was this type of mentality, the "holdout mentality," that convinced the U.S. military to lobby the president to use atomic weaponry on the Japanese in the first place.

In the end, seizing Peleliu did in fact secure MacArthur's right flank, but in hindsight, the operation appears to have been unnecessary, and the odd sequence of events regarding intelligence had little effect on the outcome of the war. The scant historical commentary on Peleliu has looked down on the campaign as accomplishing very little other than producing 9,740 U.S. casualties, including 1,790 deaths. Even to this day, many veterans of that battle remain bitter toward Nimitz for sanctioning the assault and toward MacArthur for insisting to the White House that Peleliu was essential to protect his axis of advance.

IWO JIMA AND OKINAWA

Detachment and Iceberg

Strategic Background

One month before the Marines stormed the beaches on Peleliu, the Combined Chiefs of Staff, the Joint Chiefs of Staff, Admiral Nimitz, and General MacArthur were debating where to attack next. The Marianas were secure, and the Carolines would soon be isolated. MacArthur wanted to adhere to the original U.S. Pacific war plan and seize the Philippines in the fall of 1944 in preparation for the attack on Japan by using an axis of advance through the Asian mainland and Formosa. The JCS wanted to skip the Philippines entirely and lunge straight for the Asian mainland and Formosa.

Speaking his own mind, Admiral Spruance suggested an entirely different scheme of attacking not west but north-northwest, through Iwo Jima to Okinawa, from which they could launch the final invasion of Japan. His suggestion stemmed from the belief that the Asia-Formosa route to Japan required too much time, too many men, and an excessive amount of equipment. Furthermore, following a lengthy axis of advance would allow the Japanese to consolidate their home defenses, and the European theater of operations had left Nimitz and MacArthur at times short of men and material. Spruance's line of logic—economy of force—influenced the Joint Chiefs to accept his proposed Iwo Jima–Okinawa axis of advance, thereby setting the stage for the last two amphibious combat operations of the war.[1]

Operation Detachment: Iwo Jima

Campaign Background

On 19 February 1945, the U.S. Marine Corps engaged in one of history's bloodiest amphibious assaults: the battle of Iwo Jima. Trials and tribulations faced on the island were like those of no other campaign fought in the Pacific. Unknown to Nimitz and his lieutenants, the Japanese had turned Iwo Jima into a heavily armed fortress filled with thousands of highly motivated troops dedicated to defending the island to the death. Lt. Gen. Holland Smith expected fifteen thousand casualties.[2] However, in a thirty-six-day operation,[3] Marine and Navy casualties totaled 28,686 personnel, 6,821 of whom were killed in action,[4] the highest U.S. death toll to date in the Pacific War.

Why did this happen? The marines who assaulted Iwo Jima performed beyond expectations. They fought an intense infantry battle, much of it at close range, almost nonstop for over a month. Their actions on the island were the stuff that legends are made of. True, the Japanese on Iwo Jima fought from expertly engineered defensive positions, but such positions were always difficult to overcome. Similarly, the Japanese fought unyieldingly to the death, but this was also common throughout the Pacific. So why was Iwo Jima such a tough nut to crack? One reason was that the Japanese commander on the island, Gen. Tadamichi Kuribayashi, enacted a *fukkaku* defense that covered more than 90 percent of the island. The Marine Corps had never attacked such an in-depth and comprehensively defended enemy base before. Even so, if the Marines and Navy had known about these defenses, they would have been able to plan a more effective attack, and that points to one of the main reasons for their difficulties in the battle for Iwo Jima: inadequate intelligence. For Operation Detachment, JICPOA did not produce adequate intelligence on the number of Japanese combatants on the island, their weapons, their plan of defense, or the terrain they occupied.

Target Location

Iwo Jima is approximately six hundred nautical miles north of the Marianas and about six hundred miles south of Tokyo.[5] The island itself is five miles long and two miles wide at its widest point. It is less than half a mile wide at its thinnest point. Several historians have stated the island resembles a pork chop in shape. There is a volcano at the southern tip of the island, and in 1945, magma made the soil unbearably hot on certain parts of the island.

Why Iwo Jima?

Nimitz targeted Iwo Jima for several reasons. First, Iwo Jima had to be eliminated as an enemy air base. Fighters on Iwo harassed Marianas-based B-29 bombers on the way to Japan. Simply sending bombers to destroy the fighters would not work. Iwo Jima sat close to Japan, and there were numerous island bases between the two, which allowed Tokyo to base aircraft on the island largely at will. Accordingly, Japanese aircraft could fly in from

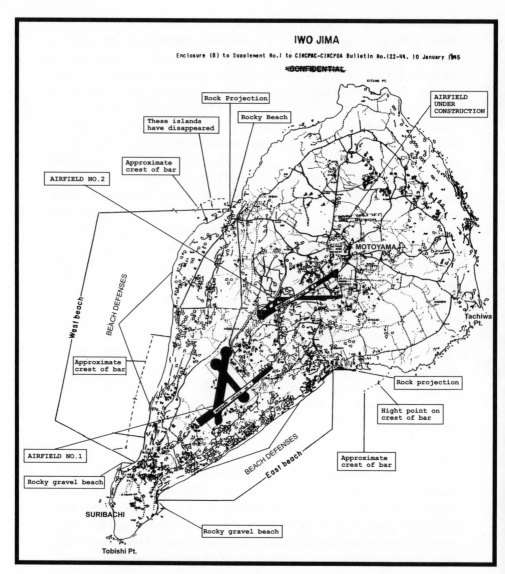

JICPOA Prebattle Map, Iwo Jima. Note the abundance of defenses pinpointed along the southeast beaches. The Marines landed on the southeast beaches, cut the island in half, seized Mt. Suribachi, and drove north to secure the rest of the island. JICPOA Information Bulletin 122-44

several locations and use Iwo as a base to ambush B-29 strategic bombing missions. Nimitz had to take it away from the Japanese in order to solve the problem.

Enemy fighters on Iwo produced indirect problems as well. B-29 pilots had to take evasive action to avoid Japanese fighters, and this required large amounts of fuel. Therefore, the bombers had to carry extra fuel to avoid the fighters. But because each bomber could fly with only so much weight, they had to reduce the number of bombs they carried. The end result was that the B-29s, if they made it past Iwo Jima, carried more fuel and fewer bombs to the target area. The combination of these impairments reduced the effectiveness of the strategic bombing raids over Japan's industrial cities.[6]

Second, bombers flying to Japan lacked cover because U.S. fighters did not have the range to fly from the Marianas to targets as far away as Tokyo. As a result, the bombers had to fly over their objectives at extremely high altitudes to avoid Japanese fighters. Harsh wind conditions prevalent in the high altitudes pushed against the large aircraft, forcing pilots to use extra power to maintain their headings and altitudes. Again, this action used an excessive amount of fuel, and bombers were forced to carry more fuel than bombs. The high altitudes also hurt bombing accuracy. With Iwo Jima as a U.S. base, however, fighters could escort the bombers all the way to Japan, eliminating the ineffective high-altitude, low-ordnance bombing.[7]

Third, damaged bombers returning from their missions needed an emergency landing field midway between Japan and the Marianas. Most bombers that pitched into the Pacific disintegrated on impact, killing the crew. As a U.S. possession, Iwo Jima would provide the sorely needed emergency landing field, therefore reducing the number of aircrew deaths and B-29 losses.[8]

Fourth, as a matter of simple strategic necessity, Nimitz needed Iwo Jima to provide a stepping-off point for the next island campaign: Okinawa. While Iwo had no port facilities to speak of, its flat terrain offered the potential for at least six airfields. The Japanese had built two there already, and there was another under construction. Such a base so close to the home islands would be invaluable to an invasion of Okinawa and Japan by providing tactical fighter cover, strategic air power, and air transport facilities.[9]

The Iwo Jima Intelligence Operation

JICPOA began collecting information on Iwo Jima after Nimitz authorized its seizure in August 1944 through Operation Detachment.[10] With this came requests for JICPOA to furnish intelligence on the island's topography, its garrison, enemy defensive plans, and other relevant information. Radio intelligence personnel conducted interception operations against the Japanese on Iwo in attempts to learn about the garrison's size. Luckily, JICPOA already possessed large quantities of intelligence on the objective taken from the Thirty-first Army headquarters on Saipan. The captured materials included maps of the island, navigational charts, and order-of-battle documents.

Aerial photographs from the summer of 1944 showed a significant enemy defensive buildup after the fall of Saipan.[11] In total, U.S. forces, including the U.S. Army's Seventh Air Force based on Saipan, flew more than two hundred photo reconnaissance missions over Iwo Jima. Unfortunately, directors of the Iwo Jima intelligence operation focused most of these flights on the area adjacent to Airfield No. 1, likely because it bordered the landing beaches. Presumably to hide reconnaissance missions, they also relied more on bombers equipped with cameras than on special photo reconnaissance aircraft such as those in the fleet; the result was mediocre coverage. Marine after-action reports stated that these photos were of no value in analyzing the whole of Iwo Jima.[12]

In addition, early photographic missions produced photos on a scale of 1:10,000, while analysts needed a scale more close-up, such as 1:5,000, in which they could better see details and shadows. Such close-ups were not available until 18 and 24 January, by which time the Iwo Jima assault force had already set to sea.[13]

P-38 Lightnings from the Twenty-eighth Photographic Reconnaissance Squadron flew missions over Iwo Jima as low as fifty feet and produced the best photographic coverage of any campaign carried out under Nimitz. These contributed to a "Joint Enemy Installations Map" printed on 11 February 1945 that was distributed to the ground element as it cycled through Guam and Saipan before sailing on to the final objective.[14] However, while this map helped battalion and company-sized elements plan their schemes of maneuver, it had no impact on the strategic planning for the campaign, and it did not help decide which division would attack what part of the island.

The submarine USS *Spearfish* circled Iwo Jima and took photographs of the island and Japanese defensive preparations well before D-Day, but the P-38 coverage produced better results.[15] Basically, then, early photographs focused on one particular area of Iwo Jima, and more comprehensive photos did not reach JICPOA in time to conduct a thorough study of the objective. The delay was unfortunate because Iwo Jima probably had the most sophisticated defenses of any Japanese-held Pacific island U.S. forces had yet encountered.

Tragically, JICPOA did not have seasoned intelligence analysts review the late photographs from the P-38 missions.[16] Toward the end of January 1945, JICPOA lost all of its experienced photographic analysts to the Advanced Intelligence Center (AIC) just starting up on Guam and to a U.S. Navy rotation policy that transferred officers in "administrative-type" occupational specialties to different locations or jobs at regular intervals. Those officers who had begun their intelligence careers at JICPOA as photo interpreters had simply arrived at their time of transfer, so they left. In his report of intelligence activities at the end of the war, General Twitty remarked about these untimely incidents:

> These two developments left JICPOA for the moment without adequate experienced personnel and, to a certain extent, handicapped the work then in progress. . . .[17]
>
> All experienced officers had either been rotated or sent to AIC, Guam, and there were insufficient officers to man the area desks or to handle the increasing volume of photographs. The first quarter of 1945 was devoted to preparing standard procedures and training folders for the new inexperienced personnel and to establishing more adequate liaison between the Geographic Section and other activities, both within JICPOA and without.[18]

Although it appears that this situation could not have been helped, essentially, JICPOA had green analysts interpreting the most important sets of photographs of Iwo Jima available since the information bulletin came out. If they had been analyzed by experienced personnel, who knows what the outcome might have been? It is possible that JICPOA would have discovered many more defenses on the island, and the plan of attack might have been altered. In addition, it may have been able to disseminate more accurate intelligence to the naval preliminary bombardment.

Despite the situation, JICPOA produced three pre-assault information bulletins on Iwo Jima. Each bulletin presented more current intelligence than the last and indicated that the Japanese were heavily fortifying the island. JICPOA published its final and most comprehensive Iwo Jima information bulletin, number 9-45, on 10 January 1945. The bulletin appeared to contain a wealth of intelligence on Iwo, but the battle would prove its numerous shortfalls.

Be that as it may, the bulletin did state that the Japanese had significant firepower regarding artillery, AA guns, and machine guns—over a hundred major weapons positions overall. It also stated that they had more than fifty pillboxes and covered artillery emplacements.[19] The fleet's own intelligence units, working in conjunction with JICPOA, discovered startling details on Iwo's defenses as neared D-Day neared. Apparently, by 10 February 1945, the Japanese had increased their firepower and defensive fortifications by 100 percent in some cases. Curiously, the number of anti-boat guns and open artillery emplacements had decreased by just over 80 percent, and machine guns had decreased by 17 percent.[20] Analysts did not know it at the time, but much of this weaponry disappeared because the Japanese were moving it underground. They were also applying extreme camouflage discipline to defense networks. The reported increases did not represent defense capabilities beyond JICPOA's original estimates for Iwo Jima, and neither Nimitz, Spruance, nor Smith recommended altering the attack plan.

Chain of Command

Nimitz assigned Spruance and his Fifth Fleet to execute the campaign plan. Turner commanded the amphibious force, and Rear Adm. Harry Hill commanded the landings. Since Lieutenant General Smith had been promoted to administrative command of all marines in the Pacific, his replacement, Maj. Gen. Harry Schmidt, would command the V Amphibious Corps—the ground assault element for Iwo Jima. However, Smith would participate in the Iwo campaign as an observer. The ground troops consisted of the Third, Fourth, and Fifth Marine Divisions. A large, two-task-force assemblage of naval ships—cruisers, destroyers, and battleships—would cover the Marine landing along with an impressive array of carrier air power.[21]

The Iwo Jima Attack Plan

The Detachment attack plan fell into four phases. In phase one, naval ships would bombard Iwo Jima for three days. In phase two, the Fourth and Fifth Marine Divisions would land on Iwo's southeast beaches and establish a beachhead. Phase three would consist of the drive inland, in which the Fifth would cut the island in half and attack Mount Suribachi, while the Fourth would seize the closest airfield and afterward sweep through the northern end of the island. During phase four, the Third Division was to land and aid in securing the objective or in furnishing fire support or combat support.[22]

The plan appeared solid but fell apart when the shooting commenced. The Fourth and Fifth Divisions did manage to secure a beachhead and cut the island in half, but with heavy casualties. The Third Division, minus the

Third Marines, had to be landed the third day of the assault to support the drive inland, and the entire scheme for taking the island had to be revised. The Fifth Division took Suribachi but then had to join the other marines in a three-division front to clear the rest of the island. The Fifth Division took the left flank, slicing through rocky and low terrain on the west side of the island. The Third Division took the center, an elevated plateau that contained Iwo's three airstrips. The Fourth Division took the right flank, or the eastern side of the island. This avenue of approach contained wicked terrain, low depressions, rocky coral ravines, steep hills, and boulder fields. In each sector, Japanese soldiers occupied every nook and cranny, and their fanatical resistance made the campaign incredibly difficult.

How Intelligence Influenced the Campaign

In some cases, the intelligence for Iwo Jima was accurate. For example, JICPOA's hydrographic survey correctly analyzed the island's surf and beach conditions and predicted a difficult but possible landing. It warned that Iwo's beaches were steep and consisted of loose volcanic sediment, an element that would slow vehicular traffic but not prohibit it.[23] Unfortunately, the report's military survey fell short of the actual situation, and JICPOA's after-action bulletin, number 136-45, demonstrated several discrepancies with pre-assault findings. Analysts grossly underestimated Iwo's garrison size, the number of support weapons it had, the number and location of its field fortifications, tunnels, and caves, the extent to which Iwo's terrain would aid the defenders, and their defensive plans.[24]

According to the prebattle information bulletin, there were 13,500 Japanese soldiers on Iwo Jima. Even though aerial reconnaissance photographs indicated a massive buildup through the fall and into the early winter of 1944, analysts claimed that "there [were] no indications that the garrison [had] been reinforced."[25] In reality, about twenty-three thousand Japanese occupied the island (as indicated by intelligence personnel who landed with assault troops and by enemy body counts).[26] This underestimate skewed the entire information bulletin concerning enemy firepower and capabilities, because JICPOA largely based these particular facets of the Japanese defense on estimates of Japanese manpower.

JICPOA classified Iwo Jima's defenses into two categories: observed defenses and reported defenses, known in today's intelligence community as "confirmed" and "probable" defenses. "Observed" meant that analysts could see it. "Reported" meant that they suspected it because of documents, POW interrogations, or similar secondary sources. Aerial and submarine reconnaissance photographs supplied the only observed defenses information. Analysts based reported defenses on POW inter-rogations, captured documents from the Thirty-first Army headquarters on Saipan that had proved useful in the past four campaigns, and wire di-agrams of Japanese units from JICPOA's Reference Section.

Observation of Japanese defenses revealed only 105 major weapon sites, including AA and dual-purpose guns, and 119 hardened weapon positions, including pillboxes, machine gun nests, and covered artillery emplace-ments. But JICPOA's analysts knew that the Japanese would defend Iwo from more than just 224 weapons positions because the island stood as the first bastion of defense of their inner Pacific defensive line.

Since observed intelligence showed only part of Japanese defenses, an-alysts relied on reported intelligence to fill the gaps.[27] The captured doc-uments from Saipan led analysts to believe that certain Japanese units oc-cupied Iwo Jima. In turn, this led them to consult Japanese unit wire diagrams for information on how many men were in each unit, how many weapons they had, and what types of weapons they had. This was the same methodology used to estimate the Japanese order of battle on Peleliu.

From analyzing reported defenses, analysts believed that in January 1945 the Japanese on Iwo possessed the following weapons: up to thirty-nine artillery pieces of 75-mm or larger, twenty-four 70-mm howitzers, eighteen mortars ranging from 81-mm to 240-mm, ten 80-mm naval guns, up to fifty-four AA guns with another possible thirty-three "other AA guns," forty-two to fifty-four 37- or 47-mm antitank guns, six rocket launcher po-sitions, and forty tanks.[28] Presumably, these made up the bulk of Japanese artillery and support weaponry.

By February, the green analysts and fleet intelligence had increased many of these estimates.[29] The number of artillery guns had risen 100 per-cent. The number of coast defense and dual-purpose guns had risen by 100 and 162 percent, respectively. Japanese AA guns had risen by at least 41 percent. On the other hand, antitank weapons had decreased by 83 per-cent, and machine guns (not on the table below) had decreased by 17 per-cent. Analysts said that there had been an 87 percent decrease in open ar-tillery positions (not on the table below) and assumed that this was because they had been moved into concrete and steel fortifications, which had also increased.[30]

Although these estimates indicated significant increases, most of them fell short of the actual situation. (There was one notable overestimation as well. See the table below regarding tanks.) In reality, the Japanese actu-ally had 361 artillery pieces of 75-mm or larger, sixty-five mortars 81-mm to 240-mm, thirty-three 80-mm naval guns, more than two hundred 20- to

25-mm AA guns, sixty-nine 37- or 47-mm AT guns, seventy rocket launchers, and twenty-two tanks. They also possessed twelve massive 320-mm mortars and ninety-four AA guns 75-mm or larger.[31]

Estimated vs. Actual Japanese Heavy Weaponry on Iwo Jima

	Estimated Support Weaponry in January	*% Increased in February*	*Actual Support Weaponry*
Artillery Guns, 75-mm or larger	39[i]	100	361
70-mm howitzers	24[ii]	100	Unknown, but enemy had 94 75-mm or larger AA
81–240-mm mortars	18[iii]	100	65
Naval guns, 80-mm or larger	10	162	33
13-, 20-, or 25-mm AA guns (plus 33 "other" guns)	54 plus 33	41	More than 200
37–47-mm AT guns	42–54	None	69
Rocket guns (200–550 lb.)	6 positions reported	None	70
Tanks	40	None	22

[i] Includes coast defense and dual-purpose weaonry except for the 80-mm naval guns.

[ii] JICPOA Information Bulletin 9-45, 1–2, "Important Errata Note," p. 11, and map, titled "Military Installations and Estimated Troops and Dispositions of Iwo Jima (Sulphur Island)."

[iii] Analysts said that, according to Japanese tables of organization and equipment, this number would decrease if the Japanese had no 70-mm infantry guns.

With these weapons, the Japanese inflicted heavy casualties on the assault forces on the beachhead and throughout the first two weeks of the operation. Historically, artillery has usually accounted for the most casualties inflicted in modern conventional battles, and this certainly proved true on Iwo Jima, especially during the fight to secure the beachhead. Furthermore, each one of these heavy guns had to be destroyed by tank-infantry teams, naval gunfire, or close air support called in by shore fire control teams. Even before the Marines landed, several of these guns pummeled the covering force for UDT operations. Of thirteen infantry landing craft converted into gunboats for close-in littoral fire support duties, eleven were hit, and one sank.[32] The cruiser USS *Pensacola* took numerous hits from a 150-mm gun that killed seventeen and wounded 120.[33]

Likewise, the high numbers of enemy soldiers meant a high volume of small-arms fire from grenades and rifles. Planners of Detachment had believed that nearly half of Iwo's presumed garrison, five thousand men, comprised its professional infantry battalions.[34] According to actual garrison numbers, they numbered as high as ten thousand. The difference seriously set back U.S. advances throughout the entire campaign.

Similarly, marines met more defensive structures than expected. All over the island, the Japanese had built blockhouses and pillboxes that held heavy machine guns and artillery. These were hardly mentioned in the pre-action information bulletin that reported only thirty-nine pillboxes, thirteen covered artillery positions with four under construction, and about 170 "rifle pits."[35] The same bulletin largely neglected blockhouses. The February intelligence report indicated that there were thirty-five blockhouses on Iwo Jima, with four under construction. It also said that there were 332 pillboxes on the island,[36] an astounding increase of fortifications during a time span of just ten weeks.

When the battle for Iwo Jima ended and JICPOA and fleet intelligence units began their analyses of the island's concrete and steel defenses, there were so many that they did not have time to plot them all on a map and count them, as they had in several past campaigns. Analysts were reduced to discussing numbers in broad terms. For example, JICPOA's 10 June 1945 Iwo Jima after-action information bulletin devoted a whole section of its analysis just to blockhouses and pillboxes, thereby indicating their abundance and successful employment by the enemy. The same report stated that, while many pillboxes commanded a scant 30-degree field of fire, "there was a sufficient number of mutually supporting pillboxes to offset the restricted field of fire of each weapon."[37] Some blockhouses and pillboxes had concrete walls from two to six feet thick, protected by as much as fifty feet of sand. To destroy these fortifications, marines had to call on main battery fire from naval ships because secondary fire failed to do the job.[38] Main battery fire came from battleships and their massive 14-inch and 12-inch guns. Secondary fire came from cruisers and their less powerful 8-inch and 6-inch guns.

Marines encountered numerous concrete fortifications in a defensive zone they called the Meat Grinder. Located on the east side of the island in the Fourth Division's area of operations, the Meat Grinder consisted of three mutually supportive strongpoints: Hill 382, another hill called Turkey Knob, and a deep, wide, natural depression in the ground called the Amphitheater. The Meat Grinder included hundreds of defensive structures and the Amphitheater, according to the JICPOA after-action report, "contained two terraces and three tiers" of concrete fortifications.[39] Overall JICPOA's Iwo Jima after-action bulletin made twenty-one references to these defenses in just five pages and summarized them in a separate five-page, ten-photo pictorial.

After-action analysis of tunnels and caves received similar treatment. Prebattle intelligence had claimed that the Japanese would use caves to shelter men, ammunition, and other supplies from destruction. JICPOA also had figured that the vast majority of caves on Iwo were located in the northern end of the island. In contrast, the after-action report stated "thousands of caves [were] used for defensive positions."[40] Indeed, most caves on the island housed guns and personnel and were nearly impervious to conventional infantry assault. Caves, man-made and natural, were so numerous on Iwo Jima that intelligence analysts said "that it was impossible to plot them all on a 1:10,000 map."[41] The after-action bulletin included caves and tunnels in almost every part of its analysis, indicating their heavy use by the enemy. In the end, it summarized tunnels and caves in a four-page, eleven-photo pictorial.

The cave pictorial focused on several underground networks. The Southeast Quarry, which was the promontory that overlooked the right flank of the beachhead, contained eight hundred yards of tunnels that led to the Meat Grinder. Guns in caves on Airfield No. 2 not only covered the airfield but the landing beach as well. On Mount Suribachi, there were hundreds of caves reinforced with concrete and protected by machine guns. Most of these connected to larger defensive structures at the base of the mountain.[42] None of these particular cave networks were located in the northern end of the island, where JICPOA's analysts had claimed they would be.

The after-action bulletin further stated that "concrete-faced caves and infantry positions in the erosion-made crevices were frequently so close together that an equally strong defensive position existed only a few yards to the rear or flank [of another]."[43] This tactic forced marines to face walls of well-defended beehive-type cave configurations that afforded the Japanese great mobility. If fire from marines grew too intense at one position, the Japanese could temporarily hide underground or move to another position until the fire subsided. Afterward, they would emerge and begin fighting again. Eventually, the marines learned to seal most caves with explosives, but the lesson cost hundreds of men killed in action.

Terrain served the enemy in a capacity similar to caves, and analysts barely mentioned it in Information Bulletin 9-45. As with Saipan and Peleliu, JICPOA did not capture the specifics of Iwo's terrain in topographical maps. Terrain provided the Japanese with excellent natural fortifications and slowed U.S. infantry movement. Loose and deep sand between the western landing beaches and the opposite shore slowed tank and infantry traffic and made them easy targets for Japanese gunners and riflemen.[44]

Similarly, the northern end of Iwo Jima did not contain man-made defensive structures because its difficult terrain provided plenty of natural defensive positions that made it just as formidable as the rest of Iwo Jima. Japanese troops hid in every hole, depression, and crevice with weapons of some sort. The island's natural armor protected each enemy soldier, and each one had to be routed out by groups of marines.

Where the terrain allowed it, several enemy soldiers clustered together in natural pillboxes and bunkers armed with machine guns. Japanese snipers found Iwo Jima an ideal place to apply their skills. In other instances, the Japanese embedded tank turrets into the island's volcanic rock to serve as improvised blockhouses. Iwo Jima's terrain also allowed for forward and reverse slope defenses on the same ridgelines.

One of the most dangerous terrain features in the island was an area called the Gorge. Located on the northwest portion of the island, the Gorge became the enemy's last stand. Consisting of a seven-hundred-foot-long washed-out crevice with hundreds of adjoining trenches, this sector resembled a miniature Grand Canyon, where enemy soldiers had dug in and established firing lanes on every avenue of approach. Accordingly, the Fifth Marine Division committed a regimental combat team, elements of an engineer battalion, and a reconnaissance company to clear the area. Fighting grew so intense there that the marines measured their progress by the yard.[45] In its after-action bulletin, JICPOA stated, "In attacking these positions no Japs were to be seen, all being in caves or crevices in the rocks and so dispersed as to give an all-round interlocking defense to each small compartment."[46] The report bolstered its findings in an eleven-photograph pictorial dealing strictly with terrain.[47] Overall, the terrain on Iwo Jima worked to the advantage of the defenders, who melded their defenses in with the earth. This tactic provided some of the most effective cover and concealment yet encountered in the Pacific and required two or three times the manpower to overwhelm. In effect, terrain provided the Japanese with a powerful force multiplier that helped them inflict massive casualties on U.S. forces.

Incorrect assumptions of the Japanese plan of defense compounded order-of-battle and terrain difficulties. JICPOA believed the Japanese planned to defend Iwo Jima with a thickly layered beach-oriented defense on the island's southern half. Information Bulletin 9-45 stated that "the heaviest concentration of infantry defenses on Iwo Jima is on the southern half of the island in the vicinity of Airfields No. 1 and No. 2 and the good beaches in that area."[48] Beach positions consisted of pillboxes and layered infantry trenches with supplementary trenches to fall back on. Analysts assumed the Japanese would focus their firepower directly on the marines as they disembarked from their LVTs and landing craft. Fire support would presumably come from the base of Suribachi, the high ground off the beaches, and from the beaches themselves, where photos indicated several covered emplacements. Analysts assumed that the few Japanese troops that occupied the northern end of the island manned only machine guns trained on small beaches.[49]

JICPOA stated that the Japanese had dispersed themselves into five sections: A, B, C, D, and a reserve area. Section A half-circled Mount Suribachi's base at the northwest, north, and southeast and covered access to its slopes and southernmost beaches on both sides of the island.[50] Section B blanketed the northern three fourths of the west beach and was covered by fire support from a south-facing bluff that stood at the beach's northernmost end. To analysts, its infantry trenches appeared less dense and commanded fewer fields of fire than those in other areas.[51] Section C protected the east beach with deeply layered infantry trenches and numerous machine-gun nests that commanded interlocking fields of fire. Fire support for this zone occupied the high ground on its northwest flank.[52] Section D occupied the entire northern portion of Iwo Jima with thinly spread positions guarding the few beaches that existed.[53] Based on captured documents dated April 1944, analysts calculated that Iwo's reserve troops were stationed in the center of the northern end of the island. However, they were not sure of their exact location, nor had they been able to locate the enemy's headquarters.[54]

In summary, analysts stated, "Above all, it is to be noted that the Japanese are learning how to fight defensively and how to get away from the rigid perimeter defense that they had so fixedly adhered to until recently."[55] This was a reference—telling, but hardly adequate—to deeply layered defenses instead of a single crust defense. The analysts also reckoned that if the Marines successfully landed and established a beachhead, an all-out night counterattack could be expected. If this failed, they thought that the remainder of the garrison might fall back to Iwo's high ground in the center of the island and engage in "the 'cornered rat' defense encountered on PELELIU."[56]

However, Japanese troop locations and defensive plans differed from what JICPOA expected. Except for those on Mt. Suribachi, Japanese defensive positions occupied the northern half of Iwo Jima in two wide belts of *fukkaku* positions. A Marine Corps after-action intelligence report stated that the entire island north of Airfield No. 1 was covered with concrete and steel fortifications and that the majority of these positions had not been picked up by photo intelligence.[57] The first belt—a thousand yards deep—began on the northwest coast above the beach and ran to the east coast a few hundred yards south of Tachiwa Point, bulging in the middle just

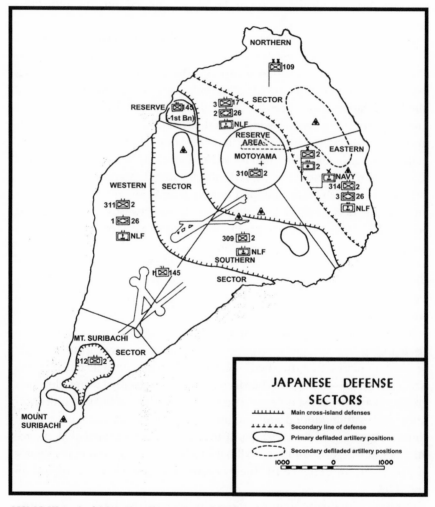

USMC Historical Map, Iwo Jima—Actual Defense Sectors. Note that most defenses are throughout the northern portion of the island. Garand and Strobridge, *Western Pacific Operations*

enough to include Airfield No. 2. The second belt was more of a thick line with defensive positions on either side. It roughly paralleled the main belt in a west-to-east line that began below Kitano Point and extended across Airfield No. 3 to a point just below Tachiwa Point.[58] Mt. Suribachi stood alone in the south with its entire surface, subsurface, and base covered with infantry, mortars, machine guns, and heavy weapons enclosed in pillboxes, caves, and blockhouses. The Japanese also planned to use Suribachi as a fire support base to cover the entire island,[59] one of the few facets of Japanese defense that JICPOA's analysts recognized accurately.

The after-action information bulletin stated that the main belt "gained its strength from its depth and its concrete and steel structures, positioned so as to obtain long fields of fire which were carefully calculated and tied into the overall defense system. Reliance on caves for shelter and fighting positions was increased here. Most of the positions showed excellent engineering and terrain appreciation."[60]

Japanese strongpoints were another item of major importance neglected by pre-action information bulletins. Strongpoints, usually one massive blockhouse supported by myriad smaller concrete fortifications and infantry positions, occupied key terrain such as hills or depressions throughout the main defensive belt. Complex strongpoints such as the Meat Grinder were linked together by tunnels, interlocking fields of fire, and hard-wire communications systems that afforded all-around defense and highly effective command and control.[61]

The northern defensive belt relied on caves and jagged terrain in lieu of man-made defensive structures.[62] JICPOA's Iwo Jima after-action bulletin noted that the terrain snaked around like a huge maze and that "attacking troops frequently were subjected to fire from flanks and rear more than from their front."[63] Pre-action intelligence wrongly indicated that this region exhibited little defensive capability. In addition, the remainder of enemy tanks on Iwo held out in this area. These obstacles made the process of clearing the northern portion of the island last for several days.

Regarding troop allocation, the Japanese deployed few soldiers at the southern end of the island where analysts expected the Japanese to make their primary defense. The heaviest concentrations of Japanese forces were in the north, and these troops fought until they were killed. The Japanese based their strategy on a simple concept: keep the U.S. forces hung up on Iwo for as long as possible and kill as many as possible in the process. This was identical to the Japanese defensive strategy for Peleliu. JICPOA's after-action bulletin concluded: "It was this simple tactic, coupled with the incredible rocky terrain and the maximum use the enemy had made of this terrain in constructing fortified positions which made the capture of Iwo Jima so difficult."[64]

Unfortunately, prebattle intelligence did not pick this up. Gen. Tadamichi Kuribayashi, the Japanese commander on Iwo Jima, established defenses to draw the Marine divisions inland where they would lose men and disintegrate. On a small scale, he hoped to destroy at least one Marine division. On a grand scale, he hoped to injure U.S. Pacific military forces enough to delay their advances into the Japanese homeland. While he did not delay the U.S. assault on Okinawa, he did manage to reduce the combat effectiveness of the Fourth Marine Division and severely injure the Fifth and Third Divisions as well.

The obvious consequences of these intelligence inadequacies were dire. The larger-than-expected garrison, greater firepower, and irregular terrain contributed to excessive casualties and delays in the operation. But intelligence flaws also affected the campaign indirectly. Intelligence on Japanese fortifications should have dictated types of special weapons that the Marines would need to secure the island. Similarly, the naval and air bombardment task force relied on JICPOA's pinpointing enemy fortifications and troop concentrations to carry out their missions effectively.

The official U.S. Marine Corps record of the assault noted that marines were trained for numerous tasks, such as destroying pillboxes and enclosed positions, overcoming mines, and utilizing support from ground based artillery and ships. As it was, this training came in handy, especially the latter, but the planning regimen did not place enough stress on combat engineering tactics, the type needed for neutralization of earthen positions, caves, and blockhouses. Likewise, combat on Iwo Jima demanded special weaponry such as flamethrowers, bazookas, and high explosives to destroy the innumerable concrete and steel fortifications that the Japanese had built. Accurate intelligence on Japanese defenses might have prompted Marine planners to supply their ground forces with more of these weapons, but JICPOA's information did not reflect the actual situation. In summary, it appears that the Marines attacked Iwo lacking an abundance of the most ideal weapons and equipment—weapons that were in such demand that they could barely be used in mop-up operations in the rear because they were sorely needed on the front.

For example, in early March, when most marines were ordered to take a day of rest to reorganize their battered ranks, the bazooka teams, flamethrower crews, and demolitioneers were sent forward into combat. Marines overcame Hill 382, the anchor of the Meat Grinder, only because bazooka teams destroyed the tanks guarding its base.[65] In the final push to secure

Iwo Jima, Marines used ten thousand gallons of flamethrower napalm per day, some in "Zippos," which were flamethrowing tanks.[66] However, in order for marines to have secured Iwo Jima in a more timely and efficient manner, they needed more of these highly effective and specialized weapons. Flamethrowers in particular were not as plentiful as they should have been.

In a similar vein, some operations planners wanted a ten-day preliminary naval bombardment to help secure the beachhead and soften enemy defenses by destroying key identified troop positions and fortifications. Unfortunately, naval gunners were allotted only three days to bombard Iwo Jima, because Nimitz wanted the assault synchronized with an aircraft-carrier attack on Japan to preempt air counterattacks against the beachhead. At the same time, he hoped to conserve limited supplies of naval ordnance for the Okinawa campaign, in an attempt to meet resource constraints. Also, Nimitz did not want supporting ships to linger too long around Iwo Jima because they made targets for Japanese air and submarine attacks.

Nonetheless, bombardment planners believed that intelligence had zeroed in on most Japanese defense installations, and they marked each one on a bombardment map and in a hard copy file system. As the bombardment progressed, gunners marked off each target after impact, and aerial spotters in light reconnaissance planes flew over the island to assess the battle damage,[67] just as they had done over Tinian.[68] However, because analysts had not discovered at least half of the enemy troop concentrations on the island, the bombardment was not as effective as it should have been. If one does not know where the enemy is, one cannot hit him, or in the case of Iwo Jima, hit him where it counts.

On D-3 and D-2, battleships (old battleships, or OBBs) *Tennessee, Nevada, Arkansas, Texas,* and *Idaho* bombarded beach areas while the *New York* fired in the vicinity of Airfield Nos. 1 and 2. OBBs used huge 14-inch and 12-inch guns. The smaller cruisers *Chester, Salt Lake City, Tuscaloosa, Pensacola,* and *Vicksburg* fired upon the remaining sectors on the northern end of Iwo. They used lighter 8-inch and 6-inch guns.[69] The same bombardment plan with little variation was used on D-1. As a result, the areas of sparse troop concentration received the heaviest bombardment, whereas the areas of heaviest troop concentration received the lightest. Specifically, the bombardment did not destroy defenses between Airfields No. 1 and 2, nor did it effectively target fortified regions of the Meat Grinder.[70] The only exception was the heavy coast-defense guns around the right flank of the landing beaches that had fired on the minesweeping force just before D-Day. The OBBs shelled these positions hard, and many of them were silent when the Marines hit the beaches. But it was not enough.

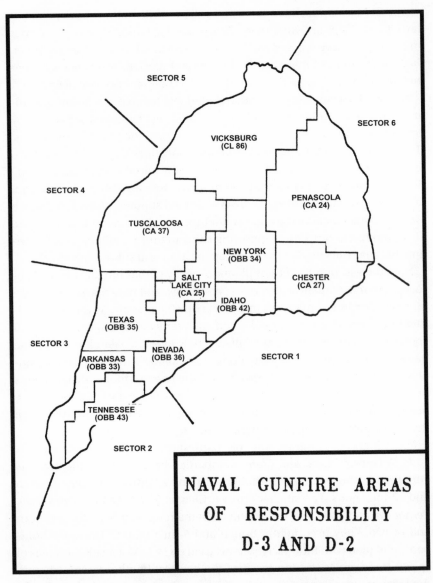

SECTOR 5

VICKSBURG
(CL 86)

SECTOR 6

SECTOR 4

PENASCOLA
(CA 24)

TUSCALOOSA
(CA 37)

NEW YORK
(OBB 34)

SALT
LAKE CITY
(CA 25)

CHESTER
(CA 27)

IDAHO
(OBB 42)

TEXAS
(OBB 35)

SECTOR 3

NEVADA
(OBB 36)

SECTOR 1

ARKANSAS
(OBB 33)

TENNESSEE
(OBB 43)

SECTOR 2

NAVAL GUNFIRE AREAS
OF RESPONSIBILITY
D-3 AND D-2

Naval Gunfire Map, D-3 and D-2, Iwo Jima. Because of faulty intelligence, battle-ships bombarded areas of sparse defenses and smaller ships bombarded areas of heavy defenses. Bartley, *Iwo Jima: Amphibious Epic*

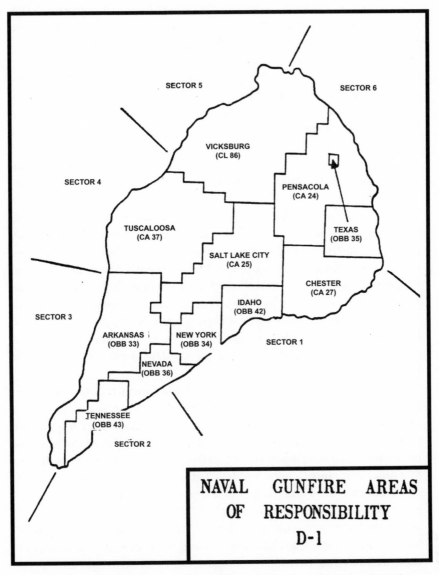

SECTOR 5

SECTOR 6

VICKSBURG
(CL 86)

SECTOR 4

PENSACOLA
(CA 24)

TUSCALOOSA
(CA 37)

TEXAS
(OBB 35)

SALT LAKE CITY
(CA 25)

CHESTER
(CA 27)

IDAHO
(OBB 42)

SECTOR 3

ARKANSAS
(OBB 33)

NEW YORK
(OBB 34)

SECTOR 1

NEVADA
(OBB 36)

TENNESSEE
(OBB 43)

SECTOR 2

NAVAL GUNFIRE AREAS OF RESPONSIBILITY
D-1

Naval Gunfire Map, D-1. The map shows little variation from the D-3 and D-2 bombardments. Bartley, *Iwo Jima: Amphibious Epic*

Because of the misplaced preliminary bombardment, marines on D-Day received intense enfilading fire from heavy weapons positions—one of the most deadly angles of fire a defender can have on an attacking enemy.[71] The bombardment did not destroy numerous defenses above Airfield No. 1, either.[72] An after-action Navy gunfire report indicated that although the bombardment accomplished its major task of providing enough fire support to allow the Marines to establish a beachhead,[73] it was not effective enough to soften up the target before they landed; sufficient fire support ideally should have cut down on casualties and the length of the battle.[74] The report concluded by stating that the bombardment suffered for three reasons: not enough ships, not enough time, and not enough accurate intelligence.[75]

On a positive note, JICPOA did contribute accurate intelligence on beach obstacles for the preliminary bombardment. Analysts spotted barbed wire, possible mine holes, and large petrol drums buried in the sand on the east beach. They thought that the petrol drums were filled with gasoline and rigged to detonate on command when the Marines landed.[76] Therefore, the Navy shelled the beaches to clear obstacles from the landing areas, effectively destroying the barbed wire and potentially deadly petrol drums that might have made the beaches unassailable.[77] As a precaution, however, the first wave of marines landed wearing fire retardant grease on their exposed skin.[78]

All told, if the operations planners of Detachment had had access to more accurate intelligence, they probably would have planned differently and made better use of increasingly scarce resources. They might have used more marines. The size of the attack force outnumbered the Japanese three to one, but the enemy's expert defenses gave them a force multiplier that upset that ratio. General Smith stated in his autobiography that "From our heavy casualties and the fact that we were scarcely moving, it was evident to me that another regiment of the Third Division was necessary to relieve the battle weary troops in the line."[79] Actually, they ended up landing two RCTs of the Third Division. General Schmidt and Gen. Graves Erskine, Third Marine Division commander, both wanted to land the remaining regiment of the Third Division to offset heavy casualties, exhaustion, and a slow operational tempo. Smith, however, overruled them because he did not want the island to become too crowded with U.S. combatants.[80]

A more accurate preliminary naval bombardment plan probably would have helped U.S. force multiplication efforts. Areas of dense infantry positions, all underground, would likely have been targeted by the OBBs' big guns, and the Navy probably would have conducted a more lengthy bombardment. Moreover, the synchronized attack on both Iwo Jima and Japan and the conservation of naval shells for Okinawa might have taken a backseat to saving the lives of thousands of Marine and Navy servicemen.

Conclusion

The intelligence mistakes on Iwo Jima occurred for six reasons, which are complex and intertwined. In brief, 1) comprehensive photographic coverage was lacking; 2) JICPOA had lost its most experienced photographic analysts; 3) many enemy construction activities took place at night; 4) captured documents showed only part of the enemy situation; 5) intelligence analysts believed the Japanese were still using a variant of the crust defense; and 6) the enemy made maximum use of highly effective camouflage techniques.

First, photo interpreters did not receive comprehensive coverage of the objective until one month before the Marines landed. Not using specialized photoreconnaissance aircraft for collection operations contributed to this shortfall. This meant two things: analysts did not have enough effective media to analyze early in the intelligence operation; and, when they did receive effective media, they had less time to analyze it because of their dissemination deadline. Second, the loss of experienced photo interpreters in late January decreased JICPOA's ability to effectively analyze February photos that showed a dramatic increase in defensive installations on the objective. The Navy rotation policy that forced the loss of the interpreters and the transfer of such valuable personnel to the AIC represents an intelligence failure.

All of this hurt the photo interpretation process, and it appears that JICPOA did not have time to conduct effective stereoscopic three-dimensional analyses. Three-dimensional imagery better revealed terrain and defenses than did two-dimensional imagery because it showed more volume and shadows. This made man-made objects easier to recognize. A succession of three-dimensional photos of a particular target on the ground gave analysts a good idea of what type of defensive construction was going on over a given period of time.

For example, stereoscopic analyses might have demonstrated, even if the activity were camouflaged, the many stages of placing an artillery piece on a plot of ground and then encasing it in a concrete and steel structure. Specifically, such activity could have been revealed by construction trails or concrete mixing and setting activities. Also, stereoscope analyses might have spotted camouflage activities by registering a dramatic increase in tufts of grass or plant life around the site in question. The point is that this type of analysis could have shown a sequence of events in one spot, the way successive frames of a motion picture show the action—stage by stage. Although the stereoscope process did not always work and required highly experienced personnel to operate, its use could increase the effectiveness of photo interpretation by as much as 50 percent.

Stereoscopes probably were not used in the intelligence operation against Iwo Jima. This is evident because they were used in the after-action analysis of the battle in Information Bulletins 136-45 and 137-45, two documents that spotted previously missed weapons positions. Of course, those who worked on this project, a joint JICPOA and Fifth Division intelligence team, had the benefit of knowing what they were analyzing. Nevertheless, both after-action bulletins demonstrated what experienced photo analysts could have done if they had had the time and effective media. For their analyses, analysts used photographs taken between 15 June 1944 and 19 February 1945.[81] Remarks from Information Bulletin 137-45 are characteristic of their observations.

After-Action Stereogram Studies of Iwo Jima

150-mm Mortar Cave Position

"Stereogram # 1—These 2 September 1944 photos show beginnings of cave entrances. Note the natural vegetation and absence of large piles of spoil [excess dirt from excavations]."

"Stereogram # 2—These 12 January 1945 pictures show an increase in digging activity."

"Stereogram # 3—These 4 February 1945 photos show large increase in spoil. Lack of camouflage would indicate digging was continuing. Amount of spoil indicates extensive works."

2 Gun Battery (one 12-cm, one 14-cm) Coast Defense (for gun positions A, B, C and D)

"Stereogram # 1—These 2 September 1944 photos show minor activity in area, at A ["A" is an area on a drawing] in particular."

"Stereogram # 2—These 11 December 1944 photos show much work had been done since stereogram 1. A has been casemated [put in concrete] and camouflaged. B, C and D appear to be empty."

"Stereogram # 3—Shadow definition on these 12 January 1945 photos make A stand out prominently. B and C have nets stretched out over them."

"Stereogram # 4—These photos of 4 February 1945 show the gun in B. The tufts of grass comprising A's camouflage are readily seen. C has a net stretched over it. D is still empty. Ground reconnaissance revealed A to be 140-mm and B to be 120-mm."

2 Gun Battery 15-cm Coast Defense Guns (for gun positions A and B)

"Stereogram # 1—These 4 July 1944 photos show the excavation for A. Uncamouflaged spoil is a giveaway to activity in this area."

"Stereogram # 2—These 2 September 1944 photos show A has been camouflaged—no evidence of casemate. There is a rectangular excavation at B. The spoil has been camouflaged with plants and bushes."

"Stereogram # 3 —These 11 December 1944 photos show the casemates finished and camouflaged. Camouflage discipline is good."

"Stereogram # 4—This 12 January 1945 photography clearly shows the direction of fire to be southwestward, covering the West Beaches. Camouflage has been improved. Shadow definition aids greatly in picking out the installations. Note the shallow communication trench leading in from the south."

"Stereogram # 5—These 4 February 1945 photos are included to show how easily the installations might be overlooked based on this one sortie."

Source: JICPOA Information Bulletin 137-45, pp. 5, 6, and 9.

If JICPOA had had the time and personnel to conduct stereoscope analyses beforehand, its analysts probably would have spotted many more enemy positions than they did. Even a thorough analysis of the late February photos could have led to a better understanding of the enemy situation and possibly a change of attack plans. Interestingly, according to the first official Marine Corps historical account of the campaign, the "American high command" did not see the Iwo Jima assault as a large and dangerous campaign at the time. Rather, it was merely a step closer to Japan, using tried-and-true amphibious assault methods and massive air and naval gunfire. The Japanese were reeling from heavy casualties throughout the Pacific, and it appears that many senior officers thought that U.S. forces could seize any island they wanted.[82] This may have been true, but it did not mean that they should have stopped applying careful thought to combat operations. Why, then, the major postbattle stereoscopic study? More than likely, the defense of Iwo Jima shocked the Pacific's operations planners, who had never before seen such a sophisticated effort on the part of the Japanese. True, the defense of Peleliu deviated from the norm, but Iwo Jima hammered the point home: the enemy had become smarter and more deadly. Information Bulletins 136-45 and 137-45 were probably lessons on what to do next time.

Regardless, the third reason that the Iwo intelligence operation did not go well was that the Japanese evidently conducted much of their construction after dark. The submarine USS *Archerfish* sat off Iwo Jima on lifeguard duty, picking up downed aircrews from planes that crashed in the sea. By periscope, its captain observed the island regularly, but he took no pictures because that was not his mission. If he had, the photos would have shown Japanese soldiers emerging from Iwo's soil like ants from an anthill shortly after sunset to build fortifications and to finish their cave gun positions.[83] Bombing missions, mostly conducted by day, had driven them underground, so photographic sorties, conducted during bombing missions, showed little surface activity. In any event, JICPOA did not have nocturnal photographic capabilities, so nighttime activity would have gone unrecorded by aerial surveillance.

Fourth, in reference to the underestimation of the Japanese garrison, analysts relied on documents to analyze the enemy's order of battle. These came from the same source that had proven reliable for the Guam, Tinian, and Peleliu operations. However, although the Iwo Jima–related documents proved correct, they showed only part of the picture. The Japanese had reinforced the island with units in addition to those listed in the captured documents. Since intelligence analysts relied largely on the documents to estimate the size of Iwo Jima's garrison, their estimates were wrong.

Oddly, analysts achieved source corroboration between the documents and photographs in three cases that dealt with Japanese weaponry. First, documents said that the IJN Guard Force on Iwo had fourteen 120-mm coast defense or dual-purpose guns, and photo analysts found all fourteen in aerial photographs. Second, documents stated that the same IJN guard force and an air defense unit had a combined strength of ten 80-mm guns, and photo analysts found all ten in aerial photographs. Lastly, the same guard unit and two other air defense units were supposed to have a combined strength of fifty-four 25-mm AA guns. Photo analysts found forty-four of them. Additionally, the increases in defenses demonstrated by the February photographs did not reflect capabilities beyond the 13,500 Japanese that were assumed to be on the island. Such evidence must have compelled JICPOA to believe that it had excellent intelligence when in fact it did not.

Interestingly enough, the documents also helped to avert a probable disaster. If JICPOA had not had access to the captured documents from Saipan, the battle for Iwo Jima might have failed. Photo analysts observed only 105 weapons and 119 weapons positions on Iwo Jima, but documents revealed that the garrison possessed about 669 weapons.[84] (These figures include machine guns, flamethrowers, antitank weapons, and artillery.) Without the analyzed documents, Nimitz and his lieutenants might have planned an assault for a garrison with only 224 heavy weapons or weapons positions, thereby using fewer troops, less air power, and less naval gunfire to seize the island. If this had happened, the attack to secure the beachhead probably would have failed, and the campaign would have been abandoned until more power could be amassed to complete it.

In a fifth intelligence miscalculation, with reference to Japanese defensive plans, intelligence planners and analysts believed that the Japanese would defend Iwo Jima from the beaches and adjacent areas. A shore-based defense (crust or layered beach area defenses, or both) had been used by the Japanese in most campaigns in the Central Pacific up to that time. Most analysts, and operations planners, for that matter, believed that the Imperial Japanese Headquarters had established this type defense as part of its tactical doctrine. Photographs of extensive layered trench lines and pillboxes just off Iwo's beaches and adjoining terrain reinforced their beliefs. Moreover, as of February 1945, the Japanese were continuing to string wire (6,700 yards) and dig trenches (42,100 yards) along Iwo's eastern beaches.[85] General Kuribayashi purposely left the trenches in the open to deceive U.S. forces, and he ordered the construction of 135 pillboxes built on or near the beaches at the request of IJN officers under his command.[86] They believed in the shore-based defense. The general did not. A Marine Corps G-2 after-action report indicated that dummy positions along the island's beaches fooled U.S. forces into thinking that the Japanese would utilize a beach defense.[87] Despite the beach defenses, however, U.S. aerial reconnaissance should not have been distracted from the massive defense construction efforts taking place on the northern portion of the island. Intelligence planners, in directing most reconnaissance aircraft to focus on the landing beaches, committed a grievous error, and this aspect of the Iwo Jima operation can be considered a failure.

Sixth, for Iwo Jima, the Japanese conducted the most effective counter-intelligence operation for any island yet attacked under Nimitz's command. Aside from deception operations just mentioned, a Marine after-action report stated that the Japanese had used camouflage to the maximum and that "most of the gun positions were totally hidden."[88] This simple but effective tactic kept hundreds of enemy positions from detection by U.S. reconnaissance efforts.[89]

What lessons can be learned from the Iwo Jima campaign? For starters, and for obvious reasons, Iwo Jima demonstrates that collection operations ideally should cover the entire battlespace on a regular basis. Looking back, it is amazing that early and mid-term photographic missions focused primarily on the area surrounding one airfield and beaches adjacent to it. If they had been more comprehensive, analysts might have discovered the actual defensive situation on Iwo Jima before the ill-timed transfer of all of their experienced photo interpreters.

Another simple lesson is that an intelligence organization should be left alone to conduct its business. That is not to say that it should have a blank check to operate any way it wants, but bureaucratic impediments from higher offices within or outside of the intelligence community can impede and even halt the intelligence cycle. The fact that JICPOA lost the expertise of its experienced photographic analysts because of administrative procedures is ridiculous. In World War II, this probably happened because higher offices did not understand the intelligence cycle and how important it was to operations planners and combatants.

Iwo Jima also points out that even the most convincing evidence can lead to the wrong conclusions—a common hazard in the intelligence business. For instance, analysts relied on captured documents and photographs to calculate the Japanese order of battle and defensive plans. Both sources seemed to corroborate one another, and they supported shore-based-defense prejudices that many analysts and planners apparently suffered from. The source corroboration convinced the beach-defense-minded analysts to believe that they had produced accurate intelligence when, in fact, they had missed the big picture.

The Strategic Implications of Operation Detachment

Despite all of the difficulties on Iwo Jima, the marines did their jobs and seized the island. Likewise, even during combat, the SeaBees landed and did their jobs. During the middle of the fight for Iwo, after the marines had secured half of the island, the SeaBees transformed Airfield No. 1 into an airstrip barely large enough to handle B-29s. Shortly thereafter, one came sputtering along, damaged from a bombing raid over Tokyo. It was the *Dinah Might,* and on 2 March 1945, it became the first U.S. bomber to use the strip. U.S. servicemen on the island erupted into massive jubilation when the plane landed. In their eyes and from what their commanders had told them, this is what they had been fighting for, an emergency landing strip close to Japan that would save the lives of countless airmen returning from Japan in damaged planes.[90]

Later, on 9 March, a huge flight of bombers left the Marianas for a first low-altitude bombing raid against Tokyo—something that would have been difficult with Japanese fighters operating from Iwo Jima's airstrips. Operation planners decided to take their chances with Japan-based fighter interceptors because they now had Iwo Jima as a safety net. The raid consisted of 334 B-29s[91] in three columns that stretched out for four hundred miles.[92] High-altitude bombing, as earlier discussed, had produced less than desired results, and the JCS probably figured that low-altitude bombing would reap the destruction desired. With Iwo now in U.S. hands, the raids could fly over the Pacific unhindered. In the 9 March raid, no bombers were shot down on the way to fire-bomb Tokyo's military industrial factories, which were surrounded by residential neighborhoods. When they arrived over the city, they dropped their bombs from altitudes ranging from 9,200 feet to 4,900 feet.[93] The raid destroyed sixteen square miles of Tokyo, killed eighty-four thousand people, destroyed 265,000 buildings, and made one million people homeless.[94] Japanese accounts claim that the temperature in and around the target zone reached a scorching 1,800 degrees and that the water in nearby canals boiled.[95] Numerous U.S. historical reports have stated that B-29 tail gunners returning to the Marianas could see the fiery glow of Tokyo from 150 miles away.[96] Few B-29s returned damaged from this raid, and only two had to land on Iwo Jima.[97] In contrast, during successive raids on cities such as Nagoya, Osaka, and Kobe, the Japanese fought harder to protect their war industries. By the end of the war, 24,761 U.S. airmen flying in damaged planes were saved by using the landing strips on Iwo Jima.[98]

Control of Iwo Jima proved to be one of the major strategic advances in the bloody war against Japan and demonstrated to the enemy two points: one, that U.S. amphibious forces were unstoppable, and two, that an invasion of the home islands would most likely occur. In this regard, JICPOA contributed to an important axis of the Central Pacific drive. The intelligence difficulties faced in the Iwo Jima operation, on the other hand, ideally should have served as warnings for the next campaign—Okinawa. Tragically, they did not.

Operation Iceberg: Okinawa
Campaign Background

On 1 April 1945, U.S. Marine Corps and Army troops landed on Okinawa in the largest amphibious operation of the Pacific War, otherwise known as Operation Iceberg.[99] The Japanese defended Okinawa as intensely as they had Iwo Jima, because it was their last line of defense between the United States and the home islands. Japanese forces fought with a fierce determination to delay what they once thought no army could ever do—invade Japan. The battle lasted for nearly three months, including all of April, May, and over half of June.[100] Massive casualties resulted. The United States suffered 7,374 KIA and 32,046 WIA and MIA. Kamikaze planes sank or heavily damaged more than twenty U.S. ships. The Japanese, including Okinawan civilians and home defense units, sustained over a hundred thousand killed in action,[101] and some estimates say as many as 107,539 enemy personnel were killed.[102]

These were the highest casualty rates of the island campaigns during the war and illustrated the horrific nature of combat experienced on Okinawa. The Japanese had burrowed into the island and set up complex kill zones with overlapping fields of fire reminiscent of Kuribayashi's death traps on Iwo Jima. U.S. forces utilized massed artillery, flamethrowers, and the highly effective tank-infantry team to root out and destroy the defenders.

Several intelligence units belonging to the fleet and U.S. Army contributed to Iceberg because it was a large, two-corps operation. However, Iceberg occurred within Admiral Nimitz's area of responsibility, so JICPOA was the lead intelligence unit for the operation. Unfortunately, JICPOA did not accurately discern Japanese defensive positions or order of battle, and the results adversely affected combat on Okinawa.[103]

Target Location

Okinawa is located 375 miles east of Formosa and three hundred miles southwest of Kyushu.[104] It is sixty miles long, has a maximum width of eighteen miles at its widest point, and a minimum width of two miles at its thinnest point.[105] The island's terrain variously features mountains, hills, swamps, woods, jungle, and flat coastal plains.

Why Okinawa?

The decision to attack Okinawa came in early October 1944.[106] The Joint Chiefs, after accepting the recommendations of the CCS and the advice of Vice Admiral Spruance, decided to attack Japan through its underside by using Okinawa as a staging area and base of operations instead of China and Formosa. Control of Okinawa also would put U.S. forces squarely in the center of Japan's lines of communication to Korea, China, and Southeast Asia. Such a maneuver would cut Japan off from its troops operating on the Asian mainland and its crumbling stocks of natural resources in countries such as Vietnam and Indonesia.[107]

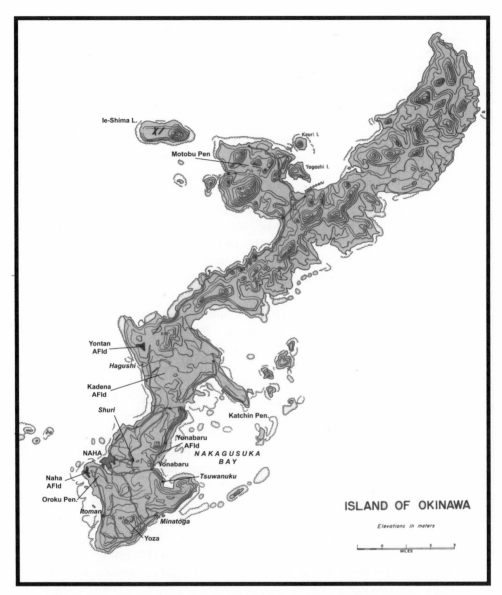

Okinawa. U.S. forces landed on the southwest shore along Hagushi and cut the island in half from west to east toward Chimu Bay. Marine forces drove north, and
Army forces drove south. Later in the campaign, the Marines returned south to assist the Army in clearing the island. Frank and Shaw, *Victory and Occupation*

The Okinawa Intelligence Operation

JICPOA began collecting information on Okinawa as soon as Nimitz received the JCS order to attack the island. Photographic reconnaissance was the main source of information that JICPOA used to formulate estimations of Japanese capabilities and intentions. Unfortunately, five major difficulties surrounded intelligence collection for Iceberg.

First, Okinawa was well protected deep inside enemy territory. Aerial reconnaissance pilots could not fly over the island with impunity and photograph it, as they had during other Pacific campaigns such as that for Tinian. The Japanese, in spite of major defeats in the past year, still retained lethal air power close to the home islands. Second, Okinawa sat 1,200 nautical miles from the nearest Allied base,[108] and the distance made reconnaissance missions complex and lengthy. (Recall that the U.S. had not yet secured Iwo Jima.) Third, poor weather plagued photographic efforts. Of nineteen days chosen for photographic coverage, only two were cloud free.[109] Fourth, pilots had to photograph a vast expanse of land—350 square miles, to be exact—to attain complete coverage.[110] This was much more difficult, over and above the disparity in size, than covering a smaller island such as Iwo Jima. Fifth, air reconnaissance missions took place under the cover of air raids, so pilots photographed Okinawa when and where operational planners wanted to strafe the island, not when and where intelligence planners wanted photographs taken. This is the same problem previously experienced on Saipan and other islands.[111]

Except for the bad weather, intelligence personnel overcame most of these obstacles. By October 1944, reconnaissance pilots had covered 90 percent of the island with vertical and oblique photographs carried out from B-29s and carrier aircraft.[112] JICPOA conducted a stereoscopic analysis of the landing beaches to analyze hydrography and plotted defenses on shore areas and near airstrips.[113] InterpRon One and Two were not able to assist because they were busy helping JICPOA with the Iwo Jima operation, and their products had a negligible impact on Okinawa.[114] A Tenth Army report stated that photo interpreters arrived at its command too late to provide intelligence for the planning phase of Iceberg, and that many of these personnel spent most of their time assisting with logistics planning and operations, further weakening the intelligence effort.[115] The same report asserted that the photo coverage of Okinawa was not good, and that commanders ultimately had to rely on Japanese maps captured during the assault to conduct certain aspects of the campaign.[116]

Aside from photographs, JICPOA additionally relied on captured hydrographic documents, POW interrogations, interviews with people who had lived on Okinawa, and articles from Japanese publications[117] to produce the main Okinawa information bulletin, number 161-44. Published on 15 November 1944,[118] it did not contain photographic intelligence from submarines. The USS *Swordfish* was supposed to reconnoiter Okinawa, but it failed to return from its mission and the crew never made port.[119]

The Okinawa information bulletin was 127 pages long and covered a standard array of subjects, such as climatology, geography, anchorages, navigational information, roads and railroads, and population. Furthermore, it warned of poisonous snakes indigenous to Okinawa that could kill a human in minutes. The information bulletin discussed the enemy order of battle and plan of defense through maps and text descriptions. In brief, JICPOA surmised that the Japanese, which numbered fifty thousand, mainly occupied the southern portion of Okinawa's coastal regions with an impressive array of coast-defense guns, dual-purpose guns, machine guns, pillboxes, and trench lines.[120]

In its search to collect hydrographic intelligence on Okinawa, JICPOA conducted interviews with U.S. citizens who had once lived there. The first was an eighty-year-old conchologist named D. D. Thaanum. Thaanum had studied shellfish on Okinawa and had intimate knowledge of its shores and surf conditions. His photographs, charts, and maps provided useful intelligence for operations planners. In addition, Thaanum gave JICPOA the name of another Okinawa conchologist, Daniel B. Langford, who had moved to Arizona. JICPOA flew one of its analysts, Lt. Cdr. N. C. Vanzant, to Arizona to interview Langford. He provided a wealth of data on Okinawa's reefs and hydrographic conditions.[121]

After publication of the Okinawa information bulletin, aerial reconnaissance continued because the attack had been scheduled to commence in March, and JICPOA needed to maintain surveillance on the Japanese and learn more about their capabilities and intentions. B-29 pilots flew photo reconnaissance missions over Okinawa on 31 December 1944, and 1–3 January 1945. Carrier pilots followed with missions on 21–22 January 1945. JICPOA's photographic analysts reviewed the new data and published an updated Okinawa information bulletin, number 53-45, on 28 February 1945. Analysts described photographs of southern Okinawa as "quite good."[122]

Regrettably, the departure of experienced photo interpreters that had marred the Iwo Jima intelligence operation had a similar impact on Okinawa. Veteran photo interpreters had analyzed photos of Okinawa for the fall 1944 information bulletin, and they had also analyzed photographs of the objective into January 1945. However, inexperienced interpreters studied photos of the objective from the end of January 1945 on. Unfortunately for U.S. forces, this was the most crucial period for the Okinawa intelligence operation, because, as later discussed, Japanese capabilities and intentions changed significantly. The results would be disastrous.

Information Bulletin 53-45 indicated increases in Japanese personnel to fifty-six thousand and gave minute detail on enemy weapons strength and troop dispositions—supposedly still on Okinawa's southern coastal regions. Analysts stated that the Japanese would use infantry with artillery support in the defense of Okinawa and that tanks had been spotted on the island as well. The information bulletin did not note any change in the Japanese defensive plan.[123]

Photo reconnaissance continued right up to L-Day and even into the attack. Photo analysts and radio intelligence personnel who had been listening to Japanese units arrive and depart from Okinawa for months revised troop estimates at least four times before the attack began. Eventually, however, they put the final Japanese manpower estimates at seventy-five thousand defenders. In total, reconnaissance squadrons flew five major photographic missions over Okinawa, and JICPOA distributed nineteen sets of photographs plus accompanying information bulletins to operations planners and the senior combat echelons involved in the operation.[124]

Chain of Command

Nimitz assigned Spruance as commander of Iceberg and Turner as commander of the amphibious task force. Lt. Gen. Simon Buckner, U.S. Army, was to command the ground element, designated as the Tenth Army.[125] The ground forces consisted of the following formations: from the Marines' III Amphibious Corps, the First, Second, and Sixth Marine Divisions; and from the U.S. Army's XXIV Corps, the Seventh, Ninety-sixth, and Seventy-seventh Divisions.[126] The Army's Twenty-seventh Division stood in reserve.[127] The entire fighting force consisted of 116,00 men. The naval support component consisted of a massive armada of ships: two carrier task forces—one U.S. and one British—an amphibious support task force, and a gunfire and covering task force.[128]

Plan of Attack

The attack plan for Iceberg entailed four main phases. In phase one, set to begin on 26 March, the Seventy-seventh Division would seize Kerama Retto, a cluster of islands just off the west coast of Okinawa, so that the U.S. Navy could use it as an anchorage and logistics base to support combat ashore. Phase one also included the seizure of nearby lesser island objectives for use as artillery support bases.[129] During phase two, naval ships and aircraft were to fire at enemy positions on and near the landing beaches for seven days. During phase three, which was set to begin on 1 April, the Second Marine Division was to conduct a feint off Minatoga Town on Okinawa's extreme southwest coast. At the same time, the First and Sixth Marine Divisions and the Seventh and Ninety-sixth Infantry Divisions would land abreast on Okinawa's central western shore near what U.S. forces called Hagushi Town.[130] Their first mission was to destroy the many enemy strongpoints along the coast to secure the beachhead and prepare to move inland. In phase four, the Marines were to secure the two airstrips nearest the beaches, sweep and clear the area north of the landing beaches, and cut the island in half. Meanwhile, the two Army divisions were tasked with clearing the enemy from the south.[131]

The plan did not go as expected, at first to the relief of combatants and then to their horror. The troops landed and experienced little or no resistance, cutting the island in half eleven days ahead of schedule. But one week later, in southern Okinawa, the U.S. Army stumbled against a series of massive, mutually supporting field fortifications, most of them subsurface emplacements. Reduction of these defenses, a grueling three-month effort, required the participation of every U.S. combat division on Okinawa. JICPOA had not foreseen the extent of, nor had it accurately pinpointed, these elaborate defense networks.

How Intelligence Influenced the Campaign

JICPOA had pinpointed enemy troop concentrations and fortifications along the shores of Okinawa's southern half in Information Bulletins 161-44 and 53-45, with the latter being the most recent. It stated that the Japanese had massed most of their troops in two areas: the beaches adjacent to Yontan and Kadena airfields, and Nakagusuku Wan, a wide bay on the southern portion of the east coast. Both were potential landing beaches.[132] Smaller troop concentrations covered adjoining shorelines where the Japanese probably thought U.S. forces less likely to land. This intelligence was based on photographs of 22 January 1945,[133] and subsequent reconnaissance never refuted it. JICPOA's troop disposition map in bulletin 53-45 categorized defensive areas by letter designations. The most important were areas "B," "C," and "D," because they contained the heaviest enemy troop concentrations.

Analysts stated that area "B," which stretched from the shores of Yontan and Kadena down to Naha City, contained heavy troop concentrations. A

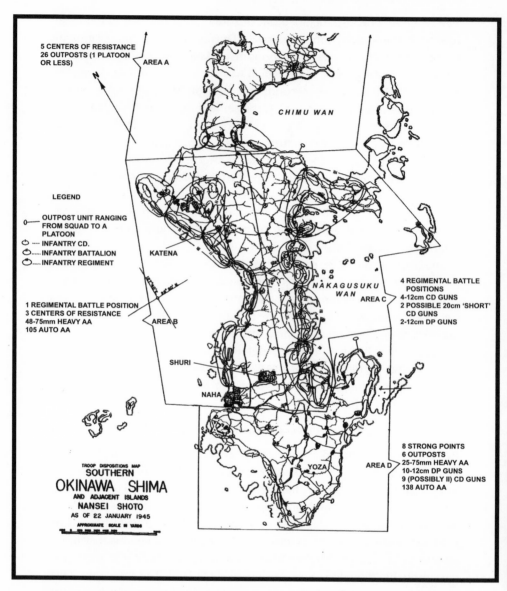

JICPOA Prebattle Map, Troop Dispositions on Southern Okinawa. Circled areas along coastlines indicate the troop dispositions. JICPOA Information Bulletin 53-43

regiment and a battalion occupied the landing beach area in three major centers of resistance that encompassed eight strongpoints. (In text, the information bulletin refers to company positions as strongpoints. Each strongpoint had layered defenses.) The regimental reserve occupied an area behind the beaches near Yontan airfield. Two battalions fortified in six strongpoints covered the southern reaches of this coastal area down to Naha Town and its airstrip.[134]

JICPOA's analysts said that there were more Japanese troops in Area "C" than in any other defensive zone on Okinawa. Located around the eastern bay, Nakagusuku Wan, defenses there were also the most organized on the island. Analysts asserted that "There is virtually an unbroken chain of foxholes and machine-gun pits at the beach along the entire length of NAKAGUSUKU Bay."[135] Almost twelve miles long, this line ran just behind a sea wall that straddled the bay. It served as the "outpost line of resistance" for the four regiments dug in behind it. Each regiment had constructed its own defense zone unique to the terrain it occupied, and together these defenses included almost three dozen company-size strongpoints.[136]

JICPOA wrote that area "D" encompassed the entire southern tip of Okinawa. Analysts presumed that it was "lightly defended" by eight companies organized into eight strongpoints and six outposts. Each outpost guarded a stretch of coastline.[137] Aerial photographs of this sector, which according to JICPOA were good, showed twenty-four artillery emplacements about three miles south of the town of Shuri. Analysts suspected that this might have been part of the enemy's central artillery base.[138]

Similarly, JICPOA estimated that the northern half of the island contained only scant resistance, with five battalions occupying five centers of resistance composed of as many as twenty-six platoon or squad-sized outposts.[139] On the other hand, analysts stated that they had not been able to figure out exactly how the Japanese were organized to defend northern Okinawa. Therefore, they assumed that U.S. forces could expect the "normal contingent of artillery, tanks, and other special troops" in this area of operations.[140]

In reality, nothing could have been further from the truth.[141] Only small enemy units opposed the landings from far inland with periodic mortar and artillery fire. In reference to the amphibious assault, Isely and Crowl wrote, "the attacking forces were given an entirely inaccurate idea of what to expect on landing."[142] Japanese troops did not occupy coastal defensive areas at the landing beaches or in southern Okinawa. Instead, they positioned their main defense forces along three ridge lines and adjoining hills that ran east to west in the interior of southern Okinawa, utilizing *fukkaku* tactics. The only facet of Japanese defense that the analysts got right was the twenty-four artillery pieces south of Shuri.

The first defensive line, the Kakazu Ridge, was just below the narrow bottleneck of the island's southern half. Three miles to the south, the enemy occupied a series of hills with Shuri Town in the center. Shuri Castle, built in 1544 to serve as the seat of power for Okinawan royalty, sat a half a mile to the east of the city. The Japanese fortified it, too. Yonabaru Town on the east coast and Naha City on the west coast anchored Shuri's flanks. Of the three lines, the Japanese had most heavily fortified this line, nicknamed the "Shuri Line," by U.S. servicemen. The Japanese placed their final line of defense about six miles south of Shuri on the Kiyan Penninsula, the southernmost tip of the island.[143] Defenses on Kiyan centered on Yaezu and Yoza hills, which, combined with nearby smaller elevations, offered an eight-kilometer front.[144] Each line had gaps of low ground, but the Japanese had turned those areas into fortified gauntlets where intruders would encounter flanking fire from both sides.

The Japanese commander on Okinawa, Lt. Gen. Mitsuru Ushijima, ordered that each line be held until it was no longer defendable. At that time, what was left of the main force would retire to the next fully manned line, leaving behind a modest suicide unit as a delaying force. Each line bristled with complex cave defenses and tunnel systems that afforded excellent cover, concealment, and mobility—identical to what the marines had faced on Iwo Jima. Caves contained powerful weapons such as heavy machine guns, light cannon, and antitank guns. Multiple machine-gun nests and infantry positions protected each cave from assault. Mortar and antitank units placed their guns to cover probable avenues of approach of U.S. tank-infantry teams. All gun emplacements commanded specific fields of fire that overlapped one another. The Japanese even fortified the reverse slope of each elevation, ensuring a difficult fight for would-be attackers.[145] This was nothing like what JICPOA had predicted, and the battle produced some of the most severe combat seen in the Pacific.

The inaccurate intelligence first affected the preliminary naval bombardment. For Iceberg, naval ships administered what the official Marine Corps record of the campaign called "the heaviest concentration of naval gunfire ever delivered in support of the landing troops."[146] Navy ships fired 3,800 tons of shells on the landing beaches. In point of fact, however, the massive bombardment fell on empty shores. The Japanese had left the beaches undefended[147] but for a few pillboxes.[148] The landing teams that hit the beaches on 1 April met almost no resistance. As they moved inland, the situation changed, but not by much. Small pockets of enemy soldiers

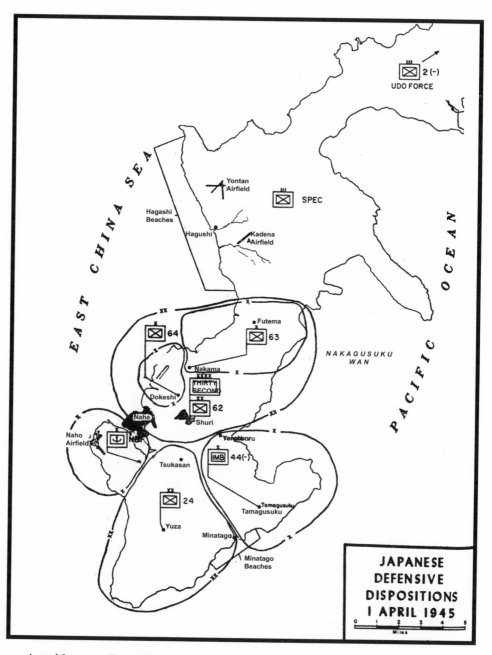

Actual Japanese Troop Dispositions on Okinawa. The Japanese lines sat within the marked areas. Frank and Shaw, *Victory and Occupation*

who engaged the landing force in firefights were quickly put down or captured.

Teams of linguists, mostly from JICPOA, interrogated numerous civilians and twenty-six captured Japanese within the first few days of the operation. None, however, were able to provide information to clear up the perplexing situation at hand and explain why the landing force met such feeble resistance. Most claimed that the Japanese occupied the southern half of Okinawa, but in what manner they did not know.[149] In just a few days, however, the Army discovered what preinvasion and operational intelligence had not.

By 4 April, the Seventh and Ninety-sixth Divisions had run up against the outskirts of the Kakazu Line, and by 7 April, they were in the thick of heavy combat. For days on end, the Japanese repelled each thrust into their lines. Even when U.S. forces took one side of an elevation, the enemy often fought them off with a reverse-slope counterattack. Artillery fire from the distant Shuri Line added to the carnage and beat back the Army's attack. By 12 April, General Buckner had to commit elements of the Twenty-seventh Division, the Corps reserves, to the right flank of the attack.[150] But the battle for the Kakazu raged so violently and produced so many casualties that on 13 April, both sides took a day of rest to consolidate their lines and reorganize.[151]

Eventually, the Kakazu fell, and by 19 April, U.S. Army units had stumbled across the soon-to-be-infamous Shuri Line. Now three full infantry divisions—the Twenty-seventh, Ninety-sixth, and Seventh—attacked the Japanese position on a wide, three-division front. But the offensive failed miserably because of heavy enemy return fire from numerous well-covered and concealed gun emplacements and accurate artillery fire. Thirty U.S. Army tanks did manage to thrust into the enemy line but were forced to withdraw because infantry troops had been unable to advance with the armored column. The tankers needed the infantry to clear out Japanese anti-tank teams, and without their support, they were left highly vulnerable. Upon retreat, the Japanese destroyed twenty-two of the tanks, an astounding loss.[152]

By 27 April, the Seventy-seventh Infantry and First Marine Divisions relieved the badly battered Ninety-sixth and Twenty-seventh for a renewed offensive against the Shuri Line. The marines had been fighting in the north but under less strenuous combat conditions. Intelligence had predicted light resistance in the north—only twenty-six platoons of Japanese—but the marines met many more than had been estimated, which made their combat operations more difficult.

Still, compared to other units, the Marine units were fresh. They linked up with both the Seventh and the Seventy-seventh and prepared to attack the Shuri, but before they could, the Japanese counterattacked on 4 May in a well-coordinated display of arms, complete with massed artillery fire and tanks supported by infantry. The enemy thrust drove through U.S. lines, trampled the Seventh Division, and retook U.S.–occupied Yonabaru Town, where the attack eventually fizzled out.[153] Obviously, JICPOA had not reported that the Japanese on Okinawa possessed such capabilities.

The attack forced another realignment of U.S. forces. The Ninety-sixth moved back to the front and relieved the Seventh, and the Sixth Marine Division joined the First for another renewed offensive. Now the U.S. line consisted of the Sixth and First Marine Divisions and the Seventy-seventh and Ninety-sixth Infantry Divisions, a massive four-division front. On 11 May, they attacked, but they became bogged down and distracted by stubborn pockets of resistance, strongpoints, and heavy rain. Such fierce and expertly engineered resistance appeared almost impenetrable at times during the fight, and it took eighteen more days of harsh combat, much of it hand-to-hand, to capture the Shuri Line.[154]

On 4 June, as U.S. forces moved farther south, the Sixth Marine Division had to attack the airport at Oroku Peninsula on Okinawa's southwest coast in a shore-to-shore amphibious operation to neutralize the five thousand Japanese dug in there. In prebattle intelligence, JICPOA had indicated stiff defenses on the peninsula, but during the battle for the Kakazu and Shuri lines, tactical aerial reconnaissance discovered even more Japanese troop positions behind the airport. It took ten days for the Marines to reduce the enemy forces on Oroku in fighting that resembled that seen on the Shuri Line.

In the meantime, the First Marine Division and the Ninety-sixth drove south to the Kiyan Peninsula, the final line of enemy defenses. By this point in the campaign, the U.S. forces had tired and became dangerously depleted of strength, but the Japanese were worse off—starving, exhausted, and lacking ammunition. To tip the scale in favor of the attackers, U.S. commanders decided to commit a regimental combat team of the Second Marine Division to the fray. After several days of brutal fighting, they had secured the remainder of the island, and the main battle for Okinawa ended on 22 June.[155]

JICPOA's inability to discern the Japanese order of battle on Okinawa added to the intelligence problems regarding the enemy's defense plans. In February, JICPOA had estimated that fifty-six thousand Japanese occupied Okinawa.[156] In March, that figure was revised upward to seventy-five thousand.[157] In reality, 114,940 Japanese, the bulk of the Thirty-second Army, and the Boeitai (Okinawan Homeguard) had occupied Okinawa.[158] The miscalculation was a 39,940-man discrepancy. The main force units that occupied Okinawa were as follows:[159]

Japanese Thirty-second Army Units on Okinawa

Unit	Unit
62d Division	Twenty-seventh Independent AA Artillery Battalion
24th Division	21st AA Headquarters (6 battalions)
63d Brigade (5 infantry battalions)	8 engineer and shipping units
64th Brigade (5 infantry battalions)	19 air force units (ground-based)
44th Independent Mixed Brigade	36th Signals Regiment (plus 8 attached units)
Twenty-seventh Tank Regiment	Various naval and miscellaneous units
7 artillery and automatic weapons units	Okinawa Naval Base Force

JICPOA also had attempted to estimate the number of weapons the Japanese possessed:[160]

Prebattle Estimate of Japanese Weaponry as of February 1945

Weapons	Numbers
Grenade dischargers	897
LMG	891
HMG	300
20-mm machine cannon	36
37-mm or 47-mm antitank guns	38
70-mm infantry guns or 81-mm mortars[i]	36
75-mm infantry guns	24
75-mm field artillery pieces	36
10-cm howitzers	48
15-cm howitzers	24

[i] Analysts said that if the infantry guns were not present, the mortars would be.

When JICPOA revised the estimated number of troops on Okinawa, weapons figures increased accordingly. Unfortunately, even that figure was incorrect. In fact, prebattle estimates misrepresented Japanese firepower on Okinawa by about a third. This included underestimations of Japanese heavy weaponry, such as artillery and high-velocity guns—the kind of firepower that could break an army. In the past, the Navy had done its best to destroy these weapons during the preliminary bombardment phase of an operation, but as with the Saipan campaign, heavy weapons on Okinawa went largely untouched. The Japanese used weapons of that kind to repulse wave after wave of U.S. assaults on the first two defensive lines.

Overall, JICPOA misinterpreted the enemy's ability to resist attack, causing operations planners to conceive a faulty scheme of maneuver. If the intelligence picture had been more accurate, planners might have proposed landing ground forces to the rear or flanks of Japanese lines. They might even have fortified the northern half of the island and waited for the Japanese to attack. Certainly, they would have used more troops. As it was, the 116,000-man invasion force did not significantly outnumber the 114,000-odd defenders; the situation was not unlike Peleliu in falling far short of the desired three-to-one ratio that U.S. forces strived to achieve. Furthermore, the Navy would not have wasted its massive preliminary bombardment on empty shores. Instead, it probably would have saved its shells to prep each Japanese defensive line with sustained fire just before U.S. forces attacked.[161] Likewise, CINCPAC or Buckner might have ordered U.S. air forces to bomb Japanese positions with high-explosive and incendiary ordnance for a lengthy amount of time well before the Tenth Army ever set foot on the island.

On a wry note, as hindsight saw the preliminary bombardment of both island assaults, inadequate intelligence and the mistakes of the Iwo Jima campaign came to haunt the Okinawa campaign as well. First, the naval shells denied at Iwo Jima and saved for Okinawa did not help in the latter assault, whereas they would have lent some degree of help in the former. Second, like the Iwo Jima campaign, the Okinawa campaign suffered grievously from naval gunners prepping areas of sparse enemy fortifications. It is unfortunate that the last two island assaults under Nimitz, and perhaps the most difficult, suffered from inadequate preliminary naval bombardments, an assault technique that had proved so useful in past battles.

Conclusion

Why did JICPOA misinterpret the enemy situation on Okinawa? Ironically, up until March, it had not. For months, most of the Japanese were exactly where JICPOA claimed they were: on the coastal regions of the island's southern half. Experienced photo interpreters had marked these positions by January 1945. The Japanese named their coastal defense plan Operation Victory. Devised by Col. Hiromichi Yahara, senior staff officer of the Thirty-second Army, the plan focused on guarding potential landing beaches in southern Okinawa. Why? Because the south contained numerous airfields, and the Japanese knew from past campaigns that U.S. forces seized air-fields for tactical exploitation as soon as possible after landing—hence the wide dispersion of Japanese troops.[162]

When U.S. combatants landed, Yahara imagined that his layered forces on the beaches would hold the attackers while all other infantry units would vacate their defenses and advance toward the battle. Upon arrival, the fresh divisions and brigades were expected to support the defense by attacking the beachhead on an alternate basis, backed by full and concentrated artillery support. This, Yahara envisioned, would provide the Japanese with consistent hard punches and a constant reserve force at the same time.[163] At sea, Japanese maritime-raiding units would attack U.S. Navy and amphibious vessels on the first night of the battle.[164]

Like a chess player thinking several moves ahead, Yahara had thought his plan through. He had even ordered construction personnel to prepare underground defenses on Okinawa's interior just in case U.S. forces managed to withstand the counterattack on their beachhead and move inland.[165] Headquarters in Tokyo added a final dimension to the plan: massive air support. Generals in Tokyo had ordered that airfields be built on Okinawa for this express purpose. Yahara knew that air support would never factor into this battle; it never had before. But he had the airfields built, nonetheless.[166]

The plan appeared logical, but a few months prior to L-Day, the Japanese lost a division, and their whole plan fell apart. Imperial Headquarters, uneasy about U.S. advances in the Philippines, removed the Ninth Division and supporting units from Okinawa and sent them south via ship toward Luzon.[167] This meant the loss of twenty-five thousand men.[168] (Some Japanese infantry divisions were quite large. The "standard" type had twenty thousand personnel, and the "strengthened" type had 29,400.)[169] Colonel Yahara's defense would not work without the Ninth, so a change in plans became necessary. On 8 March, Lieutenant General Ushijima issued "Battle Instruction Number 8" that changed the entire scope of the defense of Okinawa. The revised plan ordered that all Japanese units come off the beaches and dig in on three defensive lines formed by natural ridge lines and hills: the Kakazu, the Shuri, and the Kiyan.[170] Although the Japanese had been fortifying parts of the interior since February,[171] the main effort to fortify these lines occurred in twenty-four days that began on 8 March 1945 with the issue of order "Number 8" and ended the day U.S. forces landed.

Interestingly, JICPOA had marked some of these interior positions in its November and February information bulletins. The November bulletin marked caves and gun emplacements on its "Land Transport" target map about four thousand yards southeast of Shuri Town. It also pinpointed infantry positions such as foxholes, trenches, and machine-gun bunkers that dotted the entire island. Some of these positions were in Okinawan limestone burial tombs that the Japanese had fortified.[172] The February information bulletin, which contained photo interpretation done in late January, noted twenty-four artillery positions below Shuri in the same area where caves had earlier been spotted. These guns had been organized into four batteries, and analysts hypothesized that this zone in particular housed part of the main strength of artillery forces for Okinawa.[173]

The "Defense Installations" map from the February information bulletin pinpointed defenses on all three Japanese lines, verifying the Japanese claim that they had been fortifying the interior since before the execution of Battle Instruction Number 8. In the Kakazu area, the map displayed four covered artillery positions, a pillbox, an artillery emplacement, and numerous infantry trenches and foxholes. Shuri City showed thirteen radio towers, three artillery emplacements, an AA site, numerous trench lines, and foxholes. Shuri's left flank, Naha City and airfield, bristled with at least twenty AA guns, three coast defense guns, six artillery sites, and numerous machine-gun and infantry positions. Yonabaru, the right flank, had twelve artillery emplacements, four pillboxes, and abundant adjoining infantry trenches. The Kiyan Peninsula had about eight artillery emplacements, ten AA sites, and a few pillboxes, all spread thin throughout the area.[174] On the other hand, these defenses did not indicate main-force infantry positions for what JICPOA thought was a seventy-five-thousand-man army. Conversely, the Nakagusuku Wan, Yontan-Kadena, and associated areas did have fortifications to hold this number of troops.

Even so, it is obvious that JICPOA did not discover the massive flight of Japanese troops inland, nor did it spot the late construction effort to fortify each line. There are several possible reasons for the oversight. One concerns aerial photographic intelligence and the other, radio intelligence— the only two sources in theater that could have revealed the true situation.[175]

First, as previously discussed, photo reconnaissance missions operated under cover of bombing raids, which in this case might have precluded, except for the earliest photo reconnaissance flights, wide coverage of the island. Bombers attacked areas of military activity, and early on JICPOA had pinpointed an abundance of obvious activity on the island's southern coastal areas, specifically around the numerous airstrips under construction in those regions. This might have discouraged aerial bombardment planners from ordering missions over inland areas where they did not believe there were significant defense activities under way. But even if senior officers had ordered photographic missions over Okinawa's interior, the photos probably would not have been analyzed correctly because of the green photo analysts at JICPOA, the late-arriving analysts at Tenth Army Headquarters, and the inability of supporting units to render assistance.

Also, the intense construction activities might have led the inexperienced photo interpreters to be fooled by the obvious. First, the Japanese expected U.S. forces to attack in the spring but realized that they might come at any time. Therefore, Colonel Yahara and General Ushijima positioned all arriving troops in the coastal defensive zones in temporary positions until they assessed exactly how many troops they had at their disposal. In addition, Tokyo kept sending shiploads of troops to Okinawa piecemeal,[176] so to photo interpreters there probably appeared to be a lot of infantry activity in the coastal areas. Also, twenty-five thousand Okinawan laborers worked to build the numerous airfields in the same areas where Japanese troops were stationed. According to Colonel Yahara, they mostly used hand tools to build the airstrips, and the massive number of laborers all working at one time caused him to remark, "The sheer number of citizens and labor service students working at each of the construction sites presented quite a spectacle."[177] Again, this widespread construction activity likely added to analysts' assumptions that the Japanese had indeed entrenched themselves in Okinawa's coastal zones. Lastly, the Japanese left the coastal area trench lines and defensive positions intact when they moved inland. This probably tricked the inexperienced photo analysts into thinking that the Japanese had not changed their defense plans, not unlike what happened on Iwo Jima.

To move inland, some Japanese units marched under cover of night. Those who moved during the day used special camouflage techniques, perfected in Manchuria, that masked troop movements from prying eyes in the sky.[178] These precautionary measures hid Japanese movements from the inexperienced analysts, and, in fact, might have deceived even experienced analysts.

It seems, then, that JICPOA's photo interpreters, having pinpointed such large Japanese defense areas, thought that the enemy situation would not change, especially so close to L-Day. Why would the Japanese suddenly vacate their coastal defensive zones, which were typical in the minds of most U.S. analysts, and move inland, all in the space of three weeks? Well, why not? Deception in warfare is common, and analysts should have remained observant and intelligence planners should have ordered vigilant surveillance on the Japanese.

In like manner, radio intelligence did not detect the change in enemy defensive tactics. This probably occurred either because of strict radio discipline on the part of the Japanese or because they were using hard-line communications that Allied intelligence could not intercept. Radio intelligence personnel would not have been able to monitor enemy communiqués sent over wire, but the use of hard-line systems was nothing new. Japanese infantry forces had often used hard-line communications to link defensive positions on their island bases. Besides, Japanese officers on Okinawa were not stupid, and they obviously took precautions to hide their activities. The combined result was that JICPOA did not notice that the Japanese had changed the game plan in the bottom of the ninth, so to speak, and so the U.S. victory on Okinawa was costly.

At any rate, Okinawa represented the maturity of Japan's changing defense tactics that had begun with Biak. Because the Imperial General Headquarters had made it clear after Saipan that it could not spare naval forces to help resist U.S. amphibious assaults, island commanders had no choice but to change their tactical thinking. Therefore, they adopted effective defenses based on complex overlapping fields of fire with a special emphasis on cover and concealment. On Peleliu, the Japanese put their new tactics to the test and followed up with further refinements on Iwo Jima. Ushijima and Yahara followed suit on Okinawa and vowed to destroy a U.S. division, delay the invasion of Japan, or both. Like General Kuribayashi on Iwo Jima, General Ushijima nearly succeeded in the former.

The Okinawa model demonstrates two significant points about intelligence. First—and this lesson is directly related to the Iwo Jima operation—an intelligence organization should maintain enough power or clout to rectify administrative policies that hinder or damage its operations. If it cannot safeguard its most basic operating structure or correct its own deficiencies, then it might as well not exist. The fact that JICPOA lost all of its experienced photo analysts to an administrative rotation policy and the AIC during the Iwo Jima intelligence operation is preposterous. The fact that this same problem plagued the Okinawa operation borders on criminal negligence. Planners and senior intelligence officers at Pearl Harbor knew the effects it had had on Iwo Jima, so why did they allow it to happen again? U.S. lives were at stake. The mission was at stake. Yet nothing was done to correct the problem. General Twitty protested against having such valuable people taken from him, and he did manage to get some of them back, albeit many months later. But if he had held significant power or had had better access to those who did, he might have been able to cut through the military's dogmatic administrative red tape and maintained JICPOA's effective operational capacity.

During World War II, such restrictions did not inhibit the combat echelons. No service administrative policy ever removed a division from one of the amphibious corps en route to its objective. Why, then, did it happen with the intelligence community? In all probability, past prejudices concerning intelligence never completely went away. In essence, it seems that the U.S. military's administrative system saw intelligence as another administrative branch, not as a specialized warfighting support branch. In any event, whether because of a Navy administrative deficiency or JICPOA's inability to rectify it, this particular facet of Operation Iceberg represents an intelligence failure.

Second, the Okinawa case study demonstrates that analysts must guard against becoming complacent about the situation at hand and should instead anticipate changes in the enemy's capabilities and intentions. It is the enemy's job to trick the opponent, and one of the jobs of intelligence is to guard against trickery. On Okinawa, the enemy tricked intelligence analysts, thereby forcing the United States to fight on Japanese terms.

Whether this facet of Iceberg was an intelligence failure is a difficult question. The Japanese enacted a highly effective deception-and-denial operation to mask their change in defensive plans, something intelligence obviously failed to detect. However, the photo interpreters had no experience and little training. To say that they failed in their mission is an oversimplification; they did not have the skills to do their jobs with maximum efficiency, which is the way the majority of JICPOA's analysts entered their jobs. The war did not wait for them to obtain the necessary skill sets, and there was no quick way around this problem. Accordingly, this aspect of the Okinawa intelligence operation was a failure, for which the administrative system was largely responsible, as it had been on Iwo Jima.

6

THE HOME ISLANDS
AND THE BOMB

Olympic and Downfall

Campaign Background

After the seizure of Okinawa, the SeaBees once again began their ambitious construction duties. Like Guam, Okinawa would have sprawling military facilities such as barracks, modern air bases, roads, and ports. After all, MacArthur and Nimitz planned to use the island as the staging area for the next and final campaign—the battle of Japan. The Joint Chiefs of Staff made the decision to begin preliminary preparations for the operation in the spring of 1944, although JICPOA and MacArthur's intelligence agency had been collecting information on the home islands since the beginning of the war. Their efforts, nonetheless, would now increase on a dramatic scale. Accordingly, on 16 May 1945, Nimitz ordered the V Amphibious Corps, the Marine component of the invasion, to bring all units up to strength and to prepare for the battle of Japan that would commence in fall 1945.[1]

Target Location

The first part of the invasion of Japan focused on Kyushu. Kyushu is the southernmost island in the Japanese home islands. It is about five miles south of Honshu. Kyushu is over 120 miles wide at its widest point and about two hundred miles long.[2] With several peninsulas, it has mountainous terrain, pine forests, and plains.

Why Japan?

The Allies had agreed that Japan must accept unconditional surrender terms. They wanted to ensure that it would not rise again to make a shambles of its neighbors for economic and imperial gain. Furthermore, the United States wanted to prevent Japan's military from further attempts to annex the rest of the Pacific islands, especially Hawaii, through the use of force. Besides, traditional military thought dictates that one nation cannot

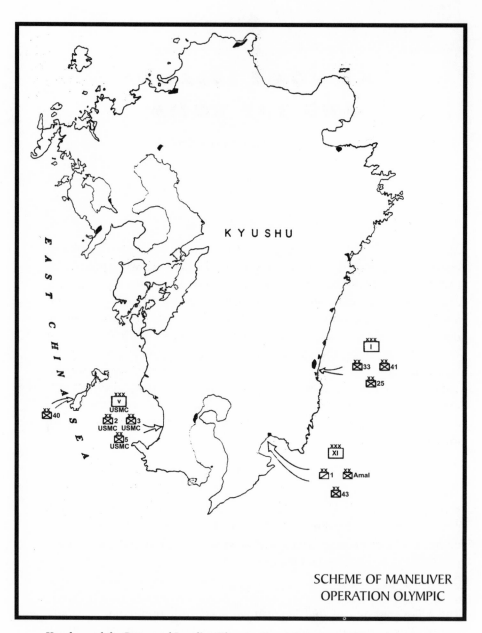

KYUSHU

EAST CHINA SEA

SCHEME OF MANEUVER
OPERATION OLYMPIC

Kyushu and the Proposed Landing Plan. Frank and Shaw, *Victory and Occupation*

bend another to its will unless the first is willing to force the second to accept its terms at bayonet point. This means that a nation can bomb the enemy's cities, it can sink the enemy's ships, and it can destroy the enemy's expeditionary forces, but it cannot guarantee the surrender of the enemy until it literally seizes the enemy's seat of government. This was the main reason for the invasion.

Chain of Command

The operation to seize Japan was named Downfall. The first phase of Downfall, code-named Olympic, entailed the invasion of Kyushu. The JCS assigned General MacArthur to command all air and ground forces for the operation and Admiral Nimitz to command all naval forces. Both would plan the operation, but MacArthur, rather than Nimitz, would take a front seat because of his experience in planning large land campaigns,[3] as opposed to the latter's primary experience with naval planning in conjunction with amphibious operations. MacArthur also had more forces at his disposal.

For Olympic, the U.S. Sixth Army, led by Gen. Walter Krueger,[4] would attack Kyushu with 815,548 men.[5] Krueger's forces consisted of four full corps: the U.S. Army's I, IX, XI Corps, and the Marines' V Amphibious Corps. Krueger also had three additional units at his disposal: the Army's Fortieth Infantry Division, the Eleventh Airborne Division, and the 158th Regimental Combat Team.[6] The VAC and I and XI Corps would spearhead the attack on southern Kyushu at three different landing sites. The other troops would serve as reserve forces or execute supporting operations associated with the giant invasion.[7] The naval component included twenty-three battleships, fifty-two cruisers, 323 destroyers, 181 submarines, twenty-six fleet carriers and sixty-four escort carriers.[8]

Plan of Attack

The entire operation would include U.S., British, Australian, and Canadian troops united under one command. Their numbers, including sailors, airmen, and infantry, totaled five million. As initially planned, Olympic consisted of five broad stages,[9] overall much larger than the invasion of France. First, naval and air power would isolate and choke Japan from outside resources, namely, its combat troops on the Asian mainland. Second, Allied air forces would bomb strategic points and high-value targets throughout Japan. These included airfields, railroads, ports, and troop concentrations. Then, on 1 November 1945, the Allies would invade Kyushu.[10] After the seizure of Kyushu, Nimitz and MacArthur would then conduct

Operation Coronet, the invasion of Honshu, in March 1946. Honshu, north of Kyushu, contained Imperial Headquarters and Tokyo.[11]

The scheme of maneuver for Kyushu specified a massive three-corps landing. The V Amphibious Corps, consisting of the Second, Third, and Fifth Marine Divisions, would land on the southwest side of Kyushu's southwest peninsula. I Corps, made up of the Thirty-third, Forty-first, and Twenty-fifth Infantry Divisions, would land on south central Kyushu's east side. And XI Corps, made up of the First Cavalry Division, the Americal, and Forty-third Divisions, would seize an east-facing bay on a peninsula parallel to VAC's area of operations.[12] Each division was to land, establish a beachhead, and move inland against airfields and Japanese troop concentrations on terrain similar to that of Iwo Jima and Okinawa. Follow-on forces would come behind them with additional infantrymen, artillery units, and logistics. According to Col. Joseph Alexander, USMC, Ret.,[13] these forces would seize only the lower third of the island, designated by the southern shelf of Kyushu's massive east-to-southwest central mountain range. U.S. forces would then establish defenses at mountain gaps and, with the support of air strikes, block Japanese forces from advancing into southern Kyushu.[14]

All Allied units knew their jobs. All Allied commanders knew the operational plan. But what about the Japanese? How many were there? Where would their units be located on D-Day, and what was their plan of defense? At first, the answers came without surprise. As time progressed, on the other hand, the answers caused shock, disbelief, and extreme concern.

How Intelligence Influenced Olympic and the Decision to Drop the Bomb

JICPOA worked in conjunction with MacArthur's G-2 (Maj. Gen. Charles Willoughby) to discover Japanese capabilities and intentions for Operation Downfall. Their overall concern for the moment, Operation Olympic, took nearly all of their resources. One of JICPOA's prime sources of intelligence was a captured document that discussed the defense of Kyushu.

Titled "Hypothetical Defense of Kyushu," it was a direct translation of a war game conducted by Imperial Military Headquarters in January 1944. JICPOA documents do not indicate how it was captured, but it might have come from the Thirty-first Army documents seized on Saipan. One of the main points of the document stated that the Japanese had to change their defensive tactics in light of what had happened at Tarawa, but it is evident that nothing changed to any serious degree until Peleliu. Regardless, while the document was only a hypothetical plan, it shed light on Japanese intentions for the defense of the home islands. It indicated that the Japanese would use in-depth defenses and *fukkaku*-like tactics to defend the homeland, and that naval and air power were essential support elements.[15]

JICPOA also published several information bulletins on Kyushu. The first and most important, titled "Southern Kyushu," Information Bulletin number 81-45, discussed every aspect of southern Kyushu that was militarily essential. Much of the topographic data in this bulletin came from a Japanese Imperial Land Survey of the region, which virtually guaranteed its accuracy. Unlike Saipan and Iwo Jima, then, topographic intelligence for the invasion would not be a problem. In addition, the Kyushu information bulletin's template differed somewhat from others because the island was highly developed, had complex terrain, a far-reaching communications system, an effective road and rail network, and several industrial centers.

The bulletin discussed essential elements of information such as trafficability, and it combined static geographic facts with analyses of what vehicle and infantry movement might be like throughout the island during combat.[16] Basically, it formulated a picture of what kind of problems U.S. forces would face. According to JICPOA, southern Kyushu consisted of rolling hills and mountains that enclosed several plains. It stated that the plains afforded areas of high maneuverability but entry onto the plains would be within range of machine guns on the surrounding elevations. If they were in range of machine guns, then they would be within the range of heavier weaponry, such as artillery. Analysts also figured that while movement on the flat coastal lowlands would be easy, they would offer little cover and concealment. The Kyushu information bulletin additionally stated that defenses were being built all over the west coast, a thin southern strip on the east coast, and in numerous positions all over the southern peninsulas. More to the point, most Japanese defenses were on top of the proposed landing beaches. The bulletin's defenses map pinpointed large concentrations of AA, coast defense, and dual-purpose weapons on key terrain and airfields throughout Kyushu.[17]

Radio intelligence added significantly to this information and provided near real-time intelligence on the defensive situation on Kyushu. In fact, in the spring of 1945, radio intelligence was providing the most crucial intelligence for Olympic and Downfall. The Japanese, perhaps resigned to the inevitability of invasion, apparently discarded strict radio security procedures and gave away over the airways the identity and location of every unit involved in the defense of Japan. Unfortunately, this excellent intelligence did not help much with tactical planning for Olympic. On the other hand, it did tell U.S. operations planners how bloody the fight was going to be.

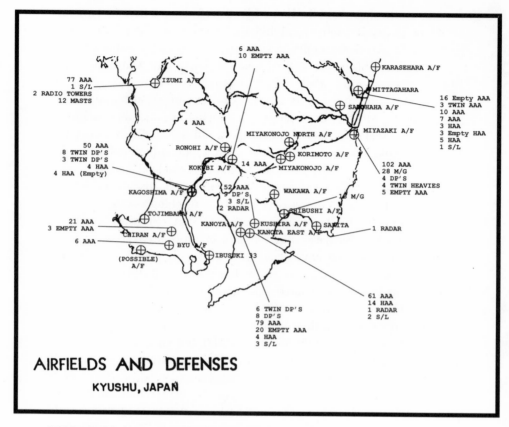

AIRFIELDS AND DEFENSES

KYUSHU, JAPAŇ

JICPOA Prebattle Map, Kyushu (Detail). The map shows defenses on or around the proposed landing beaches. JICPOA Information Bulletin 81-45

Ed Drea, an expert on World War II radio intelligence, writes that original estimates from radio intelligence put 230,000 Japanese troops on Kyushu.[18] Of these, only one hundred thousand were infantrymen. Radio intelligence also indicated that the Japanese would have 2,000 to 2,500 aircraft to oppose the U.S. landings in November.[19] Certainly, MacArthur and the JCS thought that such defenses would not be too a difficult a battle.

As the spring wore on into early June, additional troops deployed to Kyushu, and radio intelligence discovered two separate army commands on the big island. Still, this probably did not bother U.S. operations planners, who thought that they could block the northern army from aiding the southern army with air power and infantry. More troubling was that intelligence analysts had discovered that the Japanese had doubled the number of suicide aircraft designated for the defense of Kyushu.[20] The kamikazes would present a serious problem, as they had during the Okinawa campaign, but they could be dealt with through special air strike missions.

Then, in late July, the number of Japanese defenders on Kyushu increased again, this time to 525,000.[21] And that was not all. The Japanese had moved both of their army commands to southern Kyushu,[22] thereby concentrating all of their mass in the Allied area of operations. To make matters worse, many of these units established fortifications on the very landing beaches where the U.S. Sixth Army planned to land.[23] In these areas, JICPOA anticipated the same defenses encountered on Iwo Jima and Okinawa.

According to Drea, as November neared, the situation continued to look bleaker as the Japanese plan of defense for Kyushu was revealed. Again, radio intelligence broke the bad news. The Japanese planned to attack the invasion force with their multitudinous kamikaze aircraft during the ship-to-shore phase, with troop transports as the high-payoff targets. Infantry would defend the beaches from defensive fortifications such as steel reinforced concrete pillboxes, blockhouses, infantry trench lines, and antitank ditches. Reserve units would advance on the landing zones and continuously counterattack in support of beach defense units. Retreats were made illegal according to Japanese military law. Suicide squads, consisting of enlisted men and officers, were established to knock out enemy tanks.[24] The plan sounded very much like a combination of the defenses encountered at Peleliu, Iwo Jima, and Okinawa.

As MacArthur and his staff pondered their gloomy predicament, in late July through early August, intelligence revised the Japanese manpower estimate on Kyushu yet again—this time to 560,000.[25] Overall the Japanese had gathered 1,865,000 troops to defend the whole of Japan, and analysts now expected both figures to rise on a consistent basis until D-Day.[26] As a result, Nimitz, MacArthur, and the JCS discussed changing the attack plan. The number of troops chosen for the assault would not give the Allies even a two-to-one ratio for Olympic. And although many of the Japanese defenders would not be combat experienced or front-line quality, they did have a "home field advantage." No foreign army had ever defeated or occupied Japan. Otherwise known as the "land of the gods"[27] to her people, the home islands were a sacred and holy place governed by a living descendant of the gods. The Japanese were known to be a proud and racially homogeneous people, many of whom viewed themselves as superior to other Asians (an idea called Yamatoism). Knowing that the Japanese saw the white race as *gaigin*, or barbarians, intelligence analysts hypothesized that most would fight furiously to the death to protect their homeland. Besides,

Japanese soldiers had done so in almost every battle in the Pacific thus far (see table below).[28]

Number of Central Pacific Japanese Troops Garrisoned Compared to Approximate Numbers Killed in Action

Campaign	Garrison Size	Japanese KIA
Tarawa	4,836	4,800
Kwajalein	8,330	8,320
Eniwetok	3,431	3,400
Saipan	About 30,000	Nearly 30,000
Tinian	8,000	7,990
Guam	About 18,657	18,377
Peleliu	10,700	10,600
Iwo Jima	23,000	22,900
Okinawa	114,940	107,539

These horrific numbers represented only Central Pacific battles. MacArthur's South Pacific drive met similar resistance in several campaigns. The Japanese just did not quit, thereby commanding the reluctant respect of their enemies. What this meant was that, against so many troops who harbored such a fanatical spirit, many encased in formidable defensive fortifications, U.S. casualties would be high. In June, when the Japanese had fielded 280,000 troops, MacArthur figured on sustaining 105,050 casualties.[29] Now, with 560,000 Japanese prepared to fight to the death to protect Kyushu, U.S. losses might number over two hundred thousand. If the hard-won Central Pacific battles were any indication, those losses could run even higher. On Peleliu and Iwo Jima, the Marine and Army losses ranged as high as the number of defenders on each island. The same could have happened on Kyushu, resulting possibly in half a million casualties. Extended throughout the whole of Japan, the casualty count could have reached over one million Allied wounded and killed in action. To the Allies, and especially to U.S. forces that would bear the brunt of combat in Japan, the figures were unacceptable.

Enter the atomic bomb. For months in the New Mexico desert at a secret scientific facility at Los Alamos, scientists had been working on a weapon of mass destruction more powerful than any existing conventional bomb. Their work was the culmination of years of scientific research that had started at two other facilities: Hanford, Washington, and Oak Ridge, Tennessee.[30] Even before the first experimental detonation of a bomb called "Fat Man" at test site TRINITY, two hundred miles south of Los Alamos,[31] some of its makers feared the explosion might eat up the world's ozone layer. Others anticipated a giant explosion with an ultra-powerful concussion followed by an unknown degree of radiation fallout. In other words, no one was really sure of the weapon's destructive capacity, beyond a certainty that it would destroy on a massive scale. After a test detonation on 16 July 1945, the scientists no longer worried about ozone destruction, but they did realize that they had created one of the most powerful destructive devices known to man.[32]

Although the bombs took considerable time to build, the engineers would have two ready for use by late summer, just about the time radio intelligence discovered the enormous troop buildup on Kyushu. The JCS, therefore, turned to the atomic bomb as a possible alternative to invasion. They thought that if they could destroy one or two industrial cities with each bomb,[33] then the Japanese might relent in the face of certain destruction. Even though the Japanese had never before surrendered in the face of similar destruction, the atomic equation increased the power of strategic bombing on a geometric scale. One B-29 with one atomic bomb could reap just as much destruction as three hundred B-29s with thousands of conventional bombs. Such terrific economy of force coupled with such awesome and destructive power had never been achieved before; it signaled a new dawn in warfare. If the Japanese realized this, then they might surrender without a final showdown on their home islands.

So, with reducing high U.S. casualties his primary concern, President Harry S. Truman, who took office after FDR died on 12 April 1945, gave the go-ahead for the military to execute an atomic bombing mission over Japan. But before the bombings, Truman sent the Japanese a warning that stated that the United States would use a horrible weapon against them if they did not accept surrender terms. Looking far ahead, however, General Marshall ordered a contingency invasion plan that included using atomic bombs as tactical weapons in case the strategic bombing did not force surrender. In a tactical situation, the military planned to use the bombs to prep the landing beaches on Kyushu during the preliminary bombardment stages of Olympic. Their use would preclude invasion until a few days after each initial blast. The U.S. Army conceded that they could have, at the most, twelve bombs ready by D-Day.[34]

Tactical exploitation, however, depended on failure of two strategic bombing missions, the first of which the Army Air Corps executed on 8

August 1945 over Hiroshima, a large industrial city on southwest Honshu.[35] The explosion killed over eighty thousand Japanese on impact and demolished nearly the entire city. Japan's military government reacted with hypocritical defiance and cried foul on the world stage. One of the country's leading newspapers, which had obviously never heard of Japanese genocide operations such as the Rape of Nanking, called the bombing "a moral outrage against humanity."[36] Interpreting this response as a negative reply to Allied surrender terms, two days later a second B-29 dropped another bomb on Nagasaki, a port city in southwestern Kyushu.[37] It is estimated that seventy thousand civilians died in the initial blast.[38] This happened as the top members of the Japanese government met to discuss the implications of the United State's new weapon and another significant event, the Soviet invasion of Manchuria with 1,600,000 troops.[39] The Japanese had hoped to secure a peace deal with the Allies through the Soviets, who had expressed interest in brokering the transaction. Peace through the Soviets, the Japanese thought, would allow the empire to keep Manchuria and Korea, thereby easing the economic hardships and humility of defeat.

Conclusion

But now that was impossible. The Soviets had destroyed Japan's "insurance policy" by entering the Pacific War while maintaining the threat of invading northern Japan.[40] The United States had weapons that could wipe out entire cities. So, in order to avert the continued suffering of his people and complete destruction of his military, the Emperor of Japan ended the war by accepting the Allied terms of surrender.[41] In September, General MacArthur, Admiral Nimitz, hundreds of other ranking officers, and servicemen from around the world watched from the decks of the battleship USS *Missouri* as representatives of the Japanese government signed formal peace declarations that ended the war. As nearly two thousand fighters and bombers flew over in salute, JICPOA sat silent and empty but for the few officers tasked to clear and lock the building. CINCPAC had discharged or relocated its personnel to other duties upon the earliest news that the war had ended. Cdr. Donald "Mac" Showers and two linguists, Capt. Wendell Furnas, translator, and chief of the Translation Section, Cdr. John W. Steele, secured two copies of JICPOA's primary documents for storage in Washington, D.C., and had the rest burned at Honolulu's incinerator.[42] They left Makalapa Crater in silent commemoration of JICPOA's hard work that, from behind the scenes, had helped bring one of the world's bloodiest wars to a victorious close.

7

CONCLUSIONS AND
LESSONS LEARNED

With all that has been brought to light concerning JICPOA and its role in the Pacific War, it is possible to answer the questions raised in the foregoing chapters: How did JICPOA's strategic intelligence influence the overall scheme of the war? What impact did its operational intelligence have on the Central Pacific drive? How did its tactical intelligence impact the individual island campaigns under Nimitz's command? And, finally, was the organization effective?

JICPOA's Overall Impact on the War

In the overall scheme of the war, JICPOA's strategic intelligence had a tremendous influence on Nimitz and the Joint Chiefs of Staff. When World War II began, Japan was the United States' most elusive opponent. U.S. intelligence knew the basics of Germany's order of battle because the British, from the beginning of the war in September 1939, had ample opportunity to get to know their enemy. By 1941, they had fought the Germans in major land, sea, and air engagements that had yielded a mass of intelligence on Hitler's forces. The British shared this information with the United States. In comparison, the United States knew little about the Japanese military and almost nothing about its Pacific island bases such as Saipan and Iwo Jima. The Japanese held their new war technologies and infantry tactics in close secrecy, and even U.S. military attachés serving in Tokyo before 1941 collected little worthwhile intelligence on the emperor's armed forces. But information on the enemy held tremendous importance. In 1942, Japan controlled most of the Pacific Ocean and its island nations, all of Korea, Manchuria, Vietnam, Laos, Cambodia, Thailand, Burma, Malaysia, Singapore, Indonesia, Brunei, the Philippines, and half of China. It had attacked the United States and Australia. In conjunction with Hitler, the Japanese controlled half of the world. Like the Mongols, they were despotic conquerors, exerting their will on other nations, peoples, and cultures with brute force. In order to defeat the Japanese, the Allies would have to have a firm understanding of the enemy's armed forces. Otherwise, they could not draw plans for their defeat. The fate of the world sat in the hands of the Allies, a team of nations that had to use the most effective means available for killing this "global cancer."

This is where JICPOA proved invaluable. In short, it unveiled the Japanese military to an extent that strategic war planners could understand it. In doing so, JICPOA revealed the secrets of the enemy's government and military structure and provided intelligence on numerous topics: its leaders; the order of battle of each branch of the Japanese military; its combat tactics; its war technologies; the location of its troop deployments; the strength of its naval and air forces; the geography of its bases; and high-payoff targets located throughout Japan. In a broad sense, JICPOA informed the United States' senior leaders of the following essential elements of information:

who the enemy was
where the enemy was
what the enemy was capable of

Combined, this information shaped strategic planning at global and theater levels, and, in essence, provided information on how to defeat the enemy. For example, the United States knew from Japanese strength and force deployments in the Pacific that the enemy could attack in mass a single Allied axis of advance that penetrated their territory in the Pacific. The Japanese could not, on the other hand, do the same with two Allied axes of advance unless they pulled troops from China, thereby exposing both their western and southwestern flanks. (As it was, the Japanese had to pull forces from Manchuria to meet the U.S. advance in the Central Pacific, an ineffective strategy that weakened their border with Russia.) Essentially, JICPOA's intelligence provided information on how to fight the war on Allied terms—on the offensive, whereby the Japanese had to react to Allied initiatives instead of the Allies reacting to Japanese initiatives. This, in turn, contributed to the fall of the empire.

JICPOA's Impact on the
Central Pacific Drive

JICPOA's operational intelligence influenced the strategy behind the Central Pacific drive by putting the enemy situation into perspective. Its information provided a picture of the Central Pacific like pieces on a chessboard. Although it did not show all of the pieces all of the time, it showed enough of them to get the job done, so to speak. Hence, as time progressed, Nimitz knew the path to Japan. During each successive campaign, he knew where to go, when to go, how to fight upon arrival at each objective, and where to go next. The admiral's thrust into the Gilberts and then the Marshalls provides the best example. He knew from JICPOA's strategic intelligence on enemy dispositions and Pacific island geography that he needed to conduct operations to seize either Truk and Rabaul or the Marianas to gain sea control of the Pacific. From that same information, he also knew that the Marshalls would provide the platform to attack all three of these areas. However, he could not attack the Marshalls without knowing what atolls to strike and how to fight upon arrival. So he first took the Gilberts to provide a reconnaissance base to answer these operational questions.

The same type of information contributed to large-scale logistics and localization operations—Allied carrier strikes designed to tie down Japanese forces that might impede an amphibious assault. CINCPAC knew, for example, that he could establish a logistics base in the Marshalls to help seize the Marianas because, first, the Japanese themselves stored logistics in the area, and, second, the island group was close to the Marianas. For localization operations, he simply had to know the proximity of Japanese land-based aircraft to his targeted objectives. If they were close, he struck them. If they were not, he left them alone for the time being.

JICPOA's Impact on the Island Campaigns

The island campaigns are where JICPOA's intelligence had an immediate and obvious impact. Actually, this is where operational and tactical intelligence merged, and JICPOA's information played a large role in both. For Kwajalein, Eniwetok, Tinian, and Guam, it produced adequate intelligence that contributed to proficient campaigns. However, for Saipan, Peleliu, Iwo Jima, and Okinawa, the inadequacy of intelligence that JICPOA produced led to bloody campaigns. In fact, the latter were hard won under the most difficult circumstances. Does that mean that JICPOA failed in these campaigns? After all, is it not the job of intelligence to tell operations planners all there is to know about the enemy and make combat easy? Not quite.

In order to understand the impact of intelligence on the Central Pacific island assaults, such issues must be addressed. To address them, one must look at the similarities and differences of each category of campaigns: the proficient victories and the bloody, hard-won victories.

Characteristics of the Proficient Campaigns

KWAJALEIN
Enemy situation

light terrain
typical crust defense

moderate number of fortifications
moderate-sized garrison (about 7,000 but
  spread between two islands)
mediocre camouflage discipline

Intelligence operation

photographic: multiple sorties, mostly
  good weather/good analyses of terrain
  and defenses
radio: discovered enemy reinforcements
  and troop dispositions
POW interrogations: helped with a few
  tactical situations during battle

documents: documents from Betio
  helped analysts understand atoll defense tactics; helped with a few tactical
  situations during battle

ENIWETOK
Enemy situation

light terrain
typical crust defense (+ minor
  burrowing)
few fortifications
small-sized garrison (about 3,431 but
  spread between three islands)
mediocre camouflage discipline (except
  for Eniwetok Island)

Intelligence operation

photographic: short notice but good
  sorties, good weather/good analyses
  of terrain, fair analysis of defenses
radio: discovered enemy reinforcements and some troop dispositions
POW interrogations: helped verify radio
  intelligence during planning phase;
  contributed to operation and helped
  verify document intelligence
documents: hydrographic charts from
  Kwajalein and order-of-battle documents on Engebi contributed to
  victory

TINIAN
Enemy situation

mostly light terrain
shore-oriented defense, airstrip defense,
  plus defenses on three moderate
  elevations
numerous shore-based fortifications
moderate-sized garrison (about 8,000)

good camouflage discipline

Intelligence operation

photographic: unlimited sorties in good
  weather; excellent analyses of terrain
  and defenses

GUAM
Enemy situation

difficult terrain
shore-oriented defense, plus defenses
  on high ground behind beachhead,
  plus interior defense
numerous shore-based fortifications
large garrison (18,657 divided between
  high and low ground)
good camouflage discipline

Intelligence operation

photographic: aerial and submarine,
  good sorties overall in favorable
  weather; fair analyses of defenses,
  mediocre for terrain

Characteristics of the Proficient Campaigns (*continued*)

Tinian	Guam
Intelligence operation	*Intelligence operation*
radio: good but low impact	radio: good but low impact
POW interrogations: good intelligence from Japanese captured on Saipan	POW interrogations: good intelligence from Japanese captured on Saipan
documents: order-of-battle documents found on Saipan contribute to victory	documents: order-of-battle documents found on Saipan contribute to victory
human reconnaissance: both aerial and beach	special intelligence for naval preliminary bombardment

For the most part, each of these island campaigns shared certain characteristics regarding the enemy situation. For example, each target encompassed light or moderate terrain (except for Guam), each brandished mostly beach-oriented defenses, and each contained a small or divided garrison of troops. Intelligence for the proficient campaigns also had much in common. For example, terrain and enemy use of terrain did not hinder collection and analysis to a seriously harmful degree. Terrain intelligence proved accurate except for Guam, and in that case it proved at least strategically useful. Radio intelligence exposed some or all of the Japanese troops on the objective. Documents provided excellent information on enemy order of battle, except for Kwajalein, where it was not imperative. Finally, documents or photo intelligence provided effective intelligence on the enemy's defense plans.

In the difficult campaigns, the charts paint a different picture. In these cases, the positive influences present in the proficient campaigns are substandard or absent.

Characteristics of the Difficult Campaigns

Saipan	Peleliu
Enemy situation	*Enemy situation*
difficult terrain	very difficult terrain
shore-based defense with interior positions	layered defense plus *fukkaku* tactics in the mountains
moderate number of hardened fortifications, numerous makeshift fortifications	numerous hardened fortifications and natural and man-made earthworks, plus many subsurface defenses
large garrison (about 23,000)	moderate-sized garrison (about 10,700)
good camouflage discipline	excellent camouflage discipline

Characteristics of the Difficult Campaigns (*continued*)

SAIPAN
Intelligence operation

photographic: few sorties, bad weather, submarine photographs wrong beaches, lacking analyses of terrain and defenses

radio intelligence: picked up marginal garrison numbers

documents: some tactical value in midst of battle

PELELIU
Intelligence operation

photographic: several sorties but not enough to capture enemy situation, lacking analyses of terrain and defenses

radio intelligence: picked up marginal garrison numbers

documents: 1st set provided half of enemy situation, 2d set completed it but arrived too late to have positive impact on entire operation, although they did help tactically in defense of the beachhead

---

IWO JIMA
Enemy situation

very difficult terrain

radical layered *fukkaku* defense tactics

high number of hardened, earthen, and subsurface fortifications

large garrison (about 23,000)

excellent camouflage discipline plus shore deception operation

Intelligence operation

photographic: good weather, first photo missions focus on one area, later missions excellent but late, loss of experienced analysts at last phase of information processing leaves analytical capabilities impaired

radio: discovered marginal garrison numbers

documents: showed half of enemy situation, but analysts believed they showed the entire picture

OKINAWA
Enemy situation

varied terrain (difficult/light)

radical layered *fukkaku* defense tactics

high number of earthen, subsurface, and reverse slope defenses, some hardened defenses

huge garrison (about 114,940)

excellent camouflage discipline, covert troop movements, effective deception and denial operations

Intelligence operation

photographic: bad weather overcome, some good photos, some bad photos, good terrain analysis, defenses not seen due to loss of experienced photo interpreters and enemy deception operations

radio: discovered two-thirds of garrison numbers

interrogations: interviews led to excellent hydrographic intelligence; interviews with Okinawan civilians and a few POWs indicated general whereabouts of main force Japanese units

The difficult campaigns shared certain characteristics regarding the enemy situation. For example, each objective had difficult terrain. Additionally, the Japanese relied on *fukkaku* defenses, except for Saipan, which had both a shore-based defense and an interior defense. Also, each of these objectives brandished an abundant number of fortifications, and relied on caves for military use. They contained large or moderate-sized garrisons as well. Finally, the Japanese on each of these objectives exercised good to excellent camouflage discipline and deception operations. Likewise, the intelligence operations for these campaigns shared certain similarities. Each had problems with photographic surveillance, either because of bad weather, infrequent sorties, loss of experienced photo interpreters, or difficult terrain. Furthermore, radio intelligence indicated only a fraction of the enemy's numbers. Captured documents, used to a significant degree in but two of these operations, showed only part of the picture or arrived too late to make the operations more efficient.

Consequently, it appears that on the bigger islands, with their difficult terrain and large numbers of enemy troops, good intelligence was harder to obtain. But this was only partly true. While difficult terrain impeded photographic interpretation of geography and defenses and large garrisons were harder to analyze, they did not preclude effective intelligence, as the Iwo Jima after-action intelligence report demonstrates. In this case, photographs did reveal enemy dispositions, but only after the fact and by the use of an elaborate photo interpretation technology, the stereoscope. Furthermore, an administrative policy that rotated experienced photo analysts out of JICPOA proved a major impediment for the Iwo Jima and Okinawa intelligence operations, and this had nothing to do with enemy numbers or a large land mass.

Similarly, if the Japanese on a large land mass relied less on radios and more on hard-line communications, it reduced the effectiveness of radio intelligence. Collecting radio intelligence on the Japanese on the Marshalls was easier than in the Marianas, for example, because they were still reinforcing the Marshalls, which were spread out. This meant that they had to ship hundreds of troops from atoll to atoll, island to island, and ships communicate by radio, so JICPOA could "hear" them. The Japanese were more established in the Marianas, and even more so on Okinawa, and their infantry forces communicated less by radio, so there was less to intercept.

Neither the size of a Japanese force nor the area of the base it occupied had anything to do with document intelligence. Luck and chance however, did. Simply put, if the Japanese had destroyed vital military documents, JICPOA could not have obtained and exploited them. If the documents were accurate and JICPOA was able to exploit them in a timely manner, operations planners benefited. If they were inaccurate and untimely, operations planners might have benefited only partially or not at all.

Was JICPOA Effective?

Based on these case studies, it is apparent that intelligence operations are subject to the hazards of war just as combat operations are. All sorts of things can go wrong in combat operations—equipment can break down, bad weather can impede visibility, and weapons can malfunction or jam. These problems, often beyond the control of combatants, can cause disastrous results that lead to loss of life and inefficiency in battle. Similar events can plague the intelligence process. Nothing always goes as planned, even for the most victorious armies. For the most part, JICPOA could not have avoided the problems that plagued the Saipan, Peleliu, Iwo Jima, and Okinawa intelligence operations. However, several failures could have been avoided. They were caused by the denial of effective reconnaissance (Saipan); the administrative system that transferred experienced photo analysts out of JICPOA at a critical phase of the war (Iwo Jima and Okinawa); and poor intelligence direction (Iwo Jima).

Another conclusion of this study is that incompetence did not cause JICPOA's intelligence inadequacies, although it may have contributed to isolated intelligence failures. At any rate, difficulties germane to war, the nature of intelligence work, and operational priorities resulted in inadequate intelligence—that and JICPOA's now obvious handicap at not being sophisticated and professional to a certain degree. What, then, did this mean for the island campaigns? JICPOA produced good intelligence for the proficient campaigns, and good intelligence had a positive influence on combat in those cases. But what about for the difficult campaigns? Did the lack of solid intelligence have a negative influence? Not in a sense that it made the difficulties faced in these particular cases worse. True, where intelligence was lacking, combat was more difficult, but JICPOA never provided entirely worthless intelligence for any campaign, just insufficient intelligence or half of the picture in several cases. However, this is the nature of intelligence work. Intelligence is not designed to provide the commander with a 100 percent solution, and that was certainly true in the Pacific War. Additionally, the high operational tempo of the war that had a major influence on planning and logistics also impacted intelligence. Nimitz was launching major offensives that utilized tens of thousands of men and hundreds of ships on Japanese targets roughly every four months.

Time was short. This is why General Twitty remarked that JICPOA's mission was not to provide intelligence done to "apple polishing perfection," but to provide enough intelligence to get the job done. In another light, JICPOA provided at least the basics of the enemy situation for every Central Pacific campaign. In this regard, the strategy and tactics used to seize these islands was never in danger of being superseded by those of the enemy.

Although severely bloodied at times, the United States never lost a Central Pacific battle, and that was in part because Nimitz and his lieutenants had either a very good picture of the enemy situation, or a fair picture of it. In other words, in every case, JICPOA provided operational planners with enough suitable intelligence to win. Good leadership, well-trained U.S. infantrymen, competent seamen, and skilled aviators picked up the slack where intelligence left off, but this is how the system worked. U.S. combatants were trained to adapt to battlefield situations no matter how adverse, so they were able to handle extraneous circumstances—insufficient intelligence, logistical snafus, and weapons malfunctions. Therefore, JICPOA accomplished the true mission of intelligence in every Central Pacific island campaign, decreasing some of the dangerous risks inherent in these military operations by providing the commander with information about the enemy that helped him achieve his goals. The organization, as constructed and implemented, was effective. Brigadier General Twitty wrote at the end of the war, "It is my firm conviction that the Intelligence Officers and agencies of CinCPac-CinCPOA have properly used every opportunity to improve intelligence in the Pacific in coordination with agencies of neighboring theaters and that the ground, air, and naval forces of the Pacific Ocean Areas in their operations have had the advantage of detailed intelligence of the highest quality."[1]

In JICPOA's wake, the U.S. professional intelligence community began to evolve, a process that began in 1947 and continued into the 1950s. Also, the armed forces recognized intelligence as an integral part of combat operations. Each branch of service expanded the role of its own intelligence service, and at the national level the federal government created the Central Intelligence Agency to process strategic intelligence and to run clandestine operations. It formed the National Security Agency to conduct communications intelligence operations, which included code-breaking. Both organizations' structures emulated that of JICPOA and the OSS combined. Subsequent CINCPACs in future conflicts also had joint intelligence centers. During the Korean War, for example, CINCPAC had a joint intelligence division commonly referred to as the J-2. Toward the latter stages of the Korean War, it merged with CINCPACFLEET's intelligence division, commonly referred to as the N-2, to form the Joint Operational Intelligence Agency, Pacific Command, or JOINPAC.[2] However, JOINPAC was subordinate to Far East Command's intelligence center, MacArthur's Japan-based command and control center for the war.

After the close of the Korean War and several fifties-era low-intensity conflicts, it became clear that the Cold War was dominating U.S defense resources, especially intelligence, and that the CIA's military analytical capabilities were not comprehensive enough to cope with the threat. Therefore, in 1961, the Defense Department created the Defense Intelligence Agency (DIA) to focus on strategic military threats in support of national-level policy making.[3] Like its two sister organizations—the CIA and NSA—the DIA mimicked JICPOA with Cold War–era modifications. In the years following, the entire intelligence community matured and expanded with new technologies and techniques to meet a variety of threats, and several national-level intelligence agencies took on a tactical warfighting support role similar to JICPOA's in the 1940s. For example, the CIA, NSA, and DIA each provided tactical support during the Vietnam War. The DIA in particular funneled its support through CINCPAC and then onto Military Assistance Command–Vietnam in Saigon. Additionally, Pacific Command Headquarters at Pearl Harbor had its own intelligence unit. It was called Fleet Intelligence Center, Pacific, or FICPAC.[4]

By 1990, FICPAC had metamorphosed through the years and finally evolved into the Joint Intelligence Center, Pacific, or JICPAC. It has since produced actionable intelligence for the fleet on a daily basis, and it has kept all CINCPACs abreast of important developments through Asia and the Pacific through its daily intelligence briefs. As of summer 2002, JICPAC had processed intelligence on the Indonesia crisis, the 1997 coup in Cambodia, numerous naval skirmishes in the Spratly Islands, insurgent movements in the Philippines, Chinese capabilities and intentions, and various tasks in connection with the global war on terrorism. It also assists other intelligence agencies with targeting for North Korea. Each of the other joint combat commands—Central, Southern, Joint Forces (formerly Atlantic), and Europe—has its own joint intelligence center that functions similarly to JICPAC. Ultimately, JICPOA's impact had a far-reaching effect on the intelligence community into the twenty-first century and by doing so confirmed its place as one of the ground-breaking organizations that shaped the history of the United States and its national security.

JICPOA's Lessons for Future Intelligence Organizations

No intelligence organization is perfect, and JICPOA was no exception to that truism. It was, nevertheless, a successful intelligence unit that produced effective strategic, operational, and tactical intelligence a majority of the time. Its critics should remember that most of the people who helped create, staff, and operate JICPOA were intelligence novices. Regardless, even when it did not function as designed, JICPOA still produced enough beneficial intelligence to help commanders achieve victory. For that reason, JICPOA offers timeless lessons for government, military, and even corporate intelligence personnel worldwide.

Many of JICPOA's lessons certainly apply to the current U.S. intelligence community, especially in the wake of the 11 September 2001 terrorist attacks, the Pearl Harbor of a new generation. They offer valuable insights regarding the effective application of the intelligence cycle. True, today's U.S. intelligence community dwarfs JICPOA in manpower, resources, and budgets. Its operations are more complicated, and its focus is more widespread and diverse. But today's community relies on the intelligence cycle just as JICPOA did, a procedure that will never change. Intelligence agencies through history may add a streamlining step to collection or processing, or clandestine units engaged in human intelligence collection might apply innovative techniques to their operations, but the basic direction-collection-processing-dissemination cycle will remain. It is the core of intelligence work.

Three sets of lessons emerge from the study of JICPOA's organization and performance. The first set consists of general observations based on JICPOA's historical source material, organized by particular steps in the intelligence cycle, with two administrative lessons—one negative, one positive—from outside the cycle. The second and third sets come directly from the organization's most senior leaders, selected at random. Together they summarize JICPOA's legacy to the security efforts of the United States.

General Observations

1. Direction: One of JICPOA's strengths was that it served one commander, Admiral Nimitz, and his subordinate commands. Nimitz was the primary consumer of intelligence as well. This made JICPOA's scope of purpose clear and concise.
2. Direction: An additional strength of JICPOA was its short, responsive chain of command. It had one commanding officer, one second in

command, and various section heads. This scheme avoided complex layers of bureaucracy that otherwise would have caused bottlenecks in the intelligence cycle. Senior officers had ready access to subordinates and therefore understood their capabilities and needs. Subordinates understood their commander's intent.

3. Direction (theater level): JICPOA was Nimitz's primary intelligence unit, and all other intelligence organizations in his area of operations were subordinate to it. The only exception was FRUPAC, a highly specialized, single-source unit that worked in conjunction with JICPOA. This arrangement reduced duplication, curbed information overload on operations planners, and conserved resources.

4. Direction: JICPOA had the luxury of focusing on a single enemy: Imperial Japan.

5. Direction, collection, processing: General Twitty, commander of JICPOA, was a flexible leader. He frequently created temporary task forces within JICPOA to work on special projects, demonstrating the organization's requirements-driven approach. It strived to satisfy its customers' needs.

6. Direction, dissemination: JICPOA worked in close coordination with operations planners, who were integral in the direction phase of the intelligence cycle. The close relationship also helped JICPOA package intelligence in a format that its customers could use.

7. Collection, processing, dissemination (theater level): JICPOA and the fleet's subordinate intelligence units collaborated and worked well together, thereby keeping the intelligence flow unrestricted. They did not squabble over resources and engage in turf wars. On the contrary, they merged assets and manpower to form temporary intelligence cells in the field to facilitate operational and tactical intelligence when necessary.

8. Processing: As a result of the needs of Nimitz and his forces, JICPOA was organized along both geographic (such as the Geographic Section) and functional (such as the Flak Section) lines. This arrangement focused JICPOA's resources on issues directly related to the fleet's requirements.

9. Processing and dissemination: JICOPA almost exclusively produced actionable intelligence. It did not simply produce intelligence for intelligence's sake.

10. Dissemination: JICPOA disseminated its intelligence not only to planning staffs, but also to warfighters, service support echelons, and fleet intelligence units. Every military entity that needed intelligence on the enemy received it.

11. Administration/policy: JICPOA's effective hiring practices hinged on hiring personnel who had the aptitude for intelligence work (analytic, inves-

tigative, or logic-based backgrounds) or especially those who had living experience in JICPOA's area of operation (Asia-Pacific). However, on-the-job training was essential.

While these circumstances enhanced JICPOA's productivity, others impeded it:

12. Collection: JICPOA did not have complete or significant control over its key collection assets such as aerial reconnaissance. Without such control, outside interests sometimes hindered collection efforts, resulting in inadequate data gathering. This, in turn, had a negative impact on processing and production.

13. Collection: During the direction phase, JICPOA did not always make collectors aware of forthcoming operations (Peleliu, for example). Doing so would have widened the collection net and helped satisfy future information requirements. Requirements for future operations should have driven collection.

14. Administration/policy: The Navy's administrative policies hampered JICPOA's ability to complete the intelligence cycle at two critical junctures (Iwo Jima and Okinawa). The results contributed to severe U.S. casualties and inefficient campaigns. In order to avoid such a calamity, JICPOA would have needed greater autonomy.

Official Recommendations

Although at the end of the war JICPOA did not assess its impact on individual island assaults, its senior officers did evaluate the performance of the organization and published the results as advice for future U.S. intelligence agencies. The recommendations came from two publications, *Report of Intelligence Activities in the Pacific Ocean Areas* and *Narrative: Combat Intelligence, Joint Intelligence Combat Pacific Area.*

Report of Intelligence Activities

Several officers, including Commander Holmes, probably helped prepare the seventy-seven-page *Report of Intelligence Activities in the Pacific Ocean Areas;* however, Brigadier General Twitty signed and authorized it. Dated 15 October 1945, it discusses the history of JICPOA by section, demonstrates facts and figures regarding the organization, and lists its most important publications. Twitty's report presents point by point what he believed were vital lessons regarding the establishment of an effective intelligence agency:

1. The first requirement [to establish an effective military intelligence agency] is the need for a clear-cut definition of intelligence and a widespread understanding of its function. As used herein intelligence is defined as evaluated information of the enemy, his organization, equipment, capabilities, and intentions. Intelligence as defined above must be coordinated with security, censorship, and counter-espionage, but the indoctrination of regular services must obviate any possibility of confusing true intelligence with disciplinary, security or enemy spy activities.[5]

2. What is needed in peace is an organization so manned, so administered, and so organized that it can adapt itself to war circumstances with the minimum of disturbance. The first need is for an administrative organization responsible directly to the office controlling the operations requirements. Any joint intelligence organization of the future must, like JICPOA, be directly under the theater commander for functional operation with no intervening echelon. The second is for personnel familiar with all sources of intelligence: captured documents, photographs, interrogation and espionage. The third, for adequate facilities to collate, evaluate and disseminate the intelligence gained.[6]

3. One of the firmest lessons has been that intelligence is a joint function. The highest theater echelon of intelligence should encompass Army, Navy Marine, and Air Force components.[7] Intelligence is a regenerative process. An insignificant item of intelligence gained by one activity can coagulate into a significant whole many scattered bits of information. The sources of intelligence material are common to all services and separate organizations are always handicapped by not having the complete picture. Liaison and conferences are not enough; liaison is a disease, not a cure. It is necessary that all elements of this intelligence organization be gathered under one roof under the direction of one responsible officer. With the importance of political and economic information in peace times, and in view of their proven facilities for observation, the inclusion of State Department elements in this organization should be seriously considered.[8]

4. To supply well grounded, competent intelligence officers should be the objective of a training program lasting the entire service life of officers assigned. Young officers should be assigned for several years to operational forces to give them adequate military background. They should then receive adequate post-graduate intelligence instruction in a course of applied intelligence. During this course they should be instructed intensively in all forms of media of intelligence work, and on the history of potential enemies. After this instruction, suitable officers should be selected for intelligence duties only and should, from then on, work only in

the intelligence field, except for brief refresher assignments with operational forces in order to keep abreast of our own equipment and needs.[9]

5. Intelligence officers should be assigned to staff duties afloat and in the field. They should receive periodic digests of intelligence that is pertinent to their problems and their commanders. The further dissemination of the information should be rigidly controlled and adequate separate channels of communication provided. The Army Special Branch system is a model for the proper control and dissemination of intelligence.[10]

6. All of the products of intelligence must be available to all branches and all specialists.[11]

7. Collation is the heart and soul of intelligence particularly in peacetime. Centralized files are essential insofar as classification of material permits. Peacetime intelligence must insure that these files are complete, and ready for dissemination of information in useable form to expanding branches in the event of emergency. The United States started this war with hopelessly inadequate intelligence and there can be no excuse in the future for necessity of gathering static intelligence in war which could be gathered much more efficiently and less costly in peacetime. For this war, the nation had seriously inadequate information even concerning areas previously within its possession.[12]

8. Consideration should be given to the enrollment and instruction of qualified reserve personnel to feed in information from foreign sources. It is essential that all officials of all U.S. governmental agencies be obliged to collect information within their sphere of activity abroad.[13]

9. The intelligence service of CinCPac-CinCPOA was the integrated efforts of JICPOA, the Advanced Intelligence Center and the Combat Intelligence Section, CinCPac-CinCPOA. By this means, duplication was kept to a minimum.[14]

The point here is that the Pacific's intelligence architecture was proficient, streamlined, and its work was not wastefully replicated by several agencies.

10. Important intelligence billets overseas and with high commands should be reserved for professional intelligence officers, selected by the War and Navy Departments.[15]

11. In brief, intelligence must be clarified, centralized and professionalized, and so constituted and situated in relation to the top command and to those responsible for national policy that the nation can never make the disastrous mistake of not heeding its intelligence service. Atomic power will doubtless result in sweeping adjustments in the armed services and intelligence must be ahead of the field. Only thus will the observation,

based upon irrefutable past history, that the United States will never be prepared for war [be] disproved.[16]

Narrative

The second publication, titled *Narrative: Combat Intelligence Center, Joint Intelligence Pacific Ocean Area,* is rumored in historical circles to have been written by Holmes. The document is dated 8 November 1945, and in twenty pages it details the history of the Combat Intelligence Unit from its early days as station Hypo through its transformation into the backbone of JICPOA's Estimates Section. It has a communications intelligence slant, and its lessons are mentioned throughout the text of the narrative and at the end, point by point. Lessons from JICPOA's *Narrative* are as follows:

1. Ample experience has demonstrated that neither Army Intelligence nor Naval Intelligence is complete without the other. On theater and higher level, joint intelligence is necessary. Liaison and interchange of information is not enough to secure complete exploitation. Complete merger of Army and Naval Intelligence is necessary. Only in the field or at sea can intelligence afford to be exclusively Army or Navy.[17]
2. One of the first tasks of peace time intelligence organization will be to devise some means of insuring to intelligence specialists equal opportunity of promotion and recognition.[18]

   Holmes was referring to the fact that promotion boards and senior commanders often disregarded intelligence officers as unimportant, unworthy of promotion, and of little value to operations.
3. In war, censorship may be partially successful but experience has proved that it is not completely reliable. In peace any attempt at control of the press is a cure worse than the disease for the military as well as political incompetency flourishes under the cloak of secrecy. Intelligence must learn to accept these facts as part of the difficulties of the profession.[19]

Holmes was referring to the difficulties regarding keeping intelligence methods and sources secret from the press, as in the fiasco that contributed to Rochefort's professional demise.

4. [T]he preoccupation of the intelligence organization with counter intelligence duties stulified [*sic*] the growth of an organization devoted to obtaining information of the enemy. These conditions are most likely to occur again. Efforts to correct them are more important than a study of the facts surrounding the operation of any single service or unit.[20]
5. That a counter intelligence organization should exist cannot be gain-

said, but it is important that its organization should be independent of the efforts to collect and codify information of the nation's potential enemies.[21]

Although other JICPOA documents hardly mention domestic counterintelligence (CI), Holmes dedicates considerable thought and explanation to how it hindered JICPOA's efforts. He believed that it stemmed from America's psychology as an inward-looking nation, and that it gained a deep paranoia of foreign intelligence services once war began. As a result, Holmes stated that thousands of personnel entered the CI field as war exploded, and they received paltry CI or police-type training at best. Their efforts to protect U.S. intelligence activities apparently stifled the services they protected.

6. Radio intelligence must be integrated with other forms of intelligence. Radio intelligence should be a joint Army and Navy function.[22]

This is an endorsement for the utility of all-source intelligence and a reminder that single-source intelligence is less capable of completing the intelligence picture. It also means that the complexity of signals intelligence demands the resources, talent, and perspective of more than one service.[23]

NOTES

Preface

1. Michael E. Bigelow, "Intelligence in the Philippines," *Military Intelligence Professional Bulletin* (Fort Huachuca, Arizona: U.S. Army Intelligence Center), April–June 1995, 36–37.

2. Kenneth A. Campbell, "Major General Charles A. Willoughby: General MacArthur's G-2: A Biographical Sketch," in *American Intelligence Journal* 18 (nos. 1 & 2, 1998): 88.

3. Sun Tzu, *The Art of War,* trans. Samuel B. Griffith (New York: Oxford University Press, 1971), 84.

4. Carl von Clausewitz, *On War,* ed. Anatol Rapoport (New York: Penguin Books, 1982), 162.

5. *Naval Intelligence, Naval Doctrine Publication (NDP) 2* (Washington, D.C.: Department of the Navy, Office of the Chief of Naval Operations and Headquarters, United States Marine Corps), an on-line publication found at: http://sun00781.dn. net/irp/doddir/navy/ndp2.htm#c_2

6. *FM 34-3: Intelligence Analysis* (Washington, D.C.: Headquarters, Department of the Army, March 1990), 2-1.

7. Ibid., 2-1 through 2-15.

8. *Naval Intelligence,* NDP 2.

9. Benis M. Frank and Henry I. Shaw, *Victory and Occupation: History of U.S. Marine Corps Operations in World War II,* vol. 5 (Washington, D.C.: Historical Branch, G-3 Division, Headquarters, U.S. Marine Corps, 1968), 685 n.

10. Ibid.

11. Edwin E. Schwien, *Combat Intelligence: Its Acquisition and Transmission* (Washington, D.C.: The Infantry Journal Inc., 1936).

12. Dirk Anthony Ballendorf and Merrill Lewis Bartlett, *Pete Ellis: An Amphibious Warfare Prophet,* 1880–1923 (Annapolis, Md.: Naval Institute Press, 1997), 123–41.

13. *Narrative: Combat Intelligence Center, Joint Intelligence Center, Pacific Ocean Area* (Washington, D.C.: Department of the Navy, Naval Security Group Command Headquarters, 1945), 3–4.

14. Kenneth J. Clifford, *Amphibious Warfare Development in Britain and America from 1920–1940* (Laurens, N.Y.: Edgewood, 1983), 103–5.

15. Ibid.

16. Ibid., 102 and 105, and Jeter Isely and Philip Crowl, *The U.S. Marines and Amphibious War* (Princeton, N.J.: Princeton University Press, 1951), 37–44.

Chapter 1. Genesis

1. Edwin T. Layton, with Roger Pineau and John Costello, *And I Was There: Pearl Harbor and Midway—Breaking the Secrets* (New York: Quill, 1985). Layton provides a comprehensive overview of intelligence operations before the war began. Information on ONI came from pages 45–50, 68, 97, and 123–27. Information on the attachés came from pages 62–65. OP-20-G is discussed throughout the first half of the book, but information for this citation came from pages 37–46 and 56–57.

2. Wyman Packard, *A Century of U.S. Naval Intelligence* (Washington, D.C.: Department of the Navy, 1996), 180.

3. Joseph J. Twitty, *Report of Intelligence Activities in the Pacific Ocean Areas* (Pearl Harbor, HI: Joint Intelligence Center, Pacific Ocean Areas, 1945), 1–2; see "Initial Intelligence Situation" and "Development of Intelligence."

4. Layton, *And I Was There*, 37–46, 56–57.

5. John Toland, *The Rising Sun: The Decline and Fall of the Japanese Empire, 1936–1945*, vol. 1 (New York: Random House, 1970), 3.

6. Toland, *The Rising Sun*, 49–52.

7. Ibid., 53–58.

8. Dan Van Der Vat, *The Pacific Campaign: The U.S.–Japanese Naval War, 1941–1945* (New York: Simon & Schuster, 1991), 66.

9. Toland, *Rising Sun*, 81.

10. W. J. Holmes, *Double Edged Secrets: U.S. Naval Intelligence Operations during World War II* (Annapolis, Md.: Naval Institute Press, 1979), 14–15.

11. Rear Adm. Donald M. Showers, USN, Ret., interview by author, Arlington, Va., 17 December 1993 (hereafter, Showers interview).

12. Layton, *And I Was There*, 20, 113, 137.

13. Toland, *Rising Sun*, 107.

14. Layton, *And I Was There*, 38, 69, 113.

15. *Narrative: Combat Intelligence Center, Joint Intelligence Center, Pacific Ocean Area*, 7.

16. Ronald Lewin, *The American Magic: Codes, Ciphers, and the Defeat of Japan* (New York: Penguin Books, 1983), 17–18.

17. Layton, *And I Was There*, 97–101.

18. Ibid., 97, 101, 123, 137.

19. Ibid., 356–57.

20. Isely and Crowl, *The U.S. Marines and Amphibious War*, 507.

21. Twitty, "The Growth of JICPOA," in *Report of Intelligence Activities in the Pacific Ocean Areas* (Pearl Harbor, Hawaii, 15 October 1945), 3.

22. Ibid., 3–4.

23. Ibid., 4.

24. Holmes, *Double Edged Secrets*, 9–11.

25. Showers interview.

26. Ibid. This is one of the most documented stories of the Pacific War, and it is well told by Van Der Vat in *The Pacific Campaign*, 178–80.

27. Twitty, "The Growth of JICPOA," 3. See also Layton, *And I Was There*, 465.

28. Layton, *And I Was There*, 465.

29. Ibid., 465. See also Packard, *A Century of U.S. Naval Intelligence*, 399.

30. Twitty, "The Growth of JICPOA," 3.

31. Holmes, *Double Edged Secrets*, 112.

32. *Register of Commissioned and Warrant Officers of the U.S. Navy and Marine Corps* (Washington, D.C.: U.S. Government Printing Office, 1942), 5.

33. Twitty, "The Growth of JICPOA," 4.

34. Ibid.

35. Holmes, *Double Edged Secrets*, 113.

36. Twitty, "The Growth of JICPOA," 5.

37. John L. Zimmerman, *The Guadalcanal Campaign* (Headquarters, USMC: Historical Division, 1949), 4.

38. Henry I. Shaw, *First Offensive, The Marine Campaign for Guadalcanal*, Marines in WWII Commemorative Series (Washington, D.C.: USMC Historical Center, 1992), 17.

39. The AIB almost exclusively processed human intelligence later in the war.

40. Shaw, *First Offensive*, 17.

41. Zimmerman, *Guadalcanal Campaign*, 14.

42. Merrill B. Twining, *No Bended Knee: The Battle for Guadalcanal: The Memoir of General Merrill B. Twining, USMC* (Novato, Calif.: Presidio Press, 1996), 38–39.

43. Twitty, "The Growth of JICPOA," 4.

44. Zimmerman, *Guadalcanal Campaign*, 18–19.

45. Layton, *And I Was There*, 459.

46. Zimmerman, *Guadalcanal Campaign*, 14–15.

47. Ibid., 16–19.

48. Ibid.

49. Layton, *And I Was There*, 466.

50. Ibid., 468.

51. Van Der Vat, *The Pacific Campaign*, 265–66.

52. Holmes, *Double Edged Secrets*, 113.

53. Ibid., 115–16.

54. Twitty, "The Growth of JICPOA," 23.

55. Van Der Vat, *The Pacific Campaign*, 310.

56. Samuel Eliot Morison, *History of United States Naval Operations in World War II, vol. 7: Aleutians, Gilberts, and Marshalls, June 1942–April 1944* (Boston: Atlantic Monthly Press, 1955), 82.

57. Twitty, "The Growth of JICPOA," 5.

58. Ibid.

59. Ibid.

60. Ibid.

61. Ibid.

62. Ibid.

63. Ibid., 6.

64. Ibid., 5. Typically, the U.S. Army places captains in charge of companies, but in this instance, according to two sources, Twitty was an exception, a lieutenant colonel or colonel.

65. *Narrative: Combat Intelligence Unit, Joint Intelligence Center, Pacific Ocean Area,* 13.

66. Twitty, "The History of JICPOA by Sections," in *Report of Intelligence Activities in the Pacific,* 11.

67. Twitty, "The Growth of JICPOA," 6.

68. Ibid., 8.

69. Twitty, "Initial Intelligence Situation," and "Development of Intelligence," 1–2.

70. Rafael Steinberg and the Editors of Time-Life Books, *Island Fighting* (Alexandria, Va.: Time-Life Books, 1978), 118.

71. Henry Shaw, with Bernard Nalty and Edwin T. Turnbladh, *Central Pacific Drive: History of U.S. Marine Corps Operations in World War II,* vol. 3 (Washington, D.C.: Historical Branch, G-3 Division, Headquarters, U.S. Marine Corps, 1966), 103–14.

72. Ibid., 105–6.

73. Holmes, *Double Edged Secrets,* 115.

74. Twitty, "The Growth of JICPOA," 3.

75. *Narrative: Combat Intelligence Unit, Joint Intelligence Center, Pacific Ocean Area,* 13.

76. John A. Harrison, interview by author, Gainesville, Florida, 4 October 1995 (hereafter, Harrison interview). Mr. Harrison, a former officer in the Estimates Section, facetiously made the point about security when he remarked that one "could have been shot for saying the word FRUPAC."

77. Twitty, "The History of JICPOA by Sections," 12.

78. Twitty, "The Growth of JICPOA," 7. See also Wyman H. Packard, *A Century of U.S. Naval Intelligence* (Washington, D.C.: Department of the Navy, 1996), 373.

79. Packard, *A Century of U.S. Naval Intelligence,* 373.

80. G. J. A. O'Toole, *Honorable Treachery: A History of U.S. Intelligence, Espionage, and Covert Action from the American Revolution to the C.I.A.* (New York: Atlantic Monthly Press, 1991), 397–400. See also Packard, *A Century of U.S. Naval Intelligence,* 180.

81. Packard, *A Century of U.S. Naval Intelligence,* 372.

82. *Narrative: Combat Intelligence Unit, Joint Intelligence Center, Pacific Ocean Area,* 16.

83. Twitty, "The Growth of JICPOA," 8.

84. Ibid.

85. Showers interview.

86. George Dyer, *The Amphibians Came to Conquer: The Story of Admiral Richmond Kelly Turner*, vol. 2 (Washington, D.C.: U.S. Government Printing Office, 1972), 826; and March 2000 conversation with a Marine officer at the USMC Command and Staff College.

87. George Garand and Truman Strobridge, *Western Pacific Operations: History of U.S. Marine Corps Operations in World War II*, vol. 4 (Washington, D.C.: Historical Division, Headquarters, U.S. Marine Corps, 1971), 27–28.

88. Showers interview.

89. Twitty, "Development of Intelligence," 2, and Showers interview.

90. JICPOA did produce brief biographies of certain Japanese officers, but not as regular intelligence products.

91. Twitty, "Development of Intelligence," 2. According to press reports and senior level U.S. Government testimony, in the wake of 9/11/01, it does not appear that domestic law enforcement and intelligence echelons disseminated intelligence effectively, nor did they share intelligence with each other. Rivalry, turf protection, and inadequate intelligence architecture apparently inhibited the intelligence cycle. Historical documents and commentary by former JICPOA officers such as General Twitty, Commander Holmes, and now Admiral Showers demonstrate that JICPOA rarely, if at all, suffered from such problems and focused on getting intelligence to its customers in a timely manner.

92. Ibid.

93. Showers interview; Twitty, "The History of JICPOA by Sections," "The Growth of JICPOA"; *Narrative: Combat Intelligence Center, Joint Intelligence Center, Pacific Ocean Area.*

94. Ibid.

95. JICPOA Information Bulletin 9-45, *Iwo Jima: Supplement No. 1 to CINCPAC-CINCPOA Bulletin No. 122-44, Nanpo Shoto*, vol. 1 (Pearl Harbor, Hawaii, 6 January 1945), "Distribution List."

96. Robert B. Stinnett, *George Bush: His War Years* (Washington, D.C.: Brassy's U.S. Inc., 1992), 29.

97. Ibid., 203.

98. War Department, FM-21–25: *Elementary Aerial Photograph Reading* (Washington, D.C.: War Department, 15 August 1944), 92–101.

99. War Department, FM-21-26: *Advanced Map and Aerial Photography Reading* (Washington, D.C.: War Department, December 1944), 107.

100. *Narrative: Combat Intelligence Center, Joint Intelligence Center, Pacific Ocean Area*, 5.

101. War Department, FM-21-26: *Advanced Map and Aerial Photography Reading*, 125–32.

102. Keith Wheeler and the Editors of Time-Life Books, *War under the Pacific* (Alexandria, Va.: Time-Life Books, 1980), 134–35.

103. *Narrative: Combat Intelligence Center, Joint Intelligence Center, Pacific Ocean Area,* 4.

104. Twitty, "The Growth of JICPOA," 7.

105. Showers interview.

106. Twitty, "The Growth of JICPOA," 9.

107. Twitty, "History of JICPOA by Sections," 9.

108. Twitty, "Geographic Section," in "History of JICPOA by Sections," 11.

109. Ibid., 13.

110. Ibid., 11–12.

111. Ibid.

112. Ibid.

113. Ibid., 12.

114. Ibid.

115. Twitty, "Photographic Interpretation," in "History of JICPOA by Sections," 14.

116. Ibid., 14. InterpRon means Photo Interpretation Squadron. The Pacific Fleet established these commands because the farther the war progressed away from JICPOA, the longer it took to transfer raw data from the field to JICPOA and then back out into the field again for use.

117. Twitty, "Photographic Interpretation," in "History of JICPOA by Sections,"13.

118. Twitty, "Terrain Model Unit," in "History of JICPOA by Sections," 16.

119. Twitty, "Hydrographic Section," in "History of JICPOA by Sections," 17.

120. Twitty, "Geographic Section," in "History of JICPOA by Sections," 11.

121. Twitty, "Cartography Section," in "History of JICPOA by Sections," 18. JICPOA documents indicate that the Sixty-fourth Company or elements of it became the Cartography Section, while the Sixty-fourth and Thirtieth Topographic Battalions provided outsource production. Documents do not clarify if the Sixty-fourth Company later expanded and became a battalion-sized formation.

122. Twitty, "Cartography Section," 18.

123. Twitty, "Target Analysis Section," in "History of JICPOA by Sections," 17.

124. Twitty, "Reference Section," in "History of JICPOA by Sections," 15–16.

125. Twitty, "Medical Intelligence Section," in "History of JICPOA by Sections," 18–19.

126. Associated Press, "Japanese Biological Warfare Veteran Says He Cut Human 'Logs'," 16 November 2000, posted on the Internet on CNN.com at 7:06 A.M. Hong Kong time.

127. Twitty, "History of JICPOA by Sections," 21.

128. Twitty, "Enemy Air Section," in "History of JICPOA by Sections," 24.

129. Ibid.

130. Ibid.

131. Twitty, "Enemy Shipping Section," in "History of JICPOA by Sections," 24–27.

132. Twitty, "Enemy Land Section," in "History of JICPOA by Sections," 27.

133. Ibid., 26.

134. U.S. War Department, *Handbook on Japanese Military Forces* (London: Greenhill Books, 1991), 217.

135. Twitty, "Flak Intelligence," in "History of JICPOA by Sections," 27–28.

136. Twitty, "Estimate Section," in "History of JICPOA by Sections," 23–24; and *Narrative: Combat Intelligence Center, Joint Intelligence Center, Pacific Ocean Area,* 12.

137. *Narrative: Combat Intelligence Center, Joint Intelligence Center, Pacific Ocean Area,* 12–13.

138. Showers interview.

139. Ibid.

140. Twitty, "Psychological Warfare" in "History of JICPOA by Sections," 31, and "insert" at 32.

141. Ibid., 31.

142. Ibid., 32.

143. Twitty, "Escape and Evasion," in "History of JICPOA by Sections," 30–35.

144. Twitty, "Bulletin Section," in "History of JICPOA by Sections," 39.

145. Twitty, "Production Section," in "History of JICPOA by Sections," 48.

146. Twitty, "Administration Section," in "History of JICPOA by Sections," 39, 47–48, 50.

147. Twitty, "Translation Section," in "History of JICPOA by Sections," 40.

148. Ibid., 40–41.

149. Ibid., 42.

150. Ibid., 41–42.

151. Ibid., 43.

152. Ibid., 44.

153. Ibid., 45.

154. Frank Gibney, introduction to Hiromichi Yahara, *The Battle For Okinawa* (New York: John Wiley & Sons, 1995), xxi. Gibney served as a JICPOA interrogator at Hawaii and in the field on two operations: Peleliu (late in the battle) and Okinawa (early in the battle). His book provides excellent insight into the duties of a JICPOA interrogator and one of their most impressive subjects, Col. Hiromichi Yahara, the senior staff officer of the Thirty-second Japanese Army on Okinawa.

155. Frank Gibney, interview by author, California, 11 September 1997 (hereafter, Gibney interview).

156. Twitty, "Interrogation Section" in "The History of JICPOA by Sections," 45.

157. Gibney interview.

158. Frank Gibney in Yahara, *The Battle For Okinawa,* xxiii.

159. Gibney interview.

160. Twitty, "Operational Intelligence Section" in "History of JICPOA by Sections," 46–47.

161. Twitty, "Advanced Intelligence Center," in *Report of Intelligence Activities in the Pacific,* 51–56.

162. Ibid., 53.

163. Twitty, *Report of Intelligence Activities in the Pacific*, 4.

164. Ibid.

165. Holmes, *Double Edged Secrets*, 143, 150.

166. Ibid., 150.

167. Ibid., 151.

168. Ibid., 168.

169. Ibid., 176.

170. Ibid.

171. *Narration: Combat Intelligence Center, Joint Intelligence Center, Pacific Ocean Area*, 5.

172. Harrison interview.

173. Twitty, *Report of Intelligence Activities in the Pacific*, 4.

174. Ibid., 4.

175. Packard, *A Century of U.S. Naval Intelligence*, 162.

Chapter 2. The Marshalls: Flintlock and Catchpole

1. Keegan, *The Second World War* (New York: Penguin, 1990), 296.

2. Alfred T. Mahan was an American strategic naval philosopher during the age of sail, and some of his theories died with the rise of mechanically powered ships, but during World War II, his views were widely accepted as viable naval strategies. (Most of his strategies are still used in the modern age as well.) One of his theories postulated that the purpose of naval warfare was to destroy the opponent's ships, thereby undermining naval capabilities and halting maritime shipping. This, in turn, set the stage for the ultimate defeat of the enemy by other means if necessary (the land war).

3. Van Der Vat, *Pacific Campaign*, 290.

4. Ibid.

5. The Japanese could have used more men in several campaigns such as Saipan, Peleliu, and Okinawa.

6. Van Der Vat, *Pacific Campaign*, 290.

7. Keegan, *Second World War*, 302.

8. James F. Dunnigan and Albert A. Nofi, *Victory at Sea* (New York: Morrow, 1995); see chapter entitled "Ships," 79–152, and charts at 98, 106–7, 115, 118, 123, 128, 130, 137, and 140.

9. Shaw, *Central Pacific Drive*, 162, 175.

10. Ibid., 118, 120.

11. Ibid., 162, 168, 177.

12. Ibid., 180.

13. Ibid., 131.

14. Steinberg, *Island Fighting*, 21.

15. Shaw, *Central Pacific Drive*, 127.

16. Ibid., 117.

17. Isely and Crowl, *U.S. Marines and Amphibious War,* 75.

18. Shaw, *Central Pacific Drive,* 127.

19. Van Der Vat, *Pacific Campaign,* 310.

20. Ibid., 118.

21. Ibid., 117–20.

22. ICPOA Information Bulletin 30-43, *Enemy Positions; The Marshall-Gilbert Area,* vol. 2 (Pearl Harbor, Hawaii, 5 May 1943), 8.

23. Van Der Vat, *Pacific Campaign,* 302–3.

24. ICPOA Information Bulletin 30-43, 63.1.

25. Shaw, *Central Pacific Drive,* 129.

26. Ibid.

27. JICPOA Information Bulletin 53-43, *Kwajalein* (Pearl Harbor, Hawaii, 1 December 1943), "Roi and Namur Islands" and "Kwajalein Island" maps.

28. Kevin Dockery, *SEALs in Action* (New York: Avon Books, 1991), 23.

29. JICPOA Information Bulletin 53-43, "Roi and Namur Islands" and "Kwajalein Island" maps.

30. Holmes, *Double Edged Secrets,* 152.

31. Ibid., 157.

32. "Perhaps contained" means that it was still early in the war, and JICPOA's Reference Section might not have had a breadth of intelligence on Japanese units. In the coming months, however, that changed, and the Reference Section would overflow with organizational charts on enemy formations.

33. Maps in the bulletin are dated 4 December, which means that even though the bulletin itself was dated 1 December, the bulletin was disseminated after the first of the month.

34. JICPOA Information Bulletin 53-43, 11–12.

35. Ibid., 11, 17.

36. Ibid., 12.

37. Ibid., 12–18.

38. Ibid., 11–12.

39. Ibid., 35.

40. Ibid., 44.

41. Ibid., 36, 71.

42. Ibid., 35, 44.

43. ICPOA Information Bulletin 30-43, 60.

44. Ibid., 55-63, 67–69.

45. Ibid.

46. JICPOA Information Bulletin 53-43, 1.

47. Ibid., 4.

48. Isely and Crowl, *U.S. Marines and Amphibious War,* 264.

49. Shaw, *Central Pacific Drive,* 180.

50. JICPOA Information Bulletins 52-43 (Maloelap), 57-43 (Wotje); Isely and Crowl, *U.S. Marines and Amphibious War,* 256; and Holmes, *Double Edged Secrets,* 157.

51. Shaw, *Central Pacific Drive,* 121.

52. Van Der Vat, *Pacific Campaign,* 303.

53. Isely and Crowl, *U.S. Marines and Amphibious War,* 254–55.

54. Ibid.

55. Ibid., 272.

56. Van Der Vat, *Pacific Campaign,* 303.

57. Ibid., 304.

58. JICPOA Information Bulletin 53-43; "Roi and Namur Islands Map," and the "Kwajalein Island Map" compared with JICPOA Information Bulletin 48-44; map numbers 4 (Roi-Namur) and 1 (Kwajalein Island).

59. Isely and Crowl, *U.S. Marines and Amphibious War,* 260.

60. Ibid., 261–62.

61. Ibid., 262.

62. These ships did not receive the naval bombardment maps for Roi-Namur because of an unexplained foul-up. At the last minute, however, an aircraft dropped analyzed photographs of the objective that served the gunners just as well. Dyer, *Amphibians Came to Conquer,* 814.

63. Shaw, *Central Pacific Drive,* 165.

64. Ibid., 163.

65. Ibid.

66. Van Der Vat, *Pacific Campaign,* 304.

67. Shaw, *Central Pacific Drive,* 170.

68. Ibid.

69. Ibid., 177.

70. Headquarters, V Amphibious Corps, *Report by G-2 on Marshall Islands Operation* (18 February 1944), 17–18.

71. Isely and Crowl, *The U.S. Marines and Amphibious War,* 261.

72. Holmes, *Double Edged Secrets,* 158.

73. JICPOA Information Bulletin 53-43, 18.

74. Shaw, *Central Pacific Drive,* 171.

75. Isely and Crowl, *U.S. Marines and Amphibious War,* 291.

76. Shaw, *Central Pacific Drive,* 185.

77. Ibid., 186.

78. Isely and Crowl, *U.S. Marines and Amphibious War,* 75.

79. Shaw, *Central Pacific Drive,* 187.

80. Ibid., 119.

81. Ibid., 180.

82. JICPOA Information Bulletin 3-44, *Eniwetok* (Pearl Harbor, Hawaii, 20 January 1944), 7, 13–14. Although this was a JICPOA information bulletin, ICPOA had generated this particular piece of intelligence.

83. Ibid., 13.

84. Shaw, *Central Pacific Drive,* 182.

85. JICPOA Information Bulletin 3-44, 9, 22–25.

86. Shaw, *Central Pacific Drive,* 187.

87. JICPOA Information Bulletin 3-44, 1, 16–17.

88. Ibid., 1.

89. Ibid., 16.

90. Ibid.

91. Shaw, *Central Pacific Drive,* 187. The actual number of reinforcements was 3,429.

92. Robert D. Heinl Jr. and John A. Crown, *The Marshalls: Increasing the Tempo* (Washington, D.C.: Historical Branch, G-3 Division, Headquarters, United States Marine Corps, 1954), 124; and Philip A. Crowl and Edmund G. Love, *The U.S. Army in World War II: The War in the Pacific, Seizure of the Gilberts and Marshalls* (Washington, D.C.: Office of the Chief of Military History, Department of the Army, 1955), 335–36.

93. Office of the Commander, Group 3, Fifth Amphibious Force, U.S. Pacific Fleet, *Report of Amphibious Operations for the Marshalls: Capture of Roi and Namur Islands (Flintlock)* (23 February 1944), 3–4.

94. Headquarters, Fifth Amphibious Corps, *Report on Marshall Islands Operation,* 18.

95. Shaw, *Central Pacific Drive,* 181.

96. Isely and Crowl, *U.S. Marines and Amphibious War,* 291.

97. JICPOA Information Bulletin 3-44, 5.

98. Ibid., 25.

99. Ibid., 5, 9.

100. Ibid., 4.

101. Shaw, *Central Pacific Drive,* 127.

102. Dyer, *Amphibians Came to Conquer,* 830.

103. JICPOA Information Bulletin 3-44, 14.

104. Isely and Crowl, *U.S. Marines and Amphibious War,* 292.

105. Daniel P. Bolger, *Americans at War; 1975–1986, An Era of Violent Peace* (Novato, Calif.: Presidio Press, 1988), 261. The theory was made clear in a quote by Gen. George S. Patton.

106. Shaw, *Central Pacific Drive,* 182.

107. JICPOA Information Bulletin 3-44, 21–25.

108. Shaw, *Central Pacific Drive,* 183.

109. Crowl and Love, *Seizure of the Gilberts and Marshalls,* 335–36.

110. Shaw, *Central Pacific Drive,* 183.

111. Headquarters, Twenty-second Marines (Reinforced), Fifth Amphibious Corps, *Report on Catchpole Operation* (9 March 1944), 4.

112. Crowl and Love, *Seizure of the Gilberts and Marshalls,* 336.

113. Shaw, *Central Pacific Drive,* 182–87.

114. Van Der Vat, *Pacific Campaign,* 306–7.

115. Shaw, *Central Pacific Drive,* 188.

116. Van Der Vat, *Pacific Campaign,* 306–7.

117. JICPOA Information Bulletin 3-44, 5.

118. Ibid., 4–6.

119. Ibid., 4–7.

120. Heinl and Crown, *The Marshalls: Increasing the Tempo,* 128.

121. Isely and Crowl, *U.S. Marines and Amphibious War,* 294.

122. Shaw, *Central Pacific Drive,* 196.

123. JICPOA Information Bulletin 3-44, 14.

124. Ibid., 8–11.

125. Headquarters, Twenty-second Marines (Reinforced), Fifth Amphibious Corps, *Report on Catchpole Operation,* 4.

126. Isely and Crowl, *U.S. Marines and Amphibious War,* 297.

127. Shaw, *Central Pacific Drive,* 200.

128. Isely and Crowl, *U.S. Marines and Amphibious War,* 279–99.

129. Ibid., 301.

130. Shaw, *Central Pacific Drive,* 196.

131. JICPOA Information Bulletin 3-44, 20, 21.

132. Shaw, *Central Pacific Drive,* 200–201.

133. JICPOA Information Bulletin 3-44, 24–25.

134. Shaw, *Central Pacific Drive,* 206.

135. JICPOA Information Bulletin 3-44, 22–23.

136. Shaw, *Central Pacific Drive,* 211.

137. JICPOA Information Bulletin 3-44, 22.

138. JICPOA Information Bulletin 89-44, *The Japanese Defense of Eniwetok Atoll* (Pearl Harbor, Hawaii, 12 June 1944), 4–5. This information came from a translated document. The original, of course, was written in Japanese and could have been organized on the page in a different manner.

139. Holmes, *Double Edged Secrets,* 167–78. On an interesting note, both the official Marine and Army histories of the campaign state that Fifth Amphibious Corps reconnaissance personnel met and interviewed natives of Eniwetok Atoll when they attacked smaller islets in prelude to the larger island assaults. The natives claimed that there were thousands of Japanese on each of the three main islands, but precise communication with the natives was difficult, so the Marines did not regard the information as reliable. See Crowl and Love, *Seizure of the Gilberts and Marshalls,* 348.

140. The U.S. Army's official history of the campaign stated that captured documents and POWs indicated there were 556 soldiers on Eniwetok Island and 326 on Parry (based on RCT 106's report of operations at Eniwetok). These figures are too low considering the level of combat faced on these islands, as described by the Army's history of the campaign. More to the point, if the Japanese had only company-sized formations on each island, General Watson would not have altered his attack plan, and U.S. forces probably would have quickly reduced these garrisons. Furthermore, the translations that appear in the historical documents came directly from the captured documents themselves, which were included in an after-action intelligence bulletin describing the defense of Eniwetok Atoll.

141. Van Der Vat, *Pacific Campaign*, 308.

142. Holmes, *Double Edged Secrets*, 168.

143. Isely and Crowl, *U.S. Marines and Amphibious War*, 298–301.

144. Information on the sequence of events regarding the captured documents also came from: Headquarters, Twenty-second Marines (Reinforced), Fifth Amphibious Corps, *Report on Catchpole Operation* (9 March 1944), 6.

145. JICPOA Information Bulletin 3-44, 7, 16.

146. Isely and Crowl, *U.S. Marines and Amphibious War*, 293.

147. JICPOA Information Bulletin 3-44, 3–5.

148. Ibid.

149. Shaw, *Central Pacific Drive*, 197, 199, 210.

150. JICPOA Information Bulletin 3-44, 1, 3, 5.

151. Ibid., 8–11, 21–22, 25, and "Engebi Island" Map.

152. Shaw, *Central Pacific Drive*, 199–201.

153. Ibid., 213–15.

154. Ibid., 203, 215.

155. Isely and Crowl, *U.S. Marines and Amphibious War*, 300–301.

156. Ibid., 298.

157. JICPOA Information Bulletin 89-44. The entire text discusses the Japanese plan of defense, and reference is made to building spiderweb defenses, at 12–13.

158. Headquarters, Twenty-second Marines (Reinforced), Fifth Amphibious Corps, *Report on Catchpole Operation* (9 March 1944), 4–5.

159. Ibid.

160. JICPOA Information Bulletin 3-44, 14.

161. Ibid, 25.

162. Ibid., 5.

163. Holmes, *Double Edged Secrets*, 164.

164. "The commander drives intelligence" refers to directing intelligence. Specifically, the commander as planner of an operation establishes information requirements for the intelligence echelon that will help achieve specific goals and reduce operational risk. This requires a close working relationship between planning and intelligence—each has to know what the other is doing and planning to do. Most of the time, intelligence personnel help the commander develop information requirements. For Eniwetok, Nimitz "drove" intelligence by directing JICPOA to provide him with a constant picture of the enemy situation in the Marshalls because he wanted to increase his attack options. Watson "drove" intelligence by tasking operational intelligence personnel to forward him any combat intelligence that would positively influence the operation—a standard operating procedure.

165. Van Der Vat, *Pacific Campaign*, 308–9.

166. Samuel Eliot Morison, *History of United States Naval Operations in World War II*, vol. 8, *New Guinea and the Marianas, March 1944–August 1944* (Boston: Atlantic Monthly Press, 1953), 156, 164.

167. Van Der Vat, *Pacific Campaign*, 309.

168. Samuel Eliot Morison, *New Guinea and the Marianas,* 156, 164.

169. Joseph H. Alexander, *Storm Landings: Epic Amphibious Battles in the Central Pacific* (Annapolis, Md.: Naval Institute Press, 1997), 65.

170. Ibid., 158.

171. Dyer, *Amphibians Came to Conquer,* 965.

172. Ibid., 897.

173. Ibid., 875, 897.

174. Ibid., 965.

Chapter 3. The Marianas: Forager

1. Toland, *The Rising Sun,* 601–2.

2. Van Der Vat, *Pacific Campaign,* 330.

3. Ibid., 318.

4. Shaw, *Central Pacific Drive,* 346.

5. Ibid., and Philip A. Crowl, *U.S. Army in WW II, The War in the Pacific: Campaign in the Marianas* (Washington, D.C.: Office of the Chief of Military History, Department of the Army, 1960), 65.

6. Isely and Crowl, *U.S. Marines and Amphibious War,* 320.

7. Shaw, *Central Pacific Drive,* 242–43.

8. Isely and Crowl, *U.S. Marines and Amphibious War,* 320.

9. Steinberg, *Island Fighting,* 166 and map, 20–21.

10. JICPOA Information Bulletin 73-44, *Saipan, Tinian, and Rota* (Pearl Harbor, Hawaii, 10 May 1944), 6.

11. Shaw, *Central Pacific Drive,* 259 and map, 15.

12. Ibid., 232.

13. Ibid., 316.

14. Ibid.

15. Ibid., 232, 236–67.

16. The Saipan intelligence operation also included intelligence operations against the rest of the Marianas.

17. Van Der Vat, *Pacific Campaign,* 306–7, 316.

18. Headquarters, Expeditionary Troops, Task Force Fifty-Six, *G-2 Report on Forager Operation* (31 August 1944), 1.

19. Ibid., 2.

20. Carl W. Hoffman, *Saipan: The Beginning of the End* (Washington, D.C.: Historical Division, Headquarters, U.S. Marine Corps, 1950), 25.

21. Shaw, *Central Pacific Drive,* 245.

22. JICPOA Information Bulletin 73-44, 14–19.

23. Shaw, *Central Pacific Drive,* 245.

24. Hoffman, *Saipan,* 26–27.

25. Shaw, *Central Pacific Drive,* 245.

26. Hoffman, *Saipan,* 27.

27. Ibid. See also JICPOA Information Bulletin 73-44, 14–19. Fifth Amphibious

Corps maps were based on February photos; JICPOA terrain and defense maps were based on 18 April photos.

28. Shaw, *Central Pacific Drive*, 245.

29. Holmes, *Double Edged Secrets*, 175.

30. Hoffman, *Saipan*, 25.

31. Crowl, *Campaign in the Marianas*, 51–52.

32. Shaw, *Central Pacific Drive*, 246. See also Headquarters, Expeditionary Troops, Task Force Fifty-Six, *G-2 Report on Forager Operation*, 2.

33. Van Der Vat, *Pacific Campaign*, 317.

34. Hoffman, *Saipan*, 22.

35. Van Der Vat, *Pacific Campaign*, 317.

36. Dyer, *Amphibians Came to Conquer*, 846–49. Spruance, Turner, and Smith were all promoted to the next higher rank in between 16 February and 13 March 1944.

37. Ibid., 889.

38. The Japanese sent a large naval contingent to attack U.S. forces as they assaulted Saipan. Fortunately for Nimitz, the Japanese attack plan fell into U.S. hands when a senior Japanese officer who helped design the operation was captured by Philippine guerrillas after his plane crashed near Cebu. The leader of the guerrillas, a U.S. Army officer, got the Japanese attack plan reproduced with the aid of MacArthur's command without his captives' knowledge, and then, citing a lack of POW facilities, released the prisoners. Believing their plan secure, the Japanese commenced their attack, only to be ambushed by U.S. naval forces in what came to be known as the "Great Marianas Turkey Shoot." As a result, the Japanese attack failed, and Spruance supervised the Saipan operation unimpeded. For the story in detail, see S. Phil Ishio, "The Nisei Contribution to the Allied Victory in the Pacific," *American Intelligence Journal* 16, no. 1 (Spring/Summer 1995): 62–64.

39. The first was Guadalcanal.

40. Holmes, *Double Edged Secrets*, 183.

41. Shaw, *Central Pacific Drive*, 246.

42. Hoffman, *Saipan*, 11, 281–82.

43. Isely and Crowl, *U.S. Marines and Amphibious War*, 322.

44. Hoffman, *Saipan*, 84–45.

45. Shaw, *Central Pacific Drive*, 284.

46. Holland Smith and Percy Finch, *Coral and Brass* (New York: Charles Scribners' Sons, 1949), 163–64.

47. Headquarters, Northern Troops and Landing Force, *Marianas Phase I (Saipan) G-2 Report*, Enclosure D, serial number 0024A (1944), 82, 83, 84, 85, 90, 95. POW interrogations during the campaign state that some units fought to the death on the beaches, some fought a delaying action, some fell back to the interior, and some were already in the interior when the Marines landed. The same reports state that the Japanese, however, did not enact a "horseshoe defense" above a point in the upper center of the island.

48. Hoffman, *Saipan*, 12–13, map 3.

49. Ibid., map 11.

50. Isely and Crowl, *U.S. Marines and Amphibious War,* 322.

51. Ibid., 323.

52. Headquarters, Northern Troops and Landing Force, *Marianas Phase I (Saipan) G-2 Report,* 84.

53. Shaw, *Central Pacific Drive,* 310.

54. Van Der Vat, *Pacific Campaign,* 327.

55. Ibid.

56. Steinberg, *Island Fighting,* 17–21, and Van Der Vat, *Pacific Campaign,* 328.

57. Isely and Crowl, *U.S. Marines and Amphibious War,* 330.

58. JICPOA Information Bulletin 73-44, map, 17. These were part of a total of 12 coast defense, 21 dual-purpose, and 139 AA weapons, 166 machine guns, two covered artillery positions, one blockhouse, and 23 pillboxes. A significant number of these weapons positions were located north of the landing beaches and around Aslito Airfield in southern Saipan.

59. Shaw, *Central Pacific Drive,* 258, 267–77.

60. Headquarters, Northern Troops and Landing Force, *Marianas Phase I (Saipan) G-2 Report,* Enclosure D, 10.

61. Ibid.

62. Hoffman, *Saipan,* 281—compared to the JICPOA "Fortifications, Radar, and Air Facilities" map.

63. Ibid., map 3—compared to the JICPOA "Fortifications, Radar, and Air Facilities" map.

64. As in all case studies in this book, some intelligence was better than no intelligence, and most intelligence helped operations to some degree.

65. Hoffman, *Saipan,* 12–13.

66. Ibid., 281, and map 3.

67. Shaw, *Central Pacific Drive,* 269.

68. Van Der Vat, *Pacific Campaign,* 320.

69. Hoffman, *Saipan,* 69.

70. Isely and Crowl, *U.S. Marines and Amphibious War,* 331.

71. Ibid., 267.

72. Ibid., 331.

73. JICPOA Information Bulletin 77A and B-44, *Gridded Map Air Target Folder* (Pearl Harbor, Hawaii, 15 May 1944), "Saipan" sheets 1, 3, 3A, and 3B.

74. Isely and Crowl, *U.S. Marines and Amphibious War,* 331. See also Hoffman, *Saipan,* 36, 40.

75. Headquarters, Northern Troops and Landing Force, *Marianas Phase I (Saipan) G-2 Report,* 9, 10, 101.

76. Layton, *And I Was There,* 487. Layton refers to a specific Japanese counterattack as "the counterattack" on the "following evening." However, there was more than one significant counterattack during the battle.

77. JICPOA Information Bulletin 73-44, 6.

78. Hoffman, *Saipan,* 26 n.

79. Hoffman, *Saipan,* 26.

80. Isely and Crowl, *U.S. Marines and Amphibious War,* 337.

81. Shaw, *Central Pacific Drive,* 267–68.

82. JICPOA Information Bulletin 73-44, 6.

83. The distinction is clear by comparing JICPOA Information Bulletin 73-44's maps and text, pp. 6, 7, 15, 17–19, against references to terrain difficulties that marines and soldiers faced. Two distinct examples are noted in Shaw, Nalty, and Turndladh, *Central Pacific Drive,* 304–7, and Hoffman, *Saipan: The Beginning of the End,* 129, 135, and map 2.

84. Isely and Crowl, *U.S. Marines and Amphibious War,* 333.

85. Shaw, *Central Pacific Drive,* 301.

86. Isely and Crowl, *U.S. Marines and Amphibious War,* 329.

87. JICPOA Information Bulletin 73-44, 6, 8.

88. Hoffman, *Saipan,* 46–63.

89. JICPOA Information Bulletin 73-44, 6.

90. Ibid., 11.

91. JICPOA Information Bulletin 66A-44, *Target Survey: Saipan* (Pearl Harbor, Hawaii, 10 May 1944), 2.

92. Hoffman, *Saipan,* 26.

93. O. R. Lodge, *The Recapture of Guam* (Washington, D.C.: Historical Branch, G-3 Division, Headquarters, U.S. Marine Corps, 1954), 12. See also Headquarters, Northern Troops and Landing Force, *Marianas Phase I (Saipan) G-2 Report,* Enclosure D, 10.

94. Shaw, *Central Pacific Drive,* 256–57.

95. Headquarters, Northern Troops and Landing Force, *Marianas Phase I (Saipan) G-2 Report,* 10.

96. Holmes, *Double-Edged Secrets,* 168, and Twitty, "Translation Section," in "History of JICPOA by Sections," 43. Holmes believed that there were fifty tons of documents taken from Saipan.

97. Alexander, *Storm Landings,* 69.

98. Hoffman, *Saipan,* 27. Also see Headquarters, Northern Troops and Landing Force, *Marianas Phase I (Saipan) G-2 Report,* 92.

99. Ibid.

100. Headquarters, Expeditionary Troops, Task Force Fifty-Six, *G-2 Report on Forager Operation,* 1–2.

101. E. D. Forrestal, *Adm. Raymond Spruance, USN: A Study in Command* (Washington, D.C.: Government Printing Office, 1966), 125; and Thomas B. Buell, *The Quiet Warrior: A Biography of Adm. Raymond A. Spruance* (Boston: Little, Brown, 1974), 157–58.

102. Shaw, *Central Pacific Drive,* 568.

103. Ibid.

104. Lodge, *Recapture of Guam,* 197.

105. Isely and Crowl, *U.S. Marines and Amphibious War,* 311–12.

106. Ibid., 310–12, and Shaw, *Central Pacific Drive,* 431.

107. Office of the Commander, Group Three, Amphibious Forces, *CTF-53's Report of Amphibious Operations for the Capture of Guam,* Enclosure E, 10 August 1944, 3E.

108. JICPOA Information Bulletin 52-44, *Guam,* vols. 1 and 2 (Pearl Harbor, Hawaii, 15 April 1944), bibliography.

109. Ibid., 54.

110. Holmes, *Double Edged Secrets,* 170.

111. Office of the Commander, Group Three, Amphibious Forces, *CTF-53's Report of Amphibious Operations for the Capture of Guam,* Enclosure E, 2E.

112. Ibid., 3E. This particular source stated that Marine planners did not like contour and road maps. Other sources, however, state that the Marines did not like the contour maps and that they wanted to see recently built Japanese roads on the road map, but otherwise they liked the road map. More than likely, this is a case of the author of *Report of Amphibious Operations for the Capture of Guam* being vague. It appears that there was no set format for these reports, and sometimes after-action reports for the same battle contradicted one another or neglected what historians deem as vital material.

113. Ibid., 2E.

114. Shaw, *Central Pacific Drive,* 441.

115. Office of the Commander, Group Three, Amphibious Forces, *CTF-53's Report of Amphibious Operations for the Capture of Guam,* Enclosure E, 2E.

116. Commander, Task Force 53, Operational Plan A162-44, Annex "B" and Appendices, 7 June 1944.

117. Ibid., "Defense Installations; Island of Guam" map, and the intelligence appendices containing text entitled "Installations in Target Areas" and "Installations Not in Target Areas," 1–7.

118. Lodge, *The Recapture of Guam,* 23.

119. Shaw, *Central Pacific Drive,* 432, 439.

120. Headquarters, Northern Troops and Landing Force, *Marianas Phase I (Saipan) G-2 Report,* 102–8.

121. Office of the Commander, Group Three, Amphibious Forces, *CTF-53's Report of Amphibious Operations for the Capture of Guam,* Enclosure E, 2E.

122. Shaw, *Central Pacific Drive,* 433–34.

123. Ibid., 447.

124. Isely and Crowl, *U.S. Marines and Amphibious War,* 373–74.

125. Ibid., 386.

126. JICPOA Information Bulletin 52-44, 45, I-4, I-5.

127. Ibid., 44-45.

128. Ibid., 45, I-4, I-5.

129. Ibid., map entitled "Landings," small untitled map at 46, and text at 45–46.

130. Alexander, *Storm Landings,* 75.

131. JICPOA Information Bulletin 52-44, I-5.

132. Ibid., 49.

133. Alexander, *Storm Landings,* 77. See quote by General Shepherd in paragraph one.

134. Isely and Crowl, *U.S. Marines and Amphibious War,* 387.

135. JICPOA Information Bulletin 52-44, 7–10, and map at 5 in vol. 2.

136. Ibid., 31–33.

137. Commander, Task Force 53, landing zone maps, and crudely labeled "Map 9."

138. Isely and Crowl, *The U.S. Marines and Amphibious War,* 376–77.

139. JICPOA Information Bulletin 52-44, 31.

140. Ibid., 29–31.

141. This map, page 18 in volume 2 of Information Bulletin 52-44, is missing from all of the reports—original and microfilmed—that the author viewed. In this case, a "Marine Supply Depot" map included in Operation Plan 1-44, 11 May 1944, provides clear, sufficient examples of road intelligence for Guam.

142. JICPOA Information Bulletin 52-44, 29–33.

143. Shaw, *Central Pacific Drive,* 491–92.

144. Ibid., 463–65.

145. Ibid., 520–23.

146. Ibid., 540. Text here provides a clear example of the value of roads to supply echelons.

147. Isely and Crowl, *U.S. Marines and Amphibious War,* 388.

148. Lodge, *Recapture of Guam,* 197.

149. *Guam Operations of the 77th Division: 21 July–10 August 1944* in American Forces in Action Series (Washington, D.C.: War Department, Historical Division, 1946), 20–23.

150. Frank O. Hough, *The Island War: The United States Marine Corps in the Pacific* (New York: Lippincott, 1947), 262.

151. Commander, Task Force 53, *Operational Plan A162-44,* Annex "B" and Appendices, "Defense Installations; Island of Guam" map, and the intelligence appendices containing text entitled "Installations in Target Areas" and "Installations Not in Target Areas," 1–7.

152. Lodge, *Recapture of Guam,* 164–65.

153. Van Der Vat, *The Pacific Campaign,* 330.

154. Commander, Task Force 53, *Operational Plan A162-44,* Annex "B" and Appendices, "Defense Installations; Island of Guam" map, and the intelligence appendices containing text entitled "Installations in Target Areas" and "Installations Not in Target Areas," 1, 3, 5, and 6.

155. Ibid., "Defense Installations; Island of Guam" map, title page.

156. There is no evidence that radio intelligence prompted this top secret rating. More than likely, it was due to the sensitive nature of the special intelligence section combined with the fact that much of their work was done in the field.

157. Ibid., "Defense Installations; Island of Guam" map, and the intelligence appendices containing text entitled "Installations in Target Areas" and "Installations Not in Target Areas," 1–7.

158. Isely and Crowl, *U.S. Marines and Amphibious War*, 379, 381–84.

159. Shaw, *Central Pacific Drive*, 457.

160. Ibid., 460–62.

161. Isely and Crowl, *U.S. Marines and Amphibious War*, 379–84.

162. Eric Hammel, "Guam," *Leatherneck, Magazine of the Marines*, July 1994, 11.

163. Alexander, *Storm Landings*, 75.

164. Van Der Vat, *Pacific Campaign*, 330.

165. Office of the Commander, Group Three, Amphibious Forces, *CTF-53's Report of Amphibious Operations for the Capture of Guam*, Enclosure E, 5E.

166. Shaw, *Central Pacific Drive*, 435. See also Office of the Commander, Group Three, Amphibious Forces, *CTF-53's Report of Amphibious Operations for the Capture of Guam*, Enclosure E, 10 August 1944, 3E.

167. Shaw, *Central Pacific Drive*, 435–36.

168. Lodge, *The Recapture of Guam*, 23.

169. Shaw, *Central Pacific Drive*, 382.

170. Ibid., 365.

171. Ibid., 382, 400.

172. Richard Harwood, *A Close Encounter: The Marine Landing on Tinian*, Marines in World War II Commemorative Series (Washington, D.C.: Marine Corps Historical Center, 1942), 2, 4. Perhaps over a thousand Japanese died by suicide and suffocation when marines sealed off caves in which they hid.

173. Shaw, *Central Pacific Drive*, 365.

174. Steinberg, *Island Fighting*, 166, and map at 20–21.

175. JICPOA Information Bulletin 73-44, 20.

176. Shaw, *Central Pacific Drive*, 355.

177. The results of the campaign proved the report accurate.

178. JICPOA Information Bulletin 73-44, 20–28. The basic scheme of Japanese defense was revealed on 10 May in this JICPOA information bulletin—proven by comparison with the 10 May "Fortifications and Air Facilities" map to an after-action JICPOA study of Japanese defensive installations found in Carl W. Hoffman, *The Seizure of Tinian* (Washington, D.C.: Historical Branch, G-3 Division, Headquarters, U.S. Marine Corps, 1951), 15.

179. Headquarters, Fourth Marine Division, Fleet Marine Force, *Operations Report, Tinian* (25 September 1944), 5.

180. Headquarters, Northern Troops and Landing Force, *Marianas Phase I (Saipan) G-2 Report*, 84, 93, 98.

181. Ibid., 102–8.

182. Hoffman, *Seizure of Tinian*, 124.

183. Headquarters, Expeditionary Troops, Task Force Fifty Six, *G-2 Report on Forager Operation*, 136. This notation refers specifically to InterpRon 2 personnel; how-

ever, JICPOA and fleet intelligence personnel were also involved, as they were in every Central Pacific intelligence operation.

184. Headquarters, Expeditionary Troops, Task Force Fifty Six, *G-2 Report on Forager Operation*, 136.

185. Richard Harwood, *A Close Encounter*, 2, 4.

186. Shaw, *Central Pacific Drive*, 358, 366–70.

187. Ibid., 356, 366.

188. Van Der Vat, *Pacific Campaign*, 329.

189. Shaw, *Central Pacific Drive*, 370, 374.

190. Isely and Crowl, *U.S. Marines and Amphibious War*, 354.

191. Ibid., 355–57.

192. Harwood, *A Close Encounter*, 7–8.

193. Shaw, *Central Pacific Drive*, 380.

194. Isely and Crowl, *U.S. Marines and Amphibious War*, 366–68.

195. JICPOA Information Bulletin 73-44, 20.

196. Ibid., 20, and Information Bulletin 67-44, *Target Analysis Bulletin* (Pearl Harbor, Hawaii, 10 May 1944), map at 22 titled "A.A. & Coast Defense Guns."

197. Headquarters, Fourth Marine Division, Fleet Marine Force, *Operations Report, Tinian*, 2.

198. Harwood, *Close Encounter*, 11.

199. Shaw, *Central Pacific Drive*, 383.

200. Ibid., 385, 382.

201. Ibid., 328–402.

202. Ibid., 411–13.

203. Ibid., 359–60, 366.

204. JICPOA Information Bulletin 73-44, map at 25, "Fortifications and Air Facilities."

205. Isely and Crowl, *U.S. Marines and Amphibious War*, 362.

206. Shaw, *Central Pacific Drive*, 361–62.

207. Ibid., 361–62.

208. Ibid., 377–78.

209. Harwood, *Close Encounter*, 7.

210. Known today as intelligence preparation of the battlefield (IPB).

211. Keith Wheeler and the Editors of Time-Life Books, *Bombers over Japan* (Alexandria, Va.: Time-Life Books, 1982), 103.

212. Ibid., 99.

213. Ibid., 98–99.

214. Ibid., 173.

215. Ibid., 20.

216. Ibid., 70.

217. Steinberg, *Island Fighting*, 194.

218. Wheeler, *Bombers over Japan*, 74.

219. Ibid.

220. Ibid., 80.

221. Ibid., 74.

222. Ibid., 76.

223. Ibid., 83.

224. Ibid.

Chapter 4. Peleliu: Stalemate II

1. Isely and Crowl, *U.S. Marines and Amphibious War*, 395, 397, 414.

2. Ibid., 411.

3. Robert Ross Smith, *The U.S. Army in World War II: The War in the Pacific: The Approach to the Philippines* (Washington, D.C.: Office of the Chief of Military History, Department of the Army, 1953), 577. These figures include combat casualties on Anguar.

4. Isely and Crowl, *U.S Marines and Amphibious War*, 411.

5. Steinberg, *Island Fighting*, 174.

6. Garand and Strobridge, *Western Pacific Operations*, 161.

7. Isely and Crowl, *U.S. Marines and Amphibious War*, 411.

8. Steinberg, *Island Fighting*, 176.

9. Garand and Strobridge, *Western Pacific Operations*, 52–60.

10. Frank O. Hough, *The Assault on Peleliu* (Washington, D.C.: Historical Division, Headquarters, U.S. Marine Corps, 1950), 32.

11. Garand and Strobridge, *Western Pacific Operations*, 57.

12. Ibid., 51–33.

13. Ibid., 52–54.

14. The left flank, Morotai Island, stood unsecured as well and was invaded on the same day the Palau operation commenced.

15. Garand and Strobridge, *Western Pacific Operations*, 60.

16. Ibid., 56–59.

17. Ibid., 77.

18. Expeditionary Troops, Third Fleet, *F-2 Intelligence Report*, 30 September 1944, 5.

19. Garand and Strobridge, *Western Pacific Operations*, 14–15. See also First Marine Division (Reinforced), *Palau Special Action Report*, Annex B, 13 September 1944, 1.

20. First Marine Division (Reinforced), *Palau Special Action Report*, 1.

21. Garand and Strobridge, *Western Pacific Operations*, 77–79.

22. Expeditionary Troops, Third Fleet, *F-2 Intelligence Report*, 4.

23. Hough, *Assault on Peleliu*, 17.

24. JICPOA Information Bulletin 124-44, *Southern Palau* (Pearl Harbor, Hawaii, 15 August 1944), 31.

25. Ibid., 31, 42.

26. Isely and Crowl, *U.S. Marines and Amphibious War*, 395–96.

27. First Marine Division (Reinforced), *Operation Plan Number 1-44, Palau Operation, Caroline Islands*, 15 August 1944, 3.

28. Isely and Crowl, *U.S. Marines and Amphibious War*, 396–97.

29. Expeditionary Troops, Third Fleet, *F-2 Intelligence Report,* 4.

30. Garand and Strobridge, *Western Pacific Operations,* 77.

31. Hough, *Assault on Peleliu,* 10–11.

32. Isely and Crowl, *U.S. Marines and Amphibious War,* 393–94.

33. Ibid., 393.

34. Hough, *Assault on Peleliu,* 10–11, 25.

35. Garand and Strobridge, *Western Pacific Operations,* 80.

36. Hough, *Assault on Peleliu,* 109.

37. JICPOA Information Bulletin 124-44, 21.

38. Ibid.

39. Ibid., 32.

40. Ibid., 21, and "Defenses Map," 32.

41. Other JICPOA maps had merged similar data, such as for Saipan and Tinian, but not to the detailed extent of Peleliu.

42. JICPOA Information Bulletin 124-44, 21.

43. Ibid., 25, 28, 30.

44. Hough, *Assault on Peleliu,* map, 3.

45. Ibid., 40.

46. Garand and Strobridge, *Western Pacific Operations,* 111–14.

47. Ibid., 78. The Peleliu Information Bulletin's Defenses map used minutely detailed topographic lines to display Peleliu's terrain features. This was not uncommon for JICPOA's high-level planning maps, but it was not always the case. The Guam terrain map, for example, demonstrated general terrain elevations with charcoal-like shading in a sketch of the island. JICPOA did not disseminate this type of terrain intelligence to combat units. Peleliu, on the other hand, demonstrates a case where assault planners used a detailed topographic map to help them plan the campaign. JICPOA disseminated exactly this type of intelligence to assault units. In other words, for the Peleliu campaign, senior assault planners and combatants used the same topographic intelligence.

48. Expeditionary Troops, Third Fleet, *F-2 Intelligence Report,* 6.

49. JICPOA Information Bulletin 124-44, 5, 21, maps at 22 and 32.

50. Garand and Strobridge, *Western Pacific Operations,* 117.

51. JICPOA Information Bulletin 124-44, 5, 21, maps at 22 and 32.

52. Ibid., map, 32.

53. Ibid., 57.

54. Alexander, *Storm Landings,* 120.

55. Ibid.

56. Ibid. See also Hough, *Assault on Peleliu,* map 9.

57. Garand and Strobridge, *Western Pacific Operations,* 73–76. Fortified caves were not included in the report's section on Japanese defenses, either.

58. JICPOA Information Bulletin 124-44, "Topography" map and close-ups.

59. Headquarters, Third Amphibious Corps, San Francisco, *III Phib Corps Report on Palaus Operation, Intelligence,* 1 October 1944, 1.

60. JICPOA Information Bulletin 124-44, 31. One after-action report said that the quality of photographs provided for the Peleliu intelligence operation was "fair to excellent" and "very good." The same report stated that these photographs provided "detailed information on terrain, vegetation, enemy defenses, and obstacles." It went on to disapprove of the hydrographic intelligence provided. What is interesting about this report is that it contradicts JICPOA's statement about bad photographic coverage, the parallel assessments of two other intelligence reports, and the complaints from marines who said that intelligence was lacking. The author of this report was clearly wrong in his analysis and may have been confused about what actually happened—or he may not even have been involved with the operation. Still, this could have been a classic "cover-your-ass" report meant to whitewash the situation instead. The report in question is First Marine Division (Reinforced), *Palau Special Action Report*, 1.

61. JICPOA Information Bulletin 124-44, 31, and "Defenses" map, 32.

62. Ibid.

63. Ibid., 31.

64. Ibid., topography map and close-ups.

65. Ibid., 32.

66. Garand and Strobridge, *Western Pacific Operations*, 73.

67. Ibid., 73, 109–12.

68. Ibid., 109–10.

69. Hough, *Assault on Peleliu*, 88.

70. Headquarters, Third Amphibious Corps, *III Phib Corps Report on Palaus Operation, Intelligence*, 3.

71. Ibid., 2.

72. JICPOA Information Bulletin 124-44, 31, and addendum, 1.

73. Headquarters, Third Amphibious Corps, *III Phib Corps Report on Palaus Operation, Intelligence*, 2, 3.

74. Comment by Benis Frank, February 2000, Bowie, Maryland.

75. JICPOA Information Bulletin 124-44, 42.

76. Ibid.

77. Ibid. These numbers reflect the maximum numbers of weapons afforded to Japanese units as of 15 August 1944. Mortars, surprisingly, are not listed.

78. JICPOA Information Bulletin 124-44 stated that one battalion of the Fifteenth Infantry Regiment on Babelthuap might be on Peleliu.

79. Ibid.

80. Ibid.

81. Ibid., addendum titled "Defenses—Peleliu and Ngesebus Islands," 1.

82. Ibid.

83. Hough, *Assault on Peleliu*, 33–35.

84. Ibid., 17–18, 50–51.

85. Ibid., 18. See also First Marine Division (Reinforced), *Operation Plan Number 1-44, Palau Operation, Caroline Islands*, 15 August 1944, 4–5.

86. Hough, *Assault on Peleliu*, 18.

87. First Marine Division (Reinforced), *Operation Plan Number 1-44, Palau Operation, Caroline Islands*, 4–5.

88. Garand and Strobridge, *Western Pacific Operations*, 275.

89. Hough, *Assault on Peleliu*, 50.

90. Garand and Strobridge, *Western Pacific Operations*, 110.

91. Hough, *Assault on Peleliu*, 50–52. Various after-action reports indicate that ten to nineteen tanks attacked U.S. lines. The actual number remains controversial.

92. Alexander, *Storm Landings*, 118.

93. Smith, *Approach to the Philippines*, 463.

94. Harvey A. Gailey, *Peleliu, 1944* (Annapolis, Md.: Nautical and Aviation Publication Co. of America, 1983), 23.

95. Garand and Strobridge, *Western Pacific Operations*, 286. Geiger's statement was made after the operation, Inoue's before, in his estimate of U.S. attack plans.

96. JICPOA Information Bulletin 158-45, "Hypothetical Defense of Kyushu," Special Translation Number 72 (Pearl Harbor, Hawaii, 20 July 1945). JICPOA discovered this document in the summer of 1945, too late to influence any campaign except the invasion of Japan. The Japanese document claims that they realized that their defenses did not work after Tarawa, but it is evident that they did not implement these changes until Peleliu.

97. Alexander, *Storm Landings*, 110.

98. JICPOA Information Bulletin 9-45, *Iwo Jima; First Supplement to Nanpo Shoto Information Bulletin Number 122-44, 10 October 1944* (Pearl Harbor, Hawaii, 10 January 1945), 6–7.

99. Alexander, *Storm Landings*, 109.

100. Ibid., 109–11.

101. Garand and Strobridge, *Western Pacific Operations*, 71–76.

102. Similar scenarios took place in the Iwo Jima and Okinawa campaigns.

103. Garand and Strobridge, *Western Pacific Operations*, 73.

104. Hough, *Assault on Peleliu*, 181.

105. Garand and Strobridge, *Western Pacific Operations*, 275.

106. *Bulletins of the Intelligence Center, Pacific Ocean Area, Joint Intelligence Center, Pacific Ocean Area, and the Commander in Chief Pacific and Pacific Ocean Area, 1942–1946*, 30.

107. Expeditionary Troops, Third Fleet, *F-2 Intelligence Report*, 7.

108. James H. Hallas, *The Devil's Anvil; The Assault on Peleliu* (Westport, Conn.: Praeger, 1994), 280.

109. Ibid., 281.

110. Ibid., 280.

111. Ibid., 281.

112. Ibid., 283–84.

Chapter 5. Iwo Jima and Okinawa: Detachment and Iceberg

1. Dyer, *Amphibians Came to Conquer,* 972–80.

2. Karal Ann Marling and John Wetenhall, *Iwo Jima: Monuments, Memories, and the American Hero* (Cambridge, Mass.: Harvard University Press, 1991), 27.

3. Whitman S. Bartley, *Iwo Jima: Amphibious Epic* (Washington, D.C.: U.S. Government Printing Office, 1954), iii.

4. Richard Wheeler, *Iwo* (New York: Lippincott & Crowell, 1980), 234.

5. Isely and Crowl, *U.S. Marines and Amphibious War,* 75.

6. Keith Wheeler and the Editors of Time-Life Books, *The Road to Tokyo* (Alexandria, Va.: Time-Life Books, 1979), 19–24.

7. Ibid.

8. Ibid.

9. JICPOA Information Bulletin 122-44, *Nanpo Shoto (Iwo Jima)* (Pearl Harbor, Hawaii, 10 October 1945), 6.

10. Bartley, *Iwo Jima: Amphibious Epic,* 19–21.

11. Ibid., 27–28.

12. Headquarters, Expeditionary Troops, Task Force Fifty-Six, *G-2 Report on Iwo Jima Operation,* 1 April 1945, 1.

13. Ibid., 1–2.

14. Ibid., 2.

15. Ibid.

16. In some campaigns, JICPOA passed much interpretation responsibility over to other intelligence units, such as those of the Pacific Fleet or InterpRon 1 or 2. However, a Marine intelligence report indicates that JICPOA continued to be the primary photo interpretation element for this campaign. See Headquarters, Expeditionary Troops, Task Force Fifty-Six, *G-2 Report on Iwo Jima Operation,* 1–2.

17. Twitty, "The Growth of JICPOA," 7.

18. Twitty, "Geographic Section," 12.

19. JICPOA Information Bulletin 9-45, *Iwo Jima; First Supplement to Nanpo Shoto Information Bulletin Number 122-44, 10 October 1944* (Pearl Harbor, Hawaii, 10 January 1945), 1–2.

20. Headquarters, Expeditionary Troops, Task Force Fifty-Six, *State of Enemy Defenses, Iwo Jima,* Appendix A, 13 February 1945, 1–2.

21. Dyer, *Amphibians Came to Conquer,* 995–1005.

22. Ibid., 1006.

23. JICPOA Information Bulletin 9-45, *Iwo Jima; First Supplement to Nanpo Shoto Information Bulletin Number 122-44,* 12–13.

24. In this regard, it is apparent from the information bulletin that the battle for Peleliu did not have a significant impact on the analysts' thinking for Iwo. They mentioned Peleliu regarding the possibility that the Japanese might revert to a Peleliu-type defense (cornered rat) as a last-ditch attempt to delay seizure of the island, but this was only an afterthought.

25. JICPOA Information Bulletin 9-45, 2.

26. Garand and Strobridge, *Western Pacific Operations*, 458.

27. JICPOA Information Bulletin 9-45, 1.

28. Ibid., 1–2, "Important Errata Note," 11, and map, titled, "Military Installations and Estimated Troop Dispositions of Iwo Jima (Sulphur Island)." Much of this information came from a chart on the aforementioned map. On the chart, JICPOA's analysts broke defenses down into reported defenses and observed defenses, each category having its own total. The combined total is the author's.

29. It is unclear how involved fleet intelligence was in the Iwo intelligence operation, or if the same rotation policy that affected JICPOA's photo interpreters affected those of the Pacific Fleet. Regardless, it is evident that fleet intelligence was not able to pick up the slack where JICPOA proved inadequate.

30. Headquarters, Expeditionary Troops, Task Force Fifty-Six, *State of Enemy Defenses, Iwo Jima*, 13 February 1945, 1–2.

31. Garand and Strobridge, *Western Pacific Operations*, 454. This table does not include every weapon the Japanese had. They also possessed 320-mm mortars.

32. Isely and Crowl, *U.S. Marines and Amphibious War*, 468–69.

33. Garand and Strobridge, *Western Pacific Operations*, 496–97.

34. Bartley, *Iwo Jima: Amphibious Epic*, 30. This figure was arrived at by totaling the number of assumed infantry battalions on Iwo. Engineer, artillery, antitank, signal, tanker, naval guard, and medical personnel were excluded.

35. JICPOA Information Bulletin 9-45, 1, plus "Nearshore, Beach, and Soil Conditions, Iwo Jima" map, which includes minute detail on Japanese defense installations.

36. Headquarters, Expeditionary Troops, Task Force Fifty-Six, *State of Enemy Defenses, Iwo Jima*, 13 February 1945, 2. Interestingly, this fleet intelligence report stated that in December, there had been 154, and possibly 155, pillboxes on Iwo Jima. This runs contrary to two JICPOA intelligence maps and one textual analysis (see JICPOA Information Bulletin 9-45, 1, and two maps in the same bulletin: "Nearshore, Beach, and Soil Conditions, Iwo Jima" and "Military Installations and Estimated Troop Dispositions of Iwo Jima [Sulphur Island]"). These were based on photos from 2 September 1944 and 3 December 1944, the same dates claimed in the 13 February fleet estimate, when analysts compared what was on Iwo in December to what was there in February. There were not 154 or 155 pillboxes noted on these maps but only about 39. There were, however, around 150 rifle pits (different from trenches) marked on these maps with symbols that looked very similar to the one used to designate pillboxes. In all probability, analysts who wrote the February report incorrectly read the maps from 3 December 1944 and gave the Japanese many more pillboxes than had been plotted at that time.

37. JICPOA Information Bulletin 136-45, *Defense Installations on Iwo Jima* (Pearl Harbor, Hawaii, 10 June 1945), 5.

38. Ibid.

39. Ibid., 4. The vast majority of Japanese concrete fortifications on Iwo were steel reinforced structures.

40. Ibid., 19.

41. Ibid., 2.

42. Ibid., 22, 24, 30.

43. Ibid., 4.

44. The tactical battle data in the following paragraphs came from Bartley, *Iwo Jima: Amphibious Epic;* Garand and Strobridge, *Western Pacific Operations;* and the chapter on Iwo Jima in Isely and Crowl, *U.S. Marines and Amphibious War.*

45. Bartley, *Iwo Jima: Amphibious Epic,* 189.

46. JICPOA Information Bulletin 136-45, 4.

47. Ibid., 11–16.

48. JICPOA Information Bulletin 9-45, 2.

49. Ibid., 4–5.

50. Ibid., 6.

51. Ibid., 6–7.

52. Ibid., 7.

53. Ibid., 7.

54. Ibid., 7, and note on map, "Military Installations and Estimated Troop Dispositions of Iwo Jima (Sulphur Island)."

55. Ibid., 4.

56. Ibid.

57. Headquarters, Expeditionary Troops, Task Force Fifty-Six, *G-2 Report on Iwo Jima Operation,* 36.

58. Garand and Strobridge, *Western Pacific Operations,* 459.

59. JICPOA Information Bulletin 136-45, 3.

60. Ibid., 3–4.

61. Ibid.

62. Headquarters, Expeditionary Troops, Task Force Fifty-Six, *G-2 Report on Iwo Jima Operation,* 36.

63. JICPOA Information Bulletin 136-45, 4.

64. Ibid.

65. Garand and Strobridge, *Western Pacific Operations,* 690, 633, 652.

66. Bill D. Ross, *Iwo Jima: Legacy of Valor* (New York: Vanguard Press, 1985), 325.

67. Garand and Strobridge, *Western Pacific Operations,* 493.

68. Actually, they did this on most campaigns, but Tinian provides the best example.

69. *Jane's American Fighting Ships,* ed. John Moore (New York: Mallard Press, 1991), 38–50, 110–18.

70. Headquarters, Fifth Amphibious Corps, Landing Force, Iwo Jima, Special Staff Section Reports, Appendix 2, *Report of Naval Gunfire Officer,* 30 May 1945, 21.

71. Headquarters, Expeditionary Troops, Task Force Fifty-Six, *G-2 Report on Iwo Jima Operation,* 35.

72. Ibid., 36.

73. Headquarters, Fifth Amphibious Corps, Landing Force, Iwo Jima, Special Staff Section Reports, Appendix 2, *Report of Naval Gunfire Officer*, 21.

74. Ibid., 22.

75. Ibid., 21–22.

76. JICPOA Information Bulletin 9-45, 10.

77. Alexander, *Storm Landings*, 140.

78. Ibid., 134.

79. Smith, *Coral and Brass*, 266.

80. Bartley, *Iwo Jima: Amphibious Epic*, 116.

81. JICPOA Information Bulletin 137-45, *Progressive Construction and Camouflage of Defense Installations on Iwo Jima, Supplement to Bulletin No. 136-45* (Pearl Harbor, Hawaii, 13 June 1945), "Foreword." The photos are very old and were photocopied onto microfilm. Attempts to photocopy the photocopied photographs were not successful.

82. Bartley, *Iwo Jima: Amphibious Epic*, 20.

83. Holmes, *Double Edged Secrets*, 200.

84. JICPOA Information Bulletin 9-45. See notations regarding weapons throughout text.

85. Headquarters, Expeditionary Troops, Task Force Fifty-Six, *State of Enemy Defenses, Iwo Jima*, 2.

86. Alexander, *Storm Landings*, 132.

87. Headquarters, Expeditionary Troops, Task Force Fifty-Six, *G-2 Report on Iwo Jima Operation*, 1 April 1945, 35.

88. Ibid., 35–36.

89. Ibid., 36.

90. Richard F. Newcomb, *Iwo Jima* (New York: Bantam, 1982), 194–99.

91. Ibid., 223–24.

92. Wheeler, *Bombers over Japan*, 168.

93. Ibid.

94. Newcomb, *Iwo Jima*, 223–24.

95. Wheeler, *Bombers over Japan*, 168.

96. Newcomb, *Iwo Jima*, 223–24.

97. Ibid.

98. Alexander, *Storm Landings*, 147.

99. Frank and Shaw, *Victory and Occupation*, 119.

100. Isely and Crowl, *U.S. Marines and Amphibious War*, 538.

101. Frank and Shaw, *Victory and Occupation*, 369.

102. Isely and Crowl, *U.S. Marines and Amphibious War*, 551.

103. Similarly, JICPOA was unable to predict that the Japanese would mass their suicide aircraft in flights of up to three hundred at a time, that the Imperial Headquarters had dispatched the battleship *Yamato* to attack U.S. Navy ships off the coast of Okinawa, and that the enemy had developed a human-guided antiship mis-

sile just for the defense of Okinawa. However, these were intelligence issues directly related to naval operations and would not have been included in an island campaign information bulletin.

104. Dyer, *Amphibians Came to Conquer*, 1060.

105. Frank and Shaw, *Victory and Occupation*, 34.

106. Ibid., 9–13.

107. Isely and Crowl, *U.S. Marines and Amphibious War*, 533.

108. Tenth Army Action Report, *Report of Operations in the Ryukyus Campaign*, Chapter 11, Staff Section Reports, Section II—G-2, 1945, 11-II-3. At the time of these aerial photographic flights, the Marines had not yet seized Iwo Jima.

109. Ibid.

110. Ibid.

111. Frank and Shaw, *Victory and Occupation*, 78.

112. Ibid., 78–79.

113. Tenth Army Action Report, *Report of Operations in the Ryukyus Campaign*, Chapter 11, Staff Section Reports, Section II—G-2, 11-II-3.

114. Ibid.

115. Ibid., 11-II-4.

116. Ibid., 11-II-5.

117. Frank and Shaw, *Victory and Occupation*, 78.

118. JICPOA Information Bulletin 161-44, *Okinawa Gunto* (Pearl Harbor, Hawaii, 15 November 1944).

119. Frank and Shaw, *Victory and Occupation*, 80.

120. JICPOA Information Bulletin, 6, 161-44, 110–12.

121. Packard, *A Century of U.S. Naval Intelligence*, 297.

122. JICPOA Information Bulletin 53-45, *Okinawa Gunto: Second Supplement to Okinawa Information Bulletin Number 161-44* (Pearl Harbor, Hawaii, 28 February 1945), 13.

123. Ibid., "Foreword," "Summary," 2, 7–10, 14.

124. Isely and Crowl, *U.S. Marines and Amphibious War*, 552.

125. Dyer, *Amphibians Came to Conquer*, 1064.

126. Ibid., 1072–73.

127. Isely and Crowl, *U.S. Marines and Amphibious War*, 535.

128. Dyer, *Amphibians Came to Conquer*, 1073.

129. Isely and Crowl, *U.S. Marines and Amphibious War*, 533–38.

130. Japanese maps indicated that Hagushi Town at the invasion beaches was not "Hagushi" at all. It was "Tagushi." Interpreters must have mistranslated the name of the town, or there was a typo in intelligence production. Nevertheless, most U.S. histories of the battle for Okinawa list the town as Hagushi. The mistake was not caught until February 1996 when a Marine historian went to Tokyo on an exercise, and Japanese historians informed him of the error. Comment by retired Chief Historian of the Marine Corps, Benis M. Frank, February 2000.

131. Frank and Shaw, *Victory and Occupation*, 68.

132. JICPOA Information Bulletin 53-45, "Summary."

133. Ibid., map, 8.

134. Ibid., 11, map, 8.

135. Ibid., 12, map, 8.

136. Ibid., 12–13, map, 8.

137. Ibid., map, 8.

138. Ibid., 13.

139. Ibid., 9, map, 8.

140. Ibid., 9.

141. Isely and Crowl, *U.S. Marines and Amphibious War,* 553.

142. Ibid.

143. Ibid., 540, map, 23.

144. Hiromichi Yahara (with introduction and commentary by Frank Gibney), *The Battle for Okinawa* (New York: John Wiley & Sons, 1995), 67–70.

145. Isely and Crowl, *U.S. Marines and Amphibious War,* 539–41.

146. Frank and Shaw, *Victory and Occupation,* 384.

147. Ibid., 348.

148. Isely and Crowl, *U.S. Marines and Amphibious War,* 555.

149. Charles Nichols and Henry Shaw, *Okinawa: Victory in the Pacific* (Washington, D.C.: Historical Branch, G-3 Division, Headquarters, U.S. Marine Corps, 1955), 121.

150. Alexander, *Storm Landings,* 161. See also Roy E. Appleman, with James M. Burns, Russel A. Gugeler, and John Stevens, *United States Army in World War II. The War in the Pacific: Okinawa: The Last Battle* (Washington, D.C.: Historical Division, Department of the Army, 1948), Maps XXVII, XIX, and XII.

151. Isely and Crowl, *U.S. Marines and Amphibious War,* 541.

152. Ibid., 543.

153. Ibid., 544.

154. Ibid., 546–48.

155. Ibid., 549–50.

156. JICPOA Information Bulletin 53-45, 14.

157. Nichols and Shaw, *Victory and Occupation,* 81.

158. Isely and Crowl, *U.S. Marines and Amphibious War,* 551. This figure was arrived at by combining the number of Japanese killed and the number taken prisoner.

159. Nichols and Shaw, *Victory and Occupation,* 43–46 and map 3, 52, and Appleman, Burns, Gugeler, and Stevens, *Okinawa: The Last Battle,* 483–85.

160. JICPOA Information Bulletin 53-45, 14. This was assuming there were 56,000 troops on the island. The 75,000-man estimate came after the publication of this particular information bulletin.

161. Most cave positions were impervious to naval shelling and had to be blasted at point-blank range by tanks and self-propelled guns. Still, prior island campaigns such as Guam had proved that a prolonged naval bombardment could gradually de-

stroy most hardened defensive installations and shock the defender to the extent that he is incapable of putting up effective resistance.

162. Yahara, *Battle for Okinawa,* 20–23.

163. Ibid., 20–22.

164. Ibid., 22.

165. Ibid., 26.

166. Ibid., 8.

167. Nichols and Shaw, *Okinawa: Victory in the Pacific,* 54. This unit received orders to ship out to the Philippines in late November, but it probably would not have shipped out completely for several weeks later, possibly more than a month later.

168. Yahara, *Battle for Okinawa,* 31–32.

169. U.S. War Department, *Handbook on Japanese Military Forces,* 19–20.

170. Isely and Crowl, *U.S. Marines and Amphibious War,* 551–52.

171. Frank and Shaw, *Victory and Occupation,* 53.

172. JICPOA Information Bulletin 161-44, 111, and "Land Transport" map, 116.

173. JICPOA Information Bulletin 53-45, 10, 13.

174. Ibid., "Defense Installations, Southern Okinawa Shima, Nansei Shoto" as of 22 January 1945.

175. No documents could have foretold the sudden change in battle plans on Okinawa, and neither could have any previously captured POW.

176. Yahara, *Battle for Okinawa,* 14.

177. Ibid., 8.

178. Ibid., 25.

Chapter 6. The Home Islands and the Bomb: Olympic and Downfall

1. Frank and Shaw, *Victory and Occupation,* 399.

2. Alexander, *Storm Landings,* 177.

3. Frank and Shaw, *Victory and Occupation,* 401–2.

4. Ibid.

5. Ibid., 404.

6. Ibid.

7. Ibid., 404–5.

8. Ernest J. King's chapters in *The War Reports of General of the Army George C. Marshall, Chief of Staff, General of the Army; H.H. Arnold, Commanding General Army Air Forces; Fleet Admiral Ernest J. King, Commander in Chief U.S. Fleet and Chief of Naval Operations* (New York: Lippincott, 1947), 684.

9. The invasion of Honshu, set to begin in March, had yet to be formalized.

10. Frank and Shaw, *Victory and Occupation,* 399–400.

11. Ibid., 402.

12. Ibid., 404–5.

13. A recognized historical expert by the USMC Historical Center, Colonel Alexander has written several books on the U.S. Marine Corps and the Pacific War.

14. Alexander, *Storm Landings,* 176. The exact quote is: "His [MacArthur's] troops

would secure Kagoshima Bay and all other ports and airfields below this line, then bottle up Japanese troops in the north by plugging the mountain passes."

15. JICPOA Information Bulletin 158-45.

16. JICPOA Information Bulletin 81-45, *Southern Kyushu* (Pearl Harbor, Hawaii, 1945), 4, 11–12.

17. Ibid., and map, 6.

18. Edward J. Drea, "Previews of Hell: Intelligence, the Bomb, and the Invasion of Japan," *American Intelligence Journal* 16, no. 1 (Spring/Summer 1995): 52. All of the information concerning ULTRA intercepts and the Japanese buildup on Kyushu and Honshu came from this excellent article, which also appeared in *Military History Quarterly* 7, no. 3 (Spring 1995). See also Douglas J. MacEachin, *The Final Months of the War with Japan: Signals Intelligence, U.S. Invasion Planning, and the A-Bomb Decision* (Virginia: CIA publication for the Center for the Study of Intelligence, December 1998), found at: http://www.odci.gov/csi/monograph/4253605299/csi9810001.html

19. Ibid.

20. Ibid.

21. Ibid., 53.

22. Ibid.

23. Alexander, *Storm Landings*, 181–82.

24. Drea, "Previews of Hell," 54.

25. Ibid., 55.

26. Ibid., 53, 55–56.

27. Ibid., 51.

28. These are approximate numbers and do not include captured laborers, who frequently were Korean. Approximations resulted from the inability to count exactly how many Japanese were garrisoned on each island due to last minute changes in manpower, the destruction of Japanese postwar records, and the absence of those who were literally vaporized by U.S. firepower. These numbers are, however, as accurate as can be, having been based on captured Japanese documents, POW interrogations, enemy body counts, and intelligence estimations during and after the battle. Furthermore, most POWs from these islands were Korean or local laborers, or local inhabitants recruited or pressed into infantry duty, as on Okinawa.

29. Drea, "Previews of Hell," 53.

30. Keith Wheeler, *The Fall of Japan* (Alexandria, Va.: Time-Life Books, 1983), 27–29.

31. Ibid., 32.

32. Ibid., 32.

33. Some wanted to destroy Japan's ancient capital, Kyoto, their center of historical and cultural wealth. But more professional minds prevailed to focus targeting studies on cities that contained numerous war industries, like Hiroshima and Nagasaki.

34. Drea, "Previews of Hell," 55.

35. Ibid., 56.

36. Toland, *Rising Sun,* 989.

37. Drea, "Previews of Hell," 56.

38. Wheeler, *Fall of Japan,* 135.

39. Toland, *Rising Sun,* 986.

40. Ibid., 998–99.

41. Ibid., 1005–7.

42. Capt. Wendell Furnas, USN, Ret., interview by author, Bethesda, Maryland, 19 March 2002.

Chapter 7. Conclusions and Lessons Learned

1. Twitty, *Report of Intelligence Activities in the Pacific Ocean Areas,* 4.

2. Packard, *A Century of U.S. Naval Intelligence,* 403.

3. Kenneth A. Minihan, "The Defense Intelligence Agency; National and Military Intelligence for the 21st Century," *American Intelligence Journal* 16, no. 2/3 (Autumn/Winter 1995): 31.

4. Packard, *A Century of U.S. Naval Intelligence,* 446.

5. Twitty, *Report of Intelligence Activities in the Pacific Ocean Areas,* 3.

6. Ibid., 4.

7. In 1945, there was no "Air Force" in the U.S. force structure. General Twitty may have been referring to what he saw was the future USAF.

8. Twitty, *Report of Intelligence Activities in the Pacific Ocean Areas,* 4.

9. Ibid.

10. Ibid.

11. Ibid.

12. Ibid.

13. Ibid.

14. Ibid., 2.

15. Ibid.

16. Ibid.

17. *Narrative: Combat Intelligence Center, Joint Intelligence Center, Pacific Ocean Area,* 19.

18. Ibid., 4.

19. Ibid., 5.

20. Ibid., 11.

21. Ibid.

22. Ibid., 20.

23. Ibid.

BIBLIOGRAPHY

Interviews

Furnas, Wendell, Captain, USN, Ret. JICPOA Japanese linguist. Interview by author. California, 11 September 1997.

Gibney, Frank. JICPOA Japanese linguist. Interview by author. California, 11 September 1997.

Harrison, John A. JICPOA Japanese linguist. Interview by author. Gainesville, Fla., 4 October 1995.

Marine Officer, Command and Staff College, Quantico. Interview by author. March 2000.

Showers, Donald M., Rear Admiral, USN, Ret., first officer permanently assigned to JICPOA. Interview by author. Arlington, Va., 17 December 1993.

———. Interview by author. 12 January 1994.

JICPOA Information Bulletins

1943

52-43, Maleolap. Pearl Harbor, Hawaii.

53-43, Kwajalein. Pearl Harbor, Hawaii, 1 December.

57-43, Wotje. Pearl Harbor, Hawaii.

69-43, Tables, Part I: Tides and Currents. Pearl Harbor, Hawaii, 12 December.

1944

3-44, Eniwetok. Pearl Harbor, Hawaii, 20 January.

48-44, Japanese Defenses, Kwajalein Atoll. Pearl Harbor, Hawaii, 10 April.

54-44, Appendix B—Notes on Japanese Aircraft Production (NO.5) Kasei 11 and 15 Aircraft Engines. Pearl Harbor, Hawaii, 15 April.

52-44, Guam, Vol. I and II. Pearl Harbor, Hawaii, 15 April.

66A-44, Target Survey: Saipan. Pearl Harbor, Hawaii, 10 May.

67-44, Tinian: Target Analysis. Pearl Harbor, Hawaii, 10 May.

68-44, 15 cm Howitzer Emplacement, Taroa Island, Maloelap Atoll, Marshall Islands. Pearl Harbor, Hawaii, 22 April.

69-44, Captured Photographs of Japanese Ships. Pearl Harbor, Hawaii, 25 April.

73-44, Saipan, Tinian, and Rota. Pearl Harbor, Hawaii, 10 May.

77A and B-44, Gridded Map Air Target Folder: Saipan, Tinian, and Aguijan. Pearl Harbor, Hawaii, 15 May.

89-44, The Japanese Defense of Eniwetok Atoll. Pearl Harbor, Hawaii, 12 June.

122-44, Nanpo Shoto (Iwo Jima). Pearl Harbor, Hawaii, 10 October.

124-44, Southern Palau. Pearl Harbor, Hawaii, 15 August.

145-44, Iwo Jima (Sulphur Island). Pearl Harbor, Hawaii, 14 September.

151-44, Japanese Army and Navy Land Forces. Pearl Harbor, Hawaii, 6 October.

161-44, Okinawa Gunto. Pearl Harbor, Hawaii, 15 November.

167-44, Japanese Infantry Weapons. Pearl Harbor, Hawaii.

1945

6-45, Tables of Organization and Tables of Equipment of Japanese Forces, "Know Your Enemy." Pearl Harbor, Hawaii.

9-45, First Supplement to CINCPAC-CINCPOA Bulletin No. 122-44, Nanpo Shoto, Volume One, 6 January 1945. Pearl Harbor, Hawaii, 10 January.

42-45, Flak Intelligence Memorandum Number 3, Evasive Action Against Enemy Anti-Aircraft. Pearl Harbor, Hawaii, 13 February.

53-45, Okinawa Gunto: Second Supplement to Okinawa Information Bulletin Number 161-44. Pearl Harbor, Hawaii, 28 February.

81-45, Southern Kyushu. Pearl Harbor, Hawaii, 15 May.

94-45, Japanese Deliberate Fortifications: Special Translation Number 58. Pearl Harbor, Hawaii, 20 May.

105-45, Japanese Operational Aircraft: "Know Your Enemy." Pearl Harbor, Hawaii, April.

136-45, Defense Installations on Iwo Jima. Pearl Harbor, Hawaii, 10 June.

137-45, Progressive Construction and Camouflage of Defense Installations on Iwo Jima, Supplement to Bulletin No. 136-45. Pearl Harbor, Hawaii, 13 June.

158-45, Special Translation Number 72, Hypothetical Defense of Kyushu. Pearl Harbor, Hawaii, 20 July.

Other Official Sources

Bulletins of the Intelligence Center, Pacific Ocean Area, Joint Intelligence Center, Pacific Ocean Area, and the Commander in Chief Pacific, Pacific Ocean Areas, 1942–1946. Washington, D.C.: Operational Archives, U.S. Naval Historical Division, 1984.

Commander, Task Force 53. Operations Plan 1–44 (Guam), 11 May 1944.

Commander, Task Force 53. Operations Plan A162–44 (Guam), Annex "B" and Appendices, 7 June 1944.

Expeditionary Troops, Third Fleet. F–2 Intelligence Report, 30 September 1944.

First Marine Division (Reinforced). Operation Plan Number 1–44, Palau Operation, Caroline Islands, 15 August 1944.

First Marine Division (Reinforced). Palau Special Action Report, Annex B, 13 September 1944.

Headquarters, Expeditionary Troops, Task Force 56. G-2 Report on Iwo Jima Operation, 1 April 1945.

Headquarters, Expeditionary Troops, Task Force 56. State of Enemy Defenses, Iwo Jima, 13 February 1945.

Headquarters, Fifth Amphibious Corps. Report by G-2 on Marshall Islands Operation, 18 February 1944.

Headquarters, Fifth Amphibious Corps, Landing Force, Iwo Jima. Special Staff Section Reports, Appendix 2, Report of Naval Gunfire Officer, 30 May 1945.

Headquarters, Fourth Marine Division, Fleet Marine Force. Operations Report, Tinian, 25 September 1944.

Headquarters, Northern Troops and Landing Force. Marianas Phase I (Saipan) G-2 Report, Enclosure D, serial number 0024A, 1944.

Headquarters, Third Amphibious Corps. III Phib Corps Report on Palaus Operation, Intelligence, 1 October 1944.

Headquarters, 22d Marines (Reinforced), Fifth Amphibious Corps. Report on Catchpole Operation, 9 March 1944.

ICPOA Information Bulletin 30-43, Enemy Positions: The Marshall-Gilbert Area, Vol. II. Pearl Harbor, Hawaii, 5 May 1943.

King, Ernest J. Chapters in *The War Reports of General of the Army George C. Marshall, Chief of Staff, General of the Army; H. H. Arnold, Commanding General Army Air Forces; Fleet Admiral Ernest J. King, Commander in Chief U.S. Fleet and Chief of Naval Operations.* New York: J. B. Lippincott Company, 1947.

Narrative: Combat Intelligence Center, Joint Intelligence Center, Pacific Ocean Area, 8 November 1945, found in Command File, WW II. Washington, D.C.: Department of the Navy, Naval Security Group Command Headquarters letter, 5 July 1978.

Naval Intelligence, Naval Doctrine Publication (NDP) 2. Washington, D.C.: Department of the Navy, Office of the Chief of Naval Operations and Headquarters, United States Marine Corps, an on-line publication found at: http://sun00781.dn.net/irp/doddir/navy/ndp2.htm#c_2

Office of the Commander, Group Three, Amphibious Forces, U.S. Pacific Fleet. *CTF–53's Report of Amphibious Operations for the Capture of Guam,* Enclosure E, 10 August 1944.

Office of the Commander, Group 3, 5th Amphibious Force, U.S. Pacific Fleet. *Report of Amphibious Operations for the Marshalls: Capture of Roi and Namur Islands (Flintlock),* 23 February 1944.

Packard, Wyman H. *A Century of U.S. Naval Intelligence.* Washington, D.C.: Department of the Navy, 1996.

Register of Commissioned and Warrant Officers of the U.S. Navy and Marine Corps. Washington, D.C.: U.S. Government Printing Office, 1942.

Tenth Army Action Report. Report of Operations in the Ryukyus Campaign. Chapter 11, Staff Section Reports, Section II–G-2 , 1945.

Twitty, Joseph J. *Report of Intelligence Activities in the Pacific Ocean Areas,* including the articles "The Growth of JICPOA," "History of JICPOA by Sections," and "Advanced Intelligence Center." Pearl Harbor, Hawaii, 15 October 1945.

War Department. *FM-21-25: Elementary Aerial Photograph Reading.* Washington, D.C.: War Department, 15 August 1944.

War Department. *FM-21-26: Advanced Map and Aerial Photography Reading.* Washington, D.C.: War Department, December 1944.

Books

Alexander, Joseph H. *Storm Landings: Epic Amphibious Battles in the Central Pacific.* Annapolis, Md.: Naval Institute Press, 1997.

Appleman, Roy E., with James M. Burns, Russel A. Gugeler, and John Stevens. *United States Army in World War II: The War in the Pacific—Okinawa, the Last Battle.* Washington, D.C.: Historical Division, Department of the Army, 1948.

Ballendorf, Dirk Anthony, and Merrill Lewis Bartlett. *Pete Ellis: An Amphibious Warfare Prophet, 1880–1923.* Annapolis, Md.: Naval Institute Press, 1997.

Bartley, Whitman S. *Iwo Jima: Amphibious Epic.* Washington, D.C.: U.S. Government Printing Office, 1954.

Bolger, Daniel P. *Americans At War; 1975–1986: An Era of Violent Peace.* Novato, Calif.: Presidio Press, 1988.

Buell, Thomas B. *The Quiet Warrior: A Biography of Admiral Raymond A. Spruance.* Boston: Little, Brown and Company, 1974.

Clausewitz, Carl von. *On War.* Edited by Anatol Rapoport. New York: Penguin Books, 1982.

Clifford, Kenneth J. *Amphibious Warfare Development in Britain and America from 1920–1940.* Laurens, N.Y.: Edgewood, 1983.

Crowl, Philip A. *The U.S. Army in WW II: The War in the Pacific: Campaign in the Marianas.* Washington, D.C.: Office of the Chief of Military History, Department of the Army, 1960.

———, and Edmund G. Love. *The U.S. Army in World War II: The War in the Pacific; Seizure of the Gilberts and Marshalls.* Washington, D.C.: Office of the Chief of Military History, 1955.

Dockery, Kevin. *SEALS in Action.* New York: Avon Books, 1991.

Dunnigan, James F., and Albert A. Nofi. *Victory at Sea, World War II in the Pacific.* New York: William Morrow and Company, 1995.

Dyer, George. *The Amphibians Came to Conquer: The Story of Admiral Richmond Kelly Turner.* Vol. 2. Washington, D.C.: U.S. Government Printing Office, 1972.

Forrestal, E. D. *Admiral Raymond Spruance, USN: A Study in Command.* Washington, D.C.: Government Printing Office, 1966.

Frank, Benis M., and Henry I. Shaw Jr. *Victory and Occupation: History of U.S. Marine Corps Operations in World War II.* Vol. 5. Washington, D.C.: Historical Branch, G-3 Division, Headquarters, U.S. Marine Corps, 1968.

Gailey, Harvey. *Peleliu, 1944*. Annapolis, Md.: Nautical and Aviation Publication Co. of America, 1983.

Garand, George W., and Truman R. Strobridge. *Western Pacific Operations: History of U.S. Marine Corps Operations in World War II*. Vol. 4. Washington, D.C.: Historical Division, Headquarters, U.S. Marine Corps, 1971.

Guam Operations of the 77th Division: 21 July–10 August 1944. American Forces in Action Series, Washington, D.C.: War Department, Historical Division, 1946.

Hallas, James H. *The Devil's Anvil: The Assault on Peleliu*. Westport, Conn.: Praeger, 1994.

Heinel, Robert D., Jr., and John A. Crown. *The Marshalls: Increasing the Tempo*. Washington, D.C.: Historical Branch, G-3 Division, Headquarters, United States Marine Corps, 1954.

Hoffman, Carl W. *Saipan: The Beginning of the End*. Washington, D.C.: Historical Branch, G-3 Division, Headquarters, U.S. Marine Corps, 1950.

———. *The Seizure of Tinian*. Washington, D.C.: Historical Branch, G-3 Division, Headquarters, U.S. Marine Corps, 1951.

Holmes, W. J. *Double Edged Secrets: U.S. Naval Intelligence Operations in the Pacific during World War II*. Annapolis, Md.: Naval Institute Press, 1979.

Hough, Frank O. *The Assault on Peleliu*. Washington, D.C.: Historical Division, Headquarters, U.S. Marine Corps, 1950.

———. *The Island War: The United States Marine Corps in the Pacific*. New York: J. B. Lippincott Company, 1947.

Isely, Jeter, and Philip Crowl. *The U.S. Marines and Amphibious War: Its Theory and Its Practice in the Pacific*. Princeton, N.J.: Princeton University Press, 1951.

Keegan, John. *The Second World War*. New York: Penguin Books, 1990.

Layton, Edwin T., with Roger Pineau and John Costello. *And I Was There: Pearl Harbor and Midway—Breaking the Secrets*. New York: Quill, 1985.

Lewin, Ronald. *The American Magic: Codes, Ciphers, and the Defeat of Japan*. New York: Penguin Books, 1983.

Lodge, O. R. *The Recapture of Guam*. Washington, D.C.: Historical Branch, G-3 Division, Headquarters, U.S. Marine Corps, 1954.

MacEachin, Douglas J. *The Final Months of the War with Japan: Signals Intelligence, U.S. Invasion Planning, and the A-Bomb Decision*. CIA publication. Virginia: Center for the Study of Intelligence. http://www.odci.gov/csi/monograph/4253605299/csi9810001.html

Marling, Karal Ann, and John Wetenhall. *Iwo Jima: Monuments, Memories and the American Hero*. Cambridge: Harvard University Press, 1991.

Moore, Captain John, RN, ed. *Jane's American Fighting Ships of the 20th Century*. New York: Mallard Press, 1991.

Morison, Samuel Eliot. *History of United States Naval Operations in World War II*. Vol. 7. *Aleutians, Gilberts, and Marshalls, June 1942–April 1944*. Boston: Atlantic Monthly Press, 1955.

————. *History of United States Naval Operations in World War II.* Vol. 8. *New Guinea and the Marianas, March 1944–August 1944.* Boston: Atlantic Monthly Press, 1953.

Murphy, Jack. *History of the U.S. Marines.* New York: Exeter Books, 1984.

Newcomb, Richard F. *Iwo Jima.* New York: Bantam, 1982.

Nichols, Charles, and Henry Shaw. *Okinawa; Victory in the Pacific.* Washington, D.C.: Historical Branch, G-3 Division, Headquarters, U.S. Marine Corps, 1955.

O'Toole, G. J. *Honorable Treachery: A History of U.S. Intelligence, Espionage, and Covert Action from the American Revolution to the CIA.* New York: Atlantic Monthly Press, 1991.

Ross, Bill D. *Iwo Jima: Legacy of Valor.* New York: Vanguard Press, 1985.

Shaw, Henry I. *First Offensive: The Marine Campaign for Guadalcanal.* Marines in WW II Commemorative Series. Washington, D.C.: U.S. Marine Corps Historical Center, 1992.

————, with Bernard Nalty and Edwin Turnbladh. *Central Pacific Drive: History of U.S. Marine Corps Operations in World War II.* Vol. 3. Washington, D.C.: Historical Branch, G-3 Division, Headquarters, U.S. Marine Corps, 1966.

Sherrod, Robert Lee. *Tarawa; The Story of a Battle.* New York: Duell, Sloan, and Pearle, 1985.

Smith, Holland, and Percy Finch. *Coral and Brass.* New York: Charles Scribners' Sons, 1949.

Smith, Robert Ross. *The U.S. Army in World War II: The War in the Pacific: Approach to the Philippines.* Washington, D.C.: Chief of Military History, Department of the Army, 1953.

Steinberg, Rafael, and the Editors of Time-Life Books. *Island Fighting.* Alexandria, Va.: Time-Life Books, 1978.

Stinnett, Robert B. *George Bush: His War Years.* Washington, D.C.: Brassy's, U.S., Inc., 1992.

Sun Tzu. *The Art of War.* Translated by Samuel B. Griffith. New York: Oxford University Press, 1971.

Toland, John. *The Rising Sun: The Decline and Fall of the Japanese Empire, 1936–1945.* Vol. 1. New York: Random House, 1970.

Twining, Merrill B. *No Bended Knee: The Battle for Guadalcanal: The Memoir of General Merrill B. Twining, USMC.* Novato, Calif.: Presidio Press, 1996.

U.S. War Department. *Handbook on Japanese Military Forces.* London: Greenhill Books, 1991.

Van Der Vat, Dan. *The Pacific Campaign.* New York: Touchstone Books, 1991.

Weigley, Russel F. *The American Way of War: A History of United States Military Strategy and Policy.* Bloomington: Indiana University Press, 1973.

Wheeler, Keith, and the Editors of Time-Life Books. *Bombers over Japan.* Alexandria, Va.: Time-Life Books, 1982.

————. *The Fall of Japan.* Alexandria, Va.: Time-Life Books, 1983.

————. *The Road to Tokyo.* Alexandria, Va.: Time-Life Books, 1979.

———. *War under the Pacific.* Alexandria, Va: Time-Life Books, 1980.

Wheeler, Richard. *Iwo.* New York: Lippincott and Crowell Publishers, 1980.

Yahara, Hiromichi, with introduction and commentary by Frank Gibney. *The Battle for Okinawa.* New York: John Wiley and Sons, Inc., 1995.

Zich, Arthur, and the Editors of Time-Life Books. *The Rising Sun.* Alexandria, Va.: Time-Life Books, 1977.

Zimmerman, John L. *The Guadalcanal Campaign.* Headquarters, USMC: Historical Division, 1949.

Monographs and Articles

Associated Press. "Japanese Biological Warfare Veteran Says He Cut Human 'Logs'," 16 November 2000, posted on the Internet on CNN.com at 7:06 A.M. Hong Kong time.

Drea, Edward J. "Previews of Hell: Intelligence, the Bomb, and the Invasion of Japan." *American Intelligence Journal* 16, no. 1 (Spring/Summer 1995).

Hammel, Eric. "Guam." *Leatherneck; Magazine of the Marines.* July 1994.

Harwood, Richard. *A Close Encounter: The Marine Landing on Tinian.* The Marines in WW II Commemorative Series. Washington, D.C.: Marine Corps Historical Center, 1994.

Ishio, Phil S. "The Nisei Contribution to the Allied Victory in the Pacific." *American Intelligence Journal* 16, no. 1 (Spring/Summer 1995).

Minihan, Kenneth A. "The Defense Intelligence Agency: National and Military Intelligence for the 21st Century." *American Intelligence Journal* 16, nos. 2 & 3 (Autumn/Winter 1995).

Riccardelli, Richard F. "The Linguist Paradigm." *Military Intelligence Professional Bulletin* 20, no. 4 (October–December 1994).

INDEX

About the Author

A native of Greenville, North Carolina, Jeffrey Moore attended Hargrave Military Academy and then proceeded to East Carolina University, where he received a Bachelor of Arts in political science. He then earned a master's in American history with a concentration in U.S. national security affairs and U.S. involvement in Asia and the Pacific. He minored in maritime history.

In 1996–97 Moore spent a year in Vietnam teaching English and working for a market research company, where he analyzed business and regional economic conditions. In 1998 he joined a Washington, D.C.–area consultancy, where he supported several U.S. Combatant Commands, the Defense Department, and the State Department with military, political, and economic analyses. In December 2000 he began a tour on the U.S. Army Staff in the Pentagon, supporting plans and operations. He left the Pentagon in 2003 and began working for a consultancy in Asia, where he currently lives.

Moore is the author of numerous articles on political and business issues. He has spoken at the Marine Corps Command and Staff College in Quantico, Virginia, and at U.S. Pacific Command, Honolulu, Hawaii.